Egyptian
Revival in Bohemia
1850–1920

Orientalism and Egyptomania in Czech lands

with contribution
"The background of Austrian economic influence
in Egypt, Sudan, and the Levant" by Roman Míšek

*The research and completion of this publication was made possible through
the institutional and financial support from AKTION – Austrian
government programme 33 p 15 (2002), Academy of Sciences Grant
Agency Junior Research Grant No. KJB9101301,
and the Ministry of Education of the Czech Republic
(Project LN00A064, Czech National Centre for Egyptology).
Special thanks for the financial support of the publication
(covering the entire edition costs) go to UNIS, Ltd.*

Egyptian Revival in Bohemia
1850–1920

Orientalism and Egyptomania in Czech lands

with contribution
'The background of Austrian economic influence
in Egypt, Sudan, and the Levant' by Roman Míšek

SET OUT

Table of Contents

Acknowledgements

This book would not have been written without the support of many people, who took part in its creation by counsels or practical help. I wish to thank in first place all my colleagues at the Czech Institute of Egyptology and at the Czech National Centre for Egyptology.

The general conception of the work as well as the individual steps in the work that was originally developed as a master's thesis at the Faculty of Arts of Charles University proceeded with the assistance of Prof. Miroslav Verner and Prof. Zdeněk Beneš. Many valuable counsels and stimuli came also from Ass. Prof. Ladislav Bareš, PhDr. Hana Dvořáková, Dr. Jana Horneková, Dr. Jan Horský, Ass. Prof. Ivan Jakubec, Dr. Jaromír Málek, Dr. phil. Wolf B. Oerter, Prof. Jaroslava Pešková, Ass. Prof. Roman Prahl, PhDr. Jiřina Růžová, Ass. Prof. Jiří Štaif, and Ass. Prof. Břetislav Vachala. During my numerous visits in the friendly atmosphere of the Institute of Egyptology at the University of Vienna, Dr. Johanna Holaubek also played an important role in the formation of the content of the work, and I would also like to mention the help and advice of Mag. Irene Kaplan, Mrs Eveline Wabnig, Mag. Konrad Antonicek and Ass. Prof. Peter Jánosi, and, in addition, Dr. Erich Sommerauer and Dr. Gottfried Hammernik. Furthemore, I would like to mention by name my colleagues Mgr. Hana Benešovská, Dr. Jiří Janák, Adéla Macková, PhDr. Roman Míšek, Dr. František Ondráš, PhDr. Lucie Storchová and Mgr. Hana Vymazalová, who helped me with their knowledge of different fields of research and sources. Last, but not least, I would like to express my gratitude to Mgr. Renata Landgráfová, who translated this text and added a number of valuable comments. Both authors would like to thank Mr James Grimaldi for the revision of the chapter 'The background of Austrian economic influence in Egypt, Sudan and the Levant.'

While acquiring my source materials, I had to visit a number of institutions. To all their employees, who allowed me to study and publish the materials, I extend my thanks. Some I would like to mention by name. I have studied materials of the Austrian State Archives in Vienna (Dr. L. Auer, Dr. E. Petritsch), the archive of the National Museum in Prague (Prof. J. Čechura, Dr. M. Běličová, and other assistants of the study room of the archive), the archive of the National Theatre (Mgr. Z. Benešová and Mgr. T. Součková), of the Memorial of National Literacy (Dr. R. Dačeva, Mgr. Mejstříková, Mr Vaniš), of the Archive of the Charles University (Prof. J. Petráň, members of the study hall of the archive), of the Archive of Architecture of the National Technical Museum, of the National Library of the Czech Republic – Department of manuscripts, and the Náprstek Museum (above all Dr. J. Součková, director of the museum, Mgr. S. Pavlasová and Dr. Barochová). A significant part of the manuscript was written during my stay in Vienna in winter 2000–2001 supported by the scholarship of the Austrian government in terms of the programme AKTION, and additions were made during a study stay in Austrian State Archives in Vienna in May 2002, AKTION project 33 p 15.

The rich illustrations, accompanying this volume, were made possible through the kind permit from the following institutions and individuals: Mrs Alena Bílek; the City Gallery Prague (Galerie Hlavního města Prahy, Mrs Jelínková); Petr Meissner; Archives of the Czech Institute of Egyptology, Kamil Voděra; and others as indicated in photo credits.

For the financial patronnage of the book my thanks go to the Czech National Centre for Egyptology of Charles University (Project LN 00A064) and to the Unis Ltd, namely Ing. Jiří Kovář.

The publication was carefully edited and supervised by the Set Out publishing house, where I am indebted to PhDr. Roman Míšek, and Mrs Jana Kurotiková for giving the manuscript the final book form.

Finally, while I am aware that I could not have mentioned by far everyone who enabled me to publish this book or assisted at its creation on the professional level, I would like to express my gratitude to those who helped me on the personal level, above all to my family and all my friends.

Prague, 25th of November 2003

Viktor Oliva, On the edge of the Sahara desert

The background of Austrian economic influence in Egypt, Sudan and the Levant
Outline of historical survey of the 19th century

Roman Míšek

At the beginning of the 19th century, the unexplored world of the Orient changed into a world trade market, promising truly effective growth. In spite of the existence of caravan routes, slave markets and other signs of economic Middle Ages, the Near East and Levant became an area of common interest in economic policies of European powers. Moreover European cultural horizons broadened with pioneering travel reports[1], and opened gradually to the Orient. The 19th century uncovered new dimensions in European relations with Middle East, re-discovered or even newly imagined many features of this specific area. The 'Orient' – from the Levant to Sudan, from Maghrib to Persia, became part of Europe's strategic plans, and entered the economic policies of European states in a new enhanced dimension.

The Hapsburg monarchy, narrowly bound to the economic and political development of the Ottoman Empire, gradually developed its Eastern interests from the 18th century onwards, especially in the Eastern Mediterranean. The Austrian monarchy found together with other powers new horizons of expansion. European powers had great interest in importing accessible raw materials and exporting products to this area. Austria, gradually starting her own industrial revolution, was no exception.

In addition to this, the Napoleonic expedition in 1798 started a major change especially in the political and economic development of the Ottoman Empire, including both foreign relations and domestic policy. The Ottoman Empire, as the only political partner of European powers in the Middle East, had to implement substantial changes to modify its state administration and economic system. But these changes were not only a result of the long-standing contact with European trade, but also a necessity for counteracting the threat of the economic and even *de facto* political colonisation of large areas of Balkans, North Africa and the Levant.

The process of modernisation in the Ottoman Empire was accelerated by the Imperial Rescript of Gülhan in 1839. This was a decisive step made by the Sublime Porte. During the 19th century the subsequent development of the interests of European powers, especially after the Crimean war, stimulated the Ottomans to further embrace modern Europe. Thus the European allies could, following the alliance that supported the empire, develop on the Ottoman territory their economic and political influence.

Austria understood her involvement in the Levant as a specific priority of her foreign policy. The position of Austrian interests was in accordance with Austrian presence in the Balkan Peninsula and in Asia Minor, even after the Crimean war, when the monarchy was forced to search for new allies to replace the former coalition with Russia. In addition, the Hapsburg Empire could always claim long-standing and immediate diplomatic relations with the Ottoman Empire. These contacts, forced by close neighbourhood, then created a fostering milieu for the entrepreneurs of Vienna and Trieste, comparable with the activities of French and British tradesmen.

Austrian diplomacy in the Levant

The Hapsburg-Ottoman relations entered a new phase of consolidation at the end of the 17th century and at the beginning of the 18th century. The losses suffered in the struggle for the acceptance of the Pragmatic sanction accelerated the new effort of Vienna's diplomacy to achieve a strong position in European and Eastern policy. It also led to a further development of diplomatic relations between Constantinople and Vienna. Austrian diplomacy became aware of the possibility of peaceful cooperation. This task required an established professional representation, and support for diplomatic education. Therefore, Austria came into possession of an effective structure during the rule of Maria Theresia, when the Oriental Academy was founded.[2] The institution, installed by Chancellor Count Kaunitz in 1754, aimed at providing new diplomats with sufficient background for a service by the Sublime Porte. This was in fact an attempt to improve the fragile Austro-Ottoman relations.

A previous educational praxis – i.e. sending young apprentice interpreters and diplomats to Constantinople (they were called Sprachknaben) – was insufficient for the new style of diplomacy, required from the end of 18th century onwards, and characteristic for the whole 19th century. Austria needed a diplomacy that could foster her struggle with unsolved Balkan and Italian questions, and would help effectively to balance the economic difficulties of the monarchy. Thus the Oriental Academy had to create a curriculum that could fulfil these requirements. Such educational programme included and enhanced the study of foreign languages and also gave a clear preference to practical education. It even embraced horse riding and dancing lessons in the attempt to educate men with considerable language abilities and practical skills, and thus became a model, that surpassed the education policies of other European powers in the 19th century.

Moreover, there is another point that deserves our attention – Austria managed the professional administration of the Balkan areas under her control, and maintained a substantial representative establishment in the Levant. To keep running the administration in these areas with notable cultural and ethnic differences, she required a highly trained staff. Thus the Oriental Academy had an invaluable position in supporting modern diplomacy of the Metternich and post-Metternich era, because it supplied the human resources for this territory that was to be one of the most important spheres of European system of powers.

The Oriental Academy trained a large number of important individuals for Foreign Service, and possessed a unique scholarly position. First generation of teachers were mostly theologians, and set a high level that trained famous specialists in Oriental culture and languages, such as Joseph Hammer von Purgstall or Alfred von Kremer.

Purgstall can be justly compared to the leading French scholar of that time, Sylvestre de Sacy. Hammer-Purgstall, a man of scholarly talent and literary ambitions, held various diplomatic posts in Constantinople, Jassa and Cairo. He travelled to Constantinople during the Napoleonic campaign in Egypt. Hammer was sent to accompany the British fleet operating in the Eastern Mediterranean as a representative of the Hapsburg monarchy – an ally of Great Britain against the French. After a career in diplomacy he continued his professional life as a renowned translator and scholar, and author of many works dealing with the Oriental world. He not only translated classical Arab literature, but also specialised in historical topics. One of his most remarkable books is *Geschichte des Osmanischen Reiches*. It comprises ten volumes and remains a basic work for modern studies regarding the Ottoman Empire.[3] Thus he can be named alongside with his pupil Alfred von Kremer as a founding father of Austrian Oriental studies, which were firmly set in connection with diplomacy and foreign policy.

Alfred von Kremer (1828–1889) belonged to Hammer's followers and combined the skills of a scholar and diplomat. Between 1849 and 1851 he lived in Syria in order to master colloquial Arabic. After his return to Vienna he was awarded a professorship of colloquial Arabic at Vienna Polytechnic Institute. After a year he accepted a position in the diplomatic service as a lecturer and his places of work included Alexandria, Cairo, Galatia and Beirut. He reached a high diplomatic status as a member of the Committee for Egyptian State Debt in 1876. His career was crowned by a post as Minister of Commerce. Alfred von Kremer's generation included also Heinrich Haymerle (1828–1881), who began his studies in 1846, and soon became a respected orientalist and able state official. His career culminated with the position of Minister of Foreign Affairs.

An overview of Austrian oriental interests of that period cannot be complete without Anton Prokesch von Osten, the envoy to Athens in the 1830s and later an internuncio in Constantinople. Paradoxically, Prokesch never attended the Oriental Academy, yet managed to attain an exclusive position in Austrian foreign relations and in the milieu of international relations with the Eastern Mediterranean. Anton Prokesch, later Count von Osten, was born in a middle class family of a commercial inspector. Financial problems led to an early break with his university studies, at which point he entered the army, at the peak of the Napoleonic wars. His talent and abilities as a military engineer and a good observer, later documented in his memoirs and travelogues, enabled him to join the headquarters staff of General Prince Schwarzenberg. Thus he entered a circle of gifted young soldiers, as well as the elite of the Austrian army. In addition, Schwarzenberg's family took fancy in him, which granted him connections in the highest levels of Austrian society. These contacts then helped him enter a high-ranking diplomatic position, without his being of noble origin, or member of an old family with established position in diplomatic ranks. The career of Prokesch started rapidly in the 1820s, and in its entirety represents a sample of Metternich Eastern diplomacy that interconnected economic interests of the monarchy and political steps in the balance of powers. Prince Metternich, despite his not paying any exceptional attention to the Orient, aimed his plans at an economic expansionism with establishment of representatives in the Levant and Orient in general. This policy was proved during the first half of the 19th century, as Austria kept her economic positions in Asia Minor and the Levant, and moreover was able to root her interests in northern and sub-Saharan Africa.

Envoy Prokesch spent almost entire career in the Orient, and achieved successes at the court of Muhammad Ali in the 1820s and 1830s, or later in Constantinople. Despite his lacking command of Oriental languages, his materials, including his edited travelogues, represent an important source for the study of Oriental culture of his period, as well as of the European view of the Orient. His travel diaries from Egypt are of particular interest for Egyptology since they describe ancient Egyptian monuments, directly preceding any archaeological survey.[4]

The Austrian position in Africa and the Levant

'Kultusprotektorat' and the economic expansion

The Hapsburg monarchy as a member of the anti-Napoleonic alliance entered the colonial trade with North Africa and the Levant already at the beginning of the 19th century. However, the allied victory that terminated the existence of the Napoleonic Empire, actually changed the balance of powers and consistency of trade relations in the Eastern Mediterranean. Thus, although Austria could have made use of previous advantages of successful anti-Ottoman campaigns, Great Britain and France grasped the importance of Levantine trade and signed treaties with the Sublime Porte to strengthen their already growing influence in the entire Mediterranean. Moreover Britain profited from gains of Ionian Archipelago and Rhodos Island.

However, Vienna following its alliance with London, maintained her position as the primary importer and exporter in the region. The Austro-British cooperation at the Vienna Congress of 1815 successfully curbed piracy. It injected substantial help to the entrepreneurs of Vienna and Trieste, and opened for them new areas of maritime trade. Trieste thus became one of the constitutive trade partners of Alexandria in the 1820s. Although the Austro-Egyptian commercial activities shared a tradition going as far back as the 17th and 18th centuries, new impetus arrived with the era of Muhammad Ali. The Trieste-Alexandria trade route sustained notably the development of Egyptian, Sudanese and Levantine commerce. In 1828 nearly a half of Egyptian and Cypriot export wheat passed through this Italian harbour. At that time, the Hapsburg monarchy established commercial agencies in Cairo, Alexandria and Damiette.[5]

The general consulate in Cairo and the consulates in Alexandria, Damiette and Rosette backed the administration of almost thirty enterprises, connected with the main European harbours such as Trieste, Leghorn, Venice and Marseille. Convoys of trade ships, protected by the Imperial and Royal Navies followed routes from the Ionian ports and then started homeward bound from Alexandria. Although piracy still posed a significant danger, commercial activities between Austria and Egypt intensified. Austria imported Egyptian cotton, and, in turn exported wood, which was a necessary resource for Muhammad Ali's new fleet building.[6]

The markets of Cairo and Alexandria accepted not only wood – the array of commodities included coal, copper, glass, caps, cloth, nails, paper, steel, pepper, sugar, tobacco, cigarettes etc. In turn, Austrian markets welcomed gum arabic, indigo, dates, saffron and incense. Still, cotton dominated the Egyptian export, even though since the 1830s the rising cost of transportation drove up the price of cotton itself. At that time, the Trieste company 'Österreichische' Lloyd was already an established business, and as such, was much appreciated both by Vienna and by Muhammad Ali. These commercial relations proved to be stable throughout the 19th century.

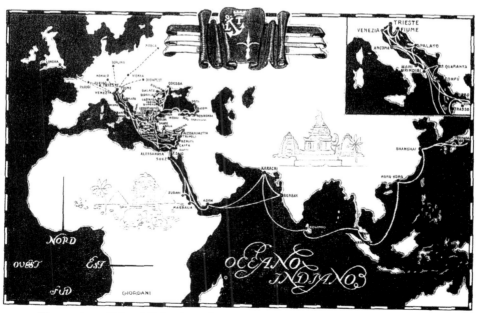

The routes of Lloyd Triestino, the 20th century heir of the Austrian Lloyd

The Austrian Lloyd deserves our further attention. The history and development of this company is a good case study for following the Austrian trade policy in the Eastern Mediterranean. The Lloyd Steamship Company was a joint-stock company. Its chief shareholder was Baron Rothschild.[7] Rothschild convinced his cousin Anton Schnapper[8] and the Wertheimstein family[9] to invest in the company shares. Thus he formed a financially strong consortium of shareholders. Moreover, Salomon Rothschild persuaded even minor entrepreneurs to become stockholders of Lloyd's. The company signed a contract with the Austrian Imperial and Royal Post in 1837, for mail delivery, besides the already established trade and passenger lines. The importance of mail service was significant even from the point of view of Austrian diplomatic relations. Vienna thus gained a tool to spread her influence over the Levant, under the suspicious eye of Paris, supporting, obviously, French ship companies in the Mediterranean. Nonetheless, the Austrian post service in its prime had 73 post offices across the Ottoman Empire.[10]

The Austrian Lloyd introduced lines from Trieste to Constantinople and Alexandria by 1837. In the 1840s, they established new routes – to Beirut and Jerusalem, followed in 1850s by Jaffa, and Haifa. In 1865 Lloyd thus had four express lines plus two regular routes.

In spite of its speedy expansion, the company was at first not a financial success, and Rothschild had to ask for governmental financial support to cover the loss. The Austrian government was aware of the advantages of maintaining the mail service and supported Lloyd with a few loans. A further successful step was a regular subsidy amounting to one million guldens yearly. The subsidy balanced the financial losses on less successful lines and enabled the introduction of a route connecting Egypt and Syria. On the other hand the Austrian government sustained this route by a war ship *Maria Anna.*

The Austrian Lloyd was a governmental *protégé.* The results of such dealing were imposing. The private company had a governmental subsidy and repaid it by cooperation including even the background for diplomatic activities.[11] Lloyd provided namely free transportation for Austrian diplomats travelling in the area of the company's coverage. Thus, it should not be surprising to read the lines of Count Stadion – in 1846 governor of Trieste – *'the governments of the Mediterranean countries are viewing with greed and jealousy the predominance of Austrian shipping in the Levant.'*[12]

Eventually, the financial effect came as well. Most lines started to earn profits in the 1850s. Finally the opening of the Suez Canal changed the structure of Lloyd's routes, and a couple of new express lines were introduced, from Trieste to Bombay.[13] Still, Lloyd was not isolated in its activities, and had to cope with Italian, French and newly established Russian competitors.[14]

The dimensions of co-operation with Muhammad Ali formed almost an exception in commercial and diplomatic relations, which is especially remarkable when compared to the situation in north-western Africa. There were no established diplomatic representations in Algeria or Morocco at the beginning of the 19th century, and hardly anything seemed to favour a change – a Moroccan bey was known to have equipped a fleet to fight merchants from Austria, Naples, Tuscany, Prussia and Hamburg. The Moroccan pirates were infamous for their cruelty across the Mediterranean. In fact, the sultan of Morocco Mawlay Suleiman avoided a raid of allied European powers in 1817 by officially banning this profession.

Austria achieved a trade agreement with Morocco only in 1830, following an incident in 1828, when an Austrian brig, 'Il Veloce', with full cargo, was prevented from continuing her voyage to Brazil. An attempt of Austrian government to liberate the ship peacefully was unsuccessful, and was followed by a blockade of Tangier and Tetouan by a fleet under the command of Admiral Francesco Bandier. In addition, his ships bombarded the forts of Larache and Arsila.[15] Once 'Il Veloce' was freed, Austria forced the sultan into a negotiation on trade agreement. The agreement granted Austrian ships free access to Moroccan harbours. Further steps, new Austrian connections to Tangier, Tetouan and Mogador, were achieved actually only after the French occupation of Algiers.

An unequivocal success of Vienna had been the maritime line to and through Constantinople. Austrians renewed their connections after the Napoleonic period and their activities surpassed even the British and French presence. The way through Constantinople guaranteed an access to Ottoman markets, both for export and import, and moreover it was an entry into the Black Sea region. Austrian trade routes led to Smyrna and the Ionian Archipelago and they continued to Constantinople and back to the Mediterranean. Moreover, Constantinople functioned as a tranship point for convoys with corn, which came from the Black Sea, and it is noteworthy that the number of Austrian ships berthing in Constantinople in 1820s were twice as high as that of Russian ships.[16]

The Greek crisis brought a temporary break of ship service. The regular service was renewed immediately after the peace of Adrianople, with lines to Constantinople and the Black Sea. The steamship company DDSG ran with the ships *Maria Dorothea* and *Fürst Metternich* the connection Smyrna – Constantinople and Trebizond and later from 1839 a line Smyrna – Thessalonica. The Austrian ships took charge of mail services between Europe and the Ottoman Empire.[17]

Meanwhile, the trade in Syria intensified. The vice-consulates in Acre and Alexandrette were supplemented by trade agencies in other harbours. Yet the position of Austria in this region was not unambiguous – attempts to establish contacts were only confirmed in 1832 to 1840 under Muhammad Ali with an official ferman, which acknowledged Austrian position as equal with Britain.

Austria developed its trade interests considerably in 1830s. Austrian commercial aims were specialised, as was already mentioned above, in raw materials. The North African region could supply Middle Egyptian sugar, sugar cane, and dates, Sudanese salt, indigo as well as the most precious gum arabic. Still, Austrian export is not to be overlooked – thus e.g. in 1836 the value of exported Austrian goods to the region amounted to 1.7 million guldens. We can follow a growing Austrian interest in the Sudan area, which was to be – for the next twenty years – an important factor in calculations of both entrepreneur and diplomatic circles in Vienna and Trieste.

The area of Sudan and the Red Sea region – i.e. the Qusseir area in particular – was even considered a possible zone of colonial expansion. As such it was viewed by Archduke Maximilian. To enhance and develop trade relations with the Sudan, the Austrian government decided to build up its diplomatic position – the vice-consulate in Khartoum was opened as early as in 1824. The commercial relations continued and it led to the establishment of Khartoum consulate in 1851. In spite of unexpected decline after 1859, when Maximilian's view was outdated, the Austrian influence in the Sudanese region remained considerable.[18]

The era of the 1850s brought another important question into the focus of Austrian trade policy. Austrian international trade interests were represented by such personalities as Archduke Ferdinand Maximilian, eager to follow colonial policy, and Minister of Finance and Commerce Baron Karl Ludwig v. Bruck, former director of the Austrian Lloyd. Bruck had strong ties to the entrepreneurs of Trieste. Thus he kept an eye on projects connected with maritime trade routes that supported the harbour of Trieste. He was a chief supporter of developing Austrian colonial interests in the 1850s and of Austrian activity regarding the Suez Canal.

The Hapsburg monarchy had its people taking active part in the Suez Canal project from the very beginning. Vienna sought in this project new opportunity for the Austrian Lloyd steamship company. The project itself had a longer history – first attempts on a study were made in 1833 by Prosper Enfantin and Dufour-Feronce, who based their observations on the work of Linant de Bellefonds. Enfantin eventually founded a society for the study of the building of the canal on the 30th of November 1846, and this society was a direct predecessor of the company that actually built the canal. The entire plan should have been shielded diplomatically by Austria, France and Germany. The planned alliance was disrupted by a rivalry between Bruck and Enfantin. Bruck and Dufour-Feronce voted for Trieste as the headquarters for the society and for Alois von Negrelli (Luigi Negrelli) as a chief engineer of the project.[19]

Luigi Negrelli was a top Austrian engineer of that time, famous for his railway projects, successfully carried out throughout the monarchy. He played an active part in various committees of the Society for the Suez Canal, but found his position seriously weakened after the Crimean war, when he supported Italian policy, which was very disagreeable to the government in Vienna. His death in 1858 ended his activities prematurely. Thus, although it was Negrelli's plan that was actually carried out in the building of the Canal, the builder *par excellence* in the eyes of posterity was to be Ferdinand de Lesseps, a cousin of Eugenie, the Empress of France.[20] De Lesseps was a man of Basque origin, and his family ruined itself by its strong pro-Napoleonic position. In spite of this, Ferdinand followed the tradition and entered diplomatic ranks, becoming a vice-consul in Egypt in 1832–1837. Although he was mostly 'renowned' as a 'Parisian dandy in the desert', his activities were broader than the nickname suggested. He acquainted himself well with the conditions and connections of the Mediterranean trade and its enterprises.

The career of de Lesseps continued successfully. In 1848, he was a plenipotentiary minister, and in the following year a chief of mission in Rome. Yet, although already interested and having studied the works of Linant de Bellefonds and Enfantin, he turned his attention fully to the Canal project, only after he was forced to leave the Foreign Service. Alexis de Tocqueville, minister of Foreign affairs charged him with supporting the Republicans, had him tried and eventually sent to pension without any financial support. De Lesseps was thus forced, after 24 years of diplomatic service, to concentrate on business. That led him back to the Canal project.

Although these European parties were interested in the Suez stage, their diplomatic opinions were far from being united in consensus. On the part of the British, Palmerston considered the project too expensive and, unlike the railway, neither practical nor reasonable. British interests in Egypt at that time concentrated on land routes. Finally it brought the only result – the railway from Alexandria to Cairo.

Viceroy Muhammad Ali kept British influence at bay for a considerable time. He aimed to eliminate the British presence and refused to build the canal on the grounds that it would endanger the balance in the Mediterranean and the Red Sea. Although even Prince Metternich tried to persuade the viceroy to sustain the Suez project, the viceroy showed no enthusiasm and justly supposed this would seriously damage the independence of Egypt. The viceroy was interested in a presupposed position of the Sublime Porte in the entire enterprise and claimed his own ability to build the canal, if that were utterly necessary, as he claimed his right to control the canal traffic and its fees.[21]

The opposition similar to Ali's view on the Canal project continued under Abbas Pasha, who followed a line of strong opposition against European influence in Egypt. His refusal of the Canal building became his strong political weapon. A change came only with the violent end of Abbas's life and reign.

As for the Austrian position, Archduke Ferdinand Maximilian, brother of Emperor Franz Joseph, was the chief protagonist of maritime interests of the monarchy. When Archduke Maximilian became the Supreme Commander of the Austrian Navy in August 1854, the colonial interests of Vienna and Trieste were substantially strengthened. At first, his position was that of a commander of the *Kriegsmarine*, but later, as he made commercial interests the foremost goal of the Austrian naval presence, he took tighter control of trade ships. Maximilian moreover supported the firm Stabilimento Tecnico in Trieste and his position was clearly in favour of the Suez Canal and of enforcing the Austrian presence in the Red Sea.

All these plans were nonetheless destined to be put into practice only after the Crimean war intermezzo, which modified remarkably the diplomatic existence of the Hapsburg monarchy.

An outline of the Austrian economic presence in the Ottoman Empire could not be complete without including the '*Kultusprotektorat*'. Austria namely gained a privileged status as a protector of the Catholic Church in Jerusalem, Upper Egypt and Sudan. Since the 18th century the missionaries and pilgrims on their way to these regions claimed Austrian protection. This was in fact derived from the capitulation, provided by the Sultan both to the King of France and to the Holy Roman Emperor. Austria covered first the hospice in Jerusalem and Tantur, later accepted as protégées the Christians of Latin and Coptic denominations in Upper Egypt and Sudan, as well as the newly established missions to the south of Khartoum.[22] Still, Austria had to compete with France for the privilege of being a protector of the Catholic Christians of Roman obedience. The Capitulations, a result of a long development of treaties regarding the Holy Places, in fact brought a sort of quasi-milet into being, which shielded European interests.

However, the French envoy achieved an authoritative position and in the 18th century he was considered as a protector not just of the pilgrims in the Holy Land, but of all Catholic Christians in the region, as they were considered to be under the protection of the King of France. [23]

Thus the Austrian 'internuncio' was only a second in command, but he claimed the authority of guarding the rights of the Catholic religious activities. It was a paradox, as the French were always affected by anti-clerical positions, and yet never ceased to use the protection of the Catholic Church as a political instrument. Vienna never achieved as dominant a stand as Paris. But Austria was for the Sultan a partner that was not to be overlooked – at least since the Zsitvatorok treaty of 1615. The text of the treaty (dedicated to clearing the position of Istvan Bocskai in Transylvania and of the Sultan in Moldavia and Wallachia) entitled the Emperor to be named as brother of the Sultan, with equal power to the King of France. In addition there was another successful step made by Emperor Matthias in religious questions, in fact an independent capitulation – the Sultan allowed the Jesuit order to build a church and perform religious services in Jerusalem. Although Societas Iesu never used the privilege in full, they built a church in Constantinople.[24]

The 19th century brought a new focus – the Hapsburg monarchy expanded the protection to the Sudan. Austria at that time still used the formal titulary of the Emperor – King of Jerusalem.[25] In spite of the degree of pure formalism inherent to that title, the Emperor did not neglect his actual duties. Franz Joseph I, while visiting the Levant in 1869, visited the Holy Places and gave a clear indication that Austria would not loose her guardian position. In the same way, Austria acted as a patron for the new installation of the Coptic Catholic Patriarch Makarios, ordained by Pope Leo XIII in 1895.[26]

Ecclesiastical institutions gained Austrian subsidies. Most of them went to the Franciscan order in Jerusalem. It was this order that founded most missions in Upper Egypt. Further subsidies went to the Armenian, Syrian, Greek and Maronite Churches. The means originated in special funds of the missionaries, and of the Ministry of Foreign Affairs in Vienna.[27] The main goal must have been that of Austrian economic penetration into the region. These activities were in fact long-term, namely a network of schools, churches, presbyteries and hospices growing in Palestine since 1837, documented by substantial correspondence between the Ministry in Vienna and its clerks.[28] Later, in the 1850s, these activities moved further south to the Sudan.

The Sudanese circumstances seem to be rather specific. The mission posts were not established by the Catholic Church but by a religious association that was given permission to organise fundraising campaigns in the monarchy and control their gains. The association, together with the first missionary post, were founded in 1851. Furthermore, the Austrian government assigned a yearly subsidy of 1000 guldens to the Sudanese missions. Moreover a part of missionary activity was to educate and Christianise Sudanese children. Austrian missionary schools in Khartoum were expected to organise and transport Sudanese children into various dioceses of the monarchy, where they would be educated. But some of the missionaries unfortunately used these transfers as a convenient veil for slavery. The slave trade chain connected even the slave market in Cairo and Lloyd Steamship Company (children declared as being of the captain's) and even the consulates of Austria, Naples, and Sardinia were very helpful in this business.

The smuggling of slave children could not be concealed for long. The church authorities soon discovered the dealings, and the slave trade chain was destroyed by a discreet intervention of the Austrian government. Nonetheless, the Sudanese colonial dream gradually broke into pieces. Missionary activities were blocked by native resistance, and high taxation, imposed by Egyptian authorities, slowed down the economic growth, which led to a gradual dissolvement of trade relations. Finally the second half of the 19th century saw only the consulate of Khartoum surviving and the last missions ended their activities after 1885, in the stormy Mahdi uprising.[29]

Nevertheless, the Sudanese model, i.e. Austrian schools and mission network, represented not only the Catholic Church, but always the Austrian political and economic interests.[30] The policy of cultural leverage via school and church subsidies was in operation from the 19th to the 20th century. It is noteworthy that this is true of a similar operation e.g. in Lebanon, where we can find a Christian school subsided by Austrian funds.

A new orientation after the Crimean war

The Austrian position after the Crimean war, regarding the Eastern question and position in the Levant, was at the crossroads of Austrian foreign and home affairs. During the Crimean war itself, Austria did not enter the armed conflict as such. In spite of having signed an alliance with France and Great Britain in 1854, Austria did not enter armed combat against Russia, since the political elite of the monarchy held an unfavourable attitude in this respect.[31] The Austrian Chancellor at that time, Count Buol-Schaunstein, tried to follow the Metternich line, i.e. cooperation with the powers. Yet, he did not possess the abilities of his predecessors, who managed to balance the Austrian position on the edge between Russia and Great Britain. He failed in actually fulfilling treaties and agreements, which kept the Hapsburg Empire as a key partner in European system of powers.[32] The Crimean War strategy, sustained also by the Emperor, relied on the fact that Austrian alliance with Great Britain should have forced Russia into modifying the Moldavia and Wallachia occupation regime. Unfortunately, this situation came into being only after the Peace of Paris in 1856.

Before that, as London and Paris entered the conflict with Russian forces, Austria was supposed to influence Russian policy in that respect. Yet, Buol-Schaunstein had not secured any pledges or guarantees from the European powers, regarding subsequent Austrian position in the Balkan area. In addition, some politicians repeatedly pointed out the long-standing cooperation with Russia, which slowed the ultimatum for Russia as well. Thus, although the text had been written already on the 3rd of July 1854, and modified on the 28th of December 1855, it remained only a piece of paper, without any political consequences.[33] The ultimatum nevertheless can be viewed as the breakpoint in the relations between Russia and Austria. The liaison between two Eastern European powers, declared since 1849, was severed and the new disequilibrium had a long-term impact – it can be reasonably named as one of the roots of the 1914 development.[34]

If we should then consider the Viennese attitude as jeopardising the very existence of the monarchy, there is more to blame than Buol-Schaunstein's inconsistent policy. The Hapsburg monarchy had no potential to enter warfare, on either side of the conflict.

The economic lability of the monarchy has been studied in detail, especially with regard to the supposed inaptitude of Austria to maintain the position of a European power with considerable influence in the Balkan and Arabian Peninsula. Actually, this opinion cannot be ruled out, since Austria did loose politically due to its economic difficulties, as the Crimean example shows. In the summer of 1853 the Austrian deficit reached 95 millions guldens. The military budget was estimated at 112 millions. However, during that year, the army asked for further 115 millions.[35] The Ministry of Finance tried to solve the situation by a loan, preferably from a foreign banker, as there was no chance to cover the expenses from any new tariff or charge. The state had a constant shortfall in its finances. The ministry decided to opt for an issue of bonds, to be covered by lottery gains. Moreover, Baron von Czernig left for Paris in March, to ensure further loans. He succeeded with Rothschild, and in addition in Frankfurt and Amsterodam. Moreover, the long-term lability of state budget had to be solved by selling state properties, and even by reducing the content of silver in the coinage.

A budget proposal for 1855, dated 15th of October 1854, had 414 millions of expenses, but only 249 millions actually covered by the state income. Thus there was a deficit of 165 millions. The military budget was estimated at 184 millions, but soon was declared insufficient, and the Army requested further 73 millions in November 1854.[36]

Austria might have gained considerably as a power and in terms of political partnerships if she had entered the Crimean conflict. However the Schaunstein government could not take part in warfare without substantially endangering the state itself. Moreover, not even Metternich thought the Crimean war to be a clash that would change the balance of powers in Europe. The Austrian hesitation was thus understandable.

Negotiations in Paris in 1856 left Austria, although formally a victorious power, facing the French and Sardinian alliance, that led the Hapsburg monarchy into developments that put an end to both Austrian great power intentions in Europe and Germany and to her colonial ambitions in Africa, Arabia and the Levant.

The Suez Canal question also signalled new developments after the Crimean war. The negotiations in the Suez Canal Company were led by Bruck and Pasquale di Revoltella, delegates of Vienna government and bankers, and entrepreneurs of Vienna and Trieste. The two representatives advocated Austrian participation on the Canal project, but they also had to aim their attention at fragile political circumstances. Austria had Italian and Prussian questions to solve. Minister of Commerce Toggenburg could not take over the subscribed shares, as the future canal neutrality was still not cleared, and this question overshadowed the renewed alliance of Austria and Great Britain.

London opposed the Canal project from the very beginning. In spite of British distrust and concerns about the route to India, the Palmerston government at length entered the project and even supplanted the position of Austria in the Company. Palmerston's concern was mainly to override the French influence.[37] The uneasiness regarding the French presence is expressed in period newspapers, such as the 1859 *Times* – '*Although there is no doubt that France has always wanted to compete with our country in Egypt, where the ambition of its governments has suffered two such significant defeats, and although it would willingly seek to make the Viceroy independent of the Porte ...*'

For Palmerston, de Lesseps and the Canal fuelled his negative attitudes toward Egypt and France, and remained the cornerstone of his political thought processes until his death in 1865. Austria indeed needed to maintain an ally against Russia, and thus satisfied Palmerston's requirements. Thus, Vienna preferred participation in the Euphrates Valley Railway project, which may have put a barrier against Russian influence, and stopped the support for de Lesseps. The situation verged on chaos, due to the developments in Italy and Poland, strongly influenced by France. Minister Bruck left his position, and was followed by Count Rechberg. In general, in the light of all these aspects, Austrian attitudes with respect to the Suez Canal changed, thus signalling a new chapter for Austrian colonial interests in Egypt, Sudan and the Levant.

The Hapsburg Monarchy and the new era of colonialism

The Hapsburg monarchy aimed at redefining its own position as a great power, and terminated several state supported projects – e.g. the colonial attempts on the White Nile, and hitherto promising expansion on Sudanese-Eritrean coastal area toward Suqutra. This last project was in operation since 1857, as Archduke Maximilian entrusted Wilhelm von Tegetthoff with the occupation mission. The project went without any official participation of the Ministry of Foreign Affairs, but with strong support of the Emperor himself, and was considered secret. The ambitious plan was nonetheless put aside after crushing defeats at Magenta and Solferino, and dissolving of the Austrian presence in Northern Italy, accompanied by strong French and Sardinian pressure on Austrian affairs.[38]

The 1860s brought alterations to Austrian trade policies as well – the Austrian government dissolved its control over international trade and support to trade activities, although it kept the administrative tasks, connected with private trade enterprises. State administration and private sector still had strong mutual ties, and interpersonal relations binding both areas, but the position of Austria as a great trade partner in the Mediterranean changed, even though it continued be the third greatest exporter and importer in the region.[39]

Conditions altered inside the Ottoman Empire as well. A sequel of uprisings and massacres in Montenegro, Bosnia and Herzegovina, Jeddah, Damascus and Beirut marked the end of 1850s. The British and French consuls were killed in

Jeddah. The Sublime Porte had to suppress a number of anti-Christian revolts and intervened in Syria with an armed action. This overstrained the Ottoman state budget and redoubled its debt, and state administration faced the problem how to finance itself.[40] The complicated home affairs of the Sublime Porte soon entered international relations as a new threat in the Eastern Question.

France and Great Britain decided, in order to protect their own investments in the region, to suppress any attempts to reopen the Eastern Question dilemma. They provided the Porte with further short termed loans, and in fact took over financial control of the empire, by means of a commission that was made a part of the Ottoman State Treasury. The powers hoped to reform the Ottoman state finances and heal them from the omnipresent corruption. This proved to be a complicated task, which needed interventions, such as that of Lord Russell. In beginning 1860s, the Ottoman Empire obtained new loans in Paris, London and Amsterodam. The finances covered mainly military expenses, but helped to establish the Ottoman financial sector as well, mainly in order to fund the military activity in Montenegro.

The death of Sultan Abdulmedjid fostered short-lived hopes in new reforms and financial rehabilitation. The reform activity was rather the result of a continuous effort of European powers than of the position of the new Sultan Abdülaziz. Inflation rose, caused at the end of 1861 by high state debt and various news and rumours such as Syria's independence and the Sultan being poisoned. An acceleration of reforms and new attitudes was brought only by a nomination of a new Grand Vizier, Fuat Pasha, a strong-minded, problem-oriented man, who was willing to cooperate with foreign investors.

The rising financial sector soon included a consortium, involving Austrian bankers. There was in fact a competition, regarding the National bank establishment, and the Vizier Fuat had to choose among consortia like Revelachi-Rodocanachi (Galatian bankers with connection to London bank Frühling and Goschen) and the Oppenheim agency.

In addition, Credit Mobilier stepped in with an offer of a loan amounting to 10,000,000 pounds, in February 1862. This company operated in London, Amsterodam, Vienna and Turin, and at that time aimed at development projects of the Marseille harbour. It was Marseille that carried out most of the French Levantine trade. Another business direction was represented by Pereira and brothers, who tried to connect the Austrian railway network to the Balkan area.[41]

The opening of the Suez Canal incited an euphoria, including Austria who subsequently became an important exporter in the Levantine maritime trade and, moreover, an important financial partner for Egypt. In spite of unsolved political, technical and economic doubts hovering over the project, the finished canal roused a new wave of interest in investments in Egypt. Credit-Anstalt thus, with the help of London bank Oppenheim, took part in the Egyptian loan of 1868 that amounted to 11,890 million pounds. In accordance with this effort the Austro-Egypt Bank was founded only a year later, as a subsidiary company of Credit-Anstalt and Anglo-Austrian Bank.[42]

At the time of the the the opening of the Suez Canal the economic situation seemed optimistic. However, a decade later, the Khedive Ismail announced state bankruptcy, which affected Austria-Hungary, Great Britain, and France, all three chief creditors. The commission controlling Egypt state debt included also an Austrian, Alfred von Kremer. Austria-Hungary, a power without colonies, was nonetheless only a member of the European concert of powers, not a conductor. The position was confirmed during the Orabi Revolt – Austrians formed a part of 'the European guard', that was to protect Austrian citizens during the revolt. Vienna found the situation aggravating, as the guard expenses only added to the already noteworthy burden of the Egyptian debt. Moreover, Austria did not gain any power or influence from the situation. On the contrary, Austria's position became ambiguous.

The 1870s and 1880s opened discussions regarding sub-Saharan Africa policies. Central Africa formed another interesting export area, besides Egypt. Nonetheless, the trade deficit steadily rose, together with opposition to further financing of colonial enterprises. As a result, much tougher control over colonial policy expenses was implemented. Thus, e.g. the support for taking part in the Belgian colonial project of King Leopold II in Congo was put to an end, as further losses were expected. Moreover, the political attention turned steadily towards the complex issues of the Balkan area.

Conclusion

Austria-Hungary did not fulfil any great colonial vision of an empire in the Levant, Egypt or Central Africa, but it did enter there in an important political partnership in Middle Eastern policy. An expansionist, albeit unsuccessful, phase of Austrian foreign policy development left a wide network of embassies and consulates ensuring the economic and financial penetration as well as safety for Austrian citizens. Austrian state citizens, coming from broad range of regions under the wings of the Hapsburg eagle, formed a substantial part of the European community in the Middle East.[43] There were 7,115 Austrians in Cairo, not including many well-known, but apparently unregistered Austrians, living e.g. on the Khedivial court.[44]

The Cairo community was not a lone runner – when the Suez Canal was under construction, von Tegetthoff estimated the number of Austrian workers at the dig to be 300, including various professions, and forming thus an important part of 1,500 Europeans present there. Austrians were a remarkable part of the Port Said European community as well. Although Africa occupied only the penultimate position in the list of destinations to which Austrians emigrated (preceding Asia), far behind the preferred United States, her position was still a remarkable one, given the conditions that awaited the émigrés there.

The monarchy thus had a distinct potential of qualified workforce in Egypt, but was not in position to use it. The Hapsburg expansion, nonetheless, due to its extent, deserves to be numbered among history's great colonial powers, and did enable the monarchy to keep its international prestige in some respects until the very end of the Austro-Hungarian era. The imprint of Austrian presence, left vigorously by Austrians, Hungarians, Czechs, Slovaks and other members of this multinational commonwealth during the 19th century, was further used and deepened by various personages, Orientalist scholars and professionals, coming from succession states, heirs of the Hapsburg monarchy after the WW I.

Notes:

1 Burckhardt, J. L., *Travels in Syria and the Holy Land,* ed. by Leake, W. M., 1822; *Travels in Arabia,* ed. by Ouseley, W., 1829; *Arabic Proverbs, or the Manners and Customs of the Modern Egyptians,* ed. by Ouseley, W., 1830; To the life of Jean Louis Burckhardt, Sim, K., *Desert Traveller, The Life of Jean Louis Burckhardt,* 2000; The subject of Austrian travellers was treated by Barnard, V., *Österreicher im Orient, Eine Bestandsaufnahme österreichischer Reiseliteratur im 19. Jahrhundert,* Wien 1996. Generally Hourani, A., *A History of the Arab Peoples,* New York 1991; Goddard, H., *A History of Christian-Muslim Relations,* Edinburgh 2000.

2 See Hammer-Purgstall, J., *Erinnerungen aus meinem Leben 1774–1852 bearbeitet von Reinhard Bachofen von Echt.* Wien – Leipzig 1940, p. 22f, also Bachmann, M., *Österreich und das osmanische Reich.* Wien 1986; Breycha-Vauthier, A., *Österreich in der Levante.* Wien – München 1972; Wandruszka, A. – Urbanitsch, P., *Die Habsburgermonarchie 1848–1914* VI/1, Wien 1989.

3 Kaiser, R., 'Josef Hammer-Purgstall, Sprachknabe, Diplomat, Orientalist', in: *Ein Lesebuch zur Ausstellung Europa und der Orient,* Berlin 1989, p. 106–115.

4 See Prokesch von Osten, *Aus den Tagebüchern des Grafen Prokesch von Osten 1830–1834,* Wien 1909; *Mehmed-Ali, Vize-König von Aegypten, Aus meinem Tagebuch 1826–1841,* Wien 1877; Prokesch von Osten, *Erinnerungen aus Ägypten und Kleinasien,* 3 Bd., Wien 1831.

5 Sauer, W., 'Schwarz-Gelb in Afrika. Habsburgermonarchie und koloniale Frage', in: *K. u. K. kolonial, Habsburgermonarchie und europäische Herrschaft in Afrika,* hg. von Sauer, W., Wien – Köln – Weimar 2002, pp. 18–23; also Angerlehner, R., *Österreichischer Schiffsverkehr und Seehandel 1815–1838,* dissertation, Wien 1968, pp. 130–145.

6 Sayyid Marsot, Afaf Lutfi, *Egypt in the reign of Muhammad* Ali, Cambridge 2001, pp. 162–170.

7 Salomon Rothschild (1774–1855), son of Mayer Amschel R. (1744–1812) and Gutel Schnapper (1735–1849), founder of the Viennese branch of Rothschild.

8 Born Frankfurt/Main, 9th of November 1790, died Vienna, 24th of November 1870, son of Mayer Wolf S. (1757–1821), the brother of Gutel S., who had married in 1822 Marie von Wertheimstein. Schnapper owned the largest money exchange in Vienna and was a highly respected bussinesman.

9 Sigmund von Wertheimstein (1796–1854), president of Austrian National Bank, Consul of Spain in Vienna, head of wholesale firm Hermann von Wertheimstein. Leopold von Wertheimstein (1802–1883), general manager of Bank Rothschild, Vienna.

10 Agstner, R., 'The Austrian Lloyd Steam Navigation Company' in: *Austrian Presence in the Holy Land in the 19th century and early 20th century,* ed. by Wrba M., Tel Aviv 1996, p. 139.

11 Breycha–Vauthier, A., *Österreich in der Levante,* Wien 1972, p. 95.

12 Agstner, R., *op. cit.,* p. 140.

13 Agstner, R., *op. cit.,* p. 144.

14 In 1840 was founded British Peninsular and Occidental Steam Navigation Company, 1840 Rubattino and L. V. Florio, the last two entered the consortium Navigazione Generale Italiana, 1851 Messageries Imperiales.

15 'Berichte des Konzul von Cadiz', in: Angerlehner, R., *op. cit.* p. 168.

16 Angerlehner, R., *op. cit.,* p. 145.

17 Angerlehner, R., *op. cit.,* pp. 146–152.

18 Sauer, *op. cit.,* p. 33.

19 *History of Suez,* p. 24.

20 Winkler, D. – Pawlik, G., *Die Dampfschiffahrtgesellschaft Österreichischer Lloyd 1836–1918*, Graz 1986, p. 10–11; Farnie, D. A., *East and West of Suez, The Suez Canal in History 1854–1956*, Oxford 1969, pp. 24, 32–33. The cultural consequences treated in following chapters by Hana Navrátilová.

21 Sauer, *op. cit.*, p. 31, *History of Suez*, p. 24.

22 McEwan, Dorothea, 'The Habsburgh Church protectorate in the Holy Land', in: *Austrian Presence.....*, Tel Aviv, p. 54.

23 McEwan, Dorothea, 'The Habsburgh Church protectorate in the Holy Land', p. 59.

24 Freeze, Ch., *Catholics and Sultan. The Church and the Ottoman Empire 1453–1923*, Cambridge 1983, p. 80.

25 Breycha-Vauthier, A., *Österreich in der Levante, Geschichte und Geschichten einer alten Freundschaft*, Wien – München, p. 54.

26 McEwan, *op. cit.*, p. 63.

27 McEwan, *op. cit.*, p. 58.

28 The correspondence between Ministry of Foreign Affairs and consuls in Orient was treated in Wandruszka, A. – Urbanitsch, P., *Die Habsburgermonarchie 1848–1914* VI/1, Wien 1989. Also the correspondence between Prokesch von Osten and Buol Schaunstein considering the Armenian church in view of French influence in the Holy Land, p. 506–510.

29 Sauer, *op. cit.*, p. 43–44.

30 Sauer, *op. cit.*, p. 40–42.

31 Hess, the head of Austrian headquaters, opined that Austria is not powerful enough to enter the war with Russia. In: Sked, A., *Úpadek a pád habsburské říše* ('Decline and Fall of the Hapsburg Empire'), Praha 1995, s. 194 (further Sked).

32 'Count Buol and the Metternich tradition', *Austrian History Yearbook*, vol. 9/10 (1973/1974), ss. 173–193. The article pointed out that Buol Schaunstein was on very good terms with Metternich. Actually he was a follower of Metternich's diplomacy style.

33 To the point of home affairs Sked, p. 194–195.

34 Rich, N., *Why the Crimean War? A Cautionary Tale*, London 1985, p. 120.

35 Beer, A., *Die Finanzen Österreichs im XIX. Jahrhundert*, Prag 1877, pp. 247–248.

36 Beer, *Die Finanzen*, p. 254.

37 In November 1858 and also at the beginning of 1859 Revolltela refused to buy 50,000 issued–shares. *History of Suez*, s. 50. There were 1246 shares in Austria which were subscribed to private investors. In: Sauer, *op. cit.*, s. 53.

38 Zach, M., 'Ein unbekannter Kolonialentwurf für Nordostafrika aus dem Jahr 1861', in: Sauer, *op. cit.*, p. 97–98.

39 Shaw, *History of the Ottoman Empire and Modern Turkey*, Cambridge 1977, p. 122.

40 Floating debt 1857 – 17,94 million, 1860 – 35 million.

41 Clay, Ch., *Gold for the Sultan, Western bankers and Ottoman Finance*, New York 2000, p. 63.

42 See Marz, E., *Österreichische Industrie- und Bankpolitik in der Zeit Franz Josephs I. am Beispiel der k.k. priv. Österreichischen Credit-Anstalt f. Handel und Gewerbe* (Wien – Frankfurt – Zürich 1968). Clay, *op. cit.*, Maria Rosa Atzenhofer-Baumgartner, *Kapitalexport der Österreichische-ungarischen Monarchie im System der internazionalen Kapitalbeziehungen* (ungedr. Phil. Diss. Wien 1980) p. 257.

43 Agstner, R., 'Die Habsburger-Monarchie und Ägypten. Eine Bestandsaufnahme', p. 14, in Agstner, R., *Österreich und Ägypten*, Cairo 1993.

44 Agstner, R., *Die österreichisch-ungarische Kolonie in Kairo vor dem ersten Weltkrieg*, Cairo 1994; s. 20–22. Also Agstner, R., 'Die Habsburger-Monarchie und Ägypten. Eine Bestandsaufnahme', pp. 23ff.

The pyramids of Saqqara in the 19th century (Francis Frith)

Introduction to the Egyptian Revival

'Se vi è l' impronta deve esserci stato qualcosa di cui è impronta, ... Non sempre un' impronta ha la stessa forma del corpo che l'ha impressa e non sempre nasce dalla pressione di un corpo. Talora riproduce l'impressione che un corpo ha lasciato nella nostra mente, è impronta di una idea. L'idea è segno delle cose, e l'immagine è segno dell'idea, segno di un segno. Ma dall' immagine ricostruisco, se non il corpo, l'idea che altri ne aveva.' [1]

'What is the origin of this peculiar attraction of the land of the pharaohs? Why is it that its name, nature, history and monuments affect us in a completely different way that is the case of other lands of the ancient times?' [2] This is the question that the Egyptologist Georg Ebers asked his readers when he wanted to awaken their interest in Egypt. His question was for many of his contemporaries an indeed rhetorical one. Egypt has already been an important tourist destination and to take part in the winter season in the Cairo hotels has become a social duty for some members of European upper classes. Despite the fact that Egypt became one of the primary destinations of modern tourism and despite the growing knowledge of ancient Egyptian culture that made accessible a great number of monuments, either directly on Egypt's territory, in the growing European museums, on the pages of educational literature or in the works of the great artists of their time, Europeans still perceived Egypt through a thick veil of the aura of a mysterious civilisation. As such, Europeans of the technical 19th century could grasp it only with extreme difficulties.

The intensive interest in ancient Egypt that grew no weaker in the course of the second half of the 19th century has a long history and complex cultural and social background. History, historiography and the past are key terms for European culture of that time. The 19th century is a century of historicism. How, however, are we to understand this growing importance of the past in everyday culture? Were people of the 19th century so attracted by history as they are now by popular figures of music or sport? Did they identify themselves with their past, and did they therefore seek for it place in their everyday lives? Did historising buildings appeal to them and did they demand historical themes in the decoration and art of theirs? Did the scholarly and political elite use historical themes to remind 'the others' of their common great past, or did the past become only a comfortable decoration, a great pattern-book from which one could choose without the necessity of new invention, as is the opinion of some modern works of art history?

It is not easy to answer all these questions. First and foremost: who were these 'people of the 19th century'? Of course, they did not form a homogeneous society with a single cultural background and identical demands; even now there exists no such human group. Culture and society are always complex, although they obey certain generally valid patterns, which their bearers accept as their own. Culture, that is '*in a sense an identity system of a certain group*'[3], a '*sum of abilities, customs, life norms, thoughts and works, that is within a certain society maintained and transmitted by learning ...*'[4] It may be more precise to speak of cultural configurations, as defined by Ruth Benedict,[5] and make more notice of their structured function in the society than only describe their manifestations.

European culture of the 19th century is a term that actually has no precisely identifiable content. We may well trace large movements, for example in art styles or social movements, but they assume different forms in different countries and often these new forms acquire new contents. This is true in the case of the term historicism that is connected with European 19th century as one of its characteristic manifestations. Today, the term historicism has many employments and definitions, some of which will still appear below. One of the more general definitions has been proposed by the Italian researcher Arnaldo Momigliano – '*... a general interest in past human deeds ...*'[6] However, Momigliano himself adds, in accord with other historians, historicism is not only this. When we need to make sense of the complex relationship of people to the past, which may, particularly now, often appear dead and unappealing, we may use the already existing and elaborated, although actually very confusing, terminology. Before we try to orient ourselves in it (see further the Appendix), we shall name the aim of our attempts to explain the relationship of the 'people of the 19th century' to the past.

With regard to the extent of the book and the topic, it was decided not to consider the entire Europe in the entire 19th century. Each social group, each nation, and the more so each state have their own multi-layered relationship to the past. The identification of state and nation is in a simplified way the result of the process of national movements,[7] which in many European countries reached its peak in the 19th century. In this context, history acquires a different meaning for a nation that is trying to prove and defend its existence, for which it fears, and a different one for a self-confident empire, whose inhabitants are the lords of their home and who feel their importance as self-evident. The historian Miroslav Hroch, who specialises in the problems of national movements, mentions that the basis for a nation's self-awareness is usually its past – 'eramus, ergo sumus.[8]' The ties to one's past are an important element. '*... The leading characters of the national movements derived from history their arguments for political struggle and for the formation of cultural and sometimes even social demands. Knowledge of the events of one's own national past was a source of pride, inspiration for national struggle, and the basis for the creation of ethical norms. It presented materials for the understanding of the present.*'[9] The situation is moreover complicated by the fact that one and the same historical fact can be regarded from several sides. Many still celebrated anniversaries of important events of world history have a dual meaning. We do not have to go too far – the anniversary of WWII will always have an ambiguous meaning, even in terms of the uniting Europe. In Czech 'national' history, the Battle at the White Mountain will always be a certain milestone (despite the fact that historians still do not agree on its interpretation), while from the point of view of the 30 years' war as a European conflict; it was just a fray, despite its certain strategic consequences.

As an example, therefore, we will focus on Czech society of the second half of the 19th century, both for its multi-levelled approach to the past and for the relationship to Czech national history. This was of great importance for Czech cultural development, since the understanding of national past on the level of rational scholarly knowledge and on the level of emotional experience strengthened the growing cultural movement within the nation. There were several streams of thought, moreover in a nation that was still searching for its identity. This work does not concentrate only on Czech national past in the narrow sense of the word. It focuses on the role of ancient Egypt for Czech minds. Why precisely this ancient Near Eastern culture? In many other European countries, the interest in Egypt combines the interest in history and in exotic countries. The so-called 'Egyptomania', as this phenomenon is not too precisely called, is also a good example of two important roles of historicism, the attempt at positivistic knowledge and desire for an escape to both in time and space distant countries.[10] To the faraway places where worlds opened for the eyes of the European, both specialist and layman. He described them with curiosity or surprise in reaction of their difference.

Could historical reminiscences and interest in ancient past fulfil these functions also in Czech environment? This role could have been played by other historical motifs. That which was abroad represented by ancient Egypt, i.e. monumentality and decorativeness,[11] motifs for the so-called archaeological painting and exotisms, could have been sought elsewhere by Czech historicism. It concentrated above all on Czech national past and such elements were sought in home styles and historical events.

We can only have a look at representative buildings of Czech historicism from the 1870s and 1880s. They are borne by the idea of monumentality and nobility, but they are Renaissance in style, understood as part of Czech cultural heritage, as we can see for example in period commentary to the design of the National Theatre in Prague, evidence of Czech national historicism *par excellence*. '*As far as the style is considered, the artistic creation of the significant assemblage of Zítek's theatre building is cast entirely in home style, in a style that was transferred to our for all that is beautiful perceptive lands from the country of the arts, namely Italy ... thus, prof. Zítek chose our, home style for his theatre ...* '[12] The decorative programme of the National Theatre chooses patterns from the national past, whether the aim of decoration is a monumental theme or decorative ornament. Parallels can be found also in other excellent buildings with a cultural role, for example in the building of the National Museum. If rich decorativeness was to be expressed, Oriental motif was only a secondary element on the Czech scene. First the end of the 19th century, the time of the retreat of historicism, seemed to bring a new wave of exotism with Oriental reminiscences.[13]

Was the role of Egypt on the European scene always only that of a decorative prop, which could easily be replaced by other motifs, especially from national past better equipped with an inner content? Or were the reasons for the development of the study of this ancient civilisation deeper? Could they then have found some reflection also in the Czech environment?

Ancient Egypt acquired an important place in European culture[14] in general and especially in European historical thinking.[15] It is present in the culture of Europe both immanently, since it stands at two of its roots, Classical and Biblical (resp. Hebrew) traditions,[16] and as a result of the varying perception of the Oriental world in European environment.[17] Some manifestations of interest in Egypt in the course of the 19th century, which are the main focus of this work, belong to the broader interest of Europeans in the Orient. In art, paintings often combine ancient and contemporary Oriental elements (or elements considered to be Oriental by the Europeans). This approach can be found for example in the work of the Austrian painter Hans Makart,[18] but also of other, for example French artists.[19] The literary scholar Edward Said subsumed the interest in Egypt under the period Orientalism of the 19th century. In his opinion, the paradigm of Orientalism is conditioned by the interest in deeper knowledge of other cultures that was stimulated by colonial policy, which brought Europeans in contact with these cultures.[20] The German Egyptologist Jan Assmann accepts this opinion only with some reserves. He considers the role of Egypt in European cultural identity to be more complex and deeper. I find Assmann's opinion more plausible, although Said is, despite his controversialist approach and razor-cut opinions, inspiring. ❖ ❖ ❖

Said stated 'Orientalism overrode the Orient'.[21] Here it is at place to ask the question to what extent in some context Egyptomania overrode the attempt to know ancient Egypt. As far as the connection of Egyptomania and manifestations of Orientalism is concerned, according to Said's list both phenomena of western culture had some shared roots. '*In the depths of this Oriental stage stands a prodigious cultural repertoire whose individual items evoke a fabulously rich world: the Sphinx, Cleopatra, Eden, Troy, Sodom and Gomorrah, Astarte, Isis and Osiris, Sheba, Babylon, … and dozens more; settings, in some cases names only, half-imagined, half-known; monsters, devils, heroes; terrors, pleasures, desires.*'[22] Said's 'Orientalism'[23] is defined as a complex of prejudices concerning the Orient that burdened the entire European regard of the Oriental world. Such an unequivocal refusal is, however, not justified. Said himself says that '*one ought never assume that the structure of Orientalism is nothing more than a structure of lies or of myths which, were the truth about them to be told, would simply blow away.*'[24] Said perceives Orientalism as a complex cultural phenomenon that influences science and popularisations of all kinds. As we will see below, it could actually be 'Orient in historical culture'. Once again there is a clear parallel to Egyptomania as one of the manifestations of the interest in Egypt. It, too, as J. M. Humbert[25] mentions and as we will see below, operates with numerous reinterpretations and misunderstood elements of ancient

Egyptian culture. Despite that, it is uneasy to declare it to be a mere confusing complex of prejudices. Both Egyptomania and Orientalism have to be studied in their proper historical context. ❖ ❖ ❖

The reflection of Egypt was therefore a longue durée phenomenon, although its forms changed and were not always stimulated by reasons that would stand the scrutiny of modern level of knowledge. Imaginary Egypt often found a more significant position in European minds than the gradually disclosed image of the real ancient culture.[26]

The romantic, mythical conception of Egypt has suffered somewhat by its systematic exploration. Positivistic researchers often declared, above all in the second half of the 19th century, that the myth of Egypt that had distorted historical reality was defeated.[27] Modern scholarship should have torn down the aureole of mystery that dominated the perception of ancient Egypt. However, it did not. ❖ ❖ ❖

If we are asking what we know and think to know of ancient Egypt, we may also ask what we think about it and what we believe to think about it and what the generations of our ancestors knew or thought about Egypt, since their view has influenced the genesis of our own opinion. Further we should know whence they derived their knowledge and how they were able to reflect it. The last question may be considered in two aspects. Firstly, how was the new specialist knowledge accepted and reflected by the general public, and second, what did the scholars themselves think of their discipline and of their own approach to the past.

Let us begin by remarking that the tradition of interest in Egypt has very deep roots, which influenced the whole following development of European relationship to this culture. Greek and Roman historians were interested in Egypt, her ethics, religion, customs and sometimes also history, and filled the pages of their books with their own experiences and with stories that were told to them by people whom they met at their journeys to Egypt. We still frequently encounter traces of the influence of Classical perception of Egypt, which was reflected in the creation of the Renaissance image of Egypt.[28] However, the Renaissance is divided from Classical Antiquity by centuries of the epoch called the Middle Ages. Mediaeval Europeans knew Egypt above all (but not exclusively) from the Bible[29] and some references that Church historians took over from ancient authors.[30]

If they indeed visited Egypt, it was often in terms of their journey to the Holy Land – that is once again in the context of the attempts to see the sites of Biblical events. The interest of pilgrims in sites connected with Biblical events was of course not limited to the Middle Ages. As we shall see below, even humanistic travellers like the Czech Kryštof Harant of Polžice, still reflected Biblical tradition. And much later, we can still find strong reminiscences of it. From Czech material, we may mention the travelogue of Jan Žvejkal from the first half of the 19th century. Similarly, or even to a greater extent, the Biblical motif loomed behind a travel motivation of many an Anglo-Saxon visitor of Egypt during the late 19th and early 20th century.

A much larger sum of knowledge was made accessible in the cultural epoch named Humanism and Renaissance by the discoveries of the manuscripts of the above mentioned Greek and Latin historians and geographers together with the broader distribution of knowledge of Classical languages – newly above all of Greek.[31] In the eyes of European scholars, Egypt continued to be a cradle of the Hermetic tradition, which was given new attention by Italian humanists.[32] Also other elements of a Classical image of Egypt were given new attention in the Renaissance. According to Classical works, wisdom and law,[33] characteristics suitable for a noble man, came from Egypt. Even pope Alexander VI of the Borgia family had, at the same time as the Hapsburgs, asked that a genealogy be made for him, reaching down to Isis and Osiris.

The significance of Humanism for the knowledge of Egypt did not lie only in the amount of material that was made accessible (many references included in the works of Classical authors were of course well known before), but also in the rise of a specialised interest in Egyptian culture. The presence of the works of Classical authors in mediaeval libraries indicates that the opportunity to study Classical texts was indeed not reserved only for humanists.[34]

The Renaissance accepted and elaborated Classical heritage.[35] In art, the image of Egypt as a land of law and wisdom appeared several times (in Italy for example in the decoration of the Vatican Borgia halls, where Isis teaches wisdom and law, and on the floor of the Siena cathedral, where Hermes Trismegistos gives legal codes to representatives of the Orient and Occident).[36] '*The year 1419 … was the year of the discovery of Horapollo's Hieroglyphica, and this discovery aroused a large enthusiasm for everything Egyptian or would-be Egyptian, but also gave birth to, or at least significantly stimulated the "emblematic spirit", so characteristic of the 16th and 17th centuries … It was exactly under the influence of the Hieroglyphica of Horapollo that a lot of books of emblems were assembled. The first one, Emblemata, was written by Andrea Alciati in 1531.*'[37] Another aspect of this Renaissance interest can be found in falsifications of Annius of Viterbo, who invented an Egyptian origin to the Borgia family in the spirit of the myths of the civilising mission of Isis and Osiris. This work then served the painter Pinturicchio as an inspiration for the decoration of the Vatican Borgia halls.[38]

No less attractive for Europeans were the attempts to explain the hieroglyphs as a symbolic writing that expressed secret truths about the world. These first studies stimulated the serious interest in the 17th century, personified by Athanasius Kircher,[39] whose work was continued by 18th century researchers, *de facto* the precursors of Champollion.

The importance of Egypt as a cradle of education is also very clearly expressed in the work of J. A. Komenský (Comenius, although he is no longer fully classifiable as a humanist scholar, which is also true of Athanasius Kircher) – '*…the art of war was developed in the time of Absolon. There followed an era of civilisation that spread in the time of Moses from the Egyptians to the Phoenicians, Chaldaeans, and Persians, and flourished. The priests, however, kept their great knowledge almost secret and did not disclose it to common people.*'[40]

Above all the last sentence is a typical manifestation of the belief that the priestly caste possessed secret knowledge that was misunderstood by the outside world. It is complementary to the concept of hieroglyphic writing as a system of signs encoding secret truths.[41]

❖ ❖ ❖

Just like in the time of imperial Rome, when the first large-scale import of Egyptian monuments to Italy can be observed,[42] the interest of period collectors was again gradually turning to Egyptian and Egyptianising[43] works. Egyptianising inspiration in Renaissance art was not limited only to the use of a peculiar Egyptianising motif, but it is also expressed by period interest in emblems[44] and symbols.[45]

Travelling also played an important part in acquiring knowledge concerning ancient Egypt. Since the Middle Ages, the primary inspiration had been the desire to visit Biblical lands. Renaissance pilgrims, despite the fact that they had the same reasons for their journey, saw Egypt more through Classical eyes and ever more often they were interested in local monuments. In Baroque times, travellers[46] collected further knowledge and drew more precise maps.[47] Among these travellers, Baroque missionaries stand out as a special group.[48]

The content of the reports of missionaries is interesting from many aspects. It allows us to appreciate the way European travellers of that time, whose journeys had a specific purpose (and who had a specific perception of the world), understood foreign countries and what they considered worth telling about them.

The reports of missionaries have become a source of information on contemporary foreign lands, or at least a source for the European approach to them. And they also allow us to understand what Europe could know about a certain territory at a given time. It is therefore necessary to stress that their messages were not the only way through which news and knowledge entered Europe. Already the 16th century witnessed the rise of newsgiving, transmitted via post lines and messengers. Important noble families, such as the Rosenbergs in Bohemia, regularly received a period version of 'newspapers', compiled by post officers in the greater cities.[49]

Today there already exist editions of missionary letters and reports published both in the original and in translation. Of crucial importance among them is the collection, which was published by J. Stoecklein already in the 18th century, namely *Der neue Welt-Bott mit allerhand Nachrichten der Missionarum Societatis Iesu etc.*[50] Almost every work concerning the Jesuite order contains a list of archives with letters and documents connected with missionary activities. Despite this fact, within the Czech province, which could have been of interest in relation to Oriental missions, there was, according to the list of J. Vraštil,[51] no missionary who had visited Egypt and the neighbouring territories. The only order where Czech members took an active part in the missions to the Middle East were the Franciscans – J. J. Římař, V. Remedius-Prutký, and K. Schneider.[52]

The attempts of missionaries to bring the Copts under the aegis of the Catholic church[53] were also connected with the new wave of interest in the Coptic language, which was correctly understood (for example by Athanasius Kircher[54]) as a language with direct links to ancient Egyptian. Besides that, though, attempts to decipher the key to the Egyptian culture – the hieroglyphic script – were hindered by beliefs in its symbolical character. This was another opinion that stemmed from the Classical tradition, which in this case had even authentic Egyptian roots.[55]

During the 17th and above all 18th centuries, Egypt entered into grand-scale volumes on history and monuments. To the same time date also the origins of freemasonry.[56] Freemasonry, too, contributed its part to the network of reinterpretations of ancient Egypt.[57] In general, it may be said that the ideas connected in European philosophy and thinking with ancient Egypt sometimes significantly influenced both the arts and material culture. For example a freemason had his so-called freemason's room furnished in an Egyptianising style, or a certain symbol, justly or unjustly connected with ancient Egypt, was reflected in architecture, etc. An example of this are sepulchral constructions connected with the idea of stability and monumental duration, ascribed to the ancient Egyptian civilisation.[58]

The fast development in the discipline of art history also played its part. For example the publication of a ten-volume art historical work of Count de Caylus[59] rated Egyptian art and culture very positively.[60] Also the opinion of J. Winckelmann concerning Egyptian art, that he mentions at various places, defined one way of seeing ancient Egypt – a basically negative assessment of her art, above all when compared with Classical antiquity.

The end of the 18th century brought a significant landmark[61] in the history of Egyptology, namely Napoleon's expedition to Egypt.

❖   ❖   ❖

Personages of the Enlightenment who belonged to Freemasonry did not hesitate to ascribe to Egypt the role of a spiritual source for Moses and for the formation of Jewish Monotheism. They sought in the religion of ancient Egypt, which they knew above all from Classical sources, primeval roots, explaining the primary knowledge of being.[62]

This variegated relationship to the country, which was part of European past, did not and could not end with the birth of Egyptological scholarship, which was developed in the course of the 19th century. With the development of scholarly knowledge, it only reached a new dimension. In the 19th century Egyptology became a positivistic historical science that made use of philological methods. It gradually discarded the centuries old myth of Egypt as a country of primeval knowledge and the origin of human education and religion. In many cases, however, Egypt did not enter general consciousness through reading of new scholarly publications. Books far outside the scope of specialised literature, such as a totally subjective experience of a journey to Egypt, or a work of art may have had a far greater influence.

How could a European, in our case an inhabitant of the Central European Hapsburg monarchy, whether in Prague or in Vienna, encounter Egypt and the Orient and get acquainted with it? One of the possibilities, undoubtedly the most important one, was a personal experience with one of Oriental countries. In the period of our interest we find in Egypt a large community of Austrian (Austro-Hungarian) citizens.

In the course of the 19th century, the community of foreigners in Egypt grew parallel to the rising importance of the contacts of Egypt with Europe. What was Egypt like at the turn of the 19th and 20th centuries? What was the role of foreigners in the life of contemporary Egyptian society? We already know the important role of Egypt in European culture. Was the opposite also true? What did a European mean in the sight of an Egyptian? We must ask these questions if we want to understand the general character of encounters of Egypt and Europe in the course of the 19th century.

It was a new meeting of two areas that carried with it the inheritance of all previous contacts. Many Europeans[63] still had a vivid memory of the Biblical heritage. Egypt and the Near East belonged to the world of the Bible and to study them was one of the tasks of the religious man. The knowledge of Classical authors also belonged to tradition, despite the fact that school education of Classical languages did not always awaken an interest in ancient cultures, and was also not generally accessible.

Practical interest in Oriental areas grew as well. Trade or political interests often preceded learned men and travellers. European trade with the Orient lasted for centuries and the weakening of the Ottoman Empire in the 18th century, which created chaos in its provinces,[64] offered new spheres of influence. Policies of Britain and France were directed at acquiring influence in the Orient. For many people, the Orient may have offered new possibilities and an easier carreer.[65] It was first necessary to know the countries in order to subsequently rule them. The interest in scholarly knowledge grew and led to the birth of Orientalist disciplines. These also opened other possibilities of communication with the Oriental world, among others also thanks to a better accessibility of language knowledge. The area of the Mediterranean also 'grew smaller', thanks to new transport possibilities.

The Hapsburg state system (and in its terms also Czech lands)[66] had already since the 16th century a powerful and expansive neighbour in the Ottoman empire, an important representative of the Oriental world, which immediately threatened the existence of the nascent Hapsburg state. First after the unsuccessful siege of Vienna in 1683 and the subsequent retreat of Turkish armies, Turkey and the whole Oriental world became distant. For the Danube monarchy and her inhabitants they will remain, above all in consequence of the interests of the Balkan empire, a close reality. A reality that had to be communicated, traded and politically used (hence the necessity to know Oriental languages). Everyday reality therefore will not play the role of exotic and decorative Orient, which attracted the French and the Britons. Austrian

'Orientalism' will necessarily differ from its British counterpart. Orientalism of German-speaking countries is generally considered, although not always with full justification, to be more scholarly and less influenced by romantic travelogues and experiences.[67]

Neither the Austrian colonial empire can be considered in the same way as British colonial empire. Despite that, Vienna also had long intensive interests in the land of the Nile.

Notes:

1 Umberto Eco, *Il nome della rosa*. Milan XLV ed. 2000, p. 319.

2 Ebers, Georg. *Egypt slovem i obrazem ve spolku s vynikajícími umělci předvádí G. Ebers*, Czech edition authorised by the author directed by dr. Otokar Hostinský. Prague 1883; p. 1.

3 Jan Assmann, *Das kulturelle Gedächtnis*. Munich 1997; p. 140 '...*Kultur als eine Art...Identitätssystem der Gruppe...*'

4 Sokol, Jan, *Malá filosofie člověka a Slovník filosofických pojmů*. Prague 1998; p. 317. Cf. also 'culture' in *Encyclopedia of Social and cultural anthropology*. (ed. A. Barnard and J. Spencer), London – New York 2002; p. 136 ff. (hereafter *Encyclopedia of anthropology*).

5 Benedict approached culture and its study in a holistic way. '*Cultures were ways of living, virtually psychological types, which she called "cultural configurations" which were said to be best perceived as integral and patterned wholes.*' – *Encyclopedia of anthropology*, p. 139.

6 Momigliano, Arnaldo, *Historicism revisited*. Mededelingen der koniklijke nederlandse Akademie van wetunschapen, Afd. Letterkunde, Nieuwe Reeks, 37/3, Amsterdam 1974.

7 Cf. Hroch, Miroslav, *V národním zájmu*. Prague 1996 and Hobsbawm, E. H., *Národy a nacionalismus*. Prague 2000.

8 Hroch, Miroslav, *V národním zájmu*. Prague 1996; p. 116.

9 Hroch, Miroslav, 'Některé metodologické poznámky ke studiu úlohy historického vedomí v národním hnutí 19. století' in *Historické vědomí v českém umění 19. století*. Prague 1981; p. 61.

10 Cf. Haja, Martina, 'Die Gesichter der Sphinx. Aspekte der ägyptomanen Malerei im 19. Jahrhundert' in Seipel, W., *Ägyptomanie. Europäische Ägyptenimagination zwischen Utopie und Phobie. Schriften des KHM 3*. Vienna 2000.

11 Cf. Werner, Friederike, *Ägyptenrezeption in der europäischen Architektur des 19. Jahrhunderts*. Weimar 1994.

12 Cf. the review of the design of the building of the National Theatre in *Národní listy*, quoted after Matějček, Antonín, *Národní divadlo a jeho výtvarníci*. Prague 1954; p. 51.

13 Cf. Vlček, Tomáš, *Praha 1900*. Prague 1986; p. 181.

14 The term 'culture' is in this context understood generally as a structure, a system of collective identity of a certain period and space, which does not necessarily have to be strictly delimited against other systems, while it can differ from them. The formation of cultural identity and some problems connected to the role of historical thought in this identity will be mentioned below, together with the citations of relevant authors. An overview of opinions and of definitions – see 'culture' in *Encyclopedia of Anthropology*, l. c.

15 The term 'historical thinking' will also be treated below. It can be understood concretely as '...*an area, where a reasoning man attempts to understand the past*' (Kutnar, František – Marek, Jaroslav, *Přehledné dějiny českého a slovenského dějepisectví*. 2. ed. Prague 1997; p. 7), or in relation to philosophical terms – cf. below H. G. Gadamer, in Appendix.

16 This thesis was generally formulated by J. Assmann, cf. Assmann, Jan, *Ägypten. Eine Sinngeschichte*. Frankfurt (M) 1999; p. 475 f. and concerning European travellers, it was expressed by Erik Hornung, *Das esoterische Ägypten*. Munich 1999; s. 100.

17 For the problem of the long-term process of contacts of Europe with the Orient cf. also the volume *Europa und der Orient 800 - 1900*, Gütersloh- München 1989, and *Europa und der Orient. Ein Lesebuch*. Berlin 1989. For a general overview of Orientalism above all in the visual arts of the entire Austrian monarchy, cf. for

example Mayr-Oehring, Erika, *Österreichische Malerei 1848–1914.* Salzburg 1997. The penetration of period Orient into the concepts of ancient Orient is well perceptible in the iconography of Biblical scenes, including those, that are set into the ancient Egyptian pattern. Cf. the plates of the article of Dirk Syndram 'Das Erbe der Pharaonen. Zur Ikonographie Ägyptens in Europa' in *Europa und der Orient*, pp. 18ff. Above all fig. on p. 27, the painting of B. Breenbergh from the year 1655. As regards the Orient in European art, there is now furthermore an excellent sourcebook, or better a sourcebook series – Les Orientalistes, a ten volume set of books publishing various schools and national groups of Orient-influenced artists, mainly painters. A good introduction is to be found in the volume by Lynne Thornton, *Les Orientalistes – Peintres voyageurs.* Paris 1985. Also see further in Chapter III.

18 One of these typical paintings entitled 'Cleopatra sails on the river Cydnus to meet Antonius' is also reproduced in the Czech edition of G. Ebers, *Egypt slovem i obrazem*, p. 17.

19 Cf. Humbert, J. M., *L'Egyptomanie dans l'art occidental.* Paris 1989; pp. 250ff.

20 Said, Edward, *Orientalism.* New York 1978, reprinted 1991; with a new Afterword 1995; quoted after the 1995 edition; passim, for the analysis of the term cf. pp. 1–73; and after the citation in Assmann, J., *Ägypten. Eine Sinngeschichte*, pp.476 and 540, note 3.

21 Quoted after Sharafuddin, M., *Islam and Romantic Orientalism.* London and New York 1994; p. XV.

22 Said, *Orientalism*, p. 63.

23 *op. cit.*, 'Introduction', passim.

24 *Orientalism*, p. 6.

25 *L'Egyptomanie dans l'art occidental*, 'Introduction'.

26 As we will see below, the emergence of ancient Egypt in the sphere of European historical knowledge brought about a certain demythisation of the perception of this culture, (for further details see J. Assmann below). A typical example can be found in Adolf Erman, whose work represents a typical opinion of an Egyptologist of the end of the 19th century of his own discipline.

27 Above all German researchers traced the veil of myth that had shaded ancient Egypt down to the influence of British romantic Orientalism. Cf. for example Adolf Erman in the introduction of his important work *Aegypten und aegyptisches Leben im Altertum.* Tübingen 1885; p. 3. These facts are summarised also in Suzanne L. Marchand, 'The End of Egyptomania: German Scholarship and the Banalization of Egypt 1830–1914.' in Seipel, W., *Ägyptomanie.*

28 Cf. Dirk Syndram, 'Das Erbe der Pharaonen. Zur Ikonographie Ägyptens in Europa' in *Europa und der Orient*, pp. 18 ff. Syndram presents an overview of the basic stages of the development of the reception of Egypt in Europe (in this Introduction, we proceed in a similar way). The basic division, Classical Antiquity – Renaissance – Enlightenment, considers Middle Ages only marginally. Both overviews are based on the same source – the classical work of Siegfried Morenz *Begegnung Europas mit Ägypten* 1968, 1969.

29 That means that together with the content of Biblical stories they necessarily had to perceive that they happened in a certain context. Of course, only few Europeans had the opportunity to acquaint themselves with this environment directly by visiting it. An early example of such a visitor can be found in the person of Egeria (Aetheria) For a bibliography, cf. Hornung, E., *Das esoterische Ägypten*, s. 99, 216–217. His bibliography on p. 216 concerns the mediaeval perception of Egypt, Hornung cites e.g. Zimmermann, F., *Die ägyptische Religion nach der Darstellung der Kirchenschriftsteller und die ägyptischen Denkmäler.* Paderborn 1912, etc.

30 The number of these references is quite significant – Felix Jacoby, *Fragmente der grie-chischen Historiker III*. E. J. Brill, Leiden 1958, (fragm. 608a–664 and Anhang 665) allows to guess the approximate number of smaller and larger fragments that were thus preserved, including also parts of the work of Manetho, hitherto known only from excerpts (excerpts from the *Aegyptiaca*, of Manetho or Manehto, an Egyptian priest who lived in the Ptolemaic period. Excerpts, above all from the second book of the work, were taken for example by Iulius Africanus, Eusebius from Caesarea and others). On Manetho cf. for example Redford, Donald B., *Pharaonic King-lists, Annals and Day-books; A Contribution to the Study of the Egyptian Sense of History*. Mississauga 1986; pp. 231 ff.

31 Carmine Ampolo, *Storie greche*. Torino 1997. For the knowledge of Greek see chapter 'Dalla riscoperta del mondo greco alle prime storie erudite', pp. 13ff. For further the publications of Czech authors, cf. for example the volume *Antika a česká kultura* ('Classical antiquity and Czech culture') Prague 1978; in the respective section.

32 Further see the views of Jan Assmann quoted above all in *Ägypten. Eine Sinngeschichte*. Cited after the edition Fischer Verlag, Frankfurt (M) 1999; E. Hornung, *Das esote-rische Ägypten*, pp. 84 ff. and above all for the Renaissance tradition pp. 89 ff.

33 The paradigm that was created in Classical tradition already by Herodotus, who men-tions the originality of some, above all religious, customs of the ancient Egyptians, in his Book II, passim, (II, 43;) and clearly also by Plato, whose reception of Egypt is mentioned among others in Assmann, Jan ed., *Stein und Zeit. Mensch und Gesellschaft im alten Ägypten*. Munich 1991; pp. 303ff. and id.: *Das kulturelle Gedächtnis*; pp. 190ff. Alexander VI had a great falsifyer at his disposal, namely Annius of Viterbo (Giovanni Nanni di Viterbo). Cf. Iversen, Erik: *The Myth of Egypt and its hieroglyphs*. Copenhagen 1961; Chapter III.

34 For Czech libraries, cf. 'Antická literatura v českých knihovnách do doby poděbrad-ské' ('Classical literature in Czech libraries of the Poděbrady period') in *Antika a česká kultura* ('Classical Antiquity and Czech culture'), Prague 1978; pp. 166f.

35 Cf. Hornung, E., 'Die Renaissance der Hermetik und der Hieroglyphen' in *Das esote-rische Ägypten*, pp. 89–98.

36 Hornung, *op. cit.,* p. 45. Cf. Baltrušaitis, Jurgis, *La Quête d'Isis*. Paris 1967; pp. 155ff.

37 Erwin Panofsky, *Meaning in the Visual Arts*; p. 159.

38 For many references to him, cf. Dirk Syndram 'Das Erbe der Pharaonen' in *Europa und der Orient*; also Patrizia Castelli, *I geroglifici e il mito dell'Egitto nel rinascimento*. Firenze 1979; illustrations. Cf. also Baltrušaitis, *La Quête d'Isis*; pp. 155ff.

39 On his museum, cf. Enrichetta Leospo 'Athanasius Kircher und das Museo Kircheriano' in *Europa und der Orient 800–1900*. For the analysis of his works, see Günther Hölbl, *Athanasius Kircher als Ägyptologe*. S. a. Vienna.

40 Komenský, J. A., 'Všenáprava. Všeobecné porady o napravení věcí lidských' ('General remedy. Common counsels on the remedy of human affairs'). Quoted after *Čítanka k dějinám dějepisectví* II. ('Reading book of the history of historiography') Prague; p. 127.

41 For Classical (and above all Hermetic) tradition cf. Assmann, J., *Weisheit und Mysterium*. Munich 2000; pp. 35ff.

42 Roullet, A., *Egyptian and Egyptianising Monuments of Imperial Rome*. EPRO 20, Leiden 1972; with other bibliography. Further a whole edition of the Leiden publishing house J. Brill entitled '*Études préliminaires aux religions orientales dans l'Empire Romain*' (EPRO).

43 Egyptianising object – one that imitates (although in some cases distortedly), or reflects the form, shape, or decoration (ornament) of ancient Egyptian origin.

44 Emblem – '*a work on the boundary of visual and literary arts, the image and text of which both conceals and reveals a message*', J. Baleka, *Výtvarné umění* ('Visual arts'), Prague 1997; p. 93.

45 Cf. Panofsky, E., 'Titian's *Allegory of Prudence:* A Postscript' in *Meaning in the Visual Arts.* 1982 (reprint of the 1955 edition); pp. 158–168, and ill. no. 32, 33, 34–43.

46 Cf. the bibliography of Jürgen Horn 'Kleine Bibliographie zur Erschliessung der Literatur der Reiseberichte über und Landesbeschreibung von Ägypten' in Minas, M. – Stöhr, S. – Schips, S. (hrsg.). *Aspekte spätägyptischer Kultur* (Fs E. Winter). Mainz 1994; pp. 169ff.

47 For the bibliography concerning old maps, cf. Pávová, Jindřiška: *Rukopisné památky české provenience k poznání zemí severovýchodní Afriky v 18. a XIX. stol.* ('Manuscript sources of Czech provenance for the knowledge of the countries of Northeast Africa in the 18th and 19th centuries') master's thesis, submitted 1984 at the Faculty of Arts, Charles University, chapter III. One of the more important maps, entitled 'Aegyptus Antiqua', was published in 1595 in Amsterodam by Abraham Ortelius.

48 Cf. Zdeněk Kalista, *Cesty ve znamení kříže* ('Voyages in the quest of the Cross'), Prague 1941; passim.

49 Cf. for example Z. Šimeček, 'Rožmberské zpravodajství o nových zemích Asie a Afriky' ('The Rosenberg newsgiving on the new lands of Asia and Africa'), *ČsČH,* XIII, 1965.

50 And a number of more recent works, in the Czech Republic for example Schulz: *Korespondence jesuitů provincie české* ('The correspondence of the members of the Societas Iesu of the Czech province') Prague, 1900. The works of Z. Kalista were published in the course of the last centuries; in both *České baroko* ('Czech Baroque') and *Cesty ve znamení kříže* ('Journeys in quest of the Cross'), missionary reports to be found in Czech translation. Already before the WW II, P. J. Vraštil published the translations of the letters of Karel Slavíček.

51 Vraštil, J., 'Účast staré české provincie Tovaryšstva Ježíšova na zámořských misiích' ('The old Czech province of the Societas Iesu on missions overseas'), *Zprávy z čs. provincie T. J.* ('News from the Czech province of the S. I.') 1927, No. 1; Vraštil, J., 'Seznam zámořských misionářů staré české provincie T. J.' ('List of overseas missionaries of the old Czech province of the S. I.') in *Zprávy z čs. provincie T. J.* 1934. No. 1.

52 For further details cf. the relevant entries in Martínek, J. – Martínek, M., *Kdo byl kdo. Naši cestovatelé a geografové* ('Who was who. Our travellers and geographers'), Prague 1999; and also in: *Čeští a slovenští orientalisté, afrikanisté a iberoamerikanisté* ('Czech and Slovak Orientalists, Africanists, and Iberoamericanists'), Prague 1999. For the reports of Remedius-Prutký on ancient Egyptian monuments, cf. Verner, M., 'Ancient Egyptian Monuments…' *Archív Orientální* 36, 1968. For observations of the topographical details contained in their works, cf. Pávová, J., *op. cit.*

53 For a systematic overview of the Coptic church, cf. Winkler, Dietmar W., *Koptische Kirche und Reichskirche. Altes Schisma und neuer Dialog.* Innsbruck – Wien 1997.

54 For a brief overview of Athanasius Kircher and his role in early scholarship, cf. *Who was who in Egyptology.* ed. by M. Bierbrier, London 1995, further Donadoni, Sergio – Donadoni-Roveri, Anna Maria – Curto, Silvio, *Egypt from Myth to Egyptology.* Milano 1990.

55 Cf. Thissen, Heinz-Josef, 'Horapollinis Hieroglyphika, Prolegomena', Minas – Stohr, *Aspekte spätägyptischer Kultur.* Mainz 1994; pp. 255ff.

56 An interesting observation on the formation of this tradition in the time of the enlightenment can be found in J. Assmann: *Moses der Ägypter.* Munich 1997. E. Hornung dedicates to it a whole chapter in his 'Das Ideal einer Bruderschaft – Die Freimaurer' in *Das esoterische Ägypten,* pp. 121ff.

57 Cf. for example Curl, J. A., 'Les thémes décoratifs égyptisants et la franc-maçonnerie' in *L'Égyptomanie à l'épreuve de l'archéologie.* Paris 1996.

58 For further details concerning Egyptian and Egyptianising motifs in European architecture, as well as their analysis, cf. Friederike Werner, *Ägyptenrezeption.* Passim.

59 For an exhaustive overview of the development in the 18th century, cf. Dirk Syndram, *Ägypten – Faszinationen. Untersuchungen zum Ägyptenbild im europäischen Klassizismus bis 1800.* Europäische Hochschulschriften, Reihe XXVIII, vol. 104. Frankfurt – Bern – New York – Paris 1990; pp. 34ff. This work also contains an annotated bibliography of older works, see chapter 'Forschungsübersicht', pp. 16f.

60 Dirk Syndram, *ibid.*

61 As Syndram stresses, not in the general interest in Egypt, which has its roots in the 18th century. Syndram cites a number of art historical works, among them also the fundamental books of De Caylus and Montfaucon. Syndram, *Ägypten – Faszinationen*, passim. Caylus, however, was neither the first nor the only European scholar to present a positive evaluation of Egyptian culture, Already the humanist Poggio Bracciolini, whose contributions to the acquaintance of Europe with ancient Egypt include a translation of Diodorus (in 1472), took a favourable stand to the Egyptian culture. Similarly Pico della Mirandola (cf. P. Castelli, *op. cit.,* and also Syndram, 'Das Erbe der Pharaonen').

62 Assmann, J., in Seipel, W., (Hrsg.). *Ägyptomanie. Schriften des KHM Wien 3.* Vienna 2000.

63 And in the 19th century also, perhaps with an even greater intensity, of Americans. Cf. B.Trigger in *American Discovery of Ancient Egypt.* Los Angeles – New York 1995.

64 For an introduction, see Buchmann, M. B., *Österreich und das Osmanische Reich.* Wien 1999; pp. 162ff. with bibliography.

65 Cf. Said, E., *Orientalism,* passim. For a general analysis of the colonies, see id. *Culture and Imperialism.* London 1994. Said's theories are, however, somewhat subjective. Moreover, he does not pay sufficient attention to the German and Austrian developments. Cf. some notes in A. L. Macfie, *Orientalism. A Reader.* Cairo 2000. Mainly text by B. Lewis and David Kopf.

66 The Czech lands were part of the Hapsburg monarchy, which was since 1804, resp. 1806, named the Austrian Empire, and since 1867 Austro-Hungarian Empire. The term 'Austrian' is also in this work used historically, signifying state citizenship. For 'Austrianness' in terms of Austrian patriotism, see also J. Kořalka, *Češi v habsburské říši a v Evropě.* ('Czechs in the Hapsburg empire and in Europe'). Prague 1997.

67 Cf. Said, *Orientalism*, p. 19.

ÆGYPTEN

WIE MAN ES AM BESTEN BEREIST

MIT 41 FARBIGEN ILLUSTRA-
TIONEN VON A. O. LAMPLOUGH

An early 20ᵗʰ century guidebook

I. Nineteenth-century Europeans in Egypt

'It is the traveller's lot to dine at many table-d'hôtes in the course of many wanderings; but it seldom befalls him to make one of a more miscellaneous gathering than that which overfills the great dining-room at Shepheard's Hotel in Cairo during the beginning and the height of the regular Egyptian season. Here assemble daily some two or three hundred persons of all ranks, nationalities, and pursuits; half of whom are Anglo-Indian homeward or outward bound, European residents, or visitors established in Cairo for the winter. The other half, it may be taken for granted, are going up the Nile.'[1]

One of rich sources, which provide information about intercultural relations, is travelling and travels. The travellers mediate impressions of their world in the visited country. On the other hand they carry a lot of knowledge about the visited country back to their own land, thus travelling and all recorded travellers' experiences are an invaluable source for the searching for stereotypes and imaginations, as well as for the sort of generally accessible information about faraway lands and their cultures. This is a contribution to the study of intercultural relations, which are now a more and more open field of research, where the Czech history already feels a debt. The travelogues are rich in impressions and knowledge gained and verified or created and refused by their authors, and give us a unique possibility of insight into an understanding of a place and time, visited by the author, and the structure in which he was able to pass his knowledge on to his audience.[2]

How easy, or rather, how difficult it was to visit Egypt? In the ensuing text, I shall mention a large number of individuals who worked in Egypt, got rich or poor there, who performed their diplomatic service in the country, who researched here or collected materials for their art projects. How, however, did all these people move through the land on the Nile, how did they cope with its unusual climate and the various difficulties that can surprise the traveller and can, despite the beauty of the Egyptian monuments, still discourage the tourist today?

Travelling and tourism[3] in Egypt date much further back than organised maintenance and protection of monuments.[4] For a long time, however, the visit of the country was no easy task. Numerous mediaeval, Renaissance, and modern pilgrims mention the difficulties of the journey; among them were the Czech noble Kryštof Harant of the 16th century, or the Prague citizen Jan Žvejkal in the first half of the 19th century. European powers were active in Egypt, above all for the reasons of commerce, and thus already the accounts of Renaissance travellers contain remarks on the French consul in Egypt and the like. The French official was allowed to stay in the country after the Ottoman conquest of Egypt in 1517, when the Sultan granted his permission. The intensive commercial activities can be explained by the strategic location of Egypt – the country was a transhipment centre for trade with India and other even more distant areas – above all for luxury items and spices.

First in the course of the 19th century, rather towards its second half, the conditions became more favourable for mass travelling to Egypt. The change can be traced back to the large-scale transformations of the society, which became more inclined to travelling, no more needing an impetus of purely utilitarian aims.[5] New and faster means of motion also played their role. Both the connection between Egypt and Europe and the intra-Egyptian traffic improved significantly since the middle of the 19th century.

It is above all the British travellers, tourists, patients seeking recovery (Egypt was considered a suitable place for the curing of TB[6] and other illnesses), researchers, and others, who left behind them rich accounts of their travels. The Britons were, however, not the only ones who recorded the impressions of their stay in Egypt. They only formed a large group, since Egypt lay on the strategical road to India. Already before the construction of the Suez Canal, numerous travellers preferred the way, which led from the British harbours to Egypt and continued by the Suez-Calcutta liners, instead of undertaking the demanding journey around whole Africa.[7] Since 1840, the Peninsular and Oriental Steam Navigation Company (P&O) provided direct connection to India precisely over the Suez. The journey from London to Bombay could thus take mere 40 days, instead of the four months long boat trip, which was the ordeal of those who chose the route along the Cape of Good Hope.[8] Consequently, numerous British merchants and other people on business trips visited Egypt, which became a kind of 'transfer station'. Florence Nightingale thus speaks of having had great luck on her journey: '*We have hardly any English, no Indians, for luckily it is not the transit week.*[9]'

Moreover, the British established themselves in Egypt as a result of the political development since the 1870s, which ended in 1882 with the unsuccessful Orabi revolt, and inaugurated the British 'veiled' occupation of Egypt.[10] In the course of these years, Egyptian officials, and above all the soldiers, increasingly criticised the growing numbers of foreigners in Egypt's administration and government. The uneasiness culminated in a clash, when part of the army, led by Colonel Orabi,[11] revolted against the government. This military revolt was defeated with the help of British forces, and the country fell under British control.[12] Although the British presence acquired a new dimension with the actual realisation of the British administration of the country, it still remained in many respects unchanged. Egypt only became an ever more socially 'compulsory' stop on tourist journeys. Since 1860, Thomas Cook has organised tourist trips to Egypt.[13] New hotels began to grow in Cairo – the famous Shepheard's had been established already earlier, in the year 1841[14]

Numerous contemporary travelogues inform us that as late as in the first half of the 19th century, visitors were faced with difficulties in the form of the quarantine (precautions against plague), or the unusual methods of travelling (donkey

Europeanised, but Orientalising, architecture of Cairo, the Khedivial palace

ride), etc.[15] In the second half of the century, travelling gradually became much easier. In Egypt, railway connection between Cairo, Alexandria and Suez was set up in the 1850s. The reign of Khedive (viceroy[16]) Ismail Pasha witnessed a boom of the rail[17] as well as the establishment of the telegraph.[18]

Naturally, European tourists and travellers of all kinds were not the only ones who profited from the new railroads and more frequent ship service (the most important route for Austria was that between Trieste and Alexandria[19]).[20] The economical and political importance of the presence of Europeans in Egypt grew steadily during the 'long nineteenth century'.[21] Above all, the extent of trade with European countries, mostly Britain and Austria, rose dramatically. The number of foreigners residing in the country was rising as well. While around 6000 Europeans were living in Egypt in 1840, in 1870 their number grew to 68 000 and finally in 1897 to 111 000.[22]

Foreigners, that is above all Europeans and Americans, streamed to Egypt in the 1860s, when cotton trade flourished, and with a renewed intensity after 1882, the first year of British occupation.[23] Khedive Ismail himself supported the influx of foreigners, until he was deposed in the political unrests that culminated later in the year 1882 with the Orabi revolt. This uprising was directed against the policy of the new Khedive Tawfik and also against the growing influence of European powers in the country.[24] The newly formed state and military apparatus of the country, boldly reorganised by Khedive Ismail, was to a large extent aided and manned by foreigners (including Austrians). On the other hand, the Egyptian government became indebted due to these changes (and due to several disadvantageous steps in the administration of the Suez canal).[25]

The political influence of European countries is interconnected with their growing economical power – both factors mutually supported one another. Ehud R. Toledano suggests the following explanation of this situation: *'The impact of European forces on the Egyptian economy can be seen as occurring in three stages: a purely commercial phase during the early decades of the nineteenth century, in which trade expanded and political influence was used to facilitate the expansion; the financial-commercial phase, in which the government of Egypt could no longer finance its reform project by taxation,*[26] had to borrow money from European creditors and consequently gave more and more way to their demands, and finally, in the last quarter of the century the third *'political-financial-commercial phase, in which direct involvement in the Egyptian economy created full dependence, as export prices, availability of credit, and the distribution of public revenues were determined by European forces.'*[27]

Khedive Ismail, the impatient Europeaniser

Thus not only tourism and the growing interest in the ancient cultures, but also commercial and political interests formed a link between the European countries and Egypt of the 19th century. Here we are also to search for the explanation of the busy connection of some countries, above all Britain, with Egypt. Their economical and political presence in turn facilitated the movement of Europeans in the country. The growth of the touristic backbone was in mutually supportive relationship with the administrative backbone above all in British Egypt.[28]

The first Cairo museum of Egyptian antiquities in Bulaq

The cultural interaction of the European and Egyptian environments influenced the gradual formation of European Orientalism[29] and the reception of Egypt. In Egypt it stimulated, e.g., the formation of several institutions,[30] above all the libraries established in the time of Khedive Ismail, or the developing research institutions (and Egyptological research projects), including the museum of Bulaq, directed by the French Egyptologist Mariette pasha.[31] Besides that, the entire Egyptian society was confronted with European behaviour and lifestyles *en masse.*

Europeans arrived with various aims and brought home with them widely differing impressions. Some of them passed them on, in word or image. A number of British and French travellers recorded their glimpses of the country in letters or travelogues, voyaging artists prepared quick sketches and aquarelles, which they elaborated after their return home.[32] On the other side stand those, who recorded a part of their travel experience in a published journal or article, or whose Oriental or Egyptian experience found a reflection in their literary work. They enabled other people to get a glimpse of the experience of the Egyptian world and formed its contemporary image in Europe.

Often the experience retold was more one of contemporary Egypt than of the monuments of ancient Egypt. The admiration for the newly discovered cultures was often intertwined with the interest in Oriental (in this context read above all as 'Near Eastern') world as such.[33] Actually, both worlds were being revealed simultaneously.

Expressions like 'to reveal', 'to uncover', 'to lift the veil' appear in many contemporaneous treatises, journals, as well as in travelogues.[34] European travellers, and possibly also researchers, perceived the ancient Oriental world as a 'Sleeping beauty', which only European man was able to awaken from a sleep that had lasted millennia, and which only he, the inheritor of Classical Antiquity and thus also of ancient Orient, was able to fully understand.[35] Ancient and modern Orient were often considered together. Above all in the case of ancient Egypt, Orientalism[36] and historicism form a homogeneous unity.

What type of observations can be found in the works of the visitors of Egypt in the course of the 19th century? A lot of the material of travelogue character is formed by letters. The collections of letters were in some cases published already during the lifetimes of their authors. The 'public destination' of a written work might always have influenced the style and views presented herein. This was the case of Lucie Duff Gordon (1821–1869),[37] an Englishwoman who came to Egypt to recover from tuberculosis. Later, she died of this disease in Cairo.

In the 1850s and 1860s, she lived in Luxor, and became integrated in the local milieu of her Egyptian neighbourhood. Local inhabitants accepted her favourably, above all thanks to her qualification as a nurse, always highly praised in areas without generally accessible medical care. Her lively description of her stay in Egypt is preserved in numerous letters addressed to the members of her family. She noticed many aspects of the Egypt that surrounded her; however, she did not forget her past, either. She is the author of the following quote: *'This country is a palimpsest, in which the Bible is written over Herodotus, and the Koran over that. In the towns the Koran is the most visible, in the country Herodotus.'*[38]

Another traveller who recorded his Egyptian experience in letters was the French writer Gustave Flaubert. His notes from his Oriental journey are often being employed to illustrate in great detail the character of some aspects of the European reception of the Orient.[39] Precisely the same aspects also shed light on contemporary perception of ancient Egypt.

Flaubert's general characterisation of the Orient is a typical example of European Orientalism, *'a synonym of escapism and sexual fantasy; the Orient is necessarily representative of the "other", foreign, exotic, violent …'*[40] Not all of Flaubert's texts were, however, published in the way he compiled them, such as letters for his friends and mother. His travelogue,[41] for example, is based on his notes concerning the journey and is influenced by the diary style. It contains mostly short, brief reflections.

Flaubert's impressions of Egypt (he visited the country in 1849–50) do not include merely the typical tourist observations of monuments and nature. He dedicated a lot of time to visiting less famous places. One of his most extensive and complete descriptions concerns his visit of the dancer Kuchuk (Kuchuk hanim)[42] in Esna. Flaubert regarded her above all as a courtesan. No wonder, then, that he later directed so much of his attention to Egyptian hospitals, where he was most interested in the syphilis departments.[43]

The 19th century saw the creation of several famous travelogues that became sources of information for whole generations of later travellers and tourists. Besides those compiled in the form of letters, there were also direct descriptions of journeys evoking the form of diaries. Among authors of the latter, we can mention for example lady Hester Stanhope[44] or later Amelia Blanford Edwards.

Some authors of travelogues and reportages not only won wide readership, but also significantly influenced the formation of the opinion of the public of their countries to the questions of maintenance and exploration of ancient Egypt. In Britain, they were Harriet Martineau, Florence Nightingale, and Amelia Blanford Edwards.[45]

Above all Amelia Edwards achieved great success in the field – for example, she collected funds for the great archaeologist and father of Egyptian archaeology Flinders Petrie,[46] and for the foundation of the first Chair of Egyptology at University College in London.[47]

Not all reports from Egypt were filled only with enthusiasm or admiration for the monuments. Accounts of some authors include notes rather similar to those of Flaubert, or concerned above all with contemporary Egypt and its comparison with Europe and the like. These include the older works (since the 1840s) of A. Kinglake, E. Warburton and others.

Especially interesting are the works of Edward Lane, above all his *Manners and Customs of Modern Egyptians* and the only recently published *Description of Egypt*. Lane's works are the result of an almost socioanthropological research, which he undertook in the years of his stay in Egypt.[48]

Lane had by the very principle of his visit more time and possibilities to observe the society *an sich*, he oriented himself in the Egyptian society, and tried to merge into it. The best source for E. W. Lane's descriptive work on Egypt – with regard to the monuments – is the newly edited *Description of Egypt*.[49] It includes the remarks on the voyage up the Nile, text regarding the reign of Muhammad Ali, and his seizing of power and a passage dedicated to Lane's description of Ancient Egypt. The *Description* is a unique work. Unfortunately, in its own time it remained unpublished, and so prived the contemporary scholarship of quite a substantial deal of knowledge[50]. It was only in parts supplanted by Lane's *Manners and Customs of the Modern Egyptians*. The draft of *Description*, which has been first published in the edition of J. Thompson in 2000, was preserved as a manuscript in the British Library. Yet the *Description* fits well into the framework of Lane's publications. The works of Lane include his *Manners and Customs of Modern Egyptians*, 1836, his translation of *The Thousand and one Nights*, 1839–41, *Selections from the Kur-an*, 1843, and the *Arabic-English Lexicon*, 1863–1893.[51]

Lane's work – the *Description* – has proved a duality – but on much more profound level, than most serious works about Egypt in that time – the modern Egypt, plus the ancient Egypt side by side.

Traditional and modern means of transport in Egypt
in the 19ᵗʰ and early 20ᵗʰ century

Lane's main trips to Nile Valley, which inspired his text, took place in 1826 and 1827, the second one he undertook with his friend Robert Hay. His purpose was to map the Egyptian monuments, so had his book been published in time, Lane would have been one of the pioneers of Egyptology – as it was only in 1822 when Champollion deciphered the hieroglyphs. Although his Egyptological knowledge was not sure in the matters of hieroglyphs and Egyptian history, his contribution was in that he described the state of monuments, as he saw them, and it was in the times in which many of them were just waning for ever, as noted Prokesch and Gliddon, for example, as well.[52]

In order to accompany his material by illustrations, he used – for the sake of accuracy – *camera lucida*, he was skilled in sketching, having originally been an engraver. His impressions of Egypt are interesting in themselves as a wittness to his personality, which proved to be open towards the Muslim society, although he himself wrote, surprisingly objectively, in the beginning:

'*I approached the beach with feelings of intense interest, though too anxious to a nature to be entirely pleasing: for I was not visiting Egypt merely with the view of enjoying the examination of its pyramids and temples and subterranean wonders, and with the intention of quitting it as soon as I have satisfied my curiosity; but I was about to take up my abode there for a period of two or three years, chiefly for the purpose of studying the language and literature of its modern inhabitants, and of familiarising myself with their manners and customs: it was requisite, therefore, that I should confine myself, almost exclusively, to the society of Moos'lims, assume their dress, and adopt their mode of life, with which I was not yet suficiently acquainted to foresee whether it would be agreeable to me or the reverse.*'[53]

His attitudes, thus are clearly expressed here, and his general attitudes towards the Muslim world, are from the very start characterised by great openmindedness and understanding.[54]

Flaubert, Lady Duff Gordon, Amelia Edwards and others are more or less random representatives of the large group of visitors to Egypt, who left a published testimony behind them. These people represent only some of the numerous opinions concerning Egypt, recorded by the nineteenth-century European visitors of the country. Some of them were no short-term visitors, but rather residents than tourists. Besides the descriptions of the monuments and exotic beauties of Egypt, we can find the accounts of diplomats and officials, to whom Egypt became the place of their service.[55] The diaries and memoirs of researchers, such as the German Egyptologist Adolf Erman, form a special group.[56]

There exist bibliographies[57] listing hundreds of accounts of journeys and stays in Egypt. Although their authors are mostly of French or Anglo-Saxon origin, there is also a numerous group of authors writing in German, including

Austrians. When in 1873 A. B. Edwards recorded the nationalities of the people whom one could meet as tourists or travellers on the Nile, she wrote: '*nine-tenths of those whom he is likely to meet up the river are English or American. The rest will be mostly German, with a sprinkling of Belgian and French.*'[58]

The presence of Austrians proves the fact that even countries that were no colonial powers and possessed no strongholds in the Near East have their place in the reception of Egypt by the European culture. In the case of the Hapsburg monarchy on the Danube, this place is rather unique.

The Subjects of His Imperial and Royal Majesty in the Orient and in Egypt

The relationship of Austrians to the Orient as a whole is rather complicated and underwent a long development. The necessity of maintaining diplomatic relationships with their neighbour, and above all the simple reality of commercial and other relationships led some of the inhabitants of the monarchy, whether they belonged to state administration or not, to learn Oriental languages. The needs of the state then brought about the support of the study of Oriental languages, which made Vienna an important Orientalist centre of the German-speaking world.[59] In the church, knowledge of Oriental languages was quite common even earlier. Hebrew was a necessity for reasons of theology, and other languages were useful tools in missionary practice (which is a Roman Church issue especially). The church past of Oriental studies was a well-known phenomenon already in the 19th century.[60]

Franz Joseph I

Since the 17th century, the need to communicate with the Ottoman Empire became an important factor for the Austrian monarchy, above all since this powerful neighbour was not always inclined to peaceful coexistence.[61] The resident of the Kaiser lived at the court of Constantinople (Istanbul) already since 1547. These envoys had long depended on the service of interpreters from amongst the Christian subjects of the Sultan, or even from the captives. Later it became common to send young boys (so-called Sprachknaben) to be educated in Istanbul, in order to become familiar with the language since their youth. Besides Turkish, Arabic and Persian were important languages in the area. Diplomatic interpreters thus became, as the first speakers of Oriental languages in the monarchy, the first authors of textbooks, grammars, and dictionaries. Often they assembled valuable collections of specialised literature, Oriental manuscripts, and objects.[62]

By founding the *Orientalische Akademie* (later, since 1898, Konsularakademie, reconstituted in 1904) in Vienna in 1754, Maria Theresia initiated the professional education of diplomats for the Orient.[63] This did not include only languages, but also the history, literature, and culture of the East (see further 'The background of Austrian economic influence', pp. 8–10).[64]

The importance of diplomats in the birth of Austrian Oriental science and in the connaissance of Oriental cultures is evident in the activities of Joseph von Hammer-Purgstall[65] (1774–1856). He began his education at the Orientalische Akademie, and is the author of numerous works on the Near Eastern world – among others, *Literaturgeschichte der Araber* (written in the course of the 1850s)[66] and the most famous *Geschichte des osmanischen Reiches* (1827–1833).[67] Another author who mediated his knowledge of the Arab world to his contemporaries was Hammer-Purgstall's student Alfred von Kremer (1828–1889), a philologist and diplomat, who served a short term as a consul in Cairo[68] and represented the Austro-Hungarian Empire in the Commision for the Control of the Egyptian public debt.[69] His other books include *Mittelsyrien und Damaskus* (1825), and *Ägypten. Forschung über Land und Volk* (1863).[70]

The Austrians travelled to various areas of the Near East for reasons of commerce, service and diplomacy. Their aims differed, and so did their occupations during their stay. We have just described the importance of the education of diplomats for the development of the study of the Orient. Another aspect that influenced it was the very stay of a number of people of Austrian origin in this area. Besides diplomats, we encounter also artists, for whom the journey to the Orient was a source of inspiration, which made them work on exotic themes. The glimpse into academic life shows us, that since the 1860s, the University of Vienna began to offer ordinary lectures on Oriental languages.[71]

The interests of the Austrian monarchy in the Orient were thus quite substantial. How about Austrian interests in Egypt herself? Rudolf Agstner, who worked with large amounts of archive materials concerning Austrian embassies in Egypt and above all their consular agenda, characterises Austrian diplomacy as follows: '*The history of the official Austrian presence in Egypt offers an interesting view at how in the course of the second half of the nineteenth century, the Ballhausplatz lost the influence they had gained during the reign of Muhammad Ali. Neither the fact that the plans for the Suez Canal were made by an Austrian, nor the existence of the largest Austro-Hungarian community in this part of the Ottoman Empire, some members of which reached an influential position at the Khedive's court, and not even the fact that the last Khedive Abbas II Hilmi[72] attended the Viennese Theresianum, were exploited politically. The monarchy nonetheless had a certain influence on some areas of economy and controlled the beer and textile trade.*'[73] This quote briefly characterises the main aspects of the Austrian (and Austro-Hungarian) presence in Egypt, both in terms of politics and general existence of the Austrian community.

If, in connection with Orientalism and Egyptomania, I mentioned the contact with the individual countries in terms of colonial and trade interests of powers such as France or Great Britain, it should be stressed that even Austria was not without political interest and influence in the area of the Near East.[74] Despite the fact that the history of Austrian representative offices in Egypt dates back to the first years of the 19th century, the enforcing of Austrian interests was not very effective. This can be explained by the political and financial situation of the monarchy.[75] At that time, Austria still played an active role in the formation of the political conceptions of the solution of the Eastern question (cf. pp. 7–19). A. Prokesch himself presents in his *Erinnerungen* a small glimpse into the extent of European, and thus also Austrian, trade. Prokesch sees Egypt as the country which has been a point of intensive trade and commerce and is going to be such one once more[76] – but with the difference, that now Egypt will have less trade with the merchandise of India and Arabia, and more of her own production. He follows the use of Egyptian ships as well – in the Levantine trade Egypt has the use of own ships now, which no doubt would spread further.

'*Egypt receives from Europe raw and worked metals, semi-metals, weapons and ammunition; cloth, products of wool, cotton, and silk; building wood; noble wood types; … knitting and ropes; water; china; glass and pottery; cheese; fruit; seeds, spices; pitch and resin; watches; clothing; colours; building stone; fish (smoked, salted, marinated); jewellery; tobacco; tea; oil; wines; household appliances and finally everything she needs from America.*'[77] He went into financial details, which were linked to his interests – the sum of European import in the year 1823 was that of 2 888 252 Spanish Thalers, he stated. This information was of value, as Austria, his mother country had quite a good deal with Egypt in the matter of weapons and military material.[78] And he continued to make his picture a complete one. Prokesch noted the imports and exports side by side– interesting is the list of what Egypt is giving to Europe[79] – '*Egypt gives to Europe: ambergris, anise, antiquities … coffee, … cassia, horses, wax, flour and corn, legumes, barley, rice, cotton and linen, untreated and spun, products of wood, linen and cotton, hemp, shawls, dates, ivory, ostrich feathers, cosmetics, rose oil, turtle shells, incense and perfumes, fine sponges, various arts of gum, linen oil, sesame oil, indigo, henna, mother-of-pearl, natron, skins, pepper and other spices, ricine oil, soap, saffron, ammonia, table and common salt, seeds, soda, sugar, rum, tobacco.*'

In comparison with that what is imported, we see clearly that for some of the products Egypt was still a place of storage and further re-selling, but some are of her own production. Egyptian export to Europe in 1823 was up to 5,518,870 Spanish Thalers. The most important European harbours have been Constantinople, Leghorn, Marseille, Malta, Sira, Trieste. The Tabelle I of *Erinnerungen* shows that Austria has been among foremost European traders with Egypt. There were two havens – Alexandria and Damiette, of which Alexandria was the more important. The Red Sea trade routes are that starting at Suez and Qusseir – the route is going to Qusseir from Qena. Prokesch noted the caravan routes as well.[80] From Assiut and Derawi started caravans for the oases, Assiut was the starting point to Darfur as well, etc. Caravan routes led even to Syria, Arabia and north-western Africa in Prokesch's times. Prokesch studied further the earnings of Egyptian caravan trade, and its routes to Africa.

The Suez Canal in the 19ᵗʰ century

Austria intended to acquire some control over the Red Sea trade already in the end of the 18ᵗʰ century[81] and again after the Napoleonic wars. At that time, however, chancellor Metternich's efforts were thwarted by the reluctance of Muhammad Ali to engage in further negotiations.[82] In connection with this problem, Metternich's subordinate and friend Anton Count Prokesch von Osten had already undertaken several journeys through the Orient in terms of the military-diplomatic mission. We will return to him in more detail in the chapter on travelogues, since he left behind very interesting memoirs of his travels. Here it is at place to cite the words that Prokesch ascribed to Muhammad Ali and that would indicate an otherwise obliging attitude of this statesman to Austria: '... *Austria and I share a common goal in today's chaos – the preservation of the Turkish empire, and I believe that together with Prince Metternich we think of the same ways that lead towards this aim*'[83] (see further the contribution by R. Míšek).

The Austrian empire played an important role in the planning of the construction of the Suez Canal. At that time, Austria already had consular representation in Alexandria and Cairo. In the mid 1840s, in connection with the development of the sailing company Austrian Lloyd,[84] the plans of the French Prosper Enfantin succeeded to appeal to the Austrian and French governments, and thus a company for the research of the possibility to construct the canal was set up in 1846. The Austrians tried to promote the plan of Alois von Negrelli. British government, however, protested.[85] During the planned division of spheres of influence, it was rather the rule to forget the Egyptian side, whose agreement was essential. First in 1854, the concession for the building was awarded to the cousin of the French Empress Eugenia,[86] Ferdinand de Lesseps.[87]

The idea of connecting two seas later intrigued also the Hapsburg Archduke, brother of the Kaiser Franz Joseph I, Ferdinand Maximilian, who visited Egypt in 1855 (and assembled a collection of aegyptiaca).[88] Ferdinand Maximilian is the later unfortunate Mexican Emperor Maximilian. As such, he supported Leo Reinisch, one of the first Austrian Egyptologists.

The original plan of the building is the result of the plan of the Austrian engineer of Italian origin Alois von Negrelli.[89] He, however, died already in the year 1858, and thus it was above all the name of Ferdinand de Lesseps that entered common knowledge. Austria also could not keep her positions in the 'Society of the Suez Canal' after she had withheld her support to Lesseps out of fear of the negative attitude of Britain.[90] Formally, the Austro-Hungarian Empire retained her face by the presence of Franz Joseph I at the celebration of the opening of the canal in 1869.[91] Later she also belonged to the greatest users of the canal.[92] The importance of Trieste as a traffic centre of the Mediterranean grew as well.[93]

The Austro-Hungarian Empire was also financially committed in Egypt. There was the *Austro-Egypt Bank*, which was closed down only in 1876 as a result of the Egyptian financial breakdown. Later, the monarchy had a representative in the Committee for the Egyptian state debt (see above the reference to Alfred von Kremer). The Austro-Egypt bank was directed by a clerk of the Austrian Credit-Anstalt, Julius Blum pasha (1843–1919). After the fall of the Egyptian state finance, he stayed in Egyptian service until 1890 and proved efficient in the sanation of the financial sector.[94]

Already since 1866, a new consular representation existed in Port Said (the one in Suez has an even longer history, it was founded in 1844). Its main task was to protect the commercial and legal interests of Austrian citizens.[95] The work of Austrian diplomats in political affairs was, however, complicated by the lack of finances and subsequent problems with representation.[96] The Austrian representative offices used to have insufficiently equipped residences. It is worth noting that later the new Czechoslovak mission in Cairo was facing similar problems, as is apparent from the letters of the first Czech ambassador Cyril Dušek and his wife Pavla.[97]

Let us now return to the time before the WW I and take a closer look at the Austrian community in Cairo. It was a large group of foreigners of European origin – the fourth largest. In 1897, it comprised of 7115 individuals, in 1907 the number grew to 7704.[98] The only preserved register book in Cairo,[99] which comes from the years 1908–1914, offers an interesting insight into the composition of the group. Although it in all likelihood does not record the entire community of citizens of the Austro-Hungarian Empire who had lived here at that time (not to speak of the entire Egypt), and it does not even include some of the very important personages who lived at the court of the Khedives, it nonetheless offers a representative sample.[100]

Among those missing are for example the physicians of Khedive Abbas II Hilmi,[101] Johann von Becher and Anton Kautzky. The court dentist, Dr. Henriette Hornik[102] is, on the other hand, recorded. A number of Austrian citizens recorded in the register worked in the Egyptian state administration as clerks. We encounter bank clerks, architects, physicians, but also servants, artisans and businessmen.[103] As far as the Austrian businessmen[104] are considered, some of them achieved high positions in Cairo, e.g. the R. Kirchmayer Company, furniture makers, who advertised in the Cairo press published in European languages.[105]

The Austrian construction companies were the most successful, e.g. Cattaui & Matasek,[106] many of whose works can (or rather could)[107] be seen in the luxury quarters of Cairo, such as Garden City. The individual architects, often educated in the history of art, even took care of the ancient monuments of Islamic art. This holds true of Max Herz[108] (the builder of the Ar-Rifa'i mosque)[109] and Julius Franz (the architect of the project of the Khedivial palace on the island

The 19th century Cairo as seen by European visitors

of Gezira, today's Hotel Marriott),[110] as well as of Antonius Lasciac,[111] who made frequent use of traditional Islamic motifs in his own architectural design. Of a somewhat older date are the works of František (Franz) Schmoranz Jr., the author of the Khedive's residence at Ismailia. Later, in 1873, he designed the Egyptian pavilions of the world exhibition in Vienna, in the decoration of which he connected both traditional Islamic and ancient Egyptian elements.[112] The common denominator of all the above-mentioned architects was a deeper interest in the cultural heritage of Egypt. M. Herz and J. Franz even directed the Museum of Islamic art.[113]

According to the visions of Khedive Ismail and his successors, Cairo should have been a 'Paris of the Orient,'[114] and as such, it should have been representative by the European character of magnificent public and residential buildings and equipment of the city. Characteristically, Classicist and Art Nouveau details prevail in these European-style buildings, which can still be found above all in Garden City, between Midan Tahrir and Midan Tala'at Harb and in the area around Qasr el-Aini or at places in the district of Doqqi.[115] They are similar to the contemporary French and Italian architecture, as well as to the Austrian floral and geometric Art Nouveau.[116] Only rarely can historical Islamising ornament be found (we saw it employed in the works of Austrian architects), Egyptian motif is even less frequent.[117]

The influence of European architecture had, both positively and negatively, shaped the face of modern Cairo at the turn of the 19th and 20th centuries.[118] Contemporary European visitors were astonished by this new face of Cairo. The new districts offered a much higher hygienical standard of living. And the description that George Ebers' guide[119] gives of the entire district of Ezbekiyeh, full of magnificent embassies and hotels, offers an entirely European impression, '... the Ezebekiyeh Square. Huge, in part imposing buildings in European style, which include the theatre, the stock market, as well as several embassies ... surround it from all sides, and the garden located in the centre of the square is one of the most beautiful ones in the world. Of course, a city like Cairo cannot lack gas lighting, and no one, who once saw the Ezebekiyeh garden lit by its 2500 lights, many of which have colourful tulip-shaped glass covers, can ever forget the sight ...' As the observant Ebers noted, this rash Europeanisation, wide boulevards, macadam streets and alleys of trees, did not have only a positive effect. The shade, that the narrow streets used to give, disappeared, and the burning-hot surface of the new streets also proved a disadvantage. New Cairo was a city of two faces, not only in architecture, but also in lifestyle. Central European travellers could not avoid encounters with this duality.

By 'Austrian citizens' we, of course, do not mean only people born on the territory of today's Austria. The above-mentioned register includes a number of Czechs, Hungarians, Slovenians and Italians.[120] The post-war Czech colony had a tradition to follow.[121]

A number of citizens of Central Europe experienced a direct encounter with the Oriental world. This does not, however, mean that they necessarily contributed to its reflection, or its reception in their home country. Unlike many Anglo-Saxons, not everyone composed a travelogue,[122] not everyone was a skilful draughtsman or photographer. The others could have let behind them a testimony in the form of correspondence, diaries, etc., such as the Czech Pavla Dušková in the 1920s. Estates form a good source of such materials. The estates of famous people are more likely to be preserved. Whether, however, we may once find the personal materials of someone from the number of people whose names fill the pages of the *Matrikelbuch des k.u.k. Konsulates*, is now in the sphere of hypotheses. We would thus be offered a view of the perception of Egypt by individual people, and perhaps even elements of personal historical culture.

Let us now take a closer look at those who recorded a part of their impression in words. Numerous[123] visitors of Egypt wrote a travelogue or an educative book. Publications of this type thus contributed to the widening of knowledge, or – in the time when Baedeker's guides and illustrated publications[124] already existed, that is chiefly in the second half of the 19th century – they presented further impressions of the visited country.[125]

Some of the travellers were literati, people trained in the written word, other testimonies are rather immediate impressions of researchers, still others only observations of curious tourists.[126] Each traveller had a different education, a different sum of previous knowledge,[127] different expectations and a different ability to reflect the visited countries and their past and present culture.

Some individuals were described in more detail in the section on 19th century Europeans in Egypt. Among the numerous Britons, mentioned so far, there were German-speaking travellers,[128] (in terms of language more accessible to the Czech lands), or authors linked with Central Europe as well. Out of the travellers-literati, Juliusz Slowacki (1809–1849), who visited Egypt in the mid 1830s,[129] is the one most closely linked to the Slavonic Central European environment. After he had unsuccessfully taken part in the Polish uprising in 1830, he lived in Paris, i. e. in an environment that offered a wide range of possibilities of encounter with the Orient.

In the Czech lands, the works of the Austrian authors were the most easily accessible. This is true in the general sense about all authors originating from the Austrian monarchy.

The long journey from the Danube and Vltava rivers to the Nile

We may divide Austrian travelogues to those, whose authors originated directly in the Czech lands, and those written by authors more or less linked to the Czech lands (above all via belonging to the Austrian monarchy). If we talk about travelogues, we must briefly introduce the background of the individual authors. We will therefore have a look at the community of travellers, who had undertaken the long journey from the Danube or Vltava rivers to the Nile.

The Czechs Žvejkal and Neruda belong to the first group. Both will be treated later in much detail.

The second group includes above all the works of aristocratic travellers, Austrian archdukes and the crown prince Rudolf, and other German language travelogues of Austrian travellers of aristocratic and middle-class origin. Sometimes their works attest knowledge of further literature, including the works of contemporary Egyptologists – this is for example the case of the travelogue of the archduke Rudolf. Motifs of aristocratic journeys usually had the character of pilgrimages – to the sacred places – or hunting expeditions. Both were typical for the journeys of the Hapsburg family.

Rudolf, the son of the Emperor Franz Joseph I and Elisabeth of Bavaria, befriended the German Egyptologist Heinrich Brugsch[130] during his journey through the Orient in 1881. He wrote a book called 'Journey through the Orient,'[131] where he makes frequent allusions to Brugsch – *'I shall use the words of my friend Brugsch pasha.'*[132] Rudolf's *Orientreise* is a relatively lively text, describing the travelling and hunting[133] experience of a small company, which was besides the prince composed of the Grand Duke of Tuscany, Count Hoyos and the painter Franz von Pausinger, whose drawings accompany the travelogue.

Even the monuments did not stay out of the traveller's interest. It was here that the influence of the prince's friend Egyptologist is the most apparent – the archduke used whole passages of his works. He was also aware of the work of other Egyptologists, during the visit of Bulaq he remembered the recently deceased French Egyptologist Mariette pasha.[134] He also knew at least several European museums with Egyptian monuments, e.g. the museum in Torino.[135]

Heinrich Brugsch was recommended to the crown prince by the Austrian consul in Cairo as one who *'belongs to the most pleasant companions and presents Egyptology to everyone in the most funny and accessible way.'*[136] Brugsch was already familiar with accompanying the nobility.[137] During the opening of the Suez Canal, he accompanied the Kaiser Franz Joseph.[138] He was favourably inclined to prince Rudolf because of his interest in Egyptology, despite the fact that Rudolf came to the country above all as a passionate ornithologist, and much less as a hunter (unlike the other members of the company). He also bought some Egyptian antiquities, following Brugsch's advice. Later, when he served in the Prague military garrison, he invited Brugsch to Prague. Brugsch recorded his visit in his autobiography. He writes very favourably about the prince and his private life, but he records no further detail about his stay in Prague.[139] There was another thing that Brugsch shared with Rudolf – both were Freemasons.[140] The Archduke's interest in Egypt included also foreign relations, which he could not influence openly, but he commented on them anonymously in the press (e.g. his reactions to the Egyptian question in 1882). Even the prince's mother, Empress Elisabeth, visited Egypt incognito as Countess von Hohenembs,[141] and published her travelogue under the name of the captain of her ship August von Almstein in 1887.[142]

The origin and aims of Austrian citizens who travelled to Egypt in the 19th and in the beginning of the 20th centuries were widely differentiated. We began our survey with the noble ones, who travelled for enjoyment and also for social duties. These noble travellers had their predecessors, who were often driven by much more various motifs.

Anton Count Prokesch von Osten

Anton Prokesch von Osten (1795–1876) is tied to the Czech environment.[143] He visited Egypt in 1826–27, and again in 1833. His travelogue *Erinnerungen aus Ägypten und Kleinasien I–III* was published between 1829–1831 in Vienna.

Anton Prokesch, Count von Osten

Prokesch's activities in Egypt were connected with the diplomatic mission of Prince Metternich.[144] Metternich's friend Prokesch-Osten had a promising military career and had already held several diplomatic posts. His second visit to Egypt in 1833 was part of a wider diplomatic-military mission. In the 1850s and 1860s, he held the high position of an internuntio and later ambassador in Constantinople. His friends included not only Prince Metternich, but also Friedrich Gentz and Franz Duke of Reichstadt, son of the emperor Napoleon I.

Prokesch von Osten was well familiar with the Oriental environment.[145] His interest in the diplomatic missions in the Orient formed gradually. The linguistically talented diplomat spoke paradoxically above all European languages. He read a lot, and was a fan of Lord Byron. He was aware of some of the European prejudices against the Islamic world.[146] His interest in ancient Egypt is apparent from his correspondence with Champollion's pupil and colleague Ippolito Rossellini. Rossellini's letters can be found in the estate of Prokesch.[147]

Rosellini tried to procure himself the German edition of *Erinnerungen*, although he could not read German. Moreover, he kept a correspondence with Prokesch. There is in Nachlass Prokesch – no. 44, Schachtel VII, 'Italien 1831–1832' a couple of letters by Rosellini,[148] devoted to a praise of *Erinnerungen*, and to a discussion of monumens both scholars were interested in. In January 1834, Rosellini was delighted at the gift of *Erinnerungen*, naming it 'sua bella e dotta opera', and 'cortese dono'. The letters contain a lot of details of Egyptological character, including a discussion about the datation of pyramids, about the Hyksos etc.

In March 1834 Rosellini tends to be even more interested in Prokesch's work, encouraging him into development of Egyptology in German-speaking countries, and criticising the weakening of the French scholarship after Champollion's death.

How does Prokesch perceive Egypt in his travelogue? Egypt is the theme of parts of the first two volumes of his *Erinnerungen aus Ägypten und Kleinasien*.[149] Prokesch von Osten was a well-prepared traveller. He acquainted himself with the history of Egypt, and observed the monument with the eyes of a knowledge-able pilgrim. In the text of his work, he cites D. V. Denon and Plinius, i.e. a contemporary and an ancient author.[150]

During his visit of Alexandria, he noticed the granite obelisks on the seashore that were known as 'Cleopatra's needles'.[151] These obelisks were originally commissioned by Thutmosis III for the temple of Heliopolis, later Ramesses II added his inscriptions to them, and finally Augustus transported them to Alexandria. Their planned further transport to Rome was never realised. As Prokesch observes, *'these obelisks were probably removed several times, and brought to Alexandria, perhaps from Memphis or Heliopolis, under the Ptolemies or Romans'*[152], Later, in Giza, Prokesch notes *'I don't know how anyone could have ever doubted that the pyramids were tombs, even before their inside was known. They stand in the middle of the large Memphite necropolis … wherever one digs, one encounters tombs and catacombs.'*[153]

Anton Prokesch von Osten was a well-informed traveller who knew his destinations. The selection is just a small one, since Prokesch travelled through the entire Egypt. These monuments were chosen so that he could be compared with other travellers, Ida Pfeifer (also Pfeiffer) and the Prague goldsmith Jan Žvejkal, who is included as a contemporary of both Austrian travellers.

Prokesch's memoirs also prove his deeper relationship to the monuments. He was aware of the dangers brought about by their constantly growing popularity, which he considers the fifth wave in the destruction of ancient Egyptian monuments. After Christian and Moslem iconoclasts and stone miners came the modern 'admirers' of antiquity, *'This fifth wave of destruction … is fully under way, and if Muhammad Ali or his son Ibrahim, in some return of barbarism, do not expel the treasure-hunting hordes out of the country, then the tombs in Thebes and Memphis and many other beautiful and unique monuments will soon be preserved only in narratives.'[154]*

Prokesch had great sense for details. He uses it to present fitting accounts of the Egyptian sites, without lengthy descriptions and at places in funny hyperboles, *'here and there a granite column, a statue of Isis, tablet inscribed with hieroglyphs, head of Mithra, here and there a palm tree with heavy bunches of dates, all this surrounded by double walls, low massive towers and French fortifications.'[155]* This should be an 'exhaustive' description of Alexandria. Cairo *'is … the seat of the rulers, enclosed by the desert … it is neither Europe nor Asia[156] … the streets are narrow, dark, and rise towards the Citadel, the bazaars are rich, … the baths numerous … "[157]*

The account of Prokesch von Osten naturally does not include only descriptions of monuments and thorough characteristics of the land and travel experiences, although they do form a predominant part of his *Erinnerungen*.[158] Interesting observations, concerning the politics and development of contemporary Egypt, can be found above all in his book *Mehmed Ali, Vizekönig von Aegypten. Aus meinem Tagebuche 1826–1841* published in Vienna in 1877. Here we can learn about the people Prokesch was meeting at that time. Among them were also Salt and Drovetti,[159] whose collections formed the foundations of the Egyptian departments of leading European museums – the Louvre in Paris and Museo Egizio in Torino. An important report is also to be found in Prokesch's letters, that he addressed to his patron and teacher Prof. Schneller.[160]

Ida Pfeifer (Pfeiffer)[161] and her contemporaries

The journey of Ida Pfeifer, daughter of a Viennese merchant, to the Holy Land and to Egypt in 1842, had a cognitive character. Her book *Reise einer Wienerin in das Heilige Land* was published in Vienna in 1844. For the Czech environment, Pfeifer is of interest also as the later travel companion of the Moravian noble B. V. Berchtold.[162] Their common journey led as far as Brazil.[163] Mrs. Pfeifer became a great fan of travelling and after her Oriental expedition she undertook several other demanding journeys, including two journeys around the world.

Ida Pfeifer (born Reyer, 1797–1858) belongs to the large number of women travellers of the 19th century.[164] The journey to the Holy Land was only one of her many long pilgrimages.[165] She managed to describe almost all of them in detailed and interesting accounts, which brought her fame, and besides the membership in the *Berlin Gesellschaft für Erdkunde* also the approval of Alexander von Humboldt.[166]

As she herself states, she prepared for her journey by reading and talking with people, who had already visited her destinations. In Egypt, just as elsewhere in the Orient, she concentrated above all on the description of her own adventures, but did not neglect the monuments and her admiration for them. In Alexandria, just like other travellers, she made sure to visit the two granite obelisks –

'Cleopatra's needles'. *'By a small detour, I came to "Cleopatra's needles", two granite obelisks. One of them is still standing, the other lies nearby in sand.'*[167]

The pyramids of Giza amazed her with their size, but she valued them not only as gigantic structures, but also as *'... the most lasting works of human art and dilligence'.*[168] It is interesting to compare her quote with that of Jan Neruda – see below, which is thirty years younger, and very disrespectful of the monuments. Mrs. Pfeifer did not forget the Biblical atmosphere of the country, but did not let it become the major part of her description of the monuments. Her travelogue evokes the English text of Harriet Martineau, including the focus on practical aspects of travelling.[169]

Ida Pfeifer is often being compared to her contemporary, Countess Ida von Hahn-Hahn, and to another very interesting personality – Anna Forneris, who spent most of her life in the Orient and wrote her memoirs in her old age.[170]

Ida Hahn-Hahn's travel conditions were, naturally, much more favourable than those of the other two women,[171] and as a member of the aristocracy, she was accepted even at embassies. The works of both ladies (Anna Forneris did not visit Egypt) contain, besides characteristics of the contemporary Oriental world, which surrounded them, also references to its ancient past. Both of them, but mainly Lady Hahn-Hahn, compare the magnificent past with the declining present.[172]

The travelogue of the Rumburk born Ignaz Pallme was another work written in the German language. Ignaz Samuel Pallme (also known as Palme, 1806 or 1810–1877)[173] also visited Egypt in the 1840s. His work on his travels through North Africa – *Beschreibungen von Kordofan und einigen angränzenden Ländern* ... etc. (1843) was later even translated to English. Pallme visited North Africa for business reasons. Also his brother, Josef Pallme, undertook business travels through Egypt, Syria, and Palestine, and he too wrote a travelogue – *Meine Reise durch Sicilien, Egypten, Syrien, und Palästina* (1841).[174] Even some Czechs (in the linguistic sense) won their traveller's spurs by visiting the Orient. Among them was the contemporary of the important Austrian travellers, Prokesch, Pfeifer, and the Pallme brothers, the Prague citizen and artisan Jan Žvejkal.

Jan Žvejkal

The Prague goldsmith Jan Žvejkal (1782–1854) wrote, and in 1844 also published, a Czech-language book on his travels, called *Popsání trojích cest po pevné zemi a po moři v Evropě, Asii a Africe roku 1818–1833 na posvátná místa v zemi svaté čili do města Jerusaléma k Božímu hrobu vykonaných od Jana Žvejkala, poutníka, mistra zlatnického a měšťana pražského* ('A description of three journeys on solid land and on the sea in Europe, Asia and Africa, to the sacred places in the Holy land or to the city of Jerusalem and to the grave of Jesus, undertaken by Jan Žvejkal, a pilgrim, master goldsmith and Prague citizen'). During his travels through Biblical sites, Žvejkal managed to visit Egypt only after several unsuccessful attempts during his third voyage through the Near East, which he undertook in the years 1831–1833.[175]

He set out for Egypt from the Holy Land. In June 1833,[176] he sailed from Jaffa (today's Tel Aviv) to Damiette, i.e. to the same site, through which also the Czech Renaissance pilgrim Kryštof Harant had entered the country. From here, Žvejkal sailed up the Nile to Cairo. Along the way, he was interested above all in the sites where the Holy Family was said to have staid.

Of the ancient monuments he visited the pyramids, but his testimony is brief and shows rather an interest in the behaviour of local people, than for the monuments themselves. He writes *'I had also visited that place, where the tomb or pyramid of Pharaoh king lies, over the Nile to the Midday side, it covers 300 steps square, and several smaller ones stand around it, and so I climbed the pyramid, the top of which Napoleon had removed in order to be able to dine there, and that area covers 14 steps square.'*[177] Following this brief description we find another account on how he was bothered by an Arab, who demanded a payment for the climbing of the pyramid. First the 'learned French', who also appeared atop the pyramid, helped him to get rid of the unwanted 'guide'.

The emphasis on Biblical connotations is apparent in his description of Cairo. *'That is the site of the jail where Joseph was arrested …'*[178] is one of its chief characteristics.

Cleopatra's Needle in Alexandria

From Cairo he continued along the common route to Alexandria, where he saw Pompeius' column. Even here, he mentions a similar story as at the pyramids '*On the top of it, 10 Frenchmen had dined*'.[179] It must be mentioned that attempts to climb the Pompeius' column belonged to the favourite occupation of the travellers to Alexandria.[180]

Among other monuments, Žvejkal noticed '*two Leopart (sic) needles, which are three-sided pointed stones of granite or sandstone, one of which lies fallen on the ground; this one the English wanted to take away, but, since for its size and weight, they could not put it aboard their ship, they decided to leave it lying on the ground. In the outskirts lies the old town, but it is buried in the ground and similar to flats and all kinds of hideaways*'.[181] One of the obelisks that Žvejkal saw now stands in London and bears the name that history assigned to it and its companion – Cleopatra's needle. He apparently thought of exotic predators rather than of the wanton Queen. Žvejkal recorded quite uncritically what others had told him about the monuments he saw, such as the tales about Napoleon's banquet atop the pyramid, or of another French feast on Pompeius' column.

The Column of Pompeius, apparently a favourite dining place of the period

Jan Neruda and his travel sketches

Almost forty years after the Prague artisan, another Czech visited Egypt and left written memoirs of his journey, namely the writer, poet and journalist Jan Neruda (1834–1891), author of *Obrazy z ciziny* ('Sketches from Abroad'), which were from the very beginning intended for publication. He recorded the journey to the Orient, which he had undertaken in the 1870s together with the father of the later famous opera singer Emmy Destinn, Emmanuel Kittl. Their voyage led over Constantinople all the way to Egypt.

His observations are of a pronounced character, focusing on details that are often the first ones that catch the eye of a tourist. In Cairo he noted, just like in the course of the entire journey, the incessant demands for 'bakshiish'.[182] In this, he does not differ from the Baedeker guide of 1929.

His two longest essays dedicated to the visit of Egypt are entitled *Průplav suesský* ('The Suez Canal') and *Masr el Kahira*, published jointly in *Obrazy z ciziny*

Another, less cosmopolitan, face of 19ᵗʰ century Cairo

in 1872.[183] They were written during the voyage in 1870.

The sketch *Průplav suesský*[184] records Neruda's arrival to the colonial port of Port Said, and includes a short history of various attempts at connecting the two seas. Neruda shows his knowledge of Herodotus[185] and Strabo, from whom he learned of the effort of King Necho II to dig through the isthmus, about the realisation of the plan in the Persian period, etc. Further he describes the journey through the canal to Ismailia and by the train to Suez.

It is interesting that when writing of Nile water (in connection with the small junction leading to the Canal), his characteristics are not unlike the description of another Czech traveller, Kryštof Harant of Polžice. Neruda writes: *'Here then, we for the first time gazed into the sacred waters of the Nile, still as muddy as millennia ago, tasty and sweet, fragrant and healing, which is said to make women fertile and healthy, men sturdy and strong …'*[186] Harant's words concerning the same topic are: *'The water cannot be praised enough for its goodness and healthiness … when drunk, it is tasty and sweet … and it is also quite fragrant … Galenus praises this Nile water above*

Jan Neruda

all waters and attests that it makes women fertile …'[187]

Neruda explicitly mentions Harant is his other sketch *Masr el Kahira.*[188] His own impressions of the capital consist above all of denunciations of poverty and dirt, contrasting with the luxury of the European colonial quarters. He was thus able to perceive the double face of Ismailean Cairo:[189] on the one hand there was the Khedive's attempt to build a 'Paris on the Nile', on the other the old town, living its own traditional life without noticing modern styles and technological conveniences. Neruda but briefly mentions the architectural wealth of Islamic buildings (paradoxically, it was above all the mosque of Muhammad Ali at the Citadel that attracted his attention).

His knowledge of ancient Egypt also sometimes comes to the foreground, for example in the sketch on dogs. *'Just as the Egyptians had a bull for a god, the Ethiopians had a dog for king … The Egyptians considered dogs sacred. If a dog died, the family cut their hair as a sign of grief. They worshipped Anubis* (feminine in Neruda's account), *who had a human body and dog's head, as a sign of wisdom connected with loyalty. Sirius, whose appearance on the sky reliably announced the rising of the Nile, was named "the Dog star"*'.[190]

And this is Neruda's view of ancient Egyptian monuments: '*The traditional trips from Cairo include the visit of the Giza cemetery. It is usually called another way, because here stands that pyramid ('p-uro-ma' = king's tomb)*[191]*... A magnificent sight indeed! Not by their artistic design, the pyramids are just mere rocks, as if cut on all four sides to form a point, ... but what a grand folly, what a miraculous heap of stupidity, what a sky-scraping, idiotically gazing monument of royal wilfulness!*[192]*... (in the burial chamber) at the back stands a sarcophagus, lidless and empty; a convenient spittoon for everyone, who remembers that 400,000 people were forced to work on the building!*[193]*... Egyptian art (which can be quite well studied in the Cairo museum, built in Bulaq) at first gives a foreign impression with its steadiness and immobility ... but the suddenly appearing impression of immense calmness and outright heavenly peace are always present and impress with their reality.*'[194]

His characteristics of the ancient Egyptians include the following account: '*The ancient Egyptians were a very cruel people, reliefs depict them beating their captives and pulling them around by their beards, and cutting off their enemies' hands and genitalia.*'[195] Although presenting a denunciation, Neruda tried to support it with direct sources. This means that he was a rather keen observer of ancient monuments. Cruelty is a trait that Europeans often assigned to the entire Orient, and the projection of these ideas into the ancient past had to lead to such harsh statements. Nonetheless, the general denunciation of the 'royal wilfulness' appears rather to be a denunciation of Neruda's royal contemporaries than to be directed straight at the ancient monarchs. Or, alternatively, Neruda wanted to indicate the superiority of his own advanced time over the despotic antiquity. This would seem to be a natural conclusion of a man of the 19th century, who often considered his own technocratic civilisation a paradigm of perfection.

Neruda learned about ancient Egyptian funerary conceptions, as they were known in his time, and he was also aware of current archaeological projects. He mentions the officials' tombs discovered at Giza, as well as Mariette's excavations.[196]

What Neruda seems to lack is a non-ironic admiration for the ancient culture. He always keeps his distance, and his accounts are sometimes even mocking. His predecessors, such as Ida Pfeifer or Anton Prokesch von Osten, who visited Egypt before him, wrote with much greater respect and understanding for the ancient monuments. Perhaps they had been better informed, although even Neruda did not arrive to Egypt fully unaware of her history. Neruda's ironic style cannot even be explained by the fact that Czech literary market would have been overflooded with similar travelogues, and there would thus be a need to take them off. This was the case of the British – or generally – English speaking – book market.[197]

Neruda's sketches are a testimony directed at the public. However, people sometimes record their personal memories of their travels, which they usually do not intend to be published. In search for such an account, we must advance to the 1920s, to the girl's lyceum teacher and ambassador's wife, Mrs. Dušková.

The letters of Mrs. Pavla Dušková – a 1st republic Czech in Egypt

The letters of the wife of the first Czech ambassador Cyril Dušek, Mrs. Pavla, are a personal testimony, which offers a glimpse of the level of individual historical culture.[198] She was a middle (or upper middle) class woman, educated in the second half of the 19th century, who moved to Egypt together with her husband in the 1920s in terms of his diplomatic mission.

Her letters do not represent a source that was accessible to the general public, since their readership remained limited to their addressees. They do, however, show a certain level of reception of a foreign country, and also of its magnificent past. Mrs. Dušková encountered the monuments of ancient Egypt on several trips organised during her stay. It appears that these trips were not stimulated by a specific interest in the monuments of ancient Egyptian culture, since she does not describe them very often (three to four longer references to them appear in her letters).[199] Their aim was rather to enliven a little the otherwise boring and demanding stay.[200] This does not, however mean, that the Dušeks, as a middle class family with a certain cultural background, had no idea about ancient Egypt.

Mrs. Dušková noticed many details in her weekly relations to her family in Prague. The impressions of her journey include the description of the menu aboard the ship.[201] She continues with all new and unexpected adventures. A journey like this was not entirely novel for the wife of a diplomat; she had

Dr Cyril Dušek, the first Czechoslovak ambassador in Egypt

already dwelled in Switzerland for some time. But in this case, she was undertaking a journey to an environment that had a scent of the exotic, although well accessible by traffic. It was not difficult to use the train connection from Prague to Trieste, whence a ship of the Lloyd Triestino Company departed for Alexandria each week. The easy traffic was the heritage of the organisation of the sails by the Austro-Hungarian Lloyd.

Along the way from Alexandria to Cairo Mrs. Dušková perceived the country as *'fully Biblical'*, but when she *'dared mention that at places the countryside was like ours on the Elbe[202]... I fared bad and earned a remark on being prejudiced'.*[203] Having

The site of Abusir today, with Giza pyramids in the background

reached Cairo, they immediately undertook a trip to the pyramids of Giza, which Mrs. Pavla admired already from the window of her hotel room. *'I was so much looking forward for the first time that I would look at the work and creation of millennia and stay at least as stunned by wonder as Loti* (sic) *or Baedekr* (sic). *I do not want to underestimate the miracle that the most ancient culture had created, and where ages speak, that afternoon, however, I had an impression and feeling of something like Krč or Liboc.*[204][205] Disillusion is quite common with the more sceptical travellers, we only need to mention the above-treated Neruda. Neruda's ironic sight and Mrs. Dušková's disillusion are, however, two different feelings. Mrs. Dušková does not describe the social background of pyramid building; she is rather disgusted by the contemporary neglected state of the environment, which is unworthy of the magnificence of the monuments.

Later during their stay, the Dušeks visited the neighbourhood of Cairo, including the important 5th Dynasty cemetery of Abusir. Several decades later, Abusir was to be permanently connected with Czech Egyptology.

'So we finally arrived,' Mrs. Dušková describes, *'to the pyramids of Abou Sir,*

where we demounted and visited the first house of Ptah, one of the higher officials of the 5ᵗʰ Dynasty. Its rooms are relatively small, with walls decorated with low relief of unusual softness … The man, lord and ruler, is always depicted as a large figure' … concerning another tomb, she writes *'… in the fallen house, there were large bathtubs made of marble… '*[206] This seems to be a description of the burial chamber with sarcophagi.

The former tomb may have been that of the vizier Ptahshepses, part of which was uncovered in 1893 by the French Egyptologist Jacques de Morgan, who was stimulated to excavate in this area by Lepsius' having marked the tomb as a pyramid no. XIX.[207] The tomb is currently under long-term exploration by the

The mastaba of Ti in Saqqara by the end of the 19ᵗʰ century

Czech Institute of Egyptology.

In the Serapeion of Cairo, the Dušeks admired the sarcophagi of the sacred Apis bulls, *'… we were stunned with fear when we imagined how much wilfulness and oppression must have been exerted by those, who were able to enslave the people to drag* (the large and heavy objects) *from somewhere, without tools or any help, to bring them to the necropolis for the sake of an animal without reason or soul'.*[208] Here we already find a similar reaction to Oriental monuments as we have seen in Jan Neruda's accounts. The 'modern civilised man' could explain their creation only by the force of a despotic government, which forced its subjects to work at the construction. In Saqqara, they also noted the *'house* (i.e. mastaba tomb) *of the architect Ti'.*[209]

References to contemporary archaeological works in Egypt do not appear too often in Dušková's letters. A note on Lord Carnarvon forms an exception, it is, however, connected to his illness. *'Speaking of Lord Carnarvon – so he is lying here in*

Hotel Continental, sick to death. He was bitten by a mosquito at those excavations.'[210] The general reference to 'those excavations' does not necessarily prove any negligence of Mrs. Dušková, it may as well mean that the addressees in Prague knew very well, what excavations she was referring to.[211]

She gives no details about the monuments of Luxor, besides the mention that she had mentally recovered *'there in front of these miracles'.[212]* She visited Luxor first after her husband's death, shortly before she left for home.

The letters of Pavla Dušková also offer a glimpse into the background of the creation of one of the private collections of aegyptiaca that found its way to two Czech museums. It is known as the Dušek and Lukjanov collection. The originally homogeneous Dušek collection was tightly connected to Prof. Lukjanov, a Russian Egyptologist living in Egypt. The inventory of its objects, which he had compiled, is now deposited at Strahov.[213] Some of the objects are now in the possession of the Náprstek Museum, recorded as 'gifts of Prof. Lukjanov'.[214]

Pavla Dušková's letters first mention a Russian named Lukjanov (transcribed as Lukianov, or sometimes as Loukianoff) in November 1922.[215] *'We are being visited by Mr. Prof. Lukianov, a Russian. He is an engineer, but a great knower of antiquities and archaeologist. He can decipher and understand hieroglyphs.'* In December of the same year, Mrs. Dušková mentions a *'visit at the Loukianofs'.[216]* A reference in the letter of January 1923 attests Lukjanov's share in creating Dušek's collections – *'And then Mr. Loukianoff, a great Egyptologist and knower of ancient art in general, brought Cyril* (i.e. Dušek) *old Greek teracotta figures.'[217]* Prof. Lukjanov was an employee of the mission.[218] Mrs. Ambassador mentions that he *'worked in our house',[219]* or elsewhere that he was present in the office of the

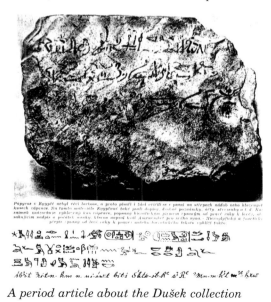

A period article about the Dušek collection

75

embassy.[220] We also learn some of the background of this befriended family namely that '*the father of Mrs. Loukianov was an aristocrat … who had a beautiful flat in Moscow in the Kremlin, and managed all restorations of the oldest monuments of the royal palace … I do not know what the profession of the family of Mr. Lukianov was, though'.*[221] Lukianov's presence at Dušek's embalming also suggests good relations of the two families. He was there at the request of Dušek's widow.[222]

Mrs. Dušková's letters also contain numerous notes on contemporary Egypt. She concentrated above all on Cairo, which she saw mainly through the eyes of a European, living in a relatively closed world. She criticised Cairo's dirt and was puzzled by the common poverty. She saw it above all as a result of the sloth of the Arabs.[223] She found it hard to understand the generally little effort to change the unfavourable situation. However, when she compares it with Europe, she is not uncritical of her home, either – '*The Cairo tram is about the same as that of Prague and accidents are frequent,*' but in Cairo '*an error here, an error there, nothing matters, malesh, malesh …*'[224]

Mostly, however, she either informs her relatives about her daily programme, a lot of which was taken up by language courses, or writes about her longing for home and the sadness that the Cairo environment awakens in her. '*In front of my windows, there is a slim minaret of a mosque, at the background the Mokattan (sic) mountains and in the distance two slim minarets of the citadel – all in the pinkish-violet light of a drowsy day in these deadly sad colours.*'[225] The romantic experience of the Orient was overpowered here, or it never entered her consciousness. We could even say that Mrs. Dušková did not very much enjoy her stay in the Orient, mostly because of her husband's illness and financial problems. She always felt separated from her usual environment.

Nostalgic memories of home did not retreat even during the journey into the desert to visit ancient monuments. '*When swallows began flying around us in a steadily growing flock and when they were flying so close to us … we felt as is we were at home.*'[226]

She noted also the Cairo bazaar Khalili.[227] She shopped for carpets and furniture, which she took to Prague after her husband's death. Otherwise, however, it seems that she developed no special liking for the city.

Her reaction to the ancient monuments combines admiration and surprise at their contemporary state (the pyramids of Giza), interest, connected with purely personal impressions (Abusir and the Serapeion), or a very generally described admiration (Luxor). Mrs. Dušková had her own way of perceiving Egypt. She knew something about her culture and history, but in general, her relationship to the monuments was guided by her personal feelings.

Her letters thus record a certain level of historical consciousness. Her reactions to the face-to-face encounters with the ancient culture are mostly at the level of historical myth, which she has construed around it (well apparent in the visit of Serapeion). Her perception of ancient Egyptian civilisation as a culture inclined to cruelty in the name of values and ideas quite incomprehensible to a European are the result of the cultural environment of the 19th century, similar to that which we have already encountered in the case of Neruda.

The above survey dealt with three travellers and their travelogues. The first and the last of them are divided almost by a century. All of them faced a different culture in Egypt and all were aware of the existence of ancient monuments in this country.

Each of them reacted in a different way. The first one perceived through the filter of a simplified Biblical tradition and expressed lively interest in what he heard on the site. The second one saw his environment through the ironical eye. And finally the third one, whose 'travelogue' is one only indirectly, since it actually comprises of private correspondence, reflects above all the personal feelings about the land and her past, and as such, it presents them to the addressees.

The above-mentioned travellers, and resident in the third case, present a selection of Czech reflection of Egypt. Their journeys also describe the conditions under which Czechs entered Egypt. Mass tourism of the Cook type and winter seasons in Cairo were not exactly a regular trait of the life of Czech society[228], which is quite comprehensible given the economical situation. On the other hand, Egypt was not an unknown country, which would be hard to visit. This is true above all for the second half of the 19th century.

So far, little has been said about the Czech aristocratic – and in general wealthy – travellers, who often travelled for fun and to increase their social prestige, such as their likes from the other countries of the monarchy. Their journeys are attested by their collections, which they brought from Egypt, and which are now scattered throughout regional museums of the Czech lands.[229] We do not know much about their impressions from their journeys. Some of them did, naturally, keep travelogues, but we are not always lucky to find an accessible and preserved source. Here we still may hope for discoveries in extensive family archives.

First hand experience and reading of travelogues, or contemporary journals, were two ways of becoming acquainted with Egypt – as an interesting Oriental country, or as an ancient civilisation, but most often both at a time.

Frequently, numerous opinions were created, influenced by previous reading, first hand experience and subjective perception. We find a completely personal level of perception of ancient Egyptian past and its remains, influenced by the values of the observer. If the traveller arrived prepared by previous reading, he could see the perceived as if through the eyes of the one whose pages he had read. Thus, when writing one's own report, he could pass on an already altered image.

The 19th century is, however, not only a time of romantic adventures – it is also the century of historical positivism. What then was the scholarly counterpart of the rich travel impressions, and what did the school have to say about ancient Egypt? Although the Prague Charles University founded a Professorship of Egyptology first in the 1920s, Czech learned society had already for some time been interested in ancient history.

Notes:

1 Edwards, A. B., *Thousand miles up the Nile*, first published 1877, 2nd edition 1891. First paragraph of chapter I, otherwise p. 1 of 2nd edition.

2 Cf. Manley, D., *The Nile – A Traveller's Anthology*. London 1991, 1996 (mainly for authors writing in English.)

3 For two different categories, see Buzard, J., *The Beaten Track*. Oxford 1993, 1998. 'Introduction'.

4 Although Muhammad Ali issued the first decree concerning protection and maintenance of monuments already in 1835, it was first the French Egyptologist Auguste Mariette who succeeded to put it to practice in the 1850s. See the overview in David, R., *Experience of Ancient Egypt*. London 2000; chapter 'Excavating the Sites'. Already some contemporaries were aware of the problems connected with the excessive interest of travellers in the monuments; the educated Austrian diplomat Anton Prokesch von Osten considered this new wave of destruction of ancient monuments (their removal, division, *en masse* destruction) as one of the worst ones in Egyptian history. Cf. below in the relevant subchapter.

5 Buzard, J., *The Beaten Track*, pp. 44–46, pp. 47ff. The development of mass transportation, above all of the rail and steam ships, stimulated a great boom of organised tourism.

6 Another patient who sought relief from this illness in Egypt was the archduke Franz Ferdinand d'Este. See Agstner, R., 'Die Habsburger-Monarchie und Ägypten. Eine Bestandsaufnahme', *Österreich und Ägypten. Beiträge zur Geschichte der Beziehungen vom 18. Jahrhundert bis 1918*. Cairo 1993; p. 18.

7 Cf. Sattin, A., *Lifting the Veil. British Society in Egypt 1786–1956*. London 1988. 'Part I' passim.

8 Ulrich Erker-Sonnabend in *Das Lüften des Schleiers – Die Oriententfahrung britischer Reisender in Ägypten und Arabien. Ein Beitrag zum Reisebericht des 19. Jahrhunderts*. Hildesheim-Zürich-New York 1987; pp. 30f.

9 Manley, D., *op. cit.*, p. 59.

10 For details on this period, cf. Vatikiotis, P. J., *The History of Modern Egypt. From Muhammad Ali to Mubarak*. Baltimore 1991 (fourth ed.), pp. 141ff. and 157ff., also Daly, M. W. ed., *The Cambridge History of Egypt II. – Modern Egypt from 1517 to the End of the Twentieth Century*, Cambridge 1998: Reid, D. M., 'The British Occupation 1882–1922'; pp. 239ff.

11 Schölch, A., *Egypt to the Egyptians! The Socio-political crisis in Egypt*. London 1981. Translation of German original from 1972. Cole, J. R. I., *Colonialism and Revolution in the Middle East*. Cairo 1999.

12 Reid, D. M., 'The Urabi revolution and British conquest, 1879–1882' in Daly, M. W., *The Cambridge History of Egypt*, Vol. II., pp. 117 ff.

13 Mostyn, T., *Egypt's Belle Epoque. Cairo 1869 – 1952*. London 1989; pp. 125ff.

14 Erker-Sonnabend, *Das Lüften des Schleiers*, p. 44. While the hotel formally changed its name several times, in the general consciousness it always remained connected with the name of its first successful owner Samuel Shepheard.

15 These troubles are described for example in the works of women travellers, such as the Austrian Ida Pfeifer and the German noble Ida von Hahn-Hahn. For their travelogues, see below.

16 Khedive is a rank title accorded by the sultan, as a hereditary title in the dynasty of Muhammad Ali, the translation 'viceroy' is only approximate. The hereditary character of the administration of Egypt was confirmed in the 1840s. Cf. Daly, M. W.,

The Cambridge History of Egypt II - Modern Egypt from 1517 to the End of the Twentieth Century.

17 Ehud R. Toledano 'Social and economic change in the 'long nineteenth century' in Daly, M. W., ed. *The Cambridge History of Egypt II;* p. 261.

18 Vatikiotis, *The History of Modern Egypt,* p. 79.

19 The ship line was run since 1837 by the Austrian Lloyd (founded in 1836). Since 1845 a ship sailed the Trieste – Alexandria line twice a month and could thus compete with the Peninsular and Oriental Steam Navigation Company (P&O). Cf. Winkler, D. – Pawlik, G., *Die Dampfschiffahrtgesellschaft Österreichischer Lloyd 1836–1918.* Graz 1986; pp. 10–11.; Farnie, D. A., *East and West of Suez. The Suez Canal in History 1854–1956.* Oxford 1969; p. 23 and Agstner, R., 'Die Habsburger-Monarchie und Ägypten. Eine Bestandsaufnahme.' In *Österreich und Ägypten. Beiträge zur Geschichte der Beziehungen vom 18. Jahrhundert bis 1918.* Cairo 1993; pp. 21f.

20 For the distinction of tourists and traveller as separate categories, cf. above all Buzard, J., *The Beaten Track,* 'Introduction'. Tourism is a kind of mass travelling, made possible by the development of new means of transportation and facilitated by the existence of guides and travel agencies (Thomas Cook & Sons, a short history of the agency can be found on its web pages <http://www.thomascookholdings.com/aboutus/history.html>), that organise tourist trips. Tourists were often already in period context criticised for their superficiality, little knowledge, unwillingness to accommodate to local conditions and the fact that they did not plan their journeys according to their own specialised interests, but made use of professional guides who created and realised their travel itineraries.

21 For details cf. Toledano, 'Social and economic change in the "long nineteenth century" ' in Daly ed. *The Cambridge History of Egypt II,* pp. 252ff. On the key period of the reign of Khedive Ismail see also Vatikiotis, 'Ismail – the impatient Europeanizer' in Vatikiotis, *The History of Modern Egypt.*

22 Cf. Toledano, 'Social and economic', p. 274.

23 Toledano, 'Social and economic', p. 254.

24 For economic context cf. Toledano in *Cambridge History of Modern Egypt,* passim.

25 Vatikiotis, *The History of Modern Egypt,* pp. 80–81ff. Since the times of Muhammad Ali, another source of lasting financial problems was the Egyptian expansive policy, above all the attempts to control Sudan.

26 Toledano, 'Social and economic', p. 275.

27 Toledano, 'Social and economic', p. 275.

28 Buzard, *The Beaten Track,* p. 323. This is true above all of the Cook travel agency, which administered the entire steam traffic on the Nile, and was also involved in the transportation of British military material and of the wounded, for example in the time of the Orabi revolt.

29 Cf. Said, *Orientalism,* passim, analysis of the term on p. 1–73. Also id. *Culture and Imperialism.* London 1994; passim and Bode, Ch. et al., *West Meets East.* Heidelberg 1997. Including a polemic with Said.

30 Cf. Vatikiotis, 'Ismail, the impatient Europeanizer', and also the section Starkey, P. – Starkey, J., 'European Influences on Egypt' in Starkey, P. – Starkey, J., *Travellers in Egypt.* London 1998; pp. 257ff. The ancient Egyptian past did not, however, become an argument for the national existence for the Egyptians until well into the 20th century. Albert Hourani traces the inclusion of ancient Egypt into Egyptian national past first to the time of the discovery of the tomb of Tutankhamun – Hourani, A., *A History of the Arab Peoples.* New York 1991; p. 342. There is now a monograph devoted entirely to the Egyptian Egyptology, its development and context, and its national perspectives and uses – Donald Reid, *Whose Pharaohs?*

Archaeology, Museums, and Egyptian National Identity from Napoleon to World War I. Cairo 2002.

31 Details on the life and works of Auguste Mariette can today be found even outside the standard handbooks *Who was who in Egyptology* (3ʳᵈ ed. Bierbrier, M., London 1995; pp. 275f.). There also exists an extensive biography of A. Mariette – Claudine Le Tourneur d'Ison, *Mariette Pacha*. Paris 1999. It describes his career, as well as the period context of Egypt in which the professional lives of Egyptologists were formed. Another book dedicated to the influential scholar is the volume of Gilles Lambert, entitled *Auguste Mariette*. Paris 1997. Finally, for the context of the history of archaeology, cf. Éve Gran-Aymerich, *Naissance de l'archéologie moderne. 1798-1945.* CNRS eds. Paris 1998. The history of the French archaeological school has been described by Jean Vercoutter, *L'École du Caire (IFAO) 1880–1980.* Cairo 1980.

32 As an example, we may mention Frank Dillon, who painted above all the Islamic architecture in Old Cairo. Cf. Briony Llewellyn, 'Two Interpretations of Domestic Islamic Interiors in Cairo: J. F. Lewis and Frank Dillon.' In P. Starkey – J. Starkey, *Travellers in Egypt.* London – New York 1998.

33 Erker-Sonnabend, *Das Lüften*, p. 5.

34 For further details cf. Erker-Sonnabend, *Das Lüften*, pp. 8–9f.

35 Erker-Sonnabend, *Das Lüften*, 'Einleitung'.

36 Cf. the term of Edward W. Said, *Orientalism.* New York 1978, reprinted 1991. For a commentary of the definition of the term, cf. also Erker-Sonnabend, *Das Lüften*, passim, and Bode, *West meets East.* Mainly the initial chapters. For a discussion see Macfie, A. L., *Orientalism. A reader.* Cairo 2001.

37 For her detailed biography, cf. Katherine Frank, *Lucie Duff Gordon. A Passage to Egypt.* London 1994. For the edition of her letters, see Lucie Duff Gordon, *Letters from Egypt.* London 1983 (reprinted 1986) after the edition of 1902. The first volume of her letters was published already in 1865. Her letters are also quoted by Amelia Edwards (cf. *Who was Who*, 3ʳᵈ ed. ; p. 132).

38 Quoted after Sattin, *Lifting the Veil*, p. 3.

39 Flaubert's approach is often considered as an example of ideal-typical Orientalism, the basic traits of which were sketched by Edward Said and revised in newer works that take into account other, less typical sources. Cf. Mary Orr, 'Flaubert's Egypt: Crucible and Crux for Textual Identity' in Starkey – Starkey, *Travellers in Egypt*, and some other articles in the same volume, for example about women-travellers.

40 Mary Orr, 'Flaubert's Egypt', p. 189. However, further in her work, Orr disputes the simplifying classification of Flaubert as a typical example of Said's 'Orientalism'. In her modified conclusion, she states that the Oriental experience enabled Flaubert to reflect those aspects of his own private life, that contemporary France would not have accepted within her own cultural context.. Orr, *op. cit.,* p. 197. For an image of ancient Egypt in artistic reflection, cf. Fischer, H., *Der Ägyptologe G. Ebers. Eine Fallstudie zum Problem Wissenschaft und Öffentlichkeit. ÄAT 25,* 1994.

41 I worked with the German edition of the travelogue Gustave Flaubert, *Reise in den Orient: Ägypten – Nubien – Palästina – Syrien – Libanon.* Frankfurt (M) 1985. Transl. by R. Werner and A. Stoll. Afterword by André Stoll.

42 Flaubert, *Reise*, pp. 96ff., pp. 100–101. The term *hanim* is a Turkish expression for 'Missis'. (Dr. F. Ondráš. Institute of Near East and Africa, Faculty of Arts, Charles University, personal communication).

43 The Qasr el-Aini hospital. Flaubert, *Reise*, p. 67.

44 For the new edition of the description of her travels, cf. James Hogg, *Travels of Lady Hester Stanhope 1–3.* Salzburg Studies in English Literature 105:4–6. Salzburg 1983. The travelogue dates to the first half of the century. The text is presented as

a narration of her physician. Egypt is to be found in the first volume, mainly in chapter IX. There is one very interesting observation in terms of the period reception of Egypt in Vol. I on p. 189: '*I had likewise surmounted another difficulty, which is apt to stand in the way of a young traveller's improvement, and which is said to accompany the English more than the people of any other nation; – that of fancying the inhabitants of other countries their inferiors in breeding, dress, mode of living, and intellectual acquirements. I could already see that a Turk, however perfidious he might be, was certainly well bred; and that an Arab, even though he were a liar, had still his glow of imagination and his eloquence.*'

45 For details on their voyages to Egypt and on their accounts cf. Joan Rees, *Writing on the Nile: Harriet Martineau, Florence Nightingale and Amelia Edwards.* The University of Birmingham – Institute for Advanced Research in the Humanities – Occasional Paper no 4. 1992; and id., *Writings on the Nile.* London 1995. A. Edwards published a travelogue entitled *A Thousand Miles up the Nile.* London Ist ed. 1877, reprint e.g. London 1982.

46 For his biography cf. Bierbrier, M. ed., *Who was who in Egyptology*, London 1995 (3rd ed); pp. 329 – 332. Ibid. also an article on Amelia Edwards, pp. 137 – 138. A publication of the letters of Flinders and Hilda Petrie is under preparation, entitled *Letters from the Desert.*

47 Cf. Rees, *Writings on the Nile*, p. 73. Also John David Wortham, *British Egyptology 1549–1906.* Univ. of Oklahoma 1971; pp. 106ff.

48 Rees, *Writings on the Nile*, pp. 7ff. Also Bode, *West meets East.*

49 See the commented first edition of Jason Thompson – Edward William Lane, *Description of Egypt*, Notes and views in Egypt and Nubia, made during the Years 1825, –26, –27 and –28, Edited by Jason Thompson. AUC Press, 2000, Cairo.

50 As Thompson – 'Editor's foreword', p. ix, in Lane, *Description.*

51 As for the biography of Lane, see Thompson on Lane, *Description,* and further Leila Ahmed, *E. W. Lane, A Study of His Life and Works and of British Ideas of the Middle East in the Nineteenth Century.*

52 See Míšek – Navrátilová, 'Prokesch von Osten, Austrian Envoy and Traveller in Orient', *Archiv Orientální,* 1/70. 2002.

53 *Description,* p. 5.

54 See instantly the narration about praying Muslims – *Description,* p. 5. As Thompson says – 'Editor's foreword', p. ix, in Lane, *Description.*

55 Most famous is the very extensive work of Evelyn Baring, Lord Cromer, the highest-ranking British official in Egypt at the turn of the 19th and 20th centuries, *Modern Egypt I-II.* London 1908. In Cromer's eyes the British presence in Egypt is often positive, since it improves the horrible living conditions of local people, who had until now experienced only inefficient administration and government (*op. cit.,* pp. 197–198). Some researchers see this thesis as one of the basic arguments for the defence of colonialism, resp. imperialism (in the sense of Said, *Imperialism and Culture.* London 1994 passim), see e.g. Rashid, A., 'Autonomie et dependance culturelle en Égypte an debut du XIXe siécle' in Vatin, J. C., *La Fuite en Egypte. Supplément aux voyages européens en Orient.* Cairo 1989; pp. 319ff. Cromer introduces his book with a quotation of Lucie Duff Gordon – '*This country is a palimpsest…*' For others cf. the bibliography in Vatikiotis, *The History of Modern Egypt.*

56 Erman, A., *Mein Werden und mein Wirken.* Leipzig 1929; pp. 205ff. Besides observations from the scholarly environment, he noted a number of details from Egypt of the 1880s.

57 For the beginning of the 19th century and Napoleonic expeditions, cf. Philippe de Meulenaere, *Bibliographie raisonnée des témoignages oculaires imprimés de l'expedition d'Egypte* (1798–1801). Paris 1993. For a general overview see Martin R. Kalfatovic, *Nile*

Notes of a Howadji. A Bibliography of Travelers' Tales from Egypt from the Earliest Times to 1918. London 1992. A relatively numerous collection of travelogues is to be found also in Burkard, G. – Rudnitzky, G., *Fachkatalog Ägyptologie*. Heidelberg 1982. For the 19th century, pp. 18ff.

58 Manley, *op. cit.*, p. 75.

59 A summary, based directly on period press and archive materials, was published by Leopold Hellmuth – 'Tradition and Major Aspects of Oriental Studies in Austria in the 19th century', in *Orient – Österreichische Malerei von 1848 bis 1914*. Ausstellungskatalog – Residenzgalerie Salzburg, ed. by Erika Mayr- Oehring.

60 Period dictionaries contain references to the meaning of *Collegium de Propaganda Fide* in Rome and the activities of the individual popes. For example the *Slovník naučný* ('Educational Dictionary'), ed. F. L. Rieger, Prague 1866, Vol. V., 'M-Ožice' on p. 1105, under the entry 'Oriental languages' (subentry of 'Oriental'), similarly also *Ottův slovník naučný-Illustrovaná encyklopedie obecných vědomostí*, ('Otto's educational dictionary – an illustrated encyclopaedia of general knowledge'), Vol. XVIII.; Prague 1902, 'Oriental philology' on pp. 864–5.

61 The following paragraph is based on Hellmuth, L., 'Tradition and Major Aspect' in *Orient. Österreichische Malerei*. For a comprehensive synthesis of Austro-Turkish relationships, cf. Buchmann, B. M., *Österreich und das Osmanische Reich*, passim, with further bibliography.

62 For example Franz von Mesgnien-Meninski (1623–1698) compiled a Turkish-Persian-Arabic dictionary, see L. Hellmuth, 'Tradition and Major Aspect'. Other personnages, too, possessed collections of manuscripts, such as the imperial general Prince Eugene of Savoy (18th cent.), or the imperial librarian Sebastian Tengnagel (16th cent.).

63 Hellmuth, *op. cit.*

64 For an overview of the study load, cf. the memoirs of Joseph von Hammer-Purgstall, *Erinnerungen aus meinem Leben 1774–1852* bearbeitet von Reinhard Bachofen von Echt. Wien – Leipzig 1940, p. 22f.

65 For further details cf. Navrátilová, H. – Míšek, R., 'Oriental Academy', in *ArOr* 2, 2003.

66 Hellmuth, *op. cit.*, pp. 333ff.

67 For further details on him cf. Kaiser, R., 'Joseph von Hammer-Purgstall' in *Europa und der Orient. Ein Lesebuch*.

68 R. Agstner, *Der Ballhausplatz und Nordafrika. Studien zum Präsenz von Österreich (Ungarn) in Kairo, Kosseir, Luxor und Bengasi*. Schriften ÖKI Band 11. Kairo 1995; p. 15 and p. 54 ff.

69 See Gombár, E., *Moderní dějiny islámských zemí* (Modern history of Islamic countries), Prague 1999; pp. 260-262. Von Kremer was a member of the commission between 1876–1880. Cf. Agstner, *Der Ballhausplatz und Nordafrika*; p. 15.

70 See further Veronika Bernard, *Österreicher im Orient: eine Bestandsaufnahme österreichischer Reiseliteratur im 19. Jahrhundert*. Wien 1996.

71 Hellmuth, *op. cit.*, pp. 338ff. Eduard Sachau (1845–1930) came to Vienna from Berlin, and another expert in Oriental languages resp. above all of Islamic epigraphics Josef von Karabacek (1845-1918) worked at the court library. On von Karabacek cf also *Kdo byl kdo. Čeští a slovenští orientalisté, afrikanisté a iberoamerikanisté* ('Who was who. Czech and Slovak Orientalists, Africanists and Iberoamericanists'). Prague 1999; p. 238. Among the students attending the lectures of E. Sachau in Berlin was also Bedřich Hrozný, who mentioned them in one of his letters to J. V. Prášek. Cf. the J. V. Prášek collection in the Archive of the National Museum, file 544, sheet no. 5.

72 Abbas II Hilmi, son of Khedive Tawfik, succeeded him in 1892. He opposed the British administration, which was at that time headed by Lord Cromer. His reign

was a time of development of Egyptian nationalism, which the Khedive himself supported. Cf. Vatikiotis, *The History of Modern Egypt*, pp. 201ff.

73 Agstner, *Der Ballhausplatz und Nordafrika*, p. 5., '*Die Geschichte der offiziellen österreichischen Präsenz in Ägypten bietet einen interessanten Einblick, wie der Ballhausplatz seinen während der Herrschaft Mohamed Alis gegebenen Einfluss in der zweiten Hälfte des 19. Jahrhunderts verspielte. Der Umstand, dass ein Österreicher die Pläne für den Suezkanal entworfen hatte, das Vorhandensein der grössten österreichisch-ungarischen Kolonie in diesem Teil des osmanischen Reiches, von denen einige Österreicher in einflussreicher Stellung am Hofe der Khediven tätig waren, sowie dass der letzte Khedive Abbas II Hilmi am Wiener Theresianum zur Schule gegangen war, wurden politisch nicht genutzt. Immerhin hatte die Monarchie in einigen Bereichen der Wirtschaft wesentlichen Einfluss und beherrschte den Markt bei Fassbier und Textilien.*'

74 One of the most important overviews of Austro-Egyptian relationships that sketch their basic outlines is Agstner, Rudolf, 'Die Habsburger-Monarchie und Ägypten. Eine Bestandsaufnahme.' In *Österreich und Ägypten. Beiträge zur Geschichte der Beziehungen vom 18. Jahrhundert bis 1918.* Cairo 1993; pp. 8ff; see further the contribution by R. Míšek, 'The background of Austrian economic influence'.

75 Cf. Skřivan, Aleš, *Císařská politika. Rakousko-Uhersko a Německo v evropské politice v letech 1906–1914* ('Imperial politics. The Austro-Hungarian Empire and Germany in European politics in the years 1906–1914'). Prague 1996.

76 *Erinnerungen* II, p. 148 ff.

77 *Erinnerungen* II, p. 149.

78 There are notes about the treaties regarding the Austro-Egyptian trade, either in Rudolf Benigni, *Österreichische Botschafts-Berichte über arabische Länder.* Wien 1974, (Register HHStA), p. 41, or in Egyptian sources – these last ones are to be searched more intensively in the future – as there are notes in the materials in the National Archives in Cairo, the publicly accessible papers of this era, microfiches fond, period of Muhammad Ali, regarding the Austrian ships and their rights. For last information, which was not easily obtained, I am indebted to Dr. František Ondráš.

79 P. 151, *Erinnerungen* II.

80 P. 158 ff. *Erinnerungen* II.

81 Crecelius, D., 'An Austrian Attempt to Develop the Red Sea Trade Route in the Late Eighteenth Century'. *Middle Eastern Studies* 30 (April 1994), pp. 262–280. Quoted after Crecelius, D., 'Egypt in the eighteenth century' in Daly, *The Cambridge History of Egypt II*, p. 69, note 24.

82 Agstner, R., *Die Geschichte der Konsulate in Suez, Ismailia und Port Said 1844–1956; 125 Jahre Suezkanal - Österreich (-Ungarn) und seine Präsenz am Istmus von Suez.* Schriften ÖKI Kairo, Bd 10. Cairo 1995; pp. 12–13.

83 Anton Graf Prokesch-Osten, *Mehmed-Ali, Vize-König von Aegypten. Aus meinem Tagebuche* 1826-1841. Wien 1877. S. 7.' *...haben Österreich und ich in den heutigen Wirren dasselbe Ziel vor Augen, die Erhaltung des türkischen Reiches, und ich glaube, Fürst Metternich und ich denken auch gleich über den Weg zu diesem Ziele.*'

84 Winkler, D. – Pawlik, G., *Die Dampfschiffahrtgesellschaft Österreichischer Lloyd 1836–1918*, S. 10–11. The name Lloyd was derived from that of a London insurance company, originally it also was an alliance of insurance companies that was founded already in 1833. In 1836, it became a company running steam ships. It soon gained the support of the Kaiser and in the course of the second half of the 19th century it belonged to successful competitors of the French, British and Italian transport companies (see further pp. 12–17). After the settlement in 1867, the company was called the 'Austro-Hungarian Lloyd', later it returned to its original name. To a certain extent, it represented the Austro-Hungarian empire. From the point of view of

the presentation of the Czech lands, it is undoubtedly interesting that the ships of the Austrian Lloyd also bore the names *Praga* (Winkler – Pawlik, p. 68), *Palacky* (Winkler – Pawlik, p. 61) and *Bohemia*. The latter ship, *Bohemia*, also sailed on the Trieste – Alexandria line. Winkler – Pawlik, *op. cit.*, passim. Czech public was proudly informed of the names of the ships, for example the launching of *Praga* was described in *Český svět*, ('Czech World'), year IV., no. 41 – 24. 7. 1908.

85 Cf. Farnie, D. A., *East and West of Suez. The Suez Canal in History 1854–1956*. Oxford 1969; pp. 24ff. and pp. 32–33.

86 The Empress played an important role at the festive opening of the Suez canal. She even became a subject of gossip because of Khedive Ismail's courtesy towards her. The pompous celebrations connected with the opening of the canal are interesting above all because the interest in the Suez enterprise brought about an intensification of the general European interest in Egypt. Above all the anecdotic and apocryphal episodes of this phase of Egyptian history are described in Trevor Mostyn, *Egypt's Belle Epoque. Cairo 1869-1952*. London 1989.

87 Farnie, *East and West of Suez*, pp. 33ff.

88 Agstner, R., *Die Geschichte der Konsulate in Suez*; p. 13.

89 Alois (von) Negrelli is known in the Czech lands as an inspector of the railways and constructor of the Olmütz–Prague rail (Agstner, *Die Geschichte der Konsulate in Suez*, p. 19).

90 Cf. Vatikiotis, *The History of Modern Egypt*, Chapter 'Ismail, the impatient Europeanizer', or *The Cambridge History of Egypt II*. According to Agstner (Agstner, *Die Geschichte der Konsulate in Suez*) and Farnie (Farnie, *East and West of Suez*, p. 40, 52) Austria was at first hesitant about the building of the canal, because of the initial negative attitude of Britain (Austria's important ally). This Austrian policy was one of the reasons for the loss of any chance of controlling the joint-stock company. The main objective of Britain was to preserve the power situation, which supported the integrity of Turkey and was thus most favourable to an undisturbed connection with India. Therefore, she did not support Lesseps' plan, which was favoured by the French court. After the completion of the canal and turn in the Egyptian policy – her inclination to Britain after the defeat of France in the Franco-Prussian war – Britain made use of the chance to acquire the share of Khedive Ismail in the Suez Canal Company and became engaged in the area (cf. Vatikiotis, *The History*, pp. 77ff.); see further pp. 18–21.

91 Agstner, *Die Geschichte der Konsulate in Suez*; pp. 31f. A description of the celebrations in the presence of the Austrian Kaiser. He cites one period monograph (Note 26 on p. 213) – Beda Dudik, *Kaiser-Reise nach dem Oriente*, Wien 1870. Unless this is an indeed peculiar coincidence, the author of the account of the journey of the Kaiser was the period Czech, resp. Moravian historiographer B. Dudík (for more details on him, cf. Kutnar – Marek, *Přehledné dějiny* ['Comprehensive history'], pp. 308–309f).

92 Farnie, *East and West of Suez*, p. 138. For some circumstances also Johann Kurzreiter, *Österreich – Ungarn und die ägyptische Frage 1881–1885*. Univ. of Vienna Dissertation 1994; pp. 43 and 192ff.

93 Farnie, *East and West of Suez*, p. 140 and p. 142 (the growth of the tonnage of the fleet of the Austrian Lloyd), next came competing with Venice.

94 J. R. Ronall in Agstner, *Österreich und Ägypten*, pp. 79ff.

95 Agstner, *Die Geschichte der Konsulate in Suez;* p. 25.

96 Agstner, *Der Ballhausplatz und Nordafrika*; passim.

97 Cf. below.

98 Agstner, 'Die Habsburger-Monarchie und Ägypten. Eine Bestandsaufnahme,' p. 14.

99 Agstner, R., *Die österreichisch-ungarische Kolonie in Kairo vor dem ersten Weltkrieg – Das Matrikelbuch des k. u. k. Konsulates Kairo*. Schriften des ÖKI Kairo, Bd. 9. Cairo 1994.

100 Agstner, *Die...Kolonie*, s. 20–22. Also Agstner, 'Die Habsburger-Monarchie und Ägypten. Eine Bestandsaufnahme.', pp. 23ff.

101 On his reign cf. Vatikiotis, *The History of Modern Egypt*, pp. 201ff.

102 Agstner, *Die...Kolonie*, p. 177.

103 The presence of Austrian entrepreneurs is also confirmed by the fact that for example Adolf Erman lived in 1885 in the boarding house of the Austrian Mrs. Fink, who also ran a tailors' workshop. A. Erman, *Mein Werden und mein Wirken*. Leipzig 1929; p. 208.

104 Agstner, *Die...Kolonie*, pp. 52ff.

105 Agstner, *Die...Kolonie*, pp. 47f.

106 Marcela Stern, 'Österreich-Ungarns Beitrag zur Architektur in Ägypten am Beispiel von drei Architekten' in *Österreich und Ägypten. Beiträge zur Geschichte der Beziehungen vom 18. Jahrhundert bis 1918*. Kairo 1993;

107 With respect to the numerous rebuildings of the older parts of Cairo. Above all after the fall of the monarchy and establishment of the Republic in the 1950s, the rushed construction activities led to the destruction of many older buildings from the second half of the 19th century and from the time of the *fin de siécle*. For the architectural history of Cairo cf. for example Mohamed Scharabi, *Kairo. Stadt und Architektur im Zeitalter des europäischen Kolonialismus*. Tübingen 1989. For the general history of Cairo, see Janet Abu-Lughod, *Cairo. 1001 years of the City Victorious*. Princeton 1971, and Max Rodenbeck, *Cairo. The City Victorious*. Cairo 1998, André Raymond, *Cairo – The City of History*. Cairo 2000.

108 Stern, *op. cit.* pp. 54ff. Herz on p. 57.

109 The mosque next to the madrasa of Sultan Hassan.

110 Agstner, 'Die Habsburger-Monarchie und Ägypten. Eine Bestandsaufnahme', p. 24, and Marcela Stern, *op. cit.,* pp. 54ff.; on Julius Franz cf. also the period testimony – Erman, *Mein Werden und mein Wirken*. p. 209. He considers Franz to belong to the German community, according to his birthplace – Wiesbaden.

111 Cf. Vatin, J. C., *La Fuite en Egypte. Supplément aux voyages européens en Orient*. Cairo 1989, pp. 265ff. Although A. Lasciac (1856–1946) was a native Austrian, he was very critical of the monarchy, and his departure for Cairo was influenced by the in-favourable situation that he had to face in Vienna because of his radical opinions.

112 Cf. further in the text, the subchapter on František Schmoranz.

113 Stern, *op. cit.*

114 Cf. Myntti, C., *Paris along the Nile*. Cairo 1999.

115 Cairo Art Nouveau is treated in the book of C. Myntti, *Paris along the Nile*. Cairo 1999.

116 Cf. C. Myntti, *op. cit.*

117 Cf. Scharabi, *Kairo*, p. 177 ('Pseudo-islamische Architektur'), p. 183, 186; pp. 119f. – characteristics of Ismailean Cairo.

118 Wirth, E., *Orientalische Stadt*. Mainz 2001. Vol. I. Development of patterns of Oriental city life, including the specific features as the suq etc.

119 Ebers, G., *Cicerone durch das alte und neue Aegypten, I-II*. Stuttgart und Leipzig 1886, Vol. II, pp. 1ff.

120 Agstner, R., *Die... Kolonie;* register in the Appendix. We can find here both Brno and Prague citizens, people born in Budějovice as well as in Rousínov u Vyškova. On p. 32, *op. cit.* the author gives an overview of Bohemians and Moravians, listing around 30 people.

121 The problem is treated by Adéla Macková in her work *Československo-egyptské vztahy 1918–1938* ('Czechoslovak-Egyptian relationships between 1918 and 1938'); prepared as a master's thesis at the Institute for Economic History of the Faculty of Arts, Charles University).

122 Or any larger written account. An interesting aspect of contemporary information on Egypt, above all concerning her period state, were also various diplomatic relations and reports. Further we shall note the activities of A. Prokesch von Osten, whose works contain, besides the travelogues mentioned here, also extensive service reports.

123 For a general overview of the travelogue-like reports from Classical antiquity to the beginning of the 20th century, published in various forms, cf. Kalfatovic, R., *Nile Notes of a Howadji*. A smaller anthology of travelogues can be found in Pick, Ch., *Egypt. A Traveller's Anthology*. London 1991.

124 The history of the now classical guide – Baedeker – dates back as far as the early 19th century – cf. Hinrichsen, A., *Baedekers Reisehandbücher 1832–1944*, Holzminden 1981, quoted after Mayr-Oehring, *Orient*, p. 22–23. The term 'pictorial volume' may for that time be understood as the pictorial collections that were published by artists above all as a result of their 'Orientreise'. For example Ludwig Karl Libay (1814–1888) published after the journey through Egypt and Asia Minor that he undertook in 1855–56 the collection 'Reisebilder aus dem Orient', Vienna 1857. After Mayr-Oehring, *Orient*, pp. 180ff.

125 The problem of an expert analysis of travelogues as a source that can make accessible one aspect of the formation of the period regard of Egypt has been formulated among others by Ulrich Erker-Sonnabend in his book *Das Lüften des Schleiers – Die Oriententfahrung britischer Reisender in Ägypten und Arabien. Ein Beitrag zum Reisebericht des 19. Jahrhunderts.* Hildesheim – Zürich – New York 1987.

126 For an anthology of such works of mostly English-writing travellers, cf. Manley, D., *The Nile – a Travellers' Anthology*.

127 Most travelogues mention the books that the authors had read before they set on the journey, or, alternatively, there are citations of literature directly in the text. Important reports and travelogues are reflected by subsequent generations. Cf. Rossi, A., *Grenz(en)erfahrungen. Frauen des deutschen Vormärz reisen in den Orient. Die Reiseberichte von Ida Pfeiffer, Anna Forneris und Gräfin Ida Hahn-Hahn.* Diplomarbeit, Geisteswissenschaftliche Fakultät, Universität Innsbruck. November 1993, bei Prof. Dr. Sigurd Paul Schleichl.
Also Prince Pückler-Muskau (Hermann, Fürst von Pückler-Muskau, *Aus Mehemed Alis Reich. Ägypten und Sudan um 1840*. Zürich 1985) quotes Anton Prokesch von Osten (*Erinnerungen aus Ägypten und Kleinasien I-III*), who for himself cites D. V. Denon (*Voyage dans la Basse et la Haute Égypte*) etc.
Biblical stories remain an important motif – above all many British travellers visited Egypt as a Biblical stage. Cf. among others Wortham, J. D., *British Egyptology 1549–1906*, pp. 92ff.

128 Among them was for example Hermann, Prince von Pückler-Muskau. His travelogue was published in a new edition in 1985. Hermann, Fürst von Pückler-Muskau, *Aus Mehemed Alis Reich. Ägypten und Sudan um 1840*. Zürich 1985. His travelogue shows evidence of his knowledge of contemporary literature, in the notes he added even the results of the expedition of Lepsius (p. 40; the first edition was published first in 1844). Besides the monuments, he also noted the manners and customs of the country. He even had some passages of the book set in upside down and marked them as being 'nicht für Damen' (not for ladies), these were above all those concerned with intimate customs etc. He also cites Prokesch von Osten, the Austrian diplomat, whose travelogue will be mentioned below. The count was a great admirer of the translator of his works to English, Sarah Austin, who was the mother of Lucie Duff Gordon. Sarah Austin exchanged a rather scandalous correspondence with him. Cf. Frank, K., *Lucie Duff Gordon. A Passage to Egypt*. London 1994; pp. 47f. The German writing

authors include also Ida von Hahn-Hahn, who visited Egypt and the Levant in the first half of the 19th century – cf. Hahn-Hahn, Ida von, *Orientalische Briefe (1844)*. Ed. and Foreword by Gabriele Habinger. Vienna 1991. On her – Rossi, A., *Grenz(en)erfahrungen. Frauen des deutschen Vormärz reisen in den Orient. Die Reiseberichte von Ida Pfeiffer, Anna Forneris und Gräfin Ida Hahn-Hahn*. Diplomarbeit, Geisteswissenschaftliche Fakultät, Universität Innsbruck. November 1993, bei Prof. Dr. Sigurd Paul Schleichl.

129 Cf. Jan W. Weryho, 'Juliusz Slowacki' in *Travellers in Egypt*, pp. 215ff.

130 Hamann, Brigitte, *Rudolf: Kronprinz u. Rebell* ('Rudolf, crown prince and rebel'), Wien 1990, passim for a general characteristic of the crown prince.

131 *Eine Orientreise vom Jahre 1881 beschrieben von Kronprinzen Rudolf von Oesterreich*, Vienna 1885.

132 *Eine Orientreise*, ed. 1885, p. 48. '...*will ich mich der Worte meines Freundes Brugsch-Pascha bedienen*'.

133 Hunting expeditions brought several other members of the Hapsburg family to Egypt – among them was for example Archduke Otto, father of the last Kaiser Karl I., Agstner, R., 'Die Habsburger-Monarchie und Ägypten. Eine Bestandsaufnahme.', p. 18.

134 *Orientreise*, p. 47.

135 *Orientreise*, p. 163.

136 Quoted in. B. Hamann, *op. cit.*

137 Adolf Erman describes other aspects of the personality of Brugsch – his courtesy and social ability were accompanied by a chronic tendency to fabrication and unreliability. Cf. Erman, A., *Mein Werden und mein Wirken*, pp. 163ff.

138 Heinrich Brugsch, *Mein Leben und mein Wandern*. Berlin (2nd ed.) 1894. Reprinted Osnabrück 1975; pp. 353ff.

139 Brugsch, H., *Mein Leben und mein Wandern*, p. 357 – '*Einer eigenhändigen Einladung meines fürstlichen Gönners folgend, nahm ich auf ein paar Wochen meinen Aufenthalt in dem Prager Schlosse, wobei ich die Ehre hatte, täglich mit dem hohen Fürstenpaare zu verkehren*.' The famous Egyptologist visited the Czech lands once more, when he underwent a treatment in Mariánské lázně (Marienbad) (*Mein Leben*, p. 374), but neither of his stays apparently brought him into contact with any personnage of the Prague university or Czech cultural life in general.

140 For the discussion on Rudolf's membership in the lodge – Hamann, *op. cit.*

141 The incognito of the imperial pair was derived form one of the little known titles of the Hapsburg monarch, which the family acquired through reversion in the course of the 19th century. O. Urban, *František Josef I.* Prague 1992, 1999; p. 196.

142 A. von Almstein, *Ein flüchtiger Zug nach dem Orient*, Vienna 1887. For noting this fact I am indebted to Dr. J. Holaubek, Universität Wien. The information first reached me in the form of notes from her lecture held on 23. 11. 1999 at the Czech Institute of Egyptology in Prague, which I acquired from H. Vymazalová. Later I had the opportunity to become more closely acquainted with the works of Austrian travellers, including A. Prokesch-Osten, during my scholarship at the Vienna University in the winter semester 2000–01.

143 Through his origin (his father grew up in Židlochovice u Brna) and his military service – he taught mathematics to the cadettes of the Olmütz garrison. Cf. as-Sayyid Omar, M., *Anton Prokesch von Osten. Ein österreichischer Diplomat im Orient*. Studien zur Geschichte Südosteuropas 11, Frankfurt (M) 1993; p. 11 and *Österreichisches Biographisches Lexikon 1815–1950*. Pet-Raž. Wien 1983; pp. 301f.

144 For details see as-Sayyid Omar, M., *Anton Prokesch von Osten. Ein österreichischer Diplomat im Orient*. Passim. For details on the life and carreer of Prokesch von Osten cf. *Österreichisches Biographisches Lexikon 1815–1950*. Pet-Raž. Wien 1983; pp. 301f.

Despite the fact that he did not master Oriental languages, unlike another Austrian diplomat in the area, Josef von Hammer-Purgstall (see above).

145 Cf. as-Sayyid Omar, M., *Anton Prokesch von Osten*, p. 38.

146 *Ibid*, pp. 55f.

147 The papers are numbered 93, 94, 96, 99; in box VII, 'Italien 1831–1832', State Archives, Vienna.

148 State Archives, cited file.

149 *Erinnerungen aus Ägypten und Kleinasien*. Vienna 1829–33.

150 Compare J. Žvejkal below.

151 The history of the London 'needle' can be found in Iversen, E., *Obelisks in Exile II – The Obelisks of Istanbul and England*. Copenhagen 1971; pp. 90f. The inscription is reproduced on pp. 144–145.

152 *Erinnerungen aus Ägypten und Kleinasien*. Vienna 1829–33. Vol. I.; pp. 13–14. '*Wahrscheinlich sind diese Obelisken mehrmals versetzt und aus Memphis oder Heliopolis, in der Zeit der Ptolemäer oder Römer, nach Alexandria gebracht worden.*'

153 *Erinnerungen*, Vol. I; p. 73. '*Ich begreife nicht, wie man jemals zweifeln konnte, dass die Pyramiden Grabdenkmale waren, auch bevor man noch das Innere derselben kannte. Sie stehen mitten in dem umgehenden Friedhofe von Memphis...wo man gräbt, stösst man auf Gräber und Katakomben...*'

154 *Erinnerungen* II, p. 49. '*Diese fünfte Hauptzerstörung ... ist im vollen Gange, und wenn nicht Mechmed Ali oder dessen Sohn Ibrahim, in einem Rückfalle in die Barbarei, das ganze schatzgrabende Gesindel aus dem Lande jagen, so werden die Königsgräber von Theben und Memphis, und so manche andere herrliche und unvergleichbare Monumente bald nur mehr in Erzählungen erhalten sein.*'

155 Prokesch, *Erinnerungen* I, p. 5....'*hie und da eine Granitsäule, eine Isisstatue, eine Hieroglyphentafel, ein Mithraskopf; – hie und da eine Palme mit schwerem Dattelsagen: dies Alles, umfangen mit doppelten Mauern, plumpen Thürmen, französischen Forts...*'

156 Prokesch, *Erinnerungen* I, p. 48. '*....ist eine Kaiserstadt und Fürstensitz, zwischen Wüste und Wüste geklemmt... ist weder Europa, noch Asien*'.

157 Prokesch, *Erinnerungen* I, p. 49. '*...Die Straßen sind enge, finster und nach dem Schlosse zu aufsteigend; die Bazars reich...Die Bäder zahlreich...*'

158 However, we can also find references to the Egyptian army and fleet, which were reformed during the reign of Muhammad Ali. Cf. *Erinnerungen* II, p. 203.

159 Cf. Prokesch, *Mehmed Ali*, p. 3. For H. Salt see *Who was Who in Egyptology*, pp. 370–371; for Drovetti cf. *Who was Who in Egyptology*, pp. 129 –130. For more details on the representatives of the so-called 'age of the consuls' and for the period approach to Egyptian monuments, cf. David, *The Experience of Ancient Egypt*, pp. 110ff. Henry Salt as a British consul and B. Drovetti as a French consul both received fermans (government license) for excavations. Muhammad Ali thus satisfied both powers.

160 Prokesch's Estate, in Haus- Hof und Staatsarchiv, Wien. Briefe aus dem Orient und Aus Italien – Schachtel III, the file with green back and gold tooling – *Briefe*, Julius Schneller, No 36.

161 I preserve the variable form of the name.

162 Whose travelogue with the description of his visit of Egypt was kept in the Brno Land Archive, where it was, according to its employees, lost. This information was given to me in spring of 2001, with the note that it is necessary to wait until the conclusion of the running revision.

163 Lněničková, J., *Čechy v době předbřeznové*. (Bohemia in the pre-March years), Prague 1999; p. 278.

164 The names of some of them have already appeared in the text, for example Lucie Duff Gordon. The tradition of these journeys dates back at least to the 18th century

and persons such as Lady Mary Wortley-Montagu or Hester Stanhope. Cf. Ida Pfeiffer, *Reise in das Heilige Land, Konstantinopel, Palaestina, Aegypten im Jahre 1842.* Vienna 1995, Introduction – Gabriele Habinger; p. 9.

165 Rossi, *Grenz(en)erfahrungen*, passim. She describes the character of Ida Pfeiffer, mentioning her willingness to travel, preparations for the journey, etc.

166 Cf. *Österreichisches Biographisches Lexikon* 1815 – 1950. Pet-Raž. Vienna 1983; p. 31.

167 Pfeiffer, Ida, *Reise in das Heilige Land. Konstantinopel, Palästina, Ägypten im Jahre 1842.* Vienna 1995; p. 226. '*Durch einen kleinen Umweg kam ich an den "Nadeln der Kleopatra" vorüber, zwei Obelisken von Granit, deren einer noch aufrecht steht, der andere in einer kleinen Entfernung im Sande liegt.*'

168 Pfeiffer, *op. cit.*, pp. 249 – 250. '*…auch ich unter die kleine Zahl gehöre, die so glücklich sind, den höchsten und unzerstörbarsten Bau der menschlichen Kunst und menschlichen Fleisses…bewundern zu können*'

169 Manley, *op. cit.*, passim

170 Rossi, *Grenz(en)erfahrungen*, passim. The entire work is dedicated to these three ladies, and compares the character of the form and content of their works. It also includes a description and context of women travelling in general. Women travelling as a specific phenomenon, the need to be protected by men, the dangers that ladies had to face according to period imagination (above all dangers to their chastity), was described by Buzard, J., *The Beaten Track,* pp. 150f. For women travelling see also Birkett, Dea, *Spinsters Abroad – Victorian Lady Explorers.* Cambridge (MA) 1989; passim.

171 Rossi, *Grenz(en)erfahrungen*, passim.

172 Rossi, *Grenz(en)erfahrungen*, e.g. pp. 209f.

173 See Pávová, J., *Rukopisné památky české provenience k poznání zemí severovýchodní Afriky v 18.–19. stol.* ('Manuscripts of Czech Provenance related to the exploration of North African countries in the 18th–19th centuries.') M. A. thesis, FF UK, 1984. Also Vachala, B., 'The Beginning of Egyptology in Czechoslovakia' in *Egitto fuori dell'Egitto, op. cit.,* pp. 441ff.

174 Cf. *Österreichisches Biographisches Lexikon 1815–1950.* Vol. VII. Vienna 1978; p. 306.

175 J. Žvejkal, *Popsání…* etc., Prague 1844, p. 40ff.

176 Žvejkal, *Popsání*, p. 76.

177 Žvejkal, *Popsání*, p. 78.

178 Žvejkal, *Popsání*, p. 78.

179 Žvejkal, *ibid.*

180 This custom is mentioned by Dr. Richard Madden as well, as quoted by Manley, *op. cit.*

181 Žvejkal, *Popsání*, p. 80.

182 'Studie orientální' (Oriental Studies), 1871, in *Obrázky z domova i ciziny* ('Pictures from at home and from abroad') Prague 1983; p. 161.

183 Quoted after the edition: Jan Neruda: *Obrazy z ciziny* ('Pictures from abroad'). Prague 1872; National Library in Prague call number 54 K 4844.

184 *Ibid.,* pp. 142ff.

185 Cf. Herodotus, Book II.

186 Neruda, *op. cit.*, p. 147.

187 Quoted after the Erben edition of 1854, Vol. II, p. 40.

188 Pp. 155ff. of the quoted edition of *Obrazy z ciziny*, 1872. Quotation of Harant on p. 159.

189 For the architectural history of Cairo see e.g. Scharabi, M., *Kairo. Stadt und Architektur.* For a general history of Cairo see Janet Abu-Lughod, *Cairo. 1000 years of the City Victorious*; Max Rodenbeck. *Cairo. The City Victorious.*

190 'Studie orientální', p. 156. The mourning over dogs is mentioned already by Herodotus – Book II, 66. Anubis (Anup) is, however, a male deity, cf. *Lexikon der*

Ägyptologie I, Wiesbaden 1972; col. 327-333. There exists a female deity called Anukis (Anuket, *Lexikon der Ägyptologie I.*, col. 333–334), so Neruda may have been misled by this name.

191 P. 173, *op. cit.*
192 P. 174, *op. cit.*
193 P. 176, *op. cit.*
194 P. 177, *op. cit.*
195 P. 172, *op. cit.*
196 For more details see *Who was Who in Egyptology.* IIIrd ed., pp. 275–276.
197 Very persuasively e.g. William M. Thackeray in his *Christmas books*, when portraying certain Mr Bulbul, not to speak about *Innocents abroad* by certain Samuel Langhorne Clemens, otherwise known as Mark Twain.
198 The term 'historical culture' is conceived after Z. Beneš, *Historický text a historická kultura* ('Historical text and historical culture'). Prague 1995, passim. See also *Appendix.*
199 January and February 1922 (19. 1. and 15. 2. 1922, 1.3. 1923, 31.1. 1924; the cited letters are kept in the Archive of the National Museum in Prague [ANM], Cyril Dušek collection, cardboard box I, files 1–40, part II – Family correspondence).
200 The establishment of the embassy as witnessed by Mrs. Pavla would be a material for a separate study – she stressed above all the tardiness of Czech administration in the furnishing of the premises of the embassy, including its material aspects – for example, basic furniture was lacking for a long time. The letter of 7. 2. 1923 pregnantly describes the unfavourable situation of Czech embassy: '...*one cannot constantly give the same excuse. People no longer believe us and they do not know anymore what country we come from and what state Cyril actually represents.*' Apparent marginalities thus acquired great importance, as we have already mentioned before. Mrs. Dušková prepared for her representative duties and after the establishment of the embassy she also fulfilled them with all due care, but her letters never ceased to contain memories of home and repeatedly expressed hope that she would soon return home.
201 The cited letters are kept in the Archive of the National Museum in Prague (ANM), Cyril Dušek collection, cardboard box I, files 1–40 (part II – Family correspondence); file 8 (brown envelope of A5 format with a printed heading 'Légation de la République Tchécoslovaque en Egypte', and inscribed in all likelihood by the hand of Hermína Dušková, cf. her manuscript in file 20, as 'selected family letters from Cairo').
202 In this, however, she does not differ from Flaubert and his reminiscences of Normandy.
203 Letter from 19.1. 1922, file 8 of the ANM collection.
204 Krč and Liboc are two almost rural suburbs of Prague at that time. The city turned into 'Greater Prague' and incorporated in 1920s many settlements of quasi-rural character.
205 The same letter from 19. 1. 1922, *ibid.*
206 Letter from 15.2. 1922, *ibid.*
207 For this monument cf. generally Verner, M., *The Realm of Osiris*, Cairo 2002. The publication of the tomb is being realised gradually. Cf. also Verner, M., (ed.), *Preliminary Report on Czechoslovak Excavations in the Mastaba of Ptahshepses at Abusir.* Prague 1976. Verner, M., *Baugraffiti der Ptahschepses Mastaba (Abusir II)*. Prague 1992. Verner, M., *The Mastaba of Ptahshepses. Reliefs (Abusir I)*. 2 vols.
208 Letter from 15. 2. 1922, in the cited file.
209 See in *Lexikon der Ägyptologie*, Bd. VI. Wiesbaden 1986; c. 551–552.
210 Letter from 21. 3. 1923, in the cited file. She, however, arrived to the theme of Carnarvon via mentioning a textile 'à la Carnarvon'.

211 Tutankhamun was a popular victim of period journalists. The discovery was even trivialised, there appeared a soap mark Tutankhamun or carnival masks reflecting the theme. (cf. e.g. the periodical *Světozor* in the course of the year 1924, passim).

212 Letter from 31. 1. 1924.

213 Archive of the Memorial of National Literacy, art collections of the Literary Archive, I accessed them thanks to Dr. R. Dačeva.

214 The connection of these materials was made possible thanks to the courtesy of Mrs. Adéla Macková, who studied both the origin of the Náprstek museum collections, that entered there through the National Museum, and also the person of Cyril Dušek, in terms of her master's thesis *Československo-egyptské vztahy 1918–1938* ('Czech-Egyptian relations 1918–1938', prepared at the Institute of Economic History, Faculty of Arts, Charles University). Lukjanov's inventory is now in the possession of the Memorial of National Literacy and was at my disposal thanks to the courtesy of Dr. R. Dačeva and other employees of the Memorial.

215 Letter from 23. 11. 1922, Box 1/1–40, file 8, 46th letter.

216 Letter from 7. 12. 1922 in the cited file.

217 Letter from 11. 1. 1923 in the cited file.

218 Cf. A. Macková, *op. cit.*

219 Letter from 7. 12. 1922 in the cited file.

220 Letter from 12. 4. 1923 in the cited file.

221 Letter probably from 7. 1. 1923 (there is only a fragment of the letter, the date has been added in pencil).

222 Note in pencil on envelope 8 in box 1. Letter from 16. 1. 1924. The body had to be prepared for a prolonged stay in Cairo and for the transfer, which was realised only several weeks later.

223 Letter from 25. 1. 1922. This may be subsumed under the frequently mentioned stereotype of the Orient (E. Said, *Orientalism*, passim), unless it is a purely empirical observation of some Cairo inhabitants.

224 Letter from 15. 2. 1922.

225 Letter from 9. 11. 1922.

226 Letter from 15. 2. 1922.

227 Letter from 15. 2. 1922.

228 Although there seem to be individuals, who afforded themselves this sort of journey. Such example would be a grammar school teacher Josef Kořenský, who attended a Cook tour at the end of 19th century. His archive is currently under research. Personal communication by Adéla Macková.

229 Cf. M. Verner, *Veřejné sbírky.*

F. Kupka, 'Histoire ancienne' (for E. Réclus, 'L'Homme et la terre')

II. Historia magistra vitae

'Im Gegensatz zu den Kulturen des Zweistromlandes ist die Kenntnis vom alten Ägypten nie völlig verlorengegangen.'[1]

'We cannot waken a perfect human being from antiquity and incorporate him in our lives ... it is far, far more because it is completely impossible for us to transport ourselves into the mind of a strange people. Such an awareness of limitations of insight or perceptiveness should never stop us from pressing forward as far we can. Research itself acquires from this barrier a particular, stimulating attraction.'[2]

European historians have been interested in Egypt already since the time of the Greek *logographoi*[3] (including, for example, Hekataios of Miletus).

The era of the 19th century witnessed a great boom of historical research as well as the formation of the methodological and theoretical foundations of historical science. The reflection of historical science, resp. of the way how to write history, dates, however, as far back as Classical Antiquity.[4] The formation of modern historical science[5] is today conceived approximately in two stages. The first stage covers the period from Humanism to the turn of the 19th and 20th centuries, when the subject itself and its methodology were formed. The second stage dates after the turn of the 19th and 20th centuries, and is characterised by interdisciplinarity. Other scholarly disciplines enter the field of historical science, cooperate with it, or make new sources available for it.

In the course of the 19th century, historical science experienced a time of formation and rapid development. This phase of its development is often called the period of historicism, which is in this connection understood as a methodical approach.[6] The historian should be basically guided by the context of the period with which he is working, and should not detach the sources from the time of their creation.

What made the 19th century a period of special importance? The development of historical science took a new direction. Historical scholarship became 'institutionalised'. It received university chairs and prestigious departments. It produced periodicals and presented itself to the public. This is also true for its individual sub disciplines – including Egyptology.

This factor – the official position of history as a respected discipline – contributed to change general attitudes toward the past.[7] Professional history acquired new authority, revising and purportedly governing the general historical consciousness.[8] Historical knowledge, once it was corroborated by the historical science, became a standard[9], according to which society would compare other levels of historical culture.

The nascent historical sciences[10] included also Egyptology.[11] For a long time, the position of this discipline was unclear. First in 1937, German Egyptologist

W. Wolf introduced his explanation of the meaning and content of Egyptology by the sentence '*Egyptology is a historical science*'.[12]

In the course of numerous modern discussions on the classification of the humanities it was concluded[13] that the methods[14] that were of utmost importance for the formation of historical science as a whole – heuristics, analysis of sources,[15] and philological methods – played the same role in Egyptology.

The period that is the object of this study covers above all two trends of historical science: positivism and historicism. Two types of historicism are being referred to in connection with 19th century historical science: historicism still influenced by romantism, and positivist historicism.[16] In German Egyptology, these approaches are represented by Heinrich Brugsch[17] (romantist historicism), and Adolf Erman (positivist type). In the case of Erman, we cannot always talk about a full and rigid positivism; i.e. the independence of Egyptian mentality was wholly unknown to him.[18]

Adolf Erman

Erman believed that the positivist Egyptology of his time purged the mythicised image of Egypt out of European consciousness ' ... *the naïve belief of the Graeco-Roman world, that saw Egypt as a land of mysterious wisdom, outlived the 17th century, today, when we ourselves know the Egyptian monuments, can read the Egyptian hieroglyphs and study Egyptian literature, this aureole is gone ... the ancient Egyptians became for us a nation that was no better or worse than the others. Their "wisdom" appears at a closer look a scarce and in part (even) inconsistent and their customs are no more peculiar than those of other nations and deserve neither our ridicule, nor our respect'.*[19] His attempt at objectivism does not differ in any significant way from the approach of the German positivist historian Leopold von Ranke, for whom the task of the historian is to answer the question '*how it actually happened*'. Adolf Erman subscribed to the opinion that we should not hesitate to assess the spiritual world of the Egyptians by our own measures.

At this point it is useful to remark that studies of mentality, and anthropological approaches to cultures, of the type that we know now, which resulted from the influence of the *Annales* school,[20] were not fully familiar to the historical science of the end of the 19th and beginning of the 20th century. Although we cannot neglect the methodologies of W. Dilthey or Max Weber,[21] or the definition of Ernst Bernheim: '*The subject of history is human activity, and it is a basic fact of the psychophysical existence of the human being, that he is driven not only by outer causes, but also, and significantly, by inner causes ...*' Furher he notices that the '*overall identity of a human being is not enough to deduce individual cases from it*'.[22]

Stephen R. Glanville advocated the position of Egyptology within historical science, arguing that the history of Egypt '*takes its place as an integral part of Ancient History and therefore of History*'[23]. Today we have even more evidence to support the position of Egyptology as a historical science. One is the interdisciplinarity, a characteristic feature of modern historical science, which is a basic trait of any Egyptological research assisting to create a structural, and more vivid picture of the past.[24]

Jean François Champollion

The development of Egyptology was at first not exactly straightforward. Not even Champollion's discovery of the way to read the Egyptian script was unequivocally accepted.[25] Many questions long remained the subject of discussions and arguments. Nor were these always limited to scholarly debates. The general public was often supplied with publications that had little in common with the growing amount of specialised knowledge. Thus, the only results of the new science for a certain part of the public comprised exclusively of the illustrations from *Description de l'Égypte*. The new discoveries and books of Egyptologists had to constantly compete with the works that advocated one of the traditional pictures of Egypt, the most prominent among which was the Biblical picture. On the other hand, the new Orientalist sciences became tools for searching evidence for and even against this traditional view.[26] Egyptology as a scholarly discipline had to defend its position in various ways, for example also by maintaining, that Egyptological research contributes to the clarification of Biblical events,[27] that the history of Egypt forms part of general history, etc.[28]

The key moments of the history of Egyptology in the 19th century thus include not only the large expeditions of Karl R. Lepsius, which resulted in the monumental work *Denkmäler aus Aegypten und Aethiopien*, published between 1849–1859, and the development of the Antiquities service in Egypt under Auguste Mariette and Gaston Maspero, but also the institutionalisation of the subject at universities.

The Austrian and German academic circles had acquired their chairs of Egyptology already in the course of the 19th century.[29] The activity, or at least stay, of some of their members in the Czech lands is attested; in this case, however, we

Karl Richard Lepsius

cannot expect too great an influence on local historical culture.[30] Their books and articles may have fared better in this respect, as long as they were accessible to readers in the Czech lands. At the Prague University, however, the discipline of Egyptology was institutionalised only in the course of the 20th century. What was the situation of the more general discipline, ancient history? At other places, for example at the Vienna University, ancient history preceded the creation of an independent discipline of Egyptology.

Gaston Maspero

Ancient history at the Prague University

The existence of a separate chair of ancient history at the Faculty of Arts of the Prague University does not date too far back in time. Ancient history was referred to in the historical and archaeological lectures at the University, but a lecturer specialised in this subject was appointed first in 1872.[31] At that time professor Constantin von Höffler (1811–1897)[32] achieved the creation of a chair of the history of Classical Antiquity, which the historian Karel Kazbunda called *'his first scholarly love'*.

The first ordinary Professor of ancient history was Otto Hirschfeld from the University of Göttingen.[33] He was succeeded by Julius Jung, who, however, left the Prague University after its split into Czech and German parts, and interrupted the development by transferring to the German University. Lectures on ancient history were then taken over by Jaroslav Goll, who was famous for his interest in ancient Greece, above all in her art. The immense time span of Goll's lectures (from antiquity to modern times) inspired doubt as to whether it was at all possible to manage such a large bulk of material. Nonetheless Goll was the only one to whom the lectures could have been entrusted after the departure of J. Jung. Above all his reading on the Roman Imperial Period[34] was on a very high level. However, Goll completely neglected ancient Orient, and despite his interests, he avoided even Greek history.[35]

The establishment of a new professorship of ancient history at the Czech faculty after the year 1882 was repeatedly delayed, and Professor Goll was even criticised for it.[36] He was, however, of the opinion that there still was no lecturer of adequate qualities at his disposal. He continued to cover the material[37] on his own and tried to establish an extraordinary professorship. He expected it to cover modern history, and he would thus be free to give lectures on Mediaeval and ancient history.

The question of manning the chair of ancient history thus became a point of argument. Gradually, two very different candidates appeared. The first one was Justin Václav Prášek (1853–1924), a well-known populariser of ancient history. He had studied Oriental languages and undertaken several study journeys to Athens, Berlin, and Munich. He presented his work entitled 'Meden und das Haus des Kyaxares'. He regularly contributed to foreign language specialised journals (*Studien für klassische Philologie und Archaeologie*, *Berliner philologische Wochenschrift*, etc.). His articles appeared also in *Listy filologické*, and later in *České museum filologické*. However, his professional work was not unequivocally accepted. While 'Meden und das Haus des Kyaxares' was a successful study, his preceding work, 'Kambýsés a podání starověké', was refuted by Prof. Dr. Rudolf Dvořák, the first Professor of Oriental Sciences at the Prague University and later supporter of František Lexa.

In 1899, Prášek submitted his recently published book *Dějiny starověkých národů východních* ('A history of the ancient Oriental nations') (Volume I) as his habilitation (higher doctorate) thesis in Oriental history. When the decision of the habilitation committee (consisting of R. Dvořák, J. Goll, and J. Král) was repeatedly delayed, Prášek asked for a *venia docendi* also in Greek and Roman history. However, the committee finally rejected both parts of his thesis. Among those who spoke in favour of Prášek was above all Prof. Kvíčala, his colleague from *České museum filologické*. He emphasised the general profile of Prášek's activities; Prášek wrote numerous popularising articles[38] for *Osvěta*, *Květy*, and *Zlatá Praha* (see the section Textbooks below).[39]

R. Dvořák took a stand against Prášek's habilitation, on the grounds of his insufficient knowledge of Egyptology, Assyriology, and Hebrew. Prof. Král criticised, as a classical Philologist, Prášek's imperfect Greek. The final decision was thus, despite the numerous objections of Prof. Kvíčala, negative.[40]

An interesting facet of the influence of J. V. Prášek on the coming generation of Czech Orientalists is his relationship with the Egyptologist Jaroslav Černý, an excellent representative of Czech scholarship in the international field, who later worked in Oxford.[41] His personal correspondence[42] reveals that as a young scholar, Černý was a great admirer of Prášek. He expressed lasting respect for him and informed him on some new books and problems that currently occupied the attention of Egyptologists. Between 1917 and 1924, Černý maintained a relatively regular correspondence with Prášek, informing him of his work etc.[43] In August 1917 Černý asked Prášek for a recommendation to be admitted at Hlávka's college.[44] In 1922 he sent him his graduation announcement and subsequently also a letter of thanks. He writes: '*It was your* History of the ancient oriental nations *that had 10 years ago opened for me a new horizon of Egyptology by teaching me that, besides Champollion, Brugsch, and the like, there were also Erman, Sethe, Steindorff, etc., and by introducing me to the maze of questions, that Egyptology of those times had asked. If I ever live to see the moment that I indeed make a difference in scholarship, I will always remember that the basis of that I owe to your life's work …*'[45] In his subsequent letters he mentions various questions that were probably of interest for Prášek, such as for example Gardiner's opinions regarding the date of the Exodus.[46]

Prášek also received altogether 40 letters from Bedřich Hrozný, both at the time when Hrozný studied in Vienna and when he travelled Asia Minor.[47] Hrozný's letters concentrate above all on the specialised literature that he borrowed from Prášek.

Prášek also maintained contact with foreign scholars. Of special interest in this respect is his correspondence with G. Maspero, J. A. Knudtzon, and other Orientalists. Prášek's estate includes four letters from G. Maspero, dated to

Jaroslav Černý

the years 1892–1898.[48] Prášek probably considered translating Maspero's *Lectures historiques*[49] to Czech. In the course of the year 1898, Prášek asked Knudtzon for an explanation of an unclear passage in the Amarna tablets.[50]

Prášek also exchanged letters, albeit sometimes very brief ones, with Theo Pinches of the Department of Oriental Antiquities of the British Museum,[51] with Professor de Gubernatis of Rome,[52] A. H. Sayce,[53] with the Egyptologist G. Steindorff,[54] the Russian scholar Turayev,[55] and also with Heinrich Schliemann.[56]

The second candidate was Dr. Emanuel Peroutka (1860–1912), who finally reached Professorship at the Czech part of the Prague University in the year 1910. His interest was directed above all to Classical Antiquity. He undertook a research journey to Italy and Greece, and visited not only archaeological sites, but also the German Archaeological Institute in Rome, where he attended the lectures of Prof. Dörpfeld.[57] He thought that Goll's school neglected Classical Antiquity, which may sound paradoxical considering Goll's interest in this period, and his letters to J. S. Machar[58] include several critical remarks concerning Goll in this respect.[59]

Since 1904 he lectured on Greek and Roman history[60] at the university as a private docent (Assistant Professor)[61]. Nonetheless, he continued, with the support of Prof. Lubor Niederle,[62] in his attempts to renew the chair of Ancient History. His effort was finally crowned with success on June 26th, 1910, when he was appointed Associate Professor. In the following year he was appointed director of the Department of Ancient History in the Seminar of History and Epigraphy, the establishment of which was in part also the work of Jaroslav Goll.[63] However, E. Peroutka died in 1912. History of ancient Egypt did not have a special place in his lectures. He lectured above all on Greek history from the Archaic Period to the Macedonian and Hellenistic times, and on Roman history, including the history of Roman state administration, in the winter semester of 1908–09 and in the summer semester of 1911; in the winter semester of 1910–11 he gave lectures on ancient religion.[64]

This was, however, already the time when the first important figure of Czech Egyptology, František Lexa, was preparing for his career. He was supported by Rudolf Dvořák, thanks to whom the secondary school teacher of Hradec Králové was in 1906 trasferred to Prague to the Malostranské gymnázium.[65] At the same time Lexa[66] married Irena, the daughter of the Classical Philologist Prof. Jan Kvíčala, who had supported J. V. Prášek.

Lexa was appointed Associate Professor of Egyptology in 1922, and in 1925 he founded the Egyptological seminar. In 1927, Lexa was appointed the first ordinary Professor of Egyptology in Czechoslovakia.[67]

To conclude this chapter on historians and university history, I shall mention several theories of an important historian and author of philosophic-historical essays on general history, Josef Šusta.[68] In my opinion, they represent the theoretical reflection of the place of the Egyptian culture in the history of mankind, seen through the eyes of a Czech historian specialised in general history.

Josef Šusta based his opinions on the works of Hrozný and Lexa. Šusta's synthesis is the result of the works of these two authors; he even explicitly cites Hrozný.[69] Šusta ascribes a lot of conservatism to Egypt. In his opinion, '*livelier tendencies*[70] *awoke in the originally conservative and rather rigid Egyptian environment*' first in the course of the Middle Kingdom. He uses expressions such as the '*Semitic (or Hamitic) element*', it is, however, unclear to what extent he derived racial typologies from them. He compares Greece with the '*rigid traditionalism of Egyptian religiosity*'.[71] And in general, '*since the beginning the Egyptian environment is distinguished by a stronger <u>traditionalism</u>* (Šusta's emphasis), *little able to part with the once acquired cultural assets, despite the fact that they had become outdated obstacles for subsequent development.*'[72] Nonetheless, Egypt was a stronghold of ancient knowledge, whose influence was subsequently widely diffused.[73]

In the second half of the 19th century, ancient history was still understood above all as the history of Classical Antiquity, as becomes clear from the content of Peroutka's lectures. However, already in the 1860s, students at the Prague philosophical faculty could learn about non-classical ancient history in the lectures on archaeology, which was then considered an auxiliary historical science. Jan Erazim Vocel, one of the founding individuals of archaeology at the Czech University, Associate Professor of Czech archaeology and art history since 1850, and later ordinary Professor of the same subjects, lectured also on ancient Egyptian art according to the works of Karl Richard Lepsius,[74] one of the founders of German, respectively Berlin, Egyptological school.

Classical archaeology, on the other hand, was established as a separate discipline under the leadership of German-speaking scholars. '*Höffler's programme of strengthening the proportion in ancient history and culture in the education of historians was connected with the establishment of the subject of Classical Archaeology by appointing the erudite O. Benndorf in 1872.*'[75] In 1877 Otto Benndorf was summoned to Vienna, and his place was taken by E. Petersen, the opponent of the habilitation thesis of Miroslav Tyrš, an art historian who was also interested in ancient Egypt. Even in terms of lectures on Classical Antiquity, students could sometimes be informed on some Near Eastern sites.[76]

In terms of lectures on cultural history (which was itself then a freshly established discipline, without even a general academic acceptance), ancient Egypt was taken into consideration by Čeněk Zíbrt, an advocate of the development of cultural history.[77] Čeněk Zíbrt (1864–1932) submitted his habilitation thesis at the faculty in the year 1893.[78] He lectured on 'general cultural history', in which he included entire antiquity. Egypt was separately treated, for example, in the winter semester of 1909–1910.[79]

The art historian Miroslav Tyrš (1832–1884) emphasised the importance of ancient Oriental art and in this respect he achieved a lasting place in the general awareness. His initial university lecture was published in the *Časopis Českého musea* (Journal of the Czech Museum) in 1883.[80] Its content can be briefly characterised as follows: Egypt and Mesopotamia are the logical predecessors and inspirers of Greek culture, which gained a lot from them in the area of art. '*A new, fresh nation had to come, with a different, more mobile and liberal social organisation, which took over the artistic heritage and with a brilliant talent, rose to once unimaginable heights.*'[81] With this nation he meant the Greeks. However, Tyrš understood clearly that Egypt and Mesopotamia were cultures with their own internal dynamics,[82] and he strongly negated any claims about the immutability or artistic rigidity of these cultures.[83]

In order to illustrate his lectures and research, Tyrš assembled a collection of pictorial documentation. '*The full and complete idea of Tyrš's collection can be achieved only by him who beheld every one of the thousands of photographs, engravings, and pictures,*' with these words Antonín Turek[84] praised the extent of his collection. Turek's contemporary report on Tyrš's collections includes actually a small overview of the history of art of the periods, which were in the centre of Tyrš's interests. On the richly represented Egyptian art Turek writes, partly imprecisely, that the collection begins '*with the pyramids of Memphis, with the granite-alabaster temple of the sphinxes and harmachises* (sic)', elsewhere he describes '*pyramids, the seven-coloured surface of which reflects light*'.[85]

After Tyrš's unexpected passing, the memories and necrologies mentioned not only his work in the *Sokol*,[86] but also the general importance of his work for the study of art history. His lectures met with a good response and entered general awareness. The numerous articles that reacted to his unexpected death regularly mention his emphasis on the knowledge of the ancient Near East as the foundation of European knowledge. F. Čenský writes: '*Through his long and rigorous research, Tyrš became an excellent expert on art history and of the ancient cultural nations, the Assyrians, Egyptians, Greeks, and Romans …*'[87], František Zákrejs:[88] '*already then he was well aware that Greek art owes a great deal to the Assyrian and Egyptian art*'.[89]

Antiquity, and thus also ancient Egypt, was also the theme of the lectures of other art historians. Among them, the Czech aesthetician Otokar Hostinský (1847–1910) must be mentioned. His lectures include *Die Musik des Altertums* ('Ancient Music, in 1879 as Assistant Professor'), *Geschichte der Musik in Altertum* ('History of Music in Antiquity', 1881/82, as Assistant Professor), *Dějiny umění starého věku I–II* ('History of Art in Antiquity, 1897–98, Professor'), or *Dějiny estetiky starověku a středověku* ('History of Aesthetics in Antiquity and the Middle Ages', 1908–9, Professor).[90]

Not even the maintenance of a Professorial chair of art history was an easy task at the Prague university. Until 1878, Professor A. Woltmann[91] lectured in Prague. After his departure, M. Tyrš could take over first in the year 1883. His death in 1884 resulted in a renewed vacancy of the chair, which was temporarily occupied by Hostinský.[92] The titles of lectures that are known from this period are relatively general[93] and do not allow us to determine with certainty whether Egypt was represented or not.

Finally, students of the faculty of arts could learn about Egypt also in terms of the lectures on historical geography by Assistant Professor, later Professor Jan Palacký,[94] son of the Czech historian and politician František Palacký.

This was a short overview of lectures, which offered to the students of the Prague Czech University some information about ancient (and, in the case of the lectures of J. Palacký, also contemporary), Egypt. In order to complete the concept of the knowledge of Oriental philology more needs to be said about the development of Oriental studies as such at the Czech University.

Oriental Studies at the Prague University[95]

Oriental studies, and above all Oriental philology, is another scholarly discipline that was a source of knowledge about the ancient Near East. Since the 19th century, Oriental studies include also Egyptology, which stays at the watershed of history and Orientalist scholarship.[96] At that time, Egyptology was not a separate scholarly discipline at the Prague University. However, there was a long tradition of Orientalist disciplines.[97] In the context of contemporary Orientalism,[98] they provided access to the knowledge about the Orient.[99] The work of Saul Isaak Kampf (1813–1892)[100] was of special importance for the development of modern Oriental science in the second half of the 19th century, when the Faculty of Arts became a separate unit in terms of the University. He lectured on the *comparative grammar of the Semitic languages, Chaldaean, Syrian, and Arabic grammar*.[101] He thus surpassed the scope of the lectures of his colleague Wolfgang Wessely.

After the split of the university, and also of the faculty, the lectures began once again in the academic year of 1884/5, when Rudolf Dvořák (1860–1920)[102] started to work there (we have already met him in connection with the rejected habilitation of J. V. Prášek). He acted first as Assistant Professor, later as Professor.[103] His lectures concentrated above all on the comparative study of Oriental languages, covering Turkish, Arabic, Hebrew, and Chinese.[104] We also encounter a *Grammar of the Ethiopic Language*.[105]

R. Dvořák,[106] the founder of modern Czech Oriental Science, worked at the Prague University precisely at the time which is the focus of the present work. The personality of R. Dvořák is connected with the mediation of contemporary European Orientalist knowledge to the Czech audience, both by means of public lectures[107] and articles, which he published in the magazine *Athenaeum*.[108] There he also published his report *Papyrusy Fajjúmské* ('The Fayyum papyri')[109] about the important discovery of papyri, which are now part of the Papyrussammlung of the Austrian National Library in Vienna.[110] Since 1903 Dvořák was also one of the keepers of the Reference Library of Oriental Philology.[111]

In the course of his wide-ranging studies, Dvořák also became acquainted with Egyptology. He attended the lectures of Georg Ebers. It is interesting to note that although he dedicated many of his lectures to, for example Chinese culture,[112] only once in the course of the years 1882–1920 (i.e. between the establishment of the separate Czech faculty to the start of the university activities of F. Lexa) there appeared the theme of the ancient Near Eastern culture: Babylonia and Assyria. There was no lecture focusing on ancient Egypt,[113] with the exception of references to Egypt in the general lectures on the history of writing,[114] which is a theme that he developed already in the aforementioned *Athenaeum*. Rudolf ; also led the so-called 'Practical Oriental Courses', dedicated above all to Arabic and Turkish.[115] These courses were probably connected with the demand for non-university courses of Oriental languages, which was itself stimulated by practical needs. For example the work of businessmen and artisans brought them in contact with the Orient. The case of the Vienna Polytechnical School was the same, and similar courses were conducted here. From what we already know about the Austrian community in Cairo, it is clear that there was a substantial basis to this demand.

Dvořák's assistant and successor was Rudolf Růžička (1878–1957).[116] He studied numerous Arabic dialects, including Egyptian Arabic,[117] but the Ancient Near East, and thus also Egypt, did not belong to the sphere of his interest.

A seminar of ancient Near Eastern History, connected with cuneiform studies, was established first with the appointment of Prof. Bedřich Hrozný as lecturer

František Lexa

in 1919[118] (he led the 'Seminar for Cuneiform Studies and History of the Ancient Near East'). In the same year, the Orientalist Alois Musil (1868–1944) returned to the Prague University,[119] to lead the Seminar for 'Associate Eastern Sciences' (a contemporary generic term for Orientalist disciplines) and newer Arabic.[120]

Finally, in the year 1920 the Orientalist discipline that is of greatest importance for the study of ancient Egypt was established. At that time, František Lexa started his lectures, after he had been appointed Assistant Professor in 1919.[121] Already in 1922 he was appointed Reader of Egyptology, and in 1925, the Egyptological seminar was established under his leadership.[122]

In the end it should be made clear that in the 19th century, Oriental languages and their teaching were not the exclusive domain of the Faculty of Arts. The Faculty of Theology (of the Czech University) offered lectures in e.g. Aramaic, and since the winter semester of 1908–09 also in Coptic[123](under the leadership of Assistant Professor Hazuka).[124]

Since 1882, there was not only one university in Prague, but actually two – Czech and German. Neither the German University lacked interest in ancient history – we have witnessed the transfer of Julius Jung after the split.

As far as Egyptology is concerned, before the downfall of the monarchy we know of the work of the pupil of Reinisch, Nathaniel Reich – who was apparently active since 1913 until the 1920s.

Later, in the 1930s, the German University employed Theodor Hopfner, Classical philologist known for his analysis of Plutarch's *De Iside et Osiride*. Besides Hopfner, however, we now know of another Egyptologist after WWI – Ludwig Keimer, who was habilitated in this discipline in the 1930s.[125]

Both sections concerned with university education – in Orientalist disciplines and in Ancient History – end with a note on the institutionalisation of the separate discipline of Egyptology.[126] None of these fields enabled a greater development of the study of ancient Egyptian history and culture, until the formation of Egyptology as a separate scholarly discipline. Ancient Egyptian – and more generally ancient Oriental – history was only a marginal theme of contemporary university education. Ancient history was concerned above all with Classical Antiquity,[127] or at least such was the case at the Czech University.

While at that time, the dictionary definition[128] of Oriental disciplines covered also Egyptology, and contemporary encyclopaedias and information of the Prague Orientalists of the time indicate their knowledge of contemporary Egyptological publications. None of them, however, focused on ancient Egyptian language, with the exception of the Coptic course at the Faculty of Theology.

It is not always the case that the institutionalisation of a discipline guarantees its widespread influence and vice versa, as the situation in Britain shows. Britain, a country with many relationships to Egypt and a wide background of reception of the ancient Egyptian culture,[129] acquired her first chair of Egyptology as late as in the 1890s.[130] In the Czech lands, however, the little general interest in these fields was probably paralleled by a non-specialised university background.

All this does not mean that none of the contemporary historians or Orientalists was aware of the importance of ancient Oriental history and languages. Their interest in this field is apparent from the popularising works, such as Rudolf Dvořák's articles or the books of J. V. Prášek. The latter also maintained intensive contacts with the future generation of scholars, for example with the later Egyptologist Jaroslav Černý. As for Rudolf Dvořák, we have already encountered him as a supporter of František Lexa.

It is not at all easy to determine the influence of university education on the historical consciousness of ancient Egypt, an area very distant from the current national history. While it was not negligible, it could not have been too great. Above all those people, who did not directly attend university lectures, received knowledge on ancient Egypt rather from lessons on Biblical history, than in terms of general history itself. Of greater interest, though, were the various books, magazines, and articles that were also accessible to a wider audience than university lectures.

Textbooks, journals and educational literature

A number of textbooks on ancient history were published in the second half of the 19th century, while towards the end of the century, more and more works were published that popularised this historical era in various contexts. The leading populariser of Egyptology was J. V. Prášek.

The bibliographies of a number of the authors show that they already worked, just as the contemporary dictionaries, with voluminous foreign literature, including specialised Egyptological books.

Karel Svoboda records the following list of textbooks: *'The Písek-born historian Karel Ninger (1827–1913) compiled Ancient History (General History I, 1863) for the lower grades of the secondary school; in accordance with the prescribed syllabus, he dedicated a lot of space to ancient legends. The Professor of the academic secondary school Jan Lepař[131] (1827–1902) – he was brother of the Jičín philologist[132]– published such a textbook for the higher classes, and so did University Professor Antonín Gindely (1829–1892), whose book, originally written in German (Lehrbuch der allgemeinen Geschichte I, 1860), was in 1877 twice translated to Czech,[133] by M. Kovář and by K. J. Jireček. Both Lepař and Gindely based their textbooks on reliable international publications and, in keeping with the contemporary demand, they took into account cultural history. In the year 1866, the poet and historian A. H. Škultéty[134] of Štúrovo prepared a "General History of the Ancient Era" for Slovak schools … but his book remained a manuscript.'[135]*

A general history of antiquity was written also by the journalist Ivan Erazim Sojka (1828–1887),[136] who published his *Ancient Times* in 1862. '*He divided antiquity in a similar way as Svoboda into the following periods: 1. from the beginning of Kyros in 560, 2. until Alexander, 3. until Augustus, and 4. until the fall of the Empire in 476; and he synchronically treated each period at a time, so that in the second period he dealt successively with Persian, Phoinician, Palestinian, Karthagine, Greek, Macedonian, and Roman history. He did not, however, acquire his knowledge from primary sources, but from recent specialised literature ...'*

František Šembera (1842–1898) worked even more intensively with literature. *'He twice attempted a detailed account of ancient history, but never finished his task – probably because of the small number of potential readers. In his History of the educated nations of Antiquity (I, 1872; it should have been the first volume of a planned 'General history'), he dealt with the eastern nations and Greek history until the colonisation; in his History of the Classical Nations (I, 1875), he covered Greek history until the end of the Peloponnesos war. Both books were based on an extensive knowledge of secondary literature ...'*[137] This is evident also from Šembera's extensive bibliography.

Both Šembera and Prášek specialised to a certain extent on ancient themes. In the case of Prášek, we may speak of a long-term focussed interest. As we have already seen, he wanted to establish the lectures on ancient history, including ancient Oriental history, at the Prague Faculty of Arts. His correspondence[138] shows that he maintained contacts with contemporary scholars working above all in the field of the history of the ancient Near East.

We will therefore concentrate above all on the activities of František Šembera and Justin V. Prášek. The work of F. Šembera[139] is older – his *Dějiny vzdělaných národů starověkých* ('History of the educated nations of Antiquity') was published in the early 1870s.[140] For our purposes, i.e. that is for the study of the place of ancient Egypt in the historical consciousness, the most important part of his book is *'Part I – Egyptians and Semites'*.

Already the bibliography indicates the meticulous care, with which F. Šembera prepared his book. It also offers us a glimpse into the level of knowledge of contemporary specialised literature in the field of the history of Ancient Near East and Egypt.[141]

How does Šembera characterise ancient Egyptian culture? Ancient Egyptians *'moved ... from Asia'*[142] to a fertile land with a considerably monotonous flora. *'Mother Nature had everywhere forced man to improve and strengthen his abilities, but hardly anywhere else had she also supported him to such an extent as in Egypt.'*[143] In his opinion, natural conditions played an important role in the formation of the national character of the Egyptians, who themselves contributed a lot to the growth of the human culture – *Nature and the character of the land had, however, also greatly influenced their character. It was relatively good, mild, and calm, and the Egyptians were similar. It did not stimulate their minds with terrible sights (such as, for example, in India), and thus their reason could easily develop and they could have been a practical and reasonable nation. It was magnificent, regular, and monotonous ... and they were lovers of the magnificent, regular, and monotonous; lovers of law and order, they were a people stable and conservative in every respect.*

A strange country she was, Egypt, and strange were her children. Their role in the formation and development of civilisation cannot be valued enough. Education is like a magnificent building, and they paved the way to it. Their history, that is a noble pylon at the entrance of the temple of Knowledge!'[144] (Emphasis F. Š.)

Šembera's text betrays his taking up the older tradition, which searched the beginnings of human education and the first luxuries of civilisation in Egypt. His views also belong to the theories about the gradual advance of mankind, for which all contributions must be acknowledged. On the other hand, such an explanation of a gradual development of civilisation was not far from beliefs in the superiority of European culture and civilisation, or from seeing the ancient, above all ancient Oriental, civilisation as having a lot in common with 'primitive', 'uncivilised' societies.[145]

Šembera used geographical specifications[146] in order to explain the character and history of a certain nation. Conservatism also belongs to traits that are very often ascribed to the ancient Egyptians, besides the old age of their culture and pride of their own achievements ('… *ancient Egyptians were very boastful …*').

The initial passage is followed by an overview of ancient Egyptian culture, including references to approximate chronological setting of Biblical events. For example Exodus is thus dated to the end of the 19th dynasty and King *'Ramessu II … he is in all probability that terrible killer of the Israelite children, on whom the Bible reports'.*[148]

Šembera uses modern terminology to talk about the Egyptian society. He says, for example, that the '*Egyptian* constitution *was despotic and* centralistic'[149], or that the '*Egyptian nation was divided into castes'.*[150] The use of he term 'despotism' in connection with the ancient Egyptian state administration has a long history, but it has not always been used in the same context.[151] It appears in the works of various historians,[152] and later it was often used by Marxist historiography.[153]

The term 'caste' is in all likelihood the result of a misinterpretation of Herodotus' text in Book II, 164 ff.: '*There are seven social classes among the Egyptians: priests, soldiers, cattle herdsmen, swineherds, merchants, interpreters, and steersmen. So many are the Egyptian caste…*'[154] Šembera had probably taken it over from another author.

Perhaps the farthest venture into modern terminology is Šembera's description of the 'entrepreneur' caste, or of 'industrialists,'[155] and further of the quality products of the Egyptian 'haberdashery' industry, which decorated the 'boudoirs of Egyptian ladies'.[156]

This, however, is only a question of the use of words, which may now appear anachronical. Of more importance is the understanding of the ancient Egyptian society as a caste system with a centralised administration. The following quotation illustrates another aspect of the contemporary conception of the Egyptian state and of the functioning of the Egyptian society. The domestic life, concentrated on the family and children, is explained thus: '*the reasons for this are probably the following. 1. Egypt was dominated by despotism and bureaucracy. Therefore, the man did not have to (and could not) care about the community as in Hellas – and he thus concentrated more on the family and society!'*[157] Interestingly enough, similar concepts appear also in newer works, in connection with the theses on the equal positions of men and women. In front of the strong state, they were 'equal'.

Šembera also describes other, very different, aspects of the character of the ancient Egyptians, which he had defined as conservative and hierarchical: *'however, there was also a great license and wild gaiety in Egypt ... It was the result (common also elsewhere) of too great an adoration of life-bearing and fertility forces in nature. As the religion, so the people (et vice versa)'.*[158]

Šembera's account of the ancient Egyptians corresponds to the idea of an educated nation, living under a strict state administration, who enjoy personal delights within their families, from which sometimes stands out common gaiety, bordering in the point of view of a European with dissoluteness. The same portrait of the ancient Egyptian appears in the works of Julius Zeyer, whose article I shall mention below.

Ten years later, in the year 1882, Justin V. Prášek published his *Všeobecný dějepis občanský* ('General Social History') I/1, with the subtitle *Dějiny východních Arijců a vzdělaných národů severoafrických*[159] ('History of East Arians and of the educated nations of North Africa'). In many respects, his work continues that of Šembera, but he wants to be, in his own words, accessible to a wider circle of readers.

Section II of Volume I/1 is entitled *Aigypťané a Aithiopové* ('The Aegyptians and the Aethiopeans' Prášek consistently retained the Graecised spelling). Like Šembera, he begins with the description of the country, but he goes on with an overview of excavations. Actually, he includes a small insight into the history of Egyptology,[160] since the decipherment attempts of A. Kircher, over the scholars of Napoleon's expedition to the Egyptologists of his time. He focuses above all on G. Ebers (Jiří Ebers),[161] above all because this scholar popularised Egypt in his historical novels (see the section on Translated Literature). He also dedicates some attention to the Prussian expedition of Lepsius of the 1840s. Until now, the inclusion of the history of the discipline and reception of Egypt remains a standard part of contemporary historical works.

Prášek also compiled an overview of Egyptian history and Egyptian society. *'Thus, the Ancient Aegyptian state grew out of the needs of the peasant population, which protected the gifts that God's hand had given them, and the later religious account considered that unification a work of divine power.'*[162] His concept of the Egyptian society is based on Diodorus and Herodotus, as the quoted historians, who were the closest to the ancient Egyptian temporal reality. Prášek could thus dedicate a lot of attention to the Egyptian kingship, following the account of Diodorus.[163]

He also described the family life of the ancient Egyptians, which he regarded favourably – he emphasised the Egyptian respect for women – *'the family originally consisted of a man and of a single wife ...'*[164]

Unlike F. Šembera, Prášek is more cautious when describing Egyptian society: *'some Hellenistic writers, above all Herodotus and Diodorus, relate extensively, that all people of Egypt were divided into social classes similar ... to the Indian castes ... The peasants usually inherited their fields, the artisans taught their sons their craft, the shepherd passed his flock over to him, and thus, hereditary work developed on the Nile ... However, the situation never degenerated in the Indian way.'*[165]

Here we can see Prášek's critical work, which was also the core of his essay 'Kambýses a podání starověké' ('Cambyses and the ancient account'), as well as of his article about the report of Herodotus in *Recueil de travaux relatifs à philologie et archéologie égyptiennes et assyriennes*. Although it surely was influenced by what other researchers maintained, it still represented an independent contribution of a Czech scholar to the study of ancient history. The book includes rich illustration material, views of the Egyptian countryside, exteriors of tombs, temples, etc.

'General history' is one of many Prášek's books dedicated to the general public. Others include *Dějiny starověkých národů východních* ('History of the ancient Oriental nations', 1899–1902), *Egypt za starých dob faraonův* ('Egypt in the ancient times of the Pharaohs', 1914), or *Ženy antické* ('Women of Antiquity', s.a.). The last work dedicates a lot of space to Egypt already in the Introduction, and then also in the profiles of Queens Hatshepsut[166] (Prášek's Hačepsu Makara), and Cleopatra.

In the Introduction, Prášek warns against extending to Egypt the *'wrong conception of subjugation and disrespectful role of women in the entire East,'*[167] which could arise from observing the contemporary Oriental world. Besides the respected role of women in the family in general,[168] he emphasises the importance of women in royal families. In keeping with the contemporary majority view, he assigns to the wife of Amenophis III, Tii (Tiyi)[169], a decisive role in the politics of the country. He did not forget to mention the Old Testament tradition of the pharaoh's wise daughter, whom he equates with the daughter of Ramesses II, Bentanat (Bint-Anat).[170] Besides these personalities, he also knows the important royal women of the times of the beginning of the New Kingdom, Queens Ahhotpe and Ahmes Nefertari (Prášek's Aahotep and Ahmesnefertari).[171]

Two chapters of the book are dedicated to Queens Hatshepsut and Cleopatra. He mentions Hatshepsut's building activities and describes the temple of Deir el-Bahri.[172] In the case of Cleopatra, he based his account on the traditional scheme of her biography, derived from a Classical source – Plutarch's *Parallel Biographies*.

Besides Czech publications, readers could acquire a lot of information in the works of foreign authors, above all from the German-speaking sphere.[173] We will mention at least the basic overviews of Egyptian history, which were accessible[174] to the Czech university environment, namely Alfred Wiedemann's[175] *Ägyptische Geschichte* from 1884 and Eduard Meyer's *Geschichte Ägyptens* (1887). Just as in the case of the Czech books, it is, however, not clear how wide their readership was.

Popularising[176] literature includes numerous articles in journals, such as *Zlatá Praha*, *Květy*, or *Osvěta*. The latter periodical, published since 1871[177] included a large sample of prose and poetry, traveller's accounts, informative articles on social and natural sciences, and new book announcements.

Although the first volume contains no article dedicated to the study of antiquity, in the course of the further existence of the magazine, its readers could gradually acquaint themselves with travel news, new archaeological discoveries,[178] and newly published literature. All these articles also contain references to Egypt.

Volume 12 of 1882 contains J. Kalousek's[179] review of Prášek's 'General Social History'. At that time, the first four volumes were published, which '*are concerned with ancient Indians, Iranians, and begin to deal with the Egyptians*'.[180] Despite criticising its somewhat overly 'learned' presentation, Kalousek praises the publication of a work '*that should be dedicated to the history of the eastern nations with a special attention to Egyptian and Assyrian history*'.[181]

As far as the extent of the production of books and articles is concerned, it is precisely J. V. Prášek, who stands foremost among the Czech popularisers of ancient Egypt, active around the turn of the century. Prášek followed foreign specialised periodicals,[182] and his articles in *Osvěta* informed for example about new archaeological discoveries, together with the summary of activities concerned with the given theme – e.g. about the discoveries from 1888 at Tell el-Amarna, the seat of the 'reformer' king Amenophis IV, Akhenaten.[183] Besides the account of the discovery of the Amarna archive, the reader also learned several facts about the time of Akhenaten (Prášek's Chu-en-aten), as well as the detail concerning the name '*aten, which is undoubtedly connected to the Hebr. Adonai*'. Prášek also reproduces part of the analysis concerned with the identification of the Egyptian names of Asian sites, and relates thus to the reader the historical aspect of Biblical times. He quotes contemporary specialised and educational literature, above all Heinrich Brugsch and his *Geschichte Aegyptens unter den Pharaonen* and also his article in *Zeitschrift für ägyptische Sprache und Altertumskunde* of 1880 about the scarab of Amenophis III.[184] Prášek also inclines to the theory of the Asian inspiration of Akhenaten's reform – among others because he postulates foreign origin of the Queen mother Tiyi, since, to use Prášek's words, '*neither her name nor that of her parents sounds in any way Egyptian*'.[185]

Another work of educational and popularising literature is Julius Zeyer's *Pohádky a romány staroegyptské* ('Fairy Tales and Novels of Ancient Egypt'), which was published in the magazine *Lumír* in 1875.[186] He described the ancient Egyptians not just as builders of gigantic monuments, but also as a nation with an independent literary tradition. Through literary sources and Egyptian art, he also tried to understand their national character. He used the works of several Egyptologists, such as Mariette, Birch, Brugsch, Chabas, and others.[187]

What, then, is Zeyer's characteristic of the ancient Egyptians? Quite paradoxically, he writes: '*the Egyptian people, so oppressed by the terrible despotism of the pharaohs, so moulded by the fines and compulsory work, so beaten by the sticks of the tax officials, this people was merry, industrious, and quietly obedient as the modern fellahin. On certain days, during the large panegyrics, above all those of the goddesses Bastet and Hathor ... all these good people succumbed to the uncontrollable drives of cynical animalism, which kicks and roars in the heart of the man most tyrannised by civilisation ...*'[188] as well as '*Who could be sad under the blue, hot and pale Egyptian sky, in that Elysian light, sweet and bright as a kiss, which seems to be created not so much for people, but for blessed shadows? Oppression and poverty meant nothing there*[189]... *everything, even the permanent awareness of death, even the contemplation about the matters of the beyond, was of a sweet and clear seriousness in Egypt. Although their religion confronted them with a very seductive concept of the Elysean blessedness, they still strongly inclined to this life[190]... It seems that as centuries passed, death became less and less easy, gloom and doubts settled in some souls ...[191]*

As the following chapter, The Egyptian Inspiration, shows, this educative description of ancient Egypt corresponds to Zeyer's literary account. Both clearly show the double-face of the Egyptian civilisation. The same view can, however, be found in contemporary specialised literature, namely in the work of the Egyptologist Heinrich Brugsch,[192] whose work Zeyer knew, since he quotes it in his essay.[193]

In the ensuing part of the text, Zeyer acquaints the reader with the *Tale of the Two Brothers* and the story of Prince Khaemwaset. He also included the love poems from papyrus Turin 1996, following Chabas' translation.[194] The whole account was supposed to illustrate the wealth of Egyptian literature, which attests the originality of the Egyptian spirit, the heritage of which was important even in Zeyer's times.[195] In a way, Zeyer's contemporaries were thus able to spiritually approach ancient Egypt in an artistic and literary way.

We cannot neglect translations. Once again, we meet the name of Georg Ebers. '*Der federflinke Ägyptologe*'[196] was not translated only as author of novels. His book entitled *Egypt slovem i obrazem* ('Egypt in text and image', two volumes) was translated by O. Hostinský and published by the František Šimáček publishing house in 1883–1884.

Egypt slovem i obrazem is remarkable also because its numerous illustrations are the work of many famous painters of historical motifs, with whom Ebers cooperated as a counsellor. They include such personalities of European historical paintings as Hans Makart or Lawrence Alma-Tadema.

Contemporary historical novel and historical painting together create a concept of ancient Egypt full of passion, luxury and cruelty, '*Egypt (= the Egyptian theme) offered the painters an opportunity to depict on large scale nude bathing women, scantily dressed dancers, sleeping harim ladies, cruelty and brutality, market with slave girls, and the offering to the Nile, simply everything that seems so distant from "progress", "humanity" and "civilisation" of the West and of modern time'.[197]*

The works of G. Ebers are different. Above all in his *Egypt slovem a obrazem*, he analysed several traditional views, which could not stand against the weight of new evidence. Thus, sometimes the text is in contrast with the illustration. He strictly opposes for example the idea that the pyramids were built using slave work, and bases his arguments also on the character and content of Old Kingdom reliefs: '*No other period of Egyptian history makes a more pleasant impression than this one, and if the pyramids are called a "sign of slavery of numerous human generations," and from Herodotus on, numerous authors condemn the ruthless tyrants who had built them, it seems to us that those who thus lament allow themselves too great a pity; for it was not a moaning crowd that was driven to work, but a fresh and youthful*

Artistic rendering of ancient Egypt in Ebers – Ägypten im Wort und Bild

nation … exerted the great excess of their power with jubilation, as to finish in front of the eyes of their king and for his divine presence this almost superhuman work.'[198] Whatever we may now think about the logic of Ebers' explanation, he tried to build an alternative opinion to the existing stereotype. The readers of his works could thus learn about Mariette's archaeological excavations in the Serapeum,[199] about Lepsius' expedition, about the decoration of Old Kingdom mastabas at Saqqara, and many other details.

The translator of the book, Ot. Hostinský, opined that '*it thus substantially contributes to our knowledge*'.[200] He emphasised that Egypt in many respects attracted the attention of Europeans. Among reasons for this growing interest were also recent political events, which changed the character of the country. Ebers' work, based on his travel experience from the 1860s and 1870s, was one of the few sources that allowed readers to access this vanishing Egypt. Otakar Hostinský's opinion that the richly illustrated and fascinating book could celebrate success, was undoubtedly right; the fact that Ebers was a popular author of novels[201] was also of importance in this respect. The size and extent of the illustrative material of the book, however, made it a publication that only few could afford.

Even encyclopaedias and dictionaries, which are the theme of the next chapter, were not a standard inventory of all common libraries, although they should have represented the generally accessible sum of knowledge.

Encyclopaedias

Dictionaries and encyclopaedias belong to the educative literature that is accessible to a relatively wide range of readers. Therefore, we will list the most important of them in a short overview. Above all the *Ottův slovník naučný* ('Otto's Educative Dictionary'), an original Czech encyclopaedia[202] was a unique achievement in education and popularisation. It was, however, not the first Czech encyclopedic dictionary. An educative dictionary, titled *Riegrův*, was published in 1862 in Prague by the Kober publishing house. It describes contemporary Egypt (its Coptic name is given as Chemi, which corresponds to Egypt's name in Bohairic)[203], her fauna and flora, and also her history. The account on history follows the line of Classical historians, above all Herodotus. For example, Ramesses II is '*Sesostris by the Greeks*'. The reader was also supported in his beliefs about the slavery of the Egyptian people, of which pyramids are, according to the authors, clear evidence. On the other hand, the problem of ancient Egyptian religion was treated with caution, since the knowledge of the ancient Egyptian language was still insufficient. The bibliography of the dictionary includes works of Egyptologists J.-F. Champollion, I. Rosselini, J. Wilkinson, G. Parthey, and H. Brugsch. The entry on Egypt was written by Mr. Novotný and Karel Tieftrunk – the Imperial and Royal secondary school teachers.

Otto's Educative Dictionary was published since 1894 in Prague. This dictionary includes a more detailed account of Egypt's history and codifies the use of Egyptian, not Greek, forms of the names of the Egyptian kings. The author of the entry worked with foreign literature; the works cited include those of Brugsch, Revillout, Birch, de Rougé, Le Page Renouf, Rossi, Kminek-Szedlo, and Ebers (in Czech translation). These works gave him an idea about the contemporary state of research, including the theses concerning the subjugation of the native Egyptian population by a different race, or the priests' monopoly on education. The so-called Small Otto's Educative Dictionary (published in 1905 under the lead of F. A. Šubert) repeats parts of the account of the preceding large edition. First *Masarykův slovník naučný* ('Masaryk's Educative Dictionary') from 1926 brought new entries on Egypt, which were written with the assistance of the Egyptologist Jaroslav Černý.

The small overview of relevant articles and encyclopaedic entries allows us to elucidate what kind of information on ancient Egypt was accessible to the general public of the second half of the 19th century. Of course, only a certain part of the society could afford to regularly purchase the *Osvěta* or the *Athenaeum*. Dictionaries and encyclopaedias could have been more widely reflected. Textbooks are tied to the school environment, but the aforementioned works of Prášek and Šembera need not necessarily have remained mere textbooks. Rather, they were well accessible educative books, although their success on the contemporary market was not certain, as we saw in the case of Šembera. Foreign works were not unknown, either. They were used by Czech authors of educative literature, who – above all J. V. Prášek – also drew from reports on new archaeological discoveries.

These works characterise the ancient Egyptians as a highly developed culture (Prášek, Šembera, Zeyer), which played an important role in the general cultural advance of mankind (consistently Šembera). The reader is introduced to it with the help of related Biblical events (Šembera, Prášek), which may still have been of crucial importance for many people, since Scripture was still part of the basic school education. The ancient Egyptians appeared in lively forms in stories and poems, which are situated in their time (Zeyer). Some forms of the Egyptian art were accessible in the illustrations of the *Ottův slovník naučný* and in the rich illustrative material of G. Ebers' books.

The contemporary European artistic reflection of Egypt, which revivified the ancient culture in the historising art, was related in the work of Ebers, as well as in several books of J. V. Prášek (e.g. *Egypt za slavných dob faraonů* – 'Egypt in the glorious times of the Pharaohs'). However, Egypt can also be found in Czech artistic reflection. Her place was not as prominent as in the case of British or French art, but still, her unmistakable influence can be perceived here.

Books, textbooks, and other educative literature of the Czech lands offered a relatively high level of knowledge of ancient Egypt in the second half of the 19th centrury, and above all in its last two decades. Dictionaries offered a basic overview. Historical works of F. Šembera and J. V. Prášek included more detailed information on the importance of the ancient Egyptian culture. Egyptian art and its significance in the cultural history of mankind were treated in the university lectures of M. Tyrš, O. Hostinský, and Č. Zíbrt.

While general history of antiquity was not outside the scope of the interest of university historians, and Oriental science was well established at the Prague university since the 1880s, it did not lead to the foundation of a chair of ancient Oriental history, or of Egyptology as an independent discipline. The reason for this could have been the difficult situation of the university, which had to fight for the retention of the existing Professorial chairs,[204] as well as the absence of a person, who would focus on ancient Egyptian history or language. As the example of the discord between Rudolf Dvořák and Justin Prášek shows, there was an awareness of the solid Orientalistic education, which was necessary for such a job.

We can not forget to appraise Prášek's work, although its scholarly value was considered controversial. He revealed a new dimension of history to the Czech readers. The fact that his effort did not remain unnoticed is apparent from the respect that the coming generation of Oriental philologists paid him.

Notes:

1 Helck, W., *Ägyptologie an deutschen Universitäten*. Wiesbaden 1969; p. 1. '*As opposed to the cultures of Mesopotamia, the knowledge of ancient Egypt was never entirely forgotten.*' However, even here the Biblical reflection of the history of Mesopotamian countries may have played some part.

2 Schäfer, H., *Principles of Egyptian Art*, Engl. transl. John R. Baines. Oxford 1997; p. 7.

3 The term used for the first Greek historians. Thucydides used it pejoratively to denote his predecessors, whom he blamed for 'non-scholarly' work (cf. C. Ampolo, *Storie greche*).

4 E.g. *Geschichtsdiskurs*, Vol. 2, Frankfurt, 1994. See also P. Veyne, L*es Grecs ont-ils cru à leurs mythes?* Paris 1983, also A. Momigliano dedicated his attention to this question. An overview by J. Rüsen, *Die Vielfalt der Kulturen*, p. 70.

5 Summary after Z. Beneš, *Historický text a historická kultura* ('Historical text and historical culture'), Prague 1995; pp. 36–37.

6 For more details cf. Rüsen, J., *Konfigurationen des Historismus*. Frankfurt (M) 1993; pp. 17–28.

7 For the formation of historiography see the brief description of Blanke, H. W., 'Die Rolle der Historik im Entstehungsprozeß modernen historischen Denkens.' in: *Geschichtsdiskurs* Vol 2. Frankfurt (M) 1995; pp. 282ff, with further relevant bibliography.

8 Rüsen, J., *Konfigurationen*, p. 22: '…*Fachleuten, die sich mit ihrer Kompetenz für historische Forschung aus dem breiten Publikum ausgrenzen, und ihm für die Produktion historischen Wissens nur noch den Status des Dilettantismus zubilligen.*' The contingent character of interest in history is also mentioned in Rüsen – p. 23, the interest of the bourgeoisie to delimit their own (historical) role and legitimise their position. A similar expression of this widely discussed opinion is to be found in Horn, J. in *GM* 12, 1974.

9 Rüsen, *op. cit.*, p. 22 '*Zum Metier von Fachleuten geworden, erhob die Geschichtswissenschaft aber zugleich einen allgemeinen, überflachlichen Bildungsanspruch: Das von ihr produzierte historische Wissen wurde als Orientierungswissen für die gesellschaftliche Praxis ihrer Zeit zu Geltung gebracht.*' This can be compared with the corresponding theory of Hroch concerning the importance of scholarly proven facts of the national past for national agitation. Cf. above – Hroch: 'Několik poznámek…'

10 Cf. also the collection of articles in *GM*, 12, 1974, and Donadoni-Curto-Donadoni: *Egypt from Myth to Egyptology*, passim.

11 For the contemporary definition of the discipline and relevant bibliography cf. Hornung, E., *Einführung in die Ägyptologie*, Darmstadt 1993 (4. verbesserte Auflage), §§ 1–6. For an older delimitation of Egyptology and short introduction in to the discipline cf. Sethe, K., 'Die Ägyptologie. Zweck, Inhalt und Bedeutung dieser Wissenschaft und Deutschlands Anteil an ihrer Entwicklung' in: *Der Alte Orient*. 23. Band, Leipzig 1923/1921 with a general definition – cf. below. For methodological questions cf. also the recent volume of Rosalie David, *The Experience of Ancient Egypt*. London 2000; 'Conclusions', above all p. 187. And Kees, H., 'Geschichte der Ägyptologie'. *Handbuch der Orientalistik*, Bd.1/1, Leiden 1959.

12 '*Die Ägyptologie ist eine historische Wissenschaft.*' 'Wesen und Wert der Ägyptologie', *Leipziger Ägyptologische Studien*, Heft 8, 1937.

13 The discussion followed the works of Peet, T. E., *The Present Position of Egyptological studies*. Oxford 1934, W. Wolf, *op. cit.,* and others (overview in *GM* 12, 1974). Relatively extensive bibliography concerning the history of Egyptology, both in general and for individual countries, can be found in note 3 of the article of

R. Grieshammer '75 Jahre Ägyptologie in Heidelberg' in: J. Assmann ed., *Problems and priorities in Egyptian archaeology*. London 1987. For the development of German, or German-speaking, Egyptology, cf. W. Helck, *Ägyptologie an deutschen Universitäten*. Wiesbaden 1969.

14 Cf. also Björkman, G., 'Egyptology and Historical method', in: *OrSu* 13, 1964; 9–23.

15 For a survey of the various methods of the evaluation of sources, cf. Droysen, J. E., (*Historik*. Eg. Berlin u. München 1943; pp. 37ff. – 'Die Heuristik'), Ernst Bernheim, *Lehrbuch der historischen Methode und der Geschichtsphilosophie*, 1908, and others.

16 *GM* 12, 1974 – introductory study.

17 For the popularising activities of Brugsch cf. Helck, W., *Ägyptologie an deutschen Universitäten*, pp. 7ff. See also above in the chapter I. Brugsch himself described his works in his autobiography *Mein Leben und Mein Wandern*. 2 erw. Auflage Berlin 1884. Reprinted Osnabrück 1975.

18 U. Köhler, *GM* 12, 1974, p. 29. It was a foreign concept also for Erman's pupils, such as A. H. Gardiner – cf. Helck, *Ägyptologie*, p. 49. Helck remarks concerning Erman's doctrine *'Letzter und bedeutendster Vertreter dieser Richtung war Sir Alan Gardiner, ein Schüler Ermans. Diese Haltung führte dazu, dass man dem Ägypter die eigene Vorstellungswelt zuschrieb und sie wie Menschen der Gegenwart leben, denken und handeln liess.'*

19 Erman, A., *Aegypten und aegyptisches Leben im Altertum*. Leipzig 1885, Tübingen 1923; 'Einleitung'; p. 3. '...*dieser naive Glaube der griechisch-römischen Welt, der in Aegypten das Land der geheimen Weisheit sah, hat siebzehn Jahrhunderte überdauert ... Heute, wo wir die Denkmäler Aegyptens selbst kennen gelernt haben, wo wir seine Inschriften lesen und seine Literatur studieren, ist jeder Nimbus dahin; ...die alten Aegypter sind uns ein Volk geworden, das um nichts besser war und um nichts schlechter als andere Völker. Seine "Weisheit" zeigt sich bei näherem Zusehen teils als gering, teils als widersinnig und seine Sitten sind nicht absonderlicher als anderer Völker und verdienen weder unseren Spott, noch unseren Respekt.'*

20 For an overview see P. Burke, *Offene Geschichte. Die Schule der 'Annales'*. Berlin 1991. G. Duby used the definition of G. Bouthoule: ' "... *a certain kind of a stable psychological residue, consisting of opinions, conceptions and beliefs, which are basically shared by all individuals of a certain society ... a system of more or less clear mental concepts, that people more or less consciously abide by in their lives.*" ' (cited after Josef Válka, 'Historikova konstruktivní imaginace' ['The constructing imagination of the historian'] – Afterword to the 3rd volume of Duby's *Vznešené paní z 12. století*. ['Noble ladies of the 12th century'] Prague 1999; p. 138). Duby himself was well aware of the problems inherent to this term, he tried to define it several times and currently the term is no longer generally accepted even by the members of the *Annales* school. A new definition appeared instead, presented by M. Foucault – '... *a more productive perspective of that shared base, that forms the rules of discourse of a certain period.*' (J. Válka), the so-called. 'archaeology of knowledge' (cf. J. Válka, *op. cit.*).

21 Cf. Horský, Jan, 'Myšlení a cítění autonomie vědomí, individuum' ('Thinking and feeling of the autonomy of consciousness, the individual') in: *id.*, ed., *Kulturní a sociální skutečnost v dějezpytném myšlení*. ('Cultural and social reality in historiographical thinking'), Ústí n. Labem 1997.

22 E. Bernheim, quoted after the Czech edition: *Úvod do studia dějepisu*, Laichter Prague 1931; p. 40. The German text of this introduction was published several times at the turn of the century. Bernheim however also expressed slightly diverging views.

23 Cit. Glanville after Müller, Ch., in *GM* 12 1974, pp. 51ff.

24 Cf. similarly Horn, J., *GM* 12, 1974, p. 46. Assmann, J., 'Einführung' in *Stein und Zeit. Mensch und Gesellschaft im alten Ägypten*, München 1997, p. 11: *'Ein Ägyptologe kann es sich nicht leisten, ganz in der Spezialisierung aufzugehen, zu der er wie jeder andere Wissenschaftler durch die Entwicklung seines Faches gezwungen wird. So wird er sich vielleicht,*

um ein beliebiges Beispiel herauszugreifen, als Philologe für eine bestimmte Textgattung interessieren. Wenn er dem Kontext dieser Texte nachgeht, wird er sich aber notgedrungen auch z. B. mit ägyptischen Gräbern beschäftigen und das bedeutet: mit Ikonographie und Architektur, Sozial- und Verwaltungsgeschichte, Totenkult und Jenseitsvorstellungen, und er wird sich im Bemühen um ein besseres Verständnis dieser Quellen auch nach Kräften in den verschiedensten Richtungen theoretischer und vergleichender Ansätze umschauen: in der Sprach- und Literaturwissenschaft, der Sozial- und Religionswissenschaft, in der Kunsttheorie und vergleichenden Rechtsgeschichte. Der Ägyptologe ist ein notorischer Dilettant: immer etwas nachhinkend in der Entwicklung theoretischer Fragestellungen und Methoden, weil er sich auf zu vielen Gebieten gleichzeitig auf Laufenden zu halten versuchen muss, aber dafür ein gern gesehener Gast im interdisziplinären Gespräch, weil von Ägypten her zu so gut wie allem Wichtiges und oft Überraschendes beizutragen ist.' Junge, F., 'Linguistik und Ägyptologie', *GM* 10, 1974 or Assmann, J., 'Ägyptologie und Linguistik', *GM* 11, 1974. Also Sethe, *Der Alte Orient,* l.c., *'Die Ägyptologie oder ägyptische Altertumskunde beschäftigt sich mit den Spuren menschlichen Lebens aus vergangener Zeit, die in Ägypten hervortreten',* pp. 8 and 35. If we want to find an insight into the opinion of modern historians, we could also cite the classical work of Marc Bloch, *Apologie pour l'histoire ou metier de l'historien.* Paris 1993 (this is a version edited by Etienne Bloch. I used its Italian edition *Apologia della storia,* Torino 1998). While for Sethe, the Egyptologist is concerned with the *'traces of human life of the past'* on Egypt's territory; the historian Bloch considers general history to be the *'science concerned with people in time'* (Bloch, M., *op. cit.,* p. 28). In terms of the formal delimitation of sources and subject of study we are, therefore, in my opinion well justified to maintain the inclusion of Egyptology into historical science, because it deals with a certain temporally and spatially delimited section of human history in its complexity, using methods that at least current historical sciences fully accept as their own. The same conclusion was reached already by D. B. Redford, 'Egyptology and History' in Weeks, K. ed. *Egyptology and Social Sciences.* Cairo 1979. The structuralist trend is also shared by more social sciences, including historical science as a whole (cf. Loprieno, Antonio, 'Einleitung', *Topos und Mimesis. Ausländer in der ägyptischen Literatur. ÄA* 48. Wiesbaden 1988; pp. 3–4).

25 His steady opponents included, despite the fact that their argumentation was in the end refuted, for example Seyffarth. Cf. the relevant entry in *Who was Who in Egyptology.* London 1995.

26 Wortham, John David, *British Egyptology 1549–1906.* Univ. of Oklahoma 1971 passim and Keel, Othmar, 'Die Rezeption ägyptischer Bilder als Dokumente der biblischen Ereignisgeschichte (Historie) im 19. Jahrhundert' in: Elisabeth Staehelin – Betrand Jaeger, *Ägypten – Bilder. OBO* 150, 1997.

27 So far I was unfortunately unable to consult the articles of F. G. Vigouroux from the 1870s and 1880s (cf. Beinlich-Seeber, Ch., *Bibliographie Altägypten 1822–1946.* Vol. II, J–Z. *ÄA* 61. Wiesbaden 1998; p. 1685 entries 20150 and 20151), which contain period commentaries of new Egyptological discoveries and their relationship to Biblical events.

28 Fischer, H., 'Ägyptologisches Wissenschaftsverständnis im Deutschland' in: Fischer, H., *Der Ägyptologe Georg Ebers. Eine Fallstudie zum Problem Wissenschaft und Öffentlichkeit,* published in the series *Ägypten und Altes Testament,* 25, 1994, directed by M. Görg, and also Sethe, 'Die Ägyptologie. Zweck, Inhalt und Bedeutung dieser Wissenschaft und Deutschlands Anteil an ihrer Entwicklung', *Der Alte Orient* 23. passim.

29 For German countries cf. Helck, *Ägyptologie,* passim. However, in 1891 Heinrich Brugsch still writes concerning Austrian Egyptology *'Der österreichische Kaiserstaat, dessen altägyptischen Sammlungen im Ambrasser Museum und in der kaiserlichen Burg zu Wien Kapitalstücke von höchsten Werthe aufweisen, hat leider nur eine kleine Zahl von*

Ägyptologen herausgebildet.' (Brugsch, H., *Die Ägyptologie. Abriss der Entzifferungen und Forschungen.* Leipzig 1891; p. 142). He mentions the work of Dr. Simon Leo Reinisch. For the life of S. L. Reinisch, cf. the monograph of H. G. Mukarovsky et al., *Leo Reinisch. Werk und Erbe.* Österreichische Akademie der Wissenschaften. Philosophisch-historische Klasse, Sitzungsberichte 492. Bd., Wien 1987. 'The father of African studies' Reinisch was invited by the Emperor Maximilian to Mexico and in 1867 he indeed arrived at the country in order to assume the post of the director of the Mexican National Museum. This project of course did not outlive Maximilian's reign.

Further also Ernst Knight Bergmann (E. von Bergmann took part in the organisation of the collection of aegyptiaca in the Evangelical lyceum in Pressburg, i.e. Bratislava. Cf. Hudec, J., *Egyptské zbierky na Slovensku* ['Egyptian Collections in Slovakia'] doktorská práca, Praha 1997 UK FF. p. IX.) Finally univ. doc. (Assistant Professor) dr. Jacob Krall (his name can be encountered in connection with one of the papyri in the collection of the Viennese Nationalbibliothek – the so-called Papyrus Krall, which he published for the first time in *Demotische Lesestücke II.* Wien 1903. For a newer publication see Bresciani, E., *Der Kampf um den Panzer des Inaros.* Wien 1964. Cf. also Bresciani, E., *Letteratura e poesia dell'antico Egitto.* Torino 1990; pp. 922ff. and also *Who was who,* 3rd ed.; p. 232).

S. L. Reinisch is also known as the founder of African Studies and his Egyptological work is always seen in the context of his African studies. (Cf. also Thausing, G. or Duchateau, A. in Mukarovsky et al., *Leo Reinisch*) and this way he also taught his students. His work was of crucial importance for the formation of Egyptology in Austria. In 1861 he was habilitated at the Faculty of Arts in the discipline 'history of ancient Orient, including Egypt' (cf. Anders, F. in Mukarovsky et al., *Leo Reinisch,* pp. 9ff. '*Geschichte des Orients im Altertum mit Einschluss Ägyptens*'. Already in 1898 the authors of the *Geschichte der Wiener Universität 1848–1898.* Wien 1898; p. 325 write that he was habilitated '*für Alte Geschichte und Ägyptologie*'). He also took active part in the organisation of collections of aegyptiaca, such as the large collection of Archduke Maximilian (in 1864) which was originally deposited in the Miramare castle at Trieste (Cf. also Anders, F. in Mukarovsky et al., *Leo Reinisch.* The Archduke acquired his collection during his visit of Egypt in 1855.). The catalogue of the collection was published in 1865 (under the title *Die Ägyptische Denkmäler in Miramar*). In 1868 Reinisch was appointed extraordinary Professor of Egyptology. In 1873, resp. 1874, (*Geschichte der Wiener Universität 1848–1898;* p. 325.) he became ordinary Professor '*der ägyptischen Sprache und Altertumskunde*' (Cf. Anders in Mukarovsky et al., *op. cit.*). Finally in 1896–7 he was the chancellor of the Vienna University (*Geschichte der Wiener Universität 1848–1898,* p. 40.). He continued to represent the field of Egyptology until the year 1881, when Jacob Krall (1857–1905) was habilitated. He in turn was appointed extraordinary Professor in 1890 – in '*ancient history of the Orient*'. Since 1897 he was ordinary Professor (*Geschichte der Wiener Universität 1848–1898,* p. 361).

30 For example the stay of Heinrich Brugsch in Prague, where he was the guest of the Crown prince, the Hapsburg Archduke Rudolf. Cf. Brugsch, H., *Mein Leben und Mein Wandern,* pp. 357ff. and B. Hamann, *op. cit.*

31 For an overview of the history of the Department of History see K. Kazbunda, *Stolice dějin na pražské univerzitě* ('The chair of history at the Prague University'). Prague I-III, 1964–68.

32 Cf. Kutnar – Marek, *Přehledné dějiny,* e.g. pp. 350–353f. Höffler also supported Jaroslav Goll who retained, just like his teacher, an interest in a very broad field of history. See Jar. Marek, *Jaroslav Goll.* Prague 1991; p. 55.

33 The employment of German professors was common in the formative phase of the

teaching of both Classical philology and ancient history. For Classical philology cf. Svatoš, M., *Česká klasická filologie* (Czech Classical philology), pp. 24–25. This way for example the Berlin Professor Georg Curtius taught at the Prague Faculty of Arts.

34 Jaroslav Marek, *Jaroslav Goll*. Prague 1991; p. 137 and pp. 141–142.

35 Marek, *Jaroslav Goll*. p. 142.

36 Kazbunda, *op. cit.*, III, pp. 243f. This was also my source for the scholarly biographies of J. V. Prášek a Emanuel Peroutka.

37 *Přehled přednášek kteréž se odbývati budou na c. k. české Karlo-Ferdinandské univerzitě v Praze.* ('List of lectures that will be held at the Imperial and Royal Czech Carlo-Ferdinand University in Prague'). Charles University Archive call numbers B 900/2 for years 1882–1892, B 901/2 for 1892–1902. B 902 for 1902–1908. Sections 'Faculty of Arts – Historical sciences'.

38 For a positive appraisal of Prášek's importance for the popularisation of ancient Oriental history in the Czech lands and of his work with primary sources, see Otakar Klíma, *ArOr* 22, 1954.

39 Cf. the complete list of Prášek's publications – Ježilová, *AUC Philologica* 3/1980.

40 The discussion around Prášek's habilitation is also mentioned by Svatoš, M., *Česká klasická filologie na pražské univerzitě 1848–1917 (Působení Jana Kvíčaly a Josefa Krále).* ('Czech classical philology at the Prague university 1848–1917 – the work of Jan Kvíčala and Josef Král'). Prague 1995; p. 122 and Svoboda, K., *Antika a česká vzdělanost od obrození do první války světové* ('Antiquity and Czech Education since the Enlightenment to the First World War'). Prague 1957; pp. 263–264.

41 For a biography of J. Černý see e.g. T. G. H. James, 'Jaroslav Černý', *JEA* 57, 1971, p. 185f.

42 Archive of the National Museum (further ANM), box 5 of the estate of J. V. Prášek, file 462.

43 E.g. in the letter of 14. 12. 1923, where he writes '*I am working on my book on the Theban Necropolis. I held one lecture about ancient Egypt, now I am preparing another one on Tutankhamun. I maintain busy correspondence with Prof. Peet of Liverpool … I am now editing* 'Egyptské čarodejnictví' (Egyptian Magic) which Prof. Lexa is about to publish, etc.', the cited file.

44 A lodging facility for distinguished students and young scholars. The candidates were admitted on the grounds of their scholarly success.

45 Letter of 21. 12. 1922, after Černý's graduation on 20. 12., file 462, box 5, J. V. Prášek collection. It may of course be considered as a very formal expression of gratitude, but on the other hand, it may express true persuasion about Prášek's contribution to the gradual development of Oriental philology in the Czech lands. The latter is indicated also by Černý's lasting respect for Prášek, seen for example in the correspondence, which he maintained until Prášek's death. Their correspondence included, moreover, usual family greetings and information. Thus we meet in these letters a fiancée of Černý's. The name of the lady is unknown, and she disappeared after a few letters. She is a hitherto unknown and completely unexplored moment in Černý's life.

46 Letter from 24. 11. 1924, cited file.

47 File 544, box no. 5. J. V. Prášek, ANM.

48 File 696, box no. 7. J. V. Prášek, ANM.

49 Cf. *Bibliographie des oeuvres de Gaston Maspero*. Paris 1922; pp. 38, 58, 82.

50 File 603, Box no. 6. J. V. Prášek, ANM. In the letter of 22. 11. 1898, Knudtzon writes: '*Sie fragten, welcher Name in der Berliner Ausgabe der El-Amarna Tafeln Nr. 39 Z.(eile) 24 u.(nd) 28 zu lesen ist, Ja-u-du oder Su-u-du. An beiden Stellen ist u-du deutlich…*' There follows an analysis of the individual signs.

51 File 760, box no. 7, cited collection.

52 File 511, box no. 5, cited collection informs on the Orientalistic Congress in Rome, planned for October 1899 and for the conditions of partaking.

53 File 828, box no. 8, cited collection.

54 File 869, box no. 8, cited collection.

55 File 936, box no. 8, cited collection.

56 File 838, box no. 8., cited collection.

57 W. Dörpfeld, German archaeologist, an important figure of the German archaeological school of the 19th century.

58 A famous poet, and later an army inspector of the Czechoslovak Republic after 1918.

59 Kazbunda, *op. cit.*, III, p. 249, note 12, and p. 252, note 18.

60 *Přehled přednášek kteréž se odbývati budou na c. k. české Karlo-Ferdinandské univerzitě v Praze.* ('List of lectures that will be held at the Imperial and Royal Czech Carlo-Ferdinand University in Prague') Since WS 1904/05 to WS 1912/13. The academic year is divided into winter and summer semester abbreviated as WS a SS with the relevant dates. I have used the lists in the archive of the Charles University with call numbers B 900/2 for years 1882–1892, B 901/2 for 1892–1902. B 902 for 1902–1908 and B 929 for 1908–1912. B 930/3 for 1912–1917. Since 1918 the volumes are not bound. Since SS 1919 the list bears the title *Seznam přednášek, které se budou konati na české universitě Karlově v Praze* ('List of lectures to be held at the Czech Charles University in Prague').

61 For J. Goll this may have brought a relief from an ever growing number of duties. This is the explanation of Jaroslav Marek, *Jaroslav Goll*, p. 227.

62 Kazbunda, *Stolice dějin* III, pp. 252–253.

63 Marek, *Jaroslav Goll*, pp. 141–142.

64 *Přehled přednášek kteréž se odbývati budou na c. k. české Karlo-Ferdinandské univerzitě v Praze.* Since WS 1904/05 to WS 1912/13.

65 Verner et al., *František Lexa, zakladatel české egyptologie* ('František Lexa, the founder of Czech Egyptology'), AUC Philosophica et Historica 4 – 1984. Prague 1989; p. 22.

66 *Ibid.*

67 For details on his life and career cf. *František Lexa, zakladatel české egyptologie.* AUC Philosophica et Historica 4 –1984. Prague 1989. For some details see also below, in the end the section *Oriental Studies at the Prague University.*

68 Josef Šusta (1874-1945), for basic biographical data cf. Kutnar – Marek, *Přehled*; pp. 502–511 His work *Úvahy o všeobecných dějinách* ('Contemplations on general history') cited according to the new edition Prague 1999.

69 Šusta, *Úvahy*, p. 40.

70 Šusta, *Úvahy*, p. 43.

71 Šusta, *Úvahy*, p. 51.

72 Šusta, *Úvahy*, p. 42.

73 Šusta, *Úvahy*, p. 44.

74 Kazbunda, *Stolice* II, p. 162.

75 Josef Petráň, *Nástin dějin filozofické fakulty Univerzity Karlovy*, ('Outline of the history of the Faculty of Arts of the Charles University'). Prague 1983; p. 178.

76 Cf. *Přehled předn.* WS 1907–1908, p. 32, Prof. Vysoký.

77 Cf. Kutnar – Marek, *Dějepisectví*, according to index.

78 Petráň, *Nástin*, p. 244.

79 *Přehled přednášek* WS 1909–1910.

80 'O významu studia dějin starého umění orientalního' ('On the importance of the study of the history of ancient Oriental art'), the inaugural lecture of Dr. Mir. Tyrš at the Prague University, *Časopis Musea království Českého* 1883; pp. 285f.

81 Tyrš, *ČČM* 1883, p. 300. A different expression of the same opinion can be found in

the works of some modern art historians, e.g. E. Gombrich, of course now without the value judgements, which Gombrich himself analyses on the basis of some older works, such as that of Schäfer (*Idem*, 'Introduction', passim).

82 Among those who believed the thesis of the deeply rooted conservatism of the Egyptian culture, which later developed into a European cultural topos (cf. the opinion of František Šembera below in the section on educational literature), we find J. J. Winckelmann (see Helck, W. *Ägyptologie*, p. 4), but also Quatremére de Quincy (French Neoclassicist architect and admirer of Greek art; alongside Egyptian art, though, he also denounced the Gothic style); whom Tyrš criticised in the cited article. Also Plato expressed his thesis of immutability being a trait of the Egyptian artistic canon – cf. Assmann, J., *Weisheit und Mysterium.* München 2000; p. 48. He appreciated the fixed norms, that allowed expression of more permanent values in art that contemporary Greek art made, according to his opinion, possible.

83 Tyrš, *ČČM*, 1883, p. 287.

84 Turek, Ant., 'Sbírky Tyršovy' ('Tyrš's collections'), *Osvěta* 15, 1885; p. 1012.

85 Turek, *op. cit.*, pp. 623–625.

86 Sokol – 'the Falcon' – mainly a sport organisation, uniting men and women under the banner of the Classical ideal of mental and physical training. It had, moreover, a somewhat paramilitary character in details. M. Tyrš was the founder of this organisation.

87 F. Čenský, *Osvěta* 14, 1884, vol. 2, p. 871.

88 Fr. Zákrejs, *Osvěta* 14, 1884 vol. 2, p. 1060.

89 For a short overview of Tyrš's activities and some brief remarks cf. also Verner et al., *František Lexa. Zakladatel české egyptologie*, p. 27 and J. Bečka, *Nový Orient*, 39, 1984.

90 Jůzl, M., *Otakar Hostinský.* Prague 1980; pp. 336ff.

91 For a brief summary of Woltmann's activities cf. Kutnar – Marek, *Přehledné dějiny*, pp. 301 and 356.

92 Jůzl, *O. Hostinský*, pp. 218-219.

93 For a list see Jůzl, *op. cit.*, p. 336. Similarly also in the case of the chapters of the book that Hostinský was preparing for publication – *Stručný přehled dějin hudby.* ('A short overview of the history of music'. *Ibid.*, p. 185).

94 Viz *Přehled přednášek kteréž se odbývati budou na c. k. české Karlo-Ferdinandské univerzitě v Praze.* WS 1882–83; p. 9. Lecture 'Egypt, geographical image'. Jan Palacký is also known as a collector of aegyptiaca – cf. the database of Náprstek Museum in Prague. Jan Palacký's collection was, however, more extensive. Numbers P 2406 to P 2410 of Náprstek Museum stand above all for eye inlays.

95 For a summary on this theme cf. also Mendel, M. – Bečka, J., *Islám a české země* ('Islam and the Czech Lands'). Prague 1997.

96 In *Riegrův slovník naučný* ('Rieger's educational dictionary' *Slovník naučný, red. Dr. F. L. Rieger,* Prague 1866, L. Kober.) 'aegyptologie' belongs to sciences, that deal with the study of Oriental languages (*op. cit.*, Vol. V; p. 1105). Similarly Egyptian is considered an Oriental language in Otto's dictionary (*Ottův slovník naučný – Illustrovaná encyklopedie všeobecných vědomostí* ('Otto's educative dictionary – an illustrated encyclopaedia of general knowledge'; Vol. XVIII Prague 1902; p. 865, entry by Rudolf Dvořák), together with Chinese, resp. Sinology.

97 Cf. Segert, S. – Beránek, K., *Orientalistik an der Prager Universität. 1348–1848.* Prague 1967. Also Zbavitel, D., *L'Orientalisme en Tchécoslovaquie.* Prague 1959; passim. Cf. also the bibliography for the history of Orientalistic disciplines in *Kdo je kdo. Čeští a slovenští orientalisté, afrikanisté a iberoamerikanisté.* (further *Orientalisté*). Prague 1999.

98 This word is to be understood historically, without its pejorative aspects.

99 For the contemporary definition of the term cf. also several very interesting obser-

vations in: *Orient. Österreichische Malerei zwischen 1848 und 1914.* Exhibition catalogue compiled by Erika Mayr-Oehring, Residenzgalerie Salzburg 1997. They occur already in the Introduction on p. 11, where the author stresses the importance of the Napoleonic expedition, resp. above all of books such as the Description of Egypt, which were its result, for the stimulation of the general interest in the Orient. Here we must note that in the context of the 19th century Orient was considered to cover the entire area of the Mediterranean, Near East, and also Greece and the Balkans. This list appears on p. 28 by Martina Haja *'Man verstand darunter alle islämischen Länder im südlichen und östlichen Mittelmeer: der Maghreb im Westen, die Levante im Osten mit Ägypten, Palästina und Syrien, ebenso Griechenland, die Balkanländer und die Krim; selbstverständlich Türkei, die Arabische Halbinsel, Mesopotamien und Persien...'* Contemporary Czech source, *Ottův slovník naučný. Illustrovaná encyklopedie všeobecných vědomostí,* Vol. XVIII Prague 1902; p. 864, writes *'Orient (lat.), east, major direction, where the sun rises, and thus also the countries lying in the east, to the east of Italy. Now Asia Minor, Syria and Egypt are called the Orient.'* The somewhat older *Slovník naučný,* ed. Dr. F. L. Rieger. Prague, L. Kober 1866. Vol. V, M-Ožice; p. 1104-5, has the following *'the term Orient thus signifies Asian countries, and sometimes also the European Turkey...'*

100 *Orientalisté,* p. 236.
101 Josef Petráň, *Nástin dějin filosofické fakulty Univerzity Karlovy v Praze (do roku 1948),* p. 160.
102 *Přehled přednášek kteréž se odbývati budou na c. k. české Karlo-Ferdinandské univerzitě v Praze.* WS 1884-85; p. 23, 'Morphology of the Arabic language', 'Practical grammar of the Turkish language', and a public lecture on Confucius. A very wide selection reaching over the scope of the contemporary definition of the Orient, but not of Oriental sciences.
103 He was habilitated in 1884, in 1890 he became extraordinary, in 1896 ordinary Professor. Cf. Petráň, *Nástin,* p. 247.
104 Petráň, *Nástin,* p. 209. The same seems to follow from the lecture plan *Přehled přednášek kteréž se odbývati budou na c. k. české Karlo-Ferdinandské univerzitě v Praze;* since 1885.
105 Cf. *Přehled přednášek kteréž se odbývati budou na c. k. české Karlo-Ferdinandské univerzitě v Praze.* WS 1886–87. p. 22.
106 Cf. *Orientalisté,* p. 117, with selected bibliography.
107 In this context we understand 'public lectures' as those marked in the list of lectures of the university as *publicum,* or *publice.*
108 Including individual articles and reviews. See *Athenaeum,* passim – the journal was published between 1883–1893.
109 *Athenaeum* 5, (1887–1888), p. 273–280.
110 For an overview and bibliography see *LÄ* IV, cols. 895-897, 'Papyrussammlung der Österreichischen Nationalbibliothek.'
111 Petráň, *Nástin,* p. 247.
112 See the list of lectures, since WS 1884/85. (*Přehled přednášek* for the relevant semesters).
113 *Přehled přednášek kteréž se odbývati budou na c. k. české Karlo-Ferdinandské univerzitě v Praze.* WS 1884–85; and following until the end of his activities in 1920.
114 E. g. *Přehled /Seznam přednášek* WS 1891–92; p. 20 and WS 1893–94; p. 22.
115 *Přehled přednášek kteréž se odbývati budou na c. k. české Karlo-Ferdinandské univerzitě v Praze.* At least since WS 1905–06.
116 *Orientalisté,* p. 420–421. He was habilitated in 1909 (Petráň, *Nástin,* p. 247). For an overview of his professional career, cf. Petráček, K., 'Prof. Dr. Rudolf Růžicka zum 75. Geburtstag', *ArOr* 22, 1954.

117 Cf. *Seznam přednášek.* Since SS 1910, Egyptian Arabic in WS 1910–1911; p. 45.

118 *Seznam přednášek.* Since SS 1919.

119 For his brief biography and bibliography see *Orientalisté,* pp. 340ff. Also one whole issue of *Archiv Orientální* – 63, 1995 – was dedicated to him, further cf. Navrátilová, H. – Míšek, R., 'Alois Musil and the Rise of Czech Oriental Studies', *ArOr* 70/4, 2002.

120 Petráň, *Nástin,* p. 331.

121 *Seznam přednášek.* SS 1920 p. 52, 'Reading and analysis of selected ancient Egyptian texts'; 'Reading and analysis of selected Coptic texts'.

122 For Lexa's biography and professional career cf. *František Lexa, zakladatel české egyptologie. AUC Philosophica et Historica* 4–1984. Prague 1989, passim.

123 This name of the language seemingly alternates with 'Egyptian'. For example *Seznam přednášek* for WS 1911–1912, p. 5, has the latter variant.

124 *Přehled přednášek kteréž se odbývati budou na c. k. české Karlo-Ferdinandské univerzitě v Praze.* WS 1908–09

125 W. B. Oerter, 'Nejnovější poznatky v dějinách pražské egyptologie' ('Most recent discoveries in the history of Prague Egyptology'), *PES* 1/2002, pp. 180–181. Also W. B. Oerter, 'Archivalische Lesefrüchte', *GM* 191/2002, pp. 71–73. New discoveries are, however, still expected in this field, as the research of W. Oerter is still in progress.

126 Due to the primarily philological orientation of František Lexa, Egyptology is for example in the *Nástin dějin filosofické fakulty Univerzity Karlovy v Praze* of Josef Petráň (Prague 1983; p. 306) grouped with comparative linguistics and Oriental sciences.

127 Despite the fact that *Ottův slovník naučný* Vol. 23, Prague 1905, p. 1064 states that '*Speaking of Classical Antiquity, above all in the political and cultural context we mean the period that covers the history of the Greeks and Romans, but at the same time also of the nations, that were in contact with these two Classical nations (Egyptians, Phoinicians, Medes, Persians, etc.)*'

128 Egyptology is included in the field of the sciences of Oriental languages, i.e. in Oriental philology, already since the 19th century. Even Czech educational dictionaries, from the so-called 'Rieger's' (1866) to that of 'Komenský' (1938) know 'Oriental philology' and include within it a broad array of disciplines from Sinology to Egyptology. Cf. *Slovník naučný, red. F. L. Rieger.* Prague 1866 L. Kober. Vol. V M-Ožice; p. 1105, entry 'orientálský'; also *Ottův slovník naučný – Encyklopedie všeobecných vědomostí* – Vol. XVIII Prague 1902; p. 864–5, entry 'oriental philology'; and *Komenského slovník naučný,* Prague 1938; p. 430 Vol. 'Míle-Perštejn', entry 'orientalistika (orientální filologie)'.

129 For a comprehensive overview see Patrick Conner, *The Inspiration of Egypt – Its Influence on British Artists, Travellers and Designers 1700–1900.* Brighton 1983 and also Wortham, *British Egyptology 1549–1906.*

130 Cf. Wortham, *British Egyptology* and the relevant entries (W. Petrie and A. Edwards) in *Who was Who in Egyptology.*

131 Jan Lepař, secondary school teacher and writer.

132 He means the Classical philologist František Lepař. For the Lepař brothers see *Ottův slovník naučný,* Vol. 15, Prague 1900; p. 887.

133 Cf. *Problémy dějin historiografie VI.* ('Problems of the history of historiography') *AUC Philosophica et Historica 3,* Studia Historica XXXIX. Prague 1993; A. Gindely's bibliography, pp. 110ff, section 3.

134 August Horislav Škultéty (1819–1892). Cf. Kutnar – Marek, *Přehledné dějiny,* p. 348.

135 Svoboda, K., *Antika a česká vzdělanost od obrození do první války světové.* ('Classical Antiquity and Czech Education from the time of the Enlightenment to the First World War'). Prague 1957; p. 151.

136 Writer Jan Erazim Sojka (1826–1887), who took part in the unrests of 1848 and also spent some time in exile.

137 Svoboda, *Antika a česká vzdělanost od obrození do první války světové*, p. 169.

138 Cf. the J. V. Prášek collection, Archive of the National Museum (ANM), boxes 5–8 and the overview of Jarmila Pešková, *J. V. Prášek 1853–1924*. Prague 1993.

139 František Šembera (1842–1898), secondary school teacher. He worked in Německý Brod, České Budějovice, and in Prague. Cf. *Ottův slovník naučný*, Vol. 24, Prague 1906; p. 584: *'Because Czech historical literature still lacked a continuous general history, he began to collect and analyse material, on the basis of which he published …'* there follows a list of textbooks written by Šembera.

140 F. Šembera, *Dějepis všeobecný – Dějiny vzdělaných národů starověkých*. ('General history – history of the educated nations of antiquity' České Budějovice 1872, further Šembera, *Dějepis*).

141 According to his own list, the author had consulted the following publications: (underlined are the names of important contemporary Egyptologists) Duncker, Geschichte des Alterthums; Weber, Allgemeine Weltgeschichte; Bumüller, Geschichte des Alterthums; Guillemin, Histoire ancienne de l'Orient; Heeren, Ideen über die Politik, den Verkehr und den Handel der alten Welt; Carriere, Die Kunst im Zusammenhang der Culturentwicklung; Lübke. Grundriss der Kunstgeschichte; Schnaase, Geschichte der bildenden Künste; Lübke, Geschichte der Architektur; Geschichte der Plastik; Visual atlas to the educational dictionary with an explanation of Dr. Müller; Vögelin, Denkmäler der Weltgeschichte; Wuttke, Geschichte des Heidenthums; Pfleiderer, Die Religion, ihr Wesen und ihre Geschichte; Max Müller, Essays; Spiegel, Zendavesta; <u>Brugsch</u>, Histoire de l'Egypte; <u>Uhlemann</u>, Handbuch der ägyptischen Alterthumskunde; <u>Reinisch</u>, Aegyptus, in Pauly Realenzyklopädie; Mowers, Phönizer; Ewald, Geschichte des Volkes Israel; Duruy, L'histoire sainte; Kalthof, Handbuch der hebr. Alterthümer; De Wette, Lehrbuch der hebr. Archäologie; Stárek, Historie zjevení bibl. ('History of the Biblical revelation'); Meier, Geschichte der poetischen Nationalliteratur der Hebräer; Gumpach, Abriss der babyl. assyr. Geschichte; Kruger, Geschichte der Assyrier und Iranier; Lassen, Indische Alterthumskunde; A. Weber, Indische Literaturgeschichte; from the ancient ones Herodotus, Diodor and the Holy Scriptures. Šembera, *Dějepis*, p. 1.

142 Šembera, *Dějepis*, p. 7.

143 Šembera, *Dějepis*, p. 11. He surely found a convenient description of Egyptian landscape and natural conditions in Uhlemann, M. *Handbuch der gesammten aegyptischen Alterthumskunde* I-IV. Leipzig 1857–58, Vol. II, pp. 38f.

144 Šembera, *Dějepis*, p. 12-13.

145 So e.g. Maspero, Gaston, *Histoire Ancienne des peuples de L'Orient*, first ed. 1875, many others above all in the 1890s, revised as *Histoire Ancienne des peuples de L'Orient Classique* in the 1890s. Translated to English – *History of the ancient peoples of the classic East I: The dawn of civilization: Egypt and Chaldaea*. London 1894; passim. For example the characterisation of the Egyptian society and family – pp. 50ff. For bibliographical details see Beinlich-Seeber, Ch., *Bibliographie Altägypten 1822–1946*. Vol. II, J-Z. ÄA 61. Wiesbaden 1998; pp. 1112–1113, entries 13139–13143.

146 Cf. the period definition of nation, note above all the underlined terms (emphasis HN) – Ottův slovník naučný, Vol. 17, Prague 1901; p. 1046.: *'nation…a collective term for the members of one race, that have a <u>common origin</u>, common language, common manners, <u>customs and traditions</u>, a common <u>literature and education</u>.'*

147 Šembera, *Dějepis*, p. 17. Cf. the very similar definition of Brugsch, H., *Geschichte Aegyptens unter den Pharaonen*. Leipzig 1877; p. 24. Cited after this German edition (or version) of *Histoire*, if the text is analogous to the French version or variant

(which is, however, entered as an independent publication for example by Beinlich-Seeber, *Bibliographie Altägypten 1822–1946*. Vol. I see pp. 342–343.), which Šembera cites in his bibliography, this note may have come precisely from Brugsch. He could, however, also have used Herodotus, who also mentions that the Egyptians were very proud of their own long past.

148 Šembera, *Dějepis*, p. 16.
149 Šembera, *Dějepis*, p. 21 (Emphasis HN).
150 Šembera, *Dějepis*, p. 23.
151 Period dictionaries, concretely Ottův (Vol. 7, Prague 1893; p. 388) define the term 'despotism' as '*an arbitrary reign disregarding legal order and ethical norms*'. However, there is also a note that despotism is not exclusive to monarchies.
152 Including one of the most important historians of the 19th century Jacob Burckhardt (1818–1897) – '*Egypt... may have been an inspiration for other ancient Asian despotic regimes.*'
153 Soon there arose a discussion concerning the terminology. Cf. for example the summary in 'Problém typu nejstarších státu' ('The problem of the type of the most ancient states') Pečírka, J. et al., *Dějiny pravěku a starověku* ('Prehistory and ancient history') I. Prague 1989; pp. 158 ff.
154 Herodotus, II, 164.
155 Šembera, *Dějepis*, p. 25.
156 *Ibid*, p. 26.
157 Šembera, *Dějepis*, p. 28. Šembera may have taken the notion of emphasis on family care by the ancient Egyptians from Max Uhlemann. See Uhlemann, M., *Handbuch der gesammten aegyptischen Alterthumskunde* I-IV. Leipzig 1857–58. Vol. II, – part VII. 'Geselliges Leben', mainly pp. 273ff. Since however both Uhlemann and Šembera worked with the ancient works of Herodotus and Diodorus, Šembera may have formed his own opinion concerning some problems.
158 Šembera, *Dějepis*, p. 28, note 15.
159 Published in 1882 in Prague.
160 J. V. Prášek, *Všeobecný dějepis občanský I/1 – Dějiny východních Arijců a vzdělaných národů severoafrických*. ('General social history I/1 – the history of east Aryans and educated nations of North Africa') Prague 1882; pp. 114–115. (Further Prášek, *Všeobecný dějepis*).
161 Prášek, *Všeobecný dějepis*, p. 116.
162 Prášek, *Všeobecný dějepis*, p. 195.
163 Prášek, *Všeobecný dějepis*, pp. 197ff.
164 Prášek, *Všeobecný dějepis*, p. 206. He may have encountered this opinion by many of his western colleagues-historians – a discussion on this theme may be found already in Uhlemann's *Handbuch*, II, pp. 273f.
165 Prášek, *Všeobecný dejepis*, p. 203.
166 Cf. *LÄ* II, cols. 1045ff.
167 J. V. Prášek, *Ženy antické* (Ancient women). Prague s. a.; 'Foreword'.
168 *Ibid*, pp. 6ff.
169 Cf. on her *LÄ* VI, cols. 306ff.
170 Prášek, *Ženy*, p. 10. The same opinion was also expressed by William Groff, an American scholar, who also made this identification (Fischer, H., *Der Ägyptologe Georg Ebers. Eine Fallstudie zum Problem Wissenschaft und Öffentlichkeit*, p. 296, note 1).
171 For further details see Ahmose – *LÄ* I, cols. 102ff., Ahhotep – *LÄ* I, cols. 98ff.
172 For more literature see *LÄ* II, cols. 1045ff.
173 For an overview of older books concerned with Egyptian history cf. Helck, *Ägyptologie*, p. 23 and Beinlich-Seeber, Ch., *Bibliographie Altägypten 1822–1946*. Vol I–II, ÄA 61. Wiesbaden 1998.
174 The Prague University Library owns also some works of H. Brugsch and A. Mariette.

Despite the fact that the catalogue entries (all here cited publications have original handwritten catalogue cards) do not mention the year when the books became part of the Clementinum collection, we may presume that it was not very long after the publication date. The General Catalogue I includes Brugsch's works *Die Aegyptologie* (Leipzig 1891, call number 23 E 24 b) or *L'Exode et les monuments égyptiens* (Leipzig 1895, call number 24 G 152), *Histoire d'Égypte* (Leipzig 1875, call number 22 D 399) and others. The books of A. Mariette include for example the work published by his pupil Maspero, *Monuments divers recueillis en Égypte et en Nubie par A. Mariette – Pacha. Texte par G. Maspero*. Paris 1889, call number 23 A 380. Bibliographical information acquired from the scanned catalogues of the National Library (http://www.nkp.cz).

175 German Egyptologist Karl Alfred Wiedemann (1856–1936) was a student of Lepsius, and worked in Bonn. His works include the still valued overview of ancient sources for Egyptian history. Cf. *Who was Who*, 3rd ed., p. 440.

176 This definition is based on the modern distinction of literary genres.

177 Published by Ed. Grégr, directed by Václav Vlček.

178 In connection with new discoveries, connected with ancient Orient in general (not just Egypt) we often meet the name of J. V. Prášek, see below.

179 *Osvěta* 12, 1882, Kalousek, 'Nové písemnictví, Dějepis a zeměpis', ('New literacy, history and geography') pp. 83ff.

180 Kalousek, *Osvěta* 12, p. 84.

181 Kalousek, *l. c.*

182 In this context the articles in Osvěta were not the only form of popularisation. Periodicals such as *ZÄS* were cited for example also in *Athenaeum* (1883–1893).

183 *Osvěta* 18, 1888, Vol. II, p. 918–927. For Amarna cf. the bibliography of Martin, G. T., *A Bibliography of the Amarna period and its Aftermath. The reigns of Akhenaten, Smenkhkare, Tutankhamun and Ay* (c. 1350–1321 B.C.). London 1991, 1992.

184 Prášek, *Osvěta* 18, p. 923 ('Geschichte') and 924 (*ZÄS*).

185 Prášek, *Osvěta* 18, p. 924.

186 *Lumír* 3, 1875, pp. 573–575; 585–587; 595–598; 606–609; 619–621. Then under the same title in the collected volume *Spisy Julia Zeyera XXXIV*. ('The works of Julius Zeyer') Prague 1907; 5th ed., 1939 – the pages in the citations here are given after this edition. On this text see also B. Vachala, 'Literární odkaz starověkého Egypta a jeho zpřístupnění českému čtenáři Františkem Lexou' ('The literary heritage of ancient Egypt and its presentation to the Czech readers by František Lexa') in *František Lexa*, pp. 67ff.

187 *Spisy Julia Zeyera XXXIV*, pp. 3ff.

188 *Spisy Julia Zeyera XXXIV*, p. 7.

189 *Spisy Julia Zeyera XXXIV*, pp. 9-10.

190 *Spisy Julia Zeyera XXXIV*, p. 11.

191 *Spisy Julia Zeyera XXXIV*, p. 13.

192 Brugsch, H., *Geschichte Aegyptens unter den Pharaonen*. Leipzig 1877; mainly pp. 21–22 for the general joyous trait in the Egyptian national character; for the substantiation of state repressions see p. 26. (Probably the German version of the work *Histoire de l'Égypte ancienne*, which was published already in 1859 and which we have encountered in the bibliography of František Šembera).

193 Viz Poucha, *op. cit.,* p. 569.

194 Viz Vachala, *op. cit.,* in *Lexa*. For modern translations and analyses see Fox, M. V., *The Song of Songs and the Ancient Egyptian Love Songs*. London – Madison. 1985 and Mathieu, B., *La poesie amoureuse de l'Égypte ancienne. Recherches sur un genre littéraire au Nouvel Empire*. Le Caire 1996.

195 *Spisy Julia Zeyera XXXIV*, pp. 63–64.

196 Morenz, *Begegnung*, p. 187.

197 Fischer, *op. cit.*, p. 94: '*In Ägypten gibt es eine Möglichkeit, nackte Badende, lichtbekleidete Tänzerinnen, schlafende Haremsdamen, Grausamkeit und Brutalität, Sklavinnenmarkt und Nilopfer, im Großformat darzustellen, alles was weit entfernt scheint, vom Fortschritt, vom "Humanismus" und der "Zivilisation" des Westens und der Moderne.*' Similar opinions can also be found by G. Frodl particularly on Hans Makart, 'Wiener Orientmalerei', *Alte und Moderne Kunst* 26 (1981) no. 178–179; pp. 19–25. P. 22: '*Er ist einer jener Künstler, für die der Orient ein gesellschaftliches Reiseabenteuer mit exotischem Austrich blieb. Der erotische Unterton, den die ägyptischen Bilder Makarts anschlagen (und nicht nur sie), wurde vom Publikum in diesem Fall gutgeheißen und begrüßt, da man wußte, daß im Orient freiere Sitten herrschten.*' In general see also Henri Marchal in the introduction to *Les Orientalistes I*, pp. 11–12; '*…pour échapper au puritanisme victorien ou au "moralisme bourgeois", les peintres transpossent sur un fond d'Orient onirique et voluptueux, les désirs, voite les phantasmes – dévoilés en des odalisques lascives – que leur génération n'osait exprimer sous les poids des conventions,*' and also Herman de Meulenaere and P. and V. Berko, *Ancient Egypt in the XIXth century painting*. Brussels 1992; pp. 88 and 94, '*All Egyptianizing paintings have one feature in common: the vision of Ancient Egypt they wish to transmit is that of a country of splendour, wealth and voluptuousness …*'

198 Ebers, G., *Egypt slovem i obrazem*, Vol. I, p. 116.

199 Ebers, *op. cit.*, pp. 130ff.

200 Cf. *Egypt slovem i obrazem II*, 'Translator's afterword'.

201 As Erman attests, *Mein Werden und mein Wirken*, 'In der Wissenschaft'.

202 Cf. also Vlček, T., *Praha 1900*. Prague 1986; p. 54.

203 For a basic overview of dialects see 'Dialects' in A. Atiya et al., *Coptic Encyclopaedia*. New York 1991.

204 Cf. Kazbunda, *Stolice dějin, I-III* passim.

The Baroque-styled Egyptian inspiration

III. The Egyptian Inspiration

'... artists strove to use the spirit of and the visual vocabulary of the dead culture in pursuit of a living art, and thus realized the potential latent for further development within a past culture, though producing an overall effect that the ancients would never have thought of. The gifted forger of antique art is doing the same. And sometimes scholars unintentionally pursue the same path in constructing hypotheses to explain a very fragmentary past.'

(Kemp, *Ancient Egypt. Anatomy of a civilization*)[1]

The artistic reflection of a historical reality

'There is no reality without interpretation, there is neither an innocent eye, nor an innocent ear.'[2]

The 19th century, in European context century of historicism, is visually represented mainly by the artistic renderings of the past. The themes, connected with, or taken from the past, were a common stratum, present in almost all European countries. However, the choice of period, and events portrayed, differs. Moreover, there are several genres or sub genres to be distinguished in the historical themes in art, both visual and literary. There are inspirations taken from the form of ancient art, there are compositions based on an attempt to paint or describe an important historical event or personality. Furthermore, the choice of space and time of history that interested the artists depends on their own sociocultural setting. A powerful moment has been national history, or the most glorious moments of a country's past. To this we must add the gradual revelation of ancient cultures and their art as well.

In order to inspire, a work of art, architecture, painting, statue, or text, need not at all be understood within the intentions of their creators. In some cases, even the author's definition of art differs from that of his contemporaries, of the subsequent generation, or of a different era.

Moreover, in the case of inspiration by ancient art, the degree of understanding of contemporary artistic conventions is also of great importance. That is, the modern artistic conventions have to be understood, in order to see to what degree they were able to modify, or to accept, the ancient art canon. This is especially clear in the case of inspiration with Egyptian art. Distortions of proportions and canon were frequent, and even the otherwise reliable publications of 19th century Egyptologists were not absolutely free from them. Heinrich Schäfer, a specialist in Egyptian art, points out the drawing of a cosmetic spoon in the works of the French scholar Prisse d'Avennes. The wooden spoon is carved into the shape of a young girl, whose chest is seen in

131

profile, and thus only the outline of one breast is indicated. Prisse, however, drew both breasts, as if the chest was depicted in a three-quarter view.[3] This error is understandable – the author of the drawing expected, and therefore also 'saw' something that corresponded to his own drawing habits.[4]

The artistic reflection of a historical reality is not limited merely to the direct or indirect inspiration with ancient art. The author of a work of art treats the past in many different ways. For example, he tries to create a copy of the original, and achieves it more or less successfully, or he finds inspiration in the works of others and either imitates them, or incorporates their motives into his own work.

He may, however, also strive to create a model of a historical event. This may serve as a decoration, or, alternatively, the author may reflect in his work his own ideas (or those of his patron) concerning a historical personality, incident, etc. Artistic reflection of a historical reality may thus create a fictitious history, or successfully support it. It may strive to evoke historicity or historical trustworthiness, or to create an impression of it. According to J. Marek,[5] art allows us to determine the presence or absence of historical consciousness. Art also enables us to trace the period development of historical knowledge. The 19th century witnessed the creation of paintings, which were characterised by the so-called archaeological precision.[6] They reflected, for example, recent archaeological discoveries, depicted museum objects, etc. On the other hand numerous works of Egyptomania belong rather to their time and its own artistic expression, than to the reflection of ancient Egypt.

Historical themes were treated both in pictorial and literary art, and in both cases, in order to interpret the works correctly, we must take into account the methods used by their authors.[7] For some genres, the methods were given, in the case of others, the author was free to choose. Nineteenth century authors reflected the general level of historical consciousness, and thus also the specialised knowledge. A century earlier, painters quite commonly dressed historical figures in modern garments. The rules changed also in literature, where a new genre – the historical novel – was born. In terms of content, it focussed above all on the European Middle Ages.

Historical Novel

Historical novels,[8] represented for example by the works of Walter Scott, are rich in descriptions. According to literary scholars, above all G. Lukács, their authors achieve historical credibility by letting their heroes act as was believed characteristic for the atmosphere of their times. This is seen as a qualitative advance against the pseudohistorical narratives of the 18th century.[9] It is questionable, whether the authors could study ancient society to the same extent as the mediaeval society. In the time, when ancient Egyptian literature and religion were only beginning to be understood, it was not easy to evoke a credible picture of ancient Egypt. A century later, working on his tetralogy *Joseph and his brothers*, Thomas Mann intensively studied Egyptological literature, cooperated with Egyptologists, and made use of his personal experience from his travels to Egypt.[10] He had, however, at his disposal an entirely different background of historical science than authors who wrote in the time when Champollion was only preparing for the final decipherment of the hieroglyphic script. Egyptological works thus, as soon as they were accessible, presented writers with new opportunities to access information about the ancient culture that fascinated them. In the second half of the 19th century, they could for example even enrich their works with paraphrases of original ancient Egyptian literary texts. Knowledge of ancient Egyptian literature[11] advanced slowly and the precision of translations grew only gradually. However, translations of some ancient Egyptian literary works began to be used quite early, in order to increase authenticity of historical novels (e.g. by B. Prus in his book *Farao*).[12]

Egyptomania had long been present in the literary field, as an example, we can mention the 18th century novel of abbé Terrasson *Sethos*. In the course of the 19th century, above all in its second half, more famous writers chose the Egyptian theme.

One of them, Boleslaw Prus (civil name Alexander Glowacki, 1847–1912), worked in the Polish environment, close to the Czech lands. His novel *Farao* is considered to have been inspired by Western literature. In 1862, Gustave Flaubert published his *Salammbo*, and this work is believed to have initiated the extension of the motifs of the historical novel outside Europe. However, this tendency did not wholly predominate the historical novel, and above all in Czech literature, nationalist themes continued to prevail. As example, we may mention the works of Alois Jirásek and V. B. Třebízský.[13]

Concerning Prus' *Farao*, which was published in 1895, literary scholar Karel Krejčí wrote: '*Now he had an opportunity to enfold a very thrilling storyline, full of unexpected twists and complications, into which he was able to originally incorporate the traditional, well-attested motifs of the genre (i.e. novel), such as the romanticism of secret societies, an underground labyrinth, a double, and exotic erotism in an almost mystery-like plot.*'[14] Mysteries, secret societies, and exotic erotism were motifs that general historical consciousness connected with ancient Egypt.[15] Just as the historical novel created its own Middle Ages, it also created its own ancient Egypt.

Historical text

A text, that carries information on a historical reality, is defined as a 'historical text'.[16] However, not every text that contains information about historical reality can be labelled as historical text in the narrow sense of the word, i.e. one that is composed in terms of the laws of historical rationalism.[17] Simplifying a little, scholarly texts can pass this definition. Historical novel can also be understood as a text that bears information on a historical reality, but not as a *stricto sensu* historical text.

If we, however, decided to conceive the term historical text in its widest sense, it would then subsume any text containing information about a historical reality or its reflection. Such an extension could in my opinion be adopted in the case we apply for it the same measure as for the iconic historical text, resp. the iconic presentation of history, which stands 'outside the limits of historical science'.[18]

While the last paragraphs were concerned above all with written text, other categories of historical text – spoken and iconic text[19] – should not be neglected either. Such a division and definition of text allows us to subject its individual forms to the rules of interpretation, which have been delimited for the individual subfields.[20] The rules of the reception of a written and iconic text, of its semiotics, are defined in the relevant publications, e.g. of Umberto Eco.[21] In short, each message, and therefore each text, is written in a certain 'code'. In order to understand the original meaning of the text, the writer and the reader-receiver must use the same code, the same system of signs. This need not necessarily be the rule, and the use of different codes is one of the reasons why one text can be read in many different ways.

The important components of semiosis include not only the direct comprehension or miscomprehension of the original code of the message, but also, and very frequently, the so-called subcodes of the recipient, which may enrich the perceived message in certain contexts, while in others, they may make it incomprehensible, or totally cloud its original content.[22]

Let us now return in more detail to the question of the appearance of the iconic text inspired by ancient Egypt. In the European environment, the Egyptian model was frequently reinterpreted, i.e. set into a new context. We must emphasise that above all in the case of the Egyptian art, it was not just the individual motifs that were subject to reinterpretation, but often also the entire canon of Egyptian art. In the iconic texts, we can trace a certain stereotype, connected with ancient Egyptian culture. This means, that when defining the stereotype, we are no longer concerned with the misunderstood or ill-reproduced conventions of the Egyptian art. We analyse the conventions that European art used to represent ancient Egypt and which are connected with certain topoi, that frequently appear in connection with the European interpretation of ancient Egypt.

In terms of text interpretation, the factors, that may have influenced an European author, who derived his inspiration from Egyptian art, were the following:

1) *misinterpretation*, respectively an erroneous semiosis of the code, i.e. of the shapes and colours of Egyptian works of art. The reason for this misinterpretation may be found in the misunderstanding of the Egyptian artistic canon[23] (apparent, for example, in the 18th century prints, as well as in the illustrations of the *Description of Egypt*), which may also have been influenced by a fixed idea.[24] The use of these misinterpreted, *de facto* distorted, shapes by other artists and their incorporation into Egyptian art is well apparent, for example in the decoration of Napoleon's service, Wedgwood porcelain[25] (both second half and the end of the 18th century and beginning of the 19th century), etc.

2) the creation of a *stereotype* of the ancient Egyptian world in European art, either under the influence of this incorrect reproduction, or its later persistence. An interesting contrast is observable. For example, books like *Egypt in word and image* of G. Ebers,[26] include besides (albeit partially incorrect) drawings of existing Egyptian monuments also the artistic interpretation of Egypt by contemporary painters.

3) In relation to our own times – the survival of this stereotype as a heritage of the historical culture of the 19th century (for example in a 20th century film).[27]

Some of the errors, or rather imprecisions, that I mentioned, need not necessarily have been committed exclusively by artists inspired by Egyptian art. Even scholars[28] are not immune to them, since they are naturally also influenced by their environment. In the ideal case, though, scholars should be aware of this influence.[29]

The stereotype of ancient Egypt

The stereotype of ancient Egypt in European art was characterised by certain motifs, structures, and by the choice of certain words and motifs in literary arts. We have already encountered some of these, as well as the problems that were inherent in the perception of Egyptian art. What did, however, ancient Egypt look like in the eyes of the beholder, 'the 19th century man'? She was most often presented as a country of monumentality and perseverance, as well as a typical representative of the Oriental exoticism, spiced with the reminiscences of *A Thousand and One nights*. We must not forget that for many Europeans, the perception of contemporary and ancient Orient were inseparable.

Many European painters saw here an open, less censored opportunity to depict a nude human body, or even an erotic motif. Among them was for example also the Austrian Hans Makart, whose paintings may serve as a didactical tool for the listing of the main traits of the Egyptian inspiration in European historical painting of the 19th century. However, Makart's Egypt is quite fanciful, and he assembles very improbable details[30] on the individual paintings. As Günther Wimmer notes, the setting of Makart's paintings is somewhere between exotism and Egyptomania.[31] These terms, however, lack a precise definition, and the main difference between them is the choice of historical Egyptian motifs, characteristic for so-called Egyptomania, and the choice of general Oriental motifs, including contemporary ones, typical for Orientalism and exoticism. Even this distinction is not absolutely clear, since many Europeans conceived of the Oriental world as of a timeless one that had not changed much between Biblical times and the era of the trips organised by the Thomas Cook and sons travel agency.[32] The works of some painters often reflected this idea. J. M. Humbert[33] notes that in the works of many period European painters, the setting of contemporary Oriental props is only occasionally augmented by ancient Egyptian or Egyptianising objects, above all when the artist wanted to shift the event further into the past.

An ancient Egyptian in European imagination of the period

As an example, let us analyse paintings of Hans Makart. They correspond to the idea of Orientalism and Egyptomania in their general intentions. G. Frodl notes: *'[Makart] is one of the painters, for whom the Orient remained a social affair, an adventurous journey with an exotical scent. The erotic undertone present in Makart's Egyptian (and not only these) paintings, was in this case accepted by the public, since the Oriental morale was known to be much freer'.*[34]

Makart's contemporaries, such as for example Leopold Carl Müller and his pupils, perceived the Orient, including Egypt, as a source of new motifs. They delighted in depicting Oriental markets, figures dressed in colourful clothes, and they made use of a more flamboyant colour palette. Müller noted that Egypt has a special light, especially suited for painting in the open air. He taught a whole group of Austrian painters[35] who were in the second half of the 19th and in the beginning of the 20th centuries working with Oriental themes, often inspired by contemporary Egypt. Among them was Rudolf Swoboda Jr., (1859–1914), who worked with Müller in Cairo. He preferred contemporary Cairene motifs, depicting the everyday life of the city. Other Müller's pupils included Charles Wilda (1854–1907)[36] and Franz Xaver Kosler (1864–1905).[37] Above all Wilda's works sold well on the Paris arts market.[38]

Works of all these authors include contemporary Egyptian themes, sometimes enriched by an ancient building in the background or by a detail, a small ancient object. Their function here is to specify the location of the action. This is true, for example, about the painting of an antiquities dealer by the Prague born Raphael von Ambros (1854–1895). This painter attended the Prague Academy between the years 1869–1872. However, he probably encountered Oriental themes in Vienna, where he was a student of Hans Makart.[39] His paintings enjoyed great success and his name can be found between those who exhibited at the Paris Salon.[40] In 1908 he also exhibited in Prague.[41] Egyptian and other Oriental landscapes attracted also some Austrian landscape painters – e.g. Ludwig Hans Fischer (1848–1915).[42] These painters, however, do not represent of the classical narrative historical Egyptomania as Makart or the Britons Edward Poynter and Lawrence Alma-Tadema.[43]

When attempting to create an Egyptian setting, European artists of that time could choose between a Biblical theme, a motif from Egyptian history, or from one of the contemporary novels set in ancient Egypt. Europeans saw in Ancient Egypt the attraction of distant past combined with exotism. How did Czech artistic environment react to these two stimuli? Both were of great importance for nineteenth-century Czech art. *'The world of the past is attractive, because it appears to be an organised world. History is narrated and historical events are introduced.'*[44] To this may be added the influence of Orientalism[45] and general exotism of the *Lumír*[46] generation and their followers at the turn of the century. The full-fledged exotic, Oriental inspiration entered the scene first in the end and at the turn of the century, when historicism had already been part of Czech art for some time.

Given the above-mentioned preconditions, did both aspects of the Egyptian inspiration, which found reflection in the works of, for example, Viennese artists,[47] find the same response in Czech art? We know that Czech Oriental inspiration had also a spiritual dimension.[48] Spirituality and spiritual depth was searched also in Egyptian art.

Egyptian motifs in architecture and building decoration

Already since Classical Antiquity, European architecture and art had taken some elements of Egyptian architectural design. They shaped them in their own intentions and to their own needs. At the same time, we should not forget that '*not all the forms associated with the Egyptian Revival were in fact based on Egyptian or even Egyptianising precedents.*'[49] Others, however, indeed had authentic, although not always clearly identifiable, ancient roots.

One of the most frequently used elements was the obelisk, originally an Egyptian cultic symbol, most frequently connected with solar deities.[50] This usually rectangular pillar with a pyramidion (small pyramid-like tip) on top appears from the Renaissance period onwards almost all over Europe.[51] We can find singular examples at gable ends, or as portal decoration (also paired as frontispiece decoration), often combined with volutes. They also finished the edges of façade cornices.[52] Their symbolism then took on a new dimension. The frequent use in architectonic compositions in front of churches (or on their façades; the motif persisted until the Baroque) is the symbol of counterreformation of the Catholic church.[53] Numerous original ancient obelisks were erected in Rome in the course of the 16th and 17th centuries to demonstrate the greatness of the Church. Since the end of the Renaissance, the use of the obelisk became more general; the gables of Renaissance and early Baroque buildings in Prague and other European cities are often decorated with them. Generally, the obelisk was understood as a monument and symbol of glory[54] and became a frequent architectural element. The Baroque has even introduced triangular obelisks, that crown, for example, the plague pillars at the Malostranské square in Prague or on the Mikulov square. The obelisk has retained its symbolism of a monument to these days, as is shown, for example, in the installation of the obelisk of Mrákotín[55] at the Prague Castle, or the recent reinstallation of the monument in front of Emaus as a memorial for the victims of World War I. Here, a pillar without a pyramidion tops the composition of Josef Mařatka from the years 1929–1932.[56] The obelisk could, however, be assigned even more prosaic functions.[57] Its form made it an ideal milestone, as we can see on the depiction of Saxon postal milestones from the 18th century.[58]

The pyramid[59] is another popular element of Egyptian origin. It had inspired architects already in Classical Antiquity (the pyramid of Cestius in Rome).[60] Classicism revived the pyramids and employed them in the function of tombstones and memorials.[61] The motif of a pyramid was known and employed in this context already by the Baroque architect J. B. Fischer von Erlach.[62] He was not the only European artist that was relatively well acquainted with ancient Egypt,[63] '*…the painter Poussin, architect Fischer and goldsmith Dinglinger share a clear*

The pyramid inspiration of Josip Plečnik, Prague castle gardens, 1920s

inclination to scholarship, a question, however, arises, whether this inclination to scholarly knowledge did not in a very significant way outreach the study of older works that is typical for artists, and above all for artists of high qualities ...'

The third member of the triptych that in general consciousness permanently symbolised Egypt was the sphinx.[64] Although it is not unique to Egypt, such forms appear also in American cultures, the European mind has connected it tightly with the land on the Nile. European explanations of the symbolism of the sphinx appear already in Classical Antiquity.[65] Early Christianity saw the sphinx as a negative symbol connected with pagan Rome. However, it could be also perceived as a positive symbol. Its dual nature represented the connection of the divine and human elements in the person of Christ. When tetraform (including bodily parts of four creatures), it symbolised the four Evangelists, four basic elements and four directions. The Renaissance understood the sphinx as a guardian, and as such it is seated on tombstones to protect the deceased and the funerary secret. The sphinx also appears on temple paving[66] and pairs of these creatures guard gates.[67]

This triad of most important motifs is present in the architecture of a number of European countries. Classical Antiquity, Gothic period, and – in the era of historicising styles – also all styles of the past, acquired a new identity connected with the purpose of the building for which they were employed. To some extent, this is true also about the Egyptianising style, although researchers still do not fully agree on this point.[68]

Obelisks crowning the National Museum in Prague

Egyptianising architecture is most often connected with three types of buildings[69]:

1. Cultic buildings that have a religious significance or suggest a spiritual heritage (i.e. religious and funerary buildings, but also Freemasons' architecture);

2. Public representative buildings (museums[70] etc.);

3. Architectural compositions that rely on an exotic and phantastic effect (gardens and zoological gardens, sometimes even private house decoration).

Such use of Egyptianising motifs is the result of connotations commonly connected with ancient Egypt. Funerary and temple architecture forms a very significant component of Egyptian building art. In the case of museums, it was important whether Egyptian objects were to be exhibited there.[71] Where Egypt is the manifestation of the exotic, however, its meaning has few connections to the Egyptian cultural forms.

For the sake of completeness let me add that the author of the cited division of the use of Egyptianising motifs, Friederike Werner, includes under the heading 'Egyptianising' only those buildings that used one or more of the following elements[72]: pyramid, pylon, cavetto cornice[73], winged sun disc, and certain types of pillars and columns. Contrary to her definition, I include to the concept of Egyptian inspiration sculpture and relief decoration inspired by ancient Egypt, and also paintings.

The types of stylisation that might influence the architectural motif have also been subjected to classification. R. Carrott identified two such general approaches. One he calls 'Romantic Classicism' and the other 'Picturesque' or even 'Commercial Picturesque'. The first he connects with the idea of nobility and permanence, which was in the eyes of some of the classicist art and architecture theoreticians characteristic for ancient Egypt. This inspiration often inclined to pure geometrical forms.[74] The second type found employment in the sphere that Friederike Werner calls 'exotic and fanciful', or even 'advertisement' architecture. It uses many more decorative elements. None of the forms may be said with certainty to involve higher or smaller archaeological precision, since for example even the famous Leeds textile factory called 'Temple Mills', a typical example of advertising architecture, has relatively credible Egyptianising forms.[75] The aforementioned facts indicate that some Egyptian architectural elements have remained part of European architecture across several architectural styles, despite the fact that their perception diverged more or less from their original meaning. In terms of Czech architecture, the decorative role of Egyptianising elements was significant above all in the Art Nouveau period, less in the period of Czech historicism.

Nineteenth century architecture is often being connected with historicism as its most distinct manifestation. While the use of architectural elements from past historical periods is not a new feature in the 19th century, it is typical for it.

Historicism in architecture[76] and art is one of several phenomena that share the common name of historicism. In art, it means '*the reception, actualised acceptation of the formal, and thus also significant elements of past styles, trends and artistic ideas*'.[77] The relationship of Roman to Greek architecture, or of Renaissance to Classical, architecture, may be called historicism. In the narrow sense of the word, however, historicism is limited to the artistic style predominating in the second half of the 19th century. Above all because it developed (or with a hitherto unusual frequency used) some peculiar approaches to the use of historising elements, and also because the 'historicism' of the 19th century serves as a name for the whole atmosphere of the period, for which artistic expression formed only one of its manifestations.

The beginnings of the historising style can be traced down to the end of the 18th century, when the so-called Neo-gothic style[78] was formed in England.

Stucco sphinxes in classical shape, Mostecká street, Prague, datation unknown

The beginning of the 19th century in Germany is marked by Neorenaissance.[79] However, first the second half of the 19th century is considered the peak of the historising styles, because in this time their use not only became a lot more intensive, but also 'normalised'. The use of the style for the individual important buildings was not absolutely accidental. '*During the choice of the styles, … a moral-associative significance was often given to one of them, e.g. Gothic style – town hall, school, Classical antiquity – administration, parliament, …*'[80] In the Czech lands, the connection is most often as follows: Neogothic (or Neoromanesque) style – church, Neorenaissance (the so-called Czech Neorenaissance, style of the National Theatre) – public buildings, Oriental (Moor) elements – synagogue.[81] Even Egypt received her place in the functional-oriented list,[82] but the evidence for this comes above all from examples outside Czech territory. Prisons, court buildings,[83] but above all cemeteries and individual tombs[84] were built in Egyptianising style. The presence of the Egyptian inspiration was at that time reflected also theoretically, and not always in a positive way. An example of an opinion against Egyptianisms is the work of Pugin entitled *An Apology for the Revival of Christian Architecture in England* (1843).[85]

The façades of private houses were, however, mostly predominated by the so-called eclecticism, where every style has its place. Egyptian elements employed as part of eclectic decoration are to be found also in Czech environment, above all on rental houses of the second half of the 19th century.[86] Despite the rise of new building techniques (the use of steel and concrete), the buildings continue to be clad in a traditional very decorative cloak, full of historising elements.[87] The following Art Nouveau epoch was, above all in the Czech lands, also tightly connected with historicism.

Historicism in art, and thus also in architecture, is an expression of the general relationship of the society to the past, and presents thus important evidence of its historical consciousness.

Historicism in the context of the Czech historical culture is noteworthy also for other specific reasons, namely the importance of national history, or myths related to it, for the national movement. National past was an argument for the existence of the nation. Historical consciousness has therefore its role also in Czech art of the 19th century, '*…since the art of the 19th century was basically the art of mimesis, which concentrated on the translation of higher ideals of national thoughts.*'[88] Historical consciousness in Czech art of the 19th century was subject to the research of historians and art historians.[89] The study of historical motifs in art – above all painting, music, and literature, revealed a prevalence of Czech historical themes.[90]

Contemporary discussion concerning the artistic styles of the 19th century[91] is already diverging from the formerly clearly prevalent critique, according to which they were a mere conglomerate of past styles, which were moreover attached to functionally and materially differing frames. Above all the plurality of styles, newly combined in one whole, is now being defended. Eclecticism, which reached its peak toward the end of the century, is also no longer so vigorously negated. Numerous examples can be found in Czech, above all in Prague architecture of the last decades of the 19th century, for example in the buildings on the Pařížská street in the Old Town.

What is the role of Egyptian elements in Czech historicising styles? We can find them most often as small details on buildings, the main style of which bears no resemblance to anything Egyptian. In terms of Neorenaissance and Neobaroque elements we find, of course, the obelisk. In some cases, it is even possible to trace with relative precision the way, through which the element had come here. Besides the direct influence of Czech Renaissance, the architects were inspired to use this decorative element also by the study of Italian Renaissance. For many Czech architects, study journeys to Italy were commonplace. They are documented by the rich pictorial documentation of the monuments they admired there.[92]

In the case of the author of the project of the bank building, now the Academy of Sciences on the Prague Národní třída,[93] the architect Ignác Ullmann, we know that he was very interested in the work of the Italian artist Jacopo Sansovin.[94] The obelisks on the attic of Ullmann's building may have been inspired by Sansovin's Venetian library of St. Marc. Stylised pillars displaying distant similarities to obelisks or slim pyramids can be also found in the exterior decoration of the National Theatre and National Museum.

Among the elements of ancient heritage was also the sphinx. An example of a sphinx in classical stylisation can be found in the painted interior decoration of the Rudolfinum.[95] Very stylised, rather Baroque[96] sphinxes, however, with the typical *nemes* headdress on their heads, guard the entrance to the Rudolfinum from the direction of the Vltava riverbank.

However, at one occasion, Egyptian architecture played the main role, namely, in the form of the temporary hall of the Land (Jubilee) Exhibition of the year 1891. Rudolf Koukola designed an exhibition hall for Czech paperworks, which in compliance with rigid historicism tried to reproduce the forms and decoration of an Egyptian temple, including a pair of obelisks at the entrance, which was decorated also with two columns with lotus-form capitals, 'hieroglyphic' inscriptions and statues.[97] The architect's precision was not, however, intended to serve as *'a classical building paradigm, but as an attraction of exotic beauty'*.[98] The reason for the selection of precisely this motif can be found in terms of the association between Egyptian papyrus and paper, or of Egypt as the land of mysterious script. Contemporary critique of the architect Fanta, as we will see below, holds both interpretations for possible. Josef Fanta, the author of the design of the Main Railway Station (cf. p. 145), maintained that the forms of the exhibition halls encompass different inspirations *'some exceptional, some inspired by the temporary nature of the exhibition buildings or by the striving for extraordinary and imaginative impressiveness. Such is the case of the paperworks exhibition hall, which was designed by the architect Koukola, and which aims by its form language and colourful external and internal decoration to evoke the homeland of papyrus, mysterious Egypt'.*[99] This was then the opinion of the period, in which the phrase *'mysterious Egypt'* is of particular interest for us. It is one of the typical attributes with which Egypt was connected at that time.[100]

Another building of temporary character was that of the Urania theatre dating to 1898–1902, the exterior of which has been described in period critiques as 'Egyptian-orthodox',[101] and a period photograph[102] indicates the inclination of walls and concave shape of the main cornice.

Let us now see particular examples of building activities, where Egyptian motifs are either to be expected or where they are found, but in slightly or even entirely different context with respect to their European counterparts.

A winged scarab and a Pharaonic head, stucco decoration, the National Museum, Prague

The decoration of the National Museum[103]

The National Museum in Prague is a good example of a representative museum building. The decoration of buildings of this type, such as those, which were built for example in France, often indicated the nature of the collections that they were supposed to hold. The ideological motivation of the internal decoration of the National Museum in Prague is focused on places of national memory and traces the important sites of Czech national history.[104] In comparison with other buildings with similar functions it is much less inspired by the museum's task to preserve also the treasures of other cultures and periods.

As we can see on the decoration of the Louvre of Paris and of the Kunsthistorisches Museum of Vienna, their decoration reflects the content of the collections to a much greater extent.[105] Above all the painted and sculptural decoration of the Vienna Museum of Cultural History includes Egyptianising motifs. Gustav Klimt is the author of a painting representing Egyptian art. The allegory takes the form of a nude woman adorned with jewels[106] and standing against the background of a free agglomeration of Egyptian monuments, which, however, do not form part of Viennese collections.[107]

In Prague, on the other hand, we find at first sight modest details on building façades, such as, for example, the Egyptian mascaron and winged scarab over the windows of the National Museum.[108] It is quite precisely executed and very different from the later Art Nouveau mascaron over the window of the Wilson railway station.

In spite of that detail, and of European museum tradition, the character of the decoration of Czech public buildings was fixed, and it is very well represented by the National Theatre – *'in place of Classical Antiquity ... the inspiration drew from prehistory and the realm of Czech mythology,'*[109] or simply, Czech national past. This was the credo of many Czech architects and interior decorators of that time.

František Schmoranz and his circle

František Schmoranz Jr. was a somewhat unique figure among Czech architects. We have already met him as one of the most interesting figures of Austrian community in Egypt. He spent several years in Egypt as architect of Khedive Ismail and subsequently played an important part in the application of *'some Orientalising tendencies in the fine arts of Central Europe in the last quarter of the 19th century,'* which was – although not in all areas of culture – *'mostly connected with the cultures of the Near East'.*[110]

Schmoranz designed above all buildings inspired with Islamic art, intended directly for the Egyptian environment. These plans are to be found in his collection of sketches and plans. Later, distinct motifs taken over from Arab

An Egyptian lady in Dušní Street, Prague

architecture appear also in the building of the synagogue in Pardubice and of the baths in Trenčianské Teplice.[111] Schmoranz was interested in original Islamic architecture, which inspired him both in details and in overall compositions. He also documented original Cairene buildings in a number of drawings.[112]

Among the cooperators of Schmoranz was Jan Machytka, who even worked in Egypt for some time. Fr. Schmoranz also inspired the painter and sculptor K. V. Mašek, above all in the overall Orientalising setting of his works.[113] Karel V. Mašek[114] is the author of the paintings in the premises of the Prague main post office (1901), where he employed rich ornamentation.[115] Mašek also cooperated with František Schmoranz Senior, father of Schmoranz Jr., in the work on the church of Vysoké Mýto. Even here we can detect Oriental inspiration.[116] The work of K. V. Mašek is already classified as belonging to the epoch of Art Nouveau, which has all over Europe found great inspiration in Egypt and Orient in general.

Egyptianising motifs on Prague façades at the turn of the 19th and 20th centuries

The style of Art Nouveau, called also Jugendstil, or Liberty (referring to its various forms in various countries) was one of the attempts to create a new artistic style. At the same time, it often did not refuse the link to preceding styles. Its typical features include wavy lines and forms inspired by natural shapes of plants. P. Wittlich describes Art Nouveau as a style of rich decorativeness, symbolism and naturalism. It is worth noticing that the Egyptian element forms a suitable encoding of each of these characteristics. The stylisation of floral motifs could be easily taken over from Egyptian art. We may believe that for example Alfons Mucha turned to this inspiration. The rich symbolism ascribed to Egyptian art had already its tradition in Europe, and the same is true about decorative ornamental motifs.

Art Nouveau permeated all areas of art, from painting and architecture all the way to applied art.[117] One of the main centres of Art Nouveau in central Europe was Vienna, from where new stimuli were diffusing also to the Czech area.

Not all Art Nouveau buildings bear exclusively traits of the new style. Mainly in the Czech environment, we may find a great number of buildings influenced by the new style, but still set firmly into the historising basis of the past period.

Here belong also the Prague Art Nouveau buildings with Egyptian motifs, for example the house designed by the architect Bedřich Bendelmayer, now standing at the corner of the streets Celetná and U Prašné brány in Prague.[118] It was built between the years 1903–1904 and at that time, it was criticised for its bold style. Its overall decoration does not include too many markedly Egyptian elements, in fact only the locket on the corner side, depicting a lady with a striped pleated headcloth and double erect cobra,[119] the so-called uraeus, on her forehead. Against her, the otherwise symmetrical facade exhibits a classical profile.[120] Both heads are made of stucco.

Compared to the head, of much greater prominence are the column capitals and the massive statue decorating the house from 1912 in Dušní street in the Old Town.[121] The triangular tympanon of this house includes a female figure in its centre, that is clad in an Egyptianising dress and wears the *nemes* headcloth. The dress is a rather complicated and elaborate composition. It possesses the significant 'Oriental' character – a decorative belt with a prominent clasp with fringes. The skirt is pleated, maybe intended to be double, fringed and decorated. Bracelets, sandals and decorated jewels covering the breasts add a touch of Oriental riches and luxury.

The following storey is supported by pillars with Egyptianising capitals. This house has its 'Greek' counterpart in the Prague street Na Moráni. However, the columns remained Egyptianising even here, where they accompany a Greek in a fantastic helmet.

An Egyptian mascaron on the façade of the main railway station, Prague

An Egyptian mascaron was used also in the decoration of the building of the main railway station (Franz Joseph Bahnhof, at that time).[122] Here too the head is adorned with the *nemes* headdress and uraeus, but this time, it is very significantly stylised. The presence of this element in the façade of the house can be explained by the extent of the iconographical programme represented on the railway building, where '*the national and city emblems meet ... where folktale figures encounter figures from classical and Christian mythology, and stylised period elements of contemporary painting and sculpture stand next to ancient symbolic types*'.[123]

Further architectural details that may seem to accord with the consciousness of the Egyptian architectural style, can be found on other Prague buildings. The conclusiveness of the existence of a real inspiration by Egyptian motifs is in this case questionable. For example the columns in the court of the so-called Štenc House in Salvátorská street 8–10 (Prague 1 – Old Town), the work of Otakar Novotný from the years 1910–1911,[124] could also have been considered the result of an artistic reflection of the shapes of Egyptian architecture. So far, however, no way was found to support such a hypothesis, and it has therefore to remain inconclusive. In a similar way, we must also consider the use of cavetto cornice on the façades of Art Nouveau buildings. A good example is to be found in the mouldings over the windows of the house in Haštalská 4 (Prague 1, Old Town, about 1905).[125]

Cemeteries

Of a totally different kind are the, mostly in all probability unconscious, reminiscences in the sepulchral architecture of the second half, respectively end, of the 19th century. Contemporary monuments repeatedly include the motif of obelisk, or of a shape that recalls a section through an obelisk. Probably the closest to the classical obelisk shape are the monuments of the Brauner and Fibich families at the Vyšehrad cemetery in Prague. Here the reason for the choice of the motif was not the decorative character of Egyptian art, but the symbolism ascribed to the shape of the obelisk and above all to the pyramid. Other, less prominent reminiscences than the obelisk are to be found in terms of memorial design, such as, for example, the lotus flowers in the decoration of the tombstone of the Benedictine monks of Emaus,[126] which is not surprising considering the artistic traditions of the Beuron congregation. This will be treated in a separate chapter below.

The decoration of the Vyšehrad cemetery in Prague includes the figure of a man carrying a lamb. He is wearing a Greek tunic, but a stylised *nemes* headdress. The motif of a good shepherd, known from Christian art, has been supplemented by an Egyptianising headdress. The figure is part of the decoration of the portico that encloses the cemetery.[127] The overall design of the building is of Neo-renaissance style. The portico was created under the direction of Antonín Weil between 1889–1890, its decoration is the work of the painter R. Říhovský.[128] He was inspired by the paintings in Roman catacombs and by Raffael's paintings in the Vatican.

Egyptian inspiration in painting and sculpture

Egyptian motifs are a quite frequent phenomenon in European historical painting. A good example is the already mentioned Austrian painter Hans Makart. Other examples can be found in Britain and in France,[129] to a smaller extent also in Germany. In terms of Art Nouveau, Egyptian motifs appear more often as sources of decorative ornaments or as symbols.

An Egyptian queen with double uraeus in Celetná street, Prague

Czech historical painting[130] can be traced down to the first half of the 19th century, above all to the painters Antonín Machek and František Tkadlík. In the following generation, Christian Ruben defended a consistent pursuit of historical painting at the Prague academy. Others took up his work (or defined themselves against it): Karel Svoboda, Petr Maixner, Karel Javůrek, František and Jaroslav Čermák. Later, in the second half of the 19th century, also Václav Brožík and Mikoláš Aleš. The works of these artists include above all motifs from Czech, or occasionally European, history. The emphasis on local themes was well characterised by Jan Neruda, who wrote '*our ancient fights were undertaken for the same ideas that now reign here*'.[131] Old Slavonic past was to be retrieved even at the costs of deceit. The so-called Manuscripts[132] had great influence on arts. Karel Svoboda[133] made illustrations to and following them, and Josef Mánes worked on the same theme. In his material studies, Josef Mánes did not neglect monuments of the arts of past epochs, and he included many of them in his paintings;[134] however, ancient art did not find direct reflection in his work. He also worked with religious motifs, but even his initials to the text of the Bible (published between 1860–1864) do not contain ancient motifs. Therefore neither the initial that depicts the 'Finding of Moses' evokes Egypt in any significant way. This is surprising considering the traditional use of Egyptian motifs in these connections in European art, for example by Gustave Doré.[135]

Josef's father Antonín Mánes painted landscapes with classical, but not Egyptian buildings. Josef's brother Quido Mánes was inspired by the period interest in Chinoiserie in his painting 'Chinese emperor Kien-long composes a hymn to the tea,' but no other Oriental themes are known from his works.

The only Czech Romantic painter to have used a theme connected with Egypt thus appears to have been Josef Navrátil with his painting 'Cleopatra'.[136]

Around the middle of the 19th century, art historians perceive the growing orientation of several artists to French art and the inclination toward the cultural centre of Paris,[137] instead of the hitherto prevalent orientation to the German artistic milieu with the important centres of Vienna and Munich. All these three cities were big centres of historical painting, where Czech painters would frequently study.

The allegory of Architecture by F. Ženíšek, National Theatre, Prague

The first Czech painter that can be compared with important painters of exotic and historical scenes was Václav Brožík, member of the generation of the National Theatre. The catalogues of Brožík's works do not, however, mention any painting with a more or less precisely executed Egyptian theme.[138] He did not even use the colour and variety of themes that Makart in Vienna, Gerôme in Paris and others took from the ancient Oriental environment.

The National Theatre generation, as the group of artists connected with the decoration of this building is usually called, were people who, like Brožík, were well acquainted with European art, since they travelled, studied, and worked outside Czech territory. The presumption of a closed Czech environment ignorant of foreign stimuli would therefore be mistaken. Almost all individuals, who took part in the decoration of the National Theatre, had spent some years studying in Paris.[139] And not only that, some even worked for French customers and were in great demand as authors. In terms of their own work, which was predominantly directed at Czech audience, they complied with the rule they chose for the decoration of the 'Golden chapel', i.e. the above quoted '*instead of Classical Antiquity, one turned to prehistory and the realm of Czech myths*'.[140] The only moment that could foster the use of Orientalising themes was the Bible. For an Egyptian connection, we must look at the use of Old Testament themes, and, actually there are few examples – such as Karel Pavlík with *Joseph and the wife of Potiphar*. [141]

Ancient and early Christian motifs were also occasionally chosen by Emanuel Krescens Liška.[142] It appears that non-classical antiquity was little known to painters of Czech historicism. Only František Ženíšek used Egyptian motifs for his allegory of 'Architecture' on the ceiling of the auditorium of the National Theatre. A female figure is carrying two Egyptian columns with open floral capitals, painted in vivid colours and supporting an architrave, in all likelihood symbolising solid architecture *par excellence*.[143] The allegorical figure herself is, however, clad in Classical robes and her head is adorned with a laurel wreath.[144]

Vojtěch Hynais[145] rendered Biblical themes, influenced by contemporary French Orientalism, but this part of his work was created during his stay in Paris. Hynais studied by J. L. Gerôme, an important Orientalist painter. However, Hynais' own work reflected the Oriental influence predominantly in a different way than the otherwise frequent great dramatic Oriental scenes, which were preferred by Gerôme. Some of his paintings indicate his interest for the art of the Far East. The Near East, on the other hand, found only a sporadic reflection in his work. An exception is represented by the biblical theme – *Ecce homo* from 1897 (National gallery, Prague).[146]

A slight influence of Egyptian inspiration can be found in the works of Alfons Mucha and Luděk Marold. In both cases, it was mainly the result of the contact with non-Czech environment.

Alfons Mucha (1860–1939) received his artistic education in Munich and Paris, where he also became famous as a maker of theatre posters and advertisements. It was there that he used Egyptian motifs as a source of rich decoration or as an eloquent symbol.[147] The first example is his 'Zodiac' from 1896, designed first for the printing company Champenois. In his 'Zodiac', Virgo is wearing the *nemes* headdress and the hairstyles of Sagittarius and Gemini may have been inspired by some Egyptian statues. The lower section of the background is decorated with a pattern of alternating buds and lilies, stylised in all likelihood according to Egyptian patterns.[148] The second example can be found in the poster for the *Société populaire des Beaux arts* from 1897. In the upper left corner of the poster is a circle with a picture of the kiosk of Traian at Philae pierced by an obelisk. In the upper right corner there is a stylised cathedral, perhaps Notre-Dame.

In 1890 was published *Costume au Théatre*, which included A. Mucha's painting of Sarah Bernhardt representing Cleopatra in E. Moreau's play.[149] As illustrator of historical works, he strived for precision like his contemporaries. He studied a lot of material, although he did not always use them in a correct way, mainly when he later employed some historical motifs in advertisement.[150] Mucha had various opportunities to encounter Egyptian antiquities, certainly also in the collections of some of his patrons, for example the American Ch. Schwab.[151]

Smaller reminiscences of ancient Egyptian motifs can be also found in other Mucha's works, but here we are already entering the sphere of hypothesis. On another poster for the Champenois Company from the year 1897, the chest of a seated female figure is adorned with a large jewel distantly evoking a winged sun disc. Of the same date is the poster for Sarah Bernhardt in the role of a Samaritan woman (play by Edmond Rostand), the upper edges of which are adorned with lotus flowers.[152] A. Mucha's son, Jiří Mucha, mentions in his memoirs some period reminiscences of Egypt. For example in 1893, during the carnival of artists (Bal des Quat'z Arts), the costumes of models for the festive procession reflect the motif of Cleopatra and her court. If we are to believe Jiří Mucha, his father belonged to the organisers of the entire happening.[153] The costumes, judging by contemporary reflection, did not present a precise artistic representation of ancient Egypt, because they were daringly sparse.

Alfons Mucha himself mentioned Egypt in several contexts, and thus we get a glimpse of what his artistic impressions of Egypt may have been, for example when he characterised the future of American architecture: '*Your architecture will be simple. Its columns will be of a single stone, it will have spatious arcades, it will evoke the magnificence of the temple of Solomon and of Egyptian pyramids ... a great, noble and impressively simple style will come*'.[154] Interestingly, he characterised Russian art as follows: '*... an endless amount of symbols, with which the Russian man became familiar to such an extent, that he read them like an Egyptian would read the hieroglyphs*'.[155] These citations can be considered as a testimony of a relatively common regard of Egypt as a country of monumental buildings and mysterious writing.

Another Czech painter who was active in Paris was Luděk Marold (1856–1898). He turned to ancient Egypt as an illustrator of period novels, such as *Tahubu, roman égyptien* of J. H. Rosny from 1893.[156] As a skilful painter, he depicted also the scene of unwrapping a mummy (1890).[157] It is a reportage painting, however, it cannot be precisely determined whether Marold worked with a pattern picture, or whether he was personally present at the scene. For both artists, Marold and Mucha, the Egyptian motif was part of advertisement or illustration, of 'potboiling' which none of them held in too high esteem. These works originated moreover in non-Czech environment, they were commissioned in France, where the audience was used to such reminiscences.

The sight of the workshops of Czech sculptors of the second half of the 19th century is similar to that given by the works of painters. Here too we find, besides themes from Czech history, also Classical inspiration, reflection of foreign trends and even an appreciation of the works by foreign critique and audience. We cannot suspect Czech provincialism or enclosement inside one's own creative circle. Above all Josef Václav Myslbek became a popular and highly regarded figure. He also exhibited at the Salon of Paris.[158] Ancient Oriental, or ancient Egyptian inspiration did not, besides several exceptions,[159] affect the works of this generation of sculptors.

The Beuron School in Prague

The so-called Beuron School is an art historians' term for the artistic activity of the members of the Beuron Benedictine congregation,[160] which is one of the branches of the Benedictine Monk order under the leadership of the archabbot of Beuron.

Several artists of the order, the most important of whom was Desiderius Lenz (1832–1928), were active in the Czech lands at the turn of the 19th and 20th centuries. One of their greatest works was the decoration of Emaus, where the community lived, and of the Smíchov monastery of St. Gabriel, the home of the women's section of the order.

This style of religious painting and applied art was also related to Art Nouveau.[161] It is likely that Alfons Mucha was familiar with works of the Beuron school, and he may have appreciated their tendency to Byzantine and ancient inspiration.

What makes these works interesting with regard to Egypt? Their inspiration by ancient art is relatively obvious, and there is also a certain ideological content. The Beuron School unveiled '*in the service of liturgy the spirit of ancient Egyptian and Babylonian reliefs, early Greek sculptures and old Christian mosaics'*.[162] For example the decoration of the temple of the monastery of St. Gabriel at Smíchov, the work on which began in the year 1895, contains paintings reflecting the knowledge of ancient Egyptian art in their rendition of angels' wings, palms lining the scenes, and many other details. However, it was not limited to decorative details. Father Desiderius Lenz was also construing an artistic canon and tried to make it a reflection of the ancient Egyptian canon.[163] The motifs used included also ornamentation, rendition of draperies and floral motifs and palm capital forms.[164] Examples of all these elements can now be found in Prague above all in the Smíchov church of St. Gabriel and in the representative premises of the monastery, because the decoration of the Emaus suffered great damage during a WW II airstrike.[165] Emaus was decorated with Beuron paintings in the course of the years 1880–90, when the whole complex was also rebuilt in Gothic style. If photographic documentation is to be accepted as reliable evidence, floral ornaments exhibit Egyptianising forms.[166]

The simple monumental expression with a tangible influence of Egyptian art did not always trigger praise. Egyptian inspiration revealed by contemporaries led for example to the order to remove the Pieta in the main nave of the temple of St. Gabriel at Smíchov, which was painted by Desiderius' follower Jan Verkade. This was done at the order of cardinal Schönborn. In the end, the painting was only covered.[167] The cardinal was above all dissatisfied with the figure of Virgin Mary evoking an Egyptian goddess. The headdress of the Holy Virgin was indeed very Egyptian in style. It would be interesting to know, why it was so hard to accept for the cardinal. Perhaps because 'pagan' Egyptian art was incompatible with Christian ideas?

Other contexts on the other hand indicate that Egyptian architecture could acquire a highly sacral character and become a bearer of new religious ideas. It appears, however, that the Prague cardinal did not share this opinion of ancient Egyptian art. It is also true that this use was not common in Catholic culture, and Egyptian motifs were rather employed in sacral objects like synagogues or freemasons' lodges.[168]

If we search for the use of Egyptian elements as expression of Christian spirituality outside church environment, we would find a good example in the Czech art of the turn of the centuries is the work of František Bílek.

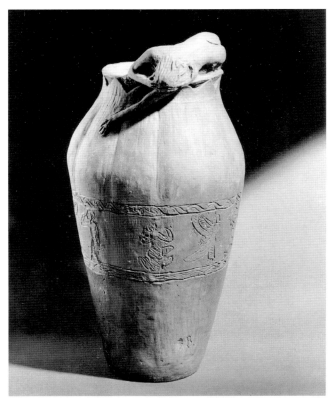

An Egyptianising vase, or jug, by František Bílek

František Bílek (1872–1914)

A representative of symbolism in sculpture, a versatile artist, sculptor, graphic designer, architect and author of applied art František Bílek went his own way in terms of Czech artistic tradition. Although he is now regarded a leading figure of Czech Art Nouveau, he did not consider himself as belonging to any specific trend in art, and even objected against the prevailing trend of Art Nouveau.[169] His work is rich in motifs and self-contained.

Many motifs that we encounter in his work do not only express deep and personally interpreted Christian faith, but also a general tendency to express spiritual values and traditions of humanity. Bílek created his own artistic, but above all religious expression. He drove not just from the Christian, but also from the Oriental spiritual tradition.[170]

Villa Bílek, a lotosoform column

How could he have become acquainted with such a broad scope of traditions? It must have been the result of the variegated influence of Bílek's education. In the years 1891–1892 he studied in Paris, where he in part sponsored his stay from a scholarship that he was awarded in Prague. In the French environment of art academies, which he was introduced to by Zdenka Braunerová and Alfons Mucha,[171] he undoubtedly acquired numerous stimuli. We often learn that

Bílek's personal mystique shares a lot with old Christians sects or with Gnosticism and Manicheism.[172] There is only a short step to a general interest in ancient mysticism. And Bílek could certainly encounter many works of ancient art in Paris, and would thus have been drawn to the study of these cultures. More probable is, however, that many of these ideas may have been passed on to Bílek by Julius Zeyer and Otokar Březina.[173] It was in all likelihood Březina who introduced to him the books of the French philosopher Edouard Schuré[174] regarding questions of spiritual traditions connecting various cultures. We do not know with certainty whether Bílek had any direct knowledge of ancient cultures, such as original works of ancient philosophers and mystics, but he could have had access to them.[175]

Bílek also used Egyptianising style, forms and motifs. They do not give a foreign impression in his work, since he was able to connect these forms well and adapt them to his own ideas. In the words of Jindřich Vybíral, Bílek began to use forms and shapes of ancient Egyptian art and chose Egyptianising columns as his favourite motif because Egypt was for him '... *a stage for Biblical events*'.[176] We do not, however, posses any evidence in support of this hypothesis. We do not know, for example, why the statue of Moses who led the Jews out of Egypt does not evoke Egyptian motifs, while the design for the Bílá hora monument, which has no direct connection to Egypt, contains evidence of Egyptian inspiration. Bílek

'*As Time Carves Wrinkles on our Face*'

Villa Bílek and its Egyptianising portico

himself wrote a testimony of his relationship to ancient Egypt, which did not play for him only the role of decorative inspiration, but became also a stimulus for his spiritual world. His book *Stavba budoucího chrámu v nás* ('Building of a future temple within us') contains the following words: '*When prehistoric man felt a desire to talk about eternity, he uttered a word so simple and in such a way, that we still admire in awe when beholding Egyptian pyramids. They created the view into eternity by mother Earth in "Isis" the earthly sphinx, and we still bow deeply before her sight. What spiritual and divine need protected the columns, corridors and halls of ancient Egyptian temples! ... the idea of the building was religiously and legally accepted by the people*'.[177] It is not without interest that Bílek regarded Classical antiquity negatively, and even denounced its art.[178]

Egyptian culture is not only spiritually rich for Bílek, but it is also able to pass down its message to the following generations. It is so because its art is eloquent in the spiritual sense of the word. '*Behold, friends, the ancient Egyptian temple. Every stone speaks here, every obelisk, every column and every pyramid.*'[179]

The symbolic Egyptian colonnade carries the idea of a temple. The first fleeting encounter with Egyptian columns comes from the year 1908, on the painting *Síň života* ('The Hall of Life'). Their shape is also reflected in the columns decorating the tomb of Nekuta designed by Bílek in Chýňov in the same year. However, the fully unfolded Egyptian inspiration is to be found in Bílek's Prague villa.

The building was finished in 1911 and Bílek introduced it personally in the review *Styl* ('Style'). He described its columns as sheaves bringing sustenance. Their shape is, however, more than just reminiscent of Egyptian lotus-formed columns, known already in the Old Kingdom.[180]

The colonnade is a dominant element in terms of Bílek's Egyptian inspiration; it is, however, not the only motif in his work. He also made frequent use of the Sphinx. It appears already in the cycle of paintings *Cesta* ('The Journey')[181] intended as a study for a monumental cycle of statues, the realisation of which has unfortunately proven impossible. Bílek created only some statues, for example that of Moses (1905). In 1909 he published a collection of drawings, which introduced the project as a whole. Egypt is represented by a graphical sheet entitled Egypt – *Sen cesty pravého života* ('Egypt – The Dream of the Journey of real life').[182] A figure wearing long robes and a headdress (it is not sure whether it is the *nemes* headdress) is sculpting the head of the Sphinx projecting over a heap of sand or over a rock. The position of the figure's hand is not very different from that of the hand of Time on the drawing entitled *Jak nám čas ryje vrásky* ('As Time Carves Wrinkles on Our Face'), which was also realised as a relief. The head of the sphinx evokes the paintings of the travellers who saw the sphinx of Giza covered with sand. The figure is holding a stonemason's mace in her other hand and is *de facto* leaning on the Sphinx. Impressed by this drawing, the author of the introduction to his cycle of paintings Miloš Marten wrote that F. Bílek let the mysterious beliefs of Egypt and India '*interrupt his chain of Biblical dreams*'.[183]

In Bílek's work, Egypt further appears very overtly in the drawing *Jak nám čas ryje vrásky* ('As Time Carves Wrinkles on Our Face') from 1902. Flowing figures of Art Nouveau style hover over the dark and already time-worn Sphinx of Giza and add with their unmerciful hands further traces of time. Two pyramids loom in the background. The general impression is somewhat that of an antithesis to the famous saying '*All fear the time, but the time fears the pyramids*', despite the fact that here Time is attacking the Sphinx, and not one of the pyramids. Tomáš Vlček perceives the opposition of the depicted figures as a symbolically expressed '*drama of life at the turn of ages*'.[184] The Sphinx appears in connection with time also on other Bílek's works – *Jak čas utíká* ('As Time Flies') and *Zloba času* ('The Wrath of Time').[185] Why such a dominant role of the Sphinx in Bílek's work? The works of some of his contemporaries, as František Kobliha and others,[186] presented the sphinx in a double role. It was a figure incorporating the Hermetic tradition and transcendence as well as a woman with all relevant associations in the eyes of men.[187] Bílek did not take into account this second meaning. Art historians explain it by the general absence of the erotic element, connected with the image of the sphinx, from Bílek's work.[188] To the contrary, for example on the woodcut *Spolupráce věků* ('The Cooperation of the Ages'), 1920 the sphinx assumes even Christ's form in agreement with her association with New Testament philosophy.[189]

In 1907 Bílek completed his famous statue *Úžas* ('Awe'), according to art historians inspired by Eduard Munch.[190] The rendition of the dress and rich composite belt could, however, be considered a reflection of Bílek's knowledge

Entrance to the temple vestibule by F. Bílek

of ancient Egyptian art. Period reviews in the periodical *Český svět*[191] expressed the same opinion. Bílek's exceptional feat was the use of the ancient Egyptian motif of a kneeling statue.[192] It was an allegory of Purity, one of the two figures flanking the access stairway in front of the main bulk of the proposed national monument for Bílá hora.[193] Other, more detailed reminiscences of Egyptian motifs, above all in column shapes, dress stylisations, etc., can be found in a number of other Bílek's sculptures, drawings and graphic works, such as for example *Síň léčivé hořkosti* ('The Hall of Healing Bitterness'), the composite statue *Budoucí dobyvatelé* ('Future conquerors'), or the woodcut *Vstup do předsíně chrámové* ('Entrance to the Temple Vestibule'), etc.

Various Egyptian motifs have clearly played an important role in the art of František Bílek. He must have been intrigued by the aesthetics of ancient Egyptian art. It is, however, likely, that he found himself most attracted by the concepts of nobility and spiritual values, which had been associated with Egyptian art since Classicism.[194] The list of Bílek's works contains several connected with the idea of a temple or the building of a temple. It was of course connected with the Old Testament concept, and in general with the idea of an ideal place to express religious respect. But besides that, it was also a symbolic expression. Bílek himself wrote that he '*would like to build a temple, extending from one horizon to the other*'.[195] He did not mean only physical span – he meant mainly the spiritual space, as is clear above all in his book *The building of a future temple within us*. Our spiritual dimension is being formed within us – we enter through the Hall of Life, pass through the Halls of Hunger and Thirst, Consecration, Awe, Terror, all the way to the Halls of Work and Creation. Almost all his graphical works expressing these ideas contain Egyptianising elements – often the elegant lotus-formed columns.

We may say that Bílek's interest in Egyptian art was not isolated, both in his own cultural background and – moreover – in the cultural setting of his generation.

A design for the Bílá hora monument, 'The past and us'

160

Ecce homo, The Church of the Elevation of the Cross, Prostějov

His friends included for example Julius Zeyer,[196] a writer with an interest in ancient Orient, and also Otokar Březina.[197] I believe that for Bílek Egypt was not only an illustration to Biblical scenes, but a bearer of a strong cultural tradition. Bílek understood and interpreted this tradition in a very specific way, just like he interpreted Christian faith.

Egyptian art influenced his works also with its monumentality. The outlines of statues and sphinxes that we often guess in his works always form the dominant feature of the whole. The case of Egyptian colonnade, appearing in a number of his works, is similar. His own works, however, indicate above all his praise for the spiritual qualities of Egyptian culture, which – like for Otokar Březina – is a precursor to further attempts to reach a really spiritual dimension of existence and the knowledge of it. For Bílek, Egypt represented a '*dream of the journey of real life*'. His reflection of Egypt was inspired more by experiences and intuitive attempts to feel the ancient culture than by a planned decorativeness. It belongs not to picturesque 'Egyptomania', but to a true spiritual artistic reflection of ancient Egypt.

161

František Kupka (1871–1857)

F. Kupka is known above all as author of symbolical and abstract paintings, but in his time he belonged to illustrators who excelled in 'archaeological' precision.[198] His work includes several paintings where Egyptian motifs play an important part. He illustrated the book of Elisée Reclus entitled '*L'Homme et la terre*',[199] a summarised history of mankind. The illustrations there belong to the archeologically precise ones, and the same is true about the illustrations for the chapter on Egypt. He worked with great feeling for detail and above all with exceptional understanding for the proportions of ancient Egyptian art. All Kupka's illustrations reflect a good knowledge of the theme and perhaps even of particular monuments.[200] This is also true of the cycle *Sedm divů světa* ('Seven Wonders of the World'), where he included also a picture of the Sphinx with Giza pyramids in the background.[201] Even the front page of *Histoire ancienne* in the work of Reclus, is dominated by Egyptian motifs – the central figure is that of an enthroned Pharaoh with full insignia.[202]

A completely different aspect of his reception of Egypt can be found in his paintings *Cesta ticha* ('The Way of Silence', 1903)[203] and *Vzdor* ('Defiance').[204] The art historians' review of the latter work does not mention any inspiration by Egyptian motifs, the shape of the figure seated on a square throne allows us to presume a reflection of Kupka's knowledge of Egyptian art. 'The Way of Silence' includes an evocation of the motif of the sphinx, connected perhaps with silence and guarding a secret. The inspiration was the same as that of František Bílek, but the resulting impression is very different. Kupka knew also the work of Edouard Schuré, which inspired him to choose the motif of a journey.[205]

F. Kupka, an illustration for 'L'Homme et la terre'

25.

חדואים נתנו־ריח ועל־פתחינו כל־מגדים
חדשים גם־ישנים דודי צפנתי לך:

מי יתנך כאח לי יונק שדי אמי אמצאך מחוץ
אשקך גם לא־יבזו לי:

אנהגך אביאך אל־בית אמי־תלמדני אשקך מיין
הרקח מעםים רמני:

F. Kupka, 'Song of Songs'

Oriental, and thus also Egyptian, inspiration played also a decisive role in the case of the illustrations for the French edition of the 'Song of Songs'.[206] As in the case of the illustrations for the work of Reclus, the paintings were not intended for Czech audience, and thus deserve their place in a book on 'Czech' reception of Egypt only through the nationality of their author. Kupka's even in this sense exceptional work turned to another audience. Of the Czech painters who were interested in the Egyptian theme, he was in all likelihood the most famous. He spent most of his life in France, where he also died.

'The Way of Silence' and his illustration work represent also two poles of the ancient inspiration – one given by the theme of the illustrated book and the other more abstract, stimulated by a contemporary collection of essays. It is also interesting to observe how different reactions were triggered by the same work by two artists – F. Kupka and F. Bílek. They shared the inspiration by ancient Egypt, and both were interested in the motif of the sphinx, but in very different contexts.

F. Kupka, 'Song of Songs'

F. Kupka, 'Seven Wonders of the World – Pyramids'

Egyptian inspiration in photography

Despite the difficulties connected with early technologies of photography, photographs allowed a relatively fast transmission of pictures of Egyptian antiquities. Photographical collections of Maxime du Camp and later Francis Frith passed down a view of ancient and Islamic monuments and, following the development of photographical technology, also a mass distribution of photography in book and postcard form.

This aspect of visits of Egypt, i.e. taking snapshots of the visited monuments, has not yet been studied by Czech travellers, since pictures of a totally different character became famous, namely, photographs of nudes taken above all by Richard Štorch[207] during his stay in the Orient. They are, however, irrelevant to ancient Egypt, and correspond to the general concepts of Europeans concerning the Orient and Oriental women, where sensuality and erotic invitation played a central role.

The topic deserves further attention. Some of the travelogues of this period are illustrated with photographs, whereas other are not, and had taken the help of an illustrator, who used photographs as a support for his work. The first is, e.g. a book by Hanuš Mayer, *Egypt – obrázky z cest* ('Egypt – Images from Voyages').[208] Mayer had used, as he himself admitted in his foreword, photographs by Emil Brugsch bey, E. Beaufort, Gustav Richter and others, but only to complete his own picture gallery. The second case, i.e., drawn or painted illustrations based on

Viktor Oliva's Oriental inspiration in an illustration for Jiří Guth

period photographs, are to be found in the book by Jiří Guth, *Na pokraji Sahary* ('On the Edge of the Sahara Desert'), Prague 1892, illustrated by a gifted painter, Viktor Oliva.[209]

A research on this issue, as well as that of an extensive survey regarding the Czech travellers in the Orient of the end of 19th century, is still in progress.[210]

Julius Zeyer and others

Julius Zeyer (1841–1901),[211] writer and poet of the Lumír generation, turned to exotic themes and elaborated on them often under the influence of older literary tradition. The heroes of his works live in Mediaeval Japan, Biblical Palestine and Pharaonic Egypt. Ancient Egypt is the setting of two Zeyer's short stories, *Asenat* and *Král Menkera* ('King Menkera').

Zeyer took the theme of the story *Asenat* (first published in 1895) from an old French original,[212] which in turn was based on the apocryphal story *Joseph and Asenat*. The high state official Joseph is supposed to comply to the will of the pharaoh and marry a noble Egyptian lady Asenat. However, he cannot accept the decision of the king, because he is unabe to tolerate the deep piety that his bride feels for the gods of her country, mere pagan symbols in his eyes.

Until Asenat met Joseph, she also entertained the thought of refusing him. After their first encounter, however, her love for him takes over and leads her in the end to denounce her own gods. Only then she can become Joseph's wife.

Zeyer enriched the story with a number of descriptions, the main task of which was to acquaint the reader with the colourful Oriental environment. He lists the deities worshipped by Asenat[213] '*together with their symbols – Amun and his goose, Maut (sic) and her vulture, Ptah and his dungbeetle, Hathor and her cow, Osiris and his ram (sic), Anubis and his jackal, Hor-M-Khut and his sphinx, Thoth and his ibis*'.[214]

It is likely that the author used in this story also his knowledge of original ancient Egyptian works of literature. For example, it seems that he inserted paraphrases of the ancient Egyptian text '*On the Salvation of Mankind*'[215] into his story. Asenat herself lives in a richly decorated tower, '*in a tower of marble of changing colours,*'[216] which stood '*besides the house*'[217] of her father, which is a motif that comes from the ancient Egyptian *Story of the Doomed Prince*. The moment where Asenat finds the sacred book recalls the scene from another Egyptian work – the *Story of Setne Khaemwaset*. These intertextual links to ancient Egyptian literature can be expected, since Zeyer himself wrote a study entitled 'Fairy Tales and Novels of Ancient Egypt', which was published in *Lumír* in 1875.

The intertextual links were also demonstrated by Pavel Poucha, who compared Zeyer's text with the translations of ancient Egyptian works present in his library. Zeyer transformed the texts so that the readers could understand the phrases without further explanations.[218] This is true above all about the texts of Egyptian hymns that the writer put into the mouths of his figures.

Zeyer's rich library[219] includes older and period Egyptological and historical publications. Besides the works of M. Rolin, M. Uhlemann and K. Schwenck we find for example also books of K. R. Lepsius, an important figure from the time of the formation of German Egyptology. Another evidence of Zeyer's interest in Egypt is the fact that he visited Coptic courses at Prague University.[220]

The motif for the second story, 'King Menkera', was in all likelihood taken from Herodotus. In the second book of his Histories, Herodotus writes about a king, whom the Gods predicted a short life and who fell in love with his own daughter. Zeyer may have encountered the motif in the works of historians M. Rolin (*Histoire ancienne des Egyptiens, des Cartaginois, des Assyriens, des Babyloniens, des Médes et des Perses de Macedonies, des Grecs*, Tome I–VIII, Amsterdam 1733–1735), and M. Uhlemann (*Handbuch der gesammten aegyptischen Altertumskunde*, I–IV, Leipzig, 1857–58).[221] In a similar way he also became acquainted with Herodotus' description of the highly unruly festivities in the city of Bubastis. He also included the story about Isis and Osiris, which he probably knew from Uhlemann's work and from the book of Konrad Schwenck (*Die Mythologie der Aegypter*, Frankfurt 1855), from which he took whole formulations.[222] This version derives a lot from Classical authors, mainly Plutarch.[223]

Zeyer skipped the part of the legend that describes the hacking of Osiris by Seth (Typhon, Zeyer retained his Greek name), and above all the passage about the phallus of Osiris. Poucha reasons that Zeyer could not have enjoyed the passage for aesthetic reasons. The atmosphere of Zeyer's period, when sexual life was subject to a social taboo, may have also played its role.[224]

Zeyer's Menkera decides to ignore the ominous oracle that forbids him to meet his own daughter. He wants at least to see her likeness, and therefore orders the making of a statue that truly depicts princess Isema. Just as the nanny of the princess, Meri-t-ma fears, the beauty of the young woman casts such a spell over the king that he decides to marry her. Meri-t-ma is trying to avoid the threatening danger by letting the princess flee with her own son Setna. The pair mingles among the crowd preparing for a festival in Bubastis, but finally they are caught and brought to the king. Setna and his mother prefer death by their own hand to the revenge of the king. The princess, whom an oracle had warned against seeing sunlight and meeting her father, looses eyesight and dies as well.

Just as in the case of the last story, Zeyer was guided by his knowledge of ancient Egyptian stories. For example the names that appear here do not lack an Egyptian foundation. King Menkera is the sovereign Menkaure (Mycerinus) of the 4th dynasty, Setna comes probably from the name of Setne Khaemwaset, Meri-t-ma probably from the name of Meritmaat[225] (even provided with an explanation 'who loves justice').

The whole text is once again full of descriptions evoking an atmosphere of the luxury of the royal palace, but also the beauty of nature (the author could have made use of travelogues – such as that of Amelia B. Edwards – the first edition of which comes from 1877) and above all the strength of emotions that the main characters succumb to. Egypt is literally painted as a picture with shadows of cruelty (for example the death of Meri-t-ma and her son Setna: the mother first throttles her son and then she knocks a heavy statue of a deity down on herself) and dissoluteness (the description of the festival in Bubastis, described with great discretion, which led Zeyer to use many indirect formulations).

Similar motifs are to be found in the works of Zeyer's European literary counterparts, for example the French writer Th. Gauthier. The same elements belonged, often in the composition of very decorative and at the same time dramatic scenes, to the general period concept of Egypt and we encounter them also in visual arts in historicising paintings of authors like Hans Makart, Antoine Rochegrosse and Lawrence Alma-Tadema.

Thanks to his library, Zeyer had at his disposal materials concerning various ancient Egyptian literary works, however, he chose two motifs that had a Biblical or Classical basis. He introduced other, original ancient Egyptian works, namely *The Story of Prince Setna Khaemwaset*[226] and *The Doomed Prince*[227] to the Czech readers in his study 'Fairy Tales and Novels of Ancient Egypt', published in *Lumír* in 1875, where he also included a treatise on ancient Egyptian love poems.[228] On the other hand he did not work on the story of Sinuhe, although he had access to relevant literature.[229]

Zeyer's work brought the Egyptian inspiration into Czech art on yet another occasion, it inspired Jan Zrzavý, who illustrated Zeyer's Oriental stories.[230]

The works of Jaroslav Vrchlický (1852–1912) included Egypt as a symbol (the collection of poems entitled *Sfinx*[231] ['Sphinx', 1883]). Vrchlický also made use of the motif of Egyptian asceticism – his *Hilarion* is '*the story of an Egyptian ascetic immersed in himself and despising humanity and the world on earth …*'[232] Another similar theme is to be found in his *Maria Aegyptiaca*.[233] In *Poslední sonety samotáře* ('The Last Sonnets of a Loner') he employed the theme of Cleopatra's story.[234]

Contemporary reviewers did not always unequivocally accept his exotic motifs. The reviewer Kuffner expressed himself concerning another of Vrchlický's works, *Noc na Karlštejně* ('A Night at Karlštejn')[235] that the poet '*perhaps merely played, perhaps merely wanted to show, what he could do, if he only wanted, perhaps only in a fleeting moment vainly played with real people from a low background within four stone walls, in order to as fast as possible fly back to the mysterious darkness of sphinxes and papyri …*'[236] Besides being a review of Vrchlický's work, these words also express a conception of ancient Egypt as a land of mystery and inaccessible, foreign exotism. A certain detachment can also be noticed, by which the reviewer may have wanted to indicate that Czech theme would have been more welcome.

The relationship of Otokar Březina (1868–1929) to Egyptian culture was somewhat obscure. Březina is a personality with an interest in the spiritual life of ancient cultures, and as such can be compared to František Bílek or František Kupka. These artists reinterpreted the spiritual heritage of antiquity in the context of their own spiritual image of the world.

Březina often mentions[237] Egypt in one breath with India. He also says that *'contemporary Arabia, India and China are the only real successors of ancient cultures …'*[238] He completes the general characteristics of the Orient with the statement that *'Orient is searching for a union with cosmos, for an immersion therein'.*[239] His interest in the mystique brought him even to the book of Helena Petrovna Blavatskaya,[240] whom Březina held in high esteem.

He was persuaded that the cultural integrity and tradition of faith and even clerical organisation remained uninterrupted from the times of ancient Egypt. This way we may understand his words concerning the church, which he characterises as follows: *'the priestly class … with their two thousand years of tradition, to which we may add also the four thousand years of experience of the Egyptian priesthood.'*[241] The essays of Otokar Březina, above all the one entitled *Skryté dějiny* ('Hidden History')[242] expresses his continuous persuasion about the spiritual continuity that follows and unites all cultural assets of mankind.

M. Dvořák mentions the following Březina's utterance concerning spiritual continuity: *'There are only two great spiritual sources, two mighty streams of spiritual tradition on earth: Buddhism and Catholicism. My art belongs to Catholicism, the Catholicism that sprouted in Egypt and reached our lands through the Near East and the Mediterranean. It is basically an active spiritual trend, that includes in it also Protestantism and other philosophical systems, that are based on it and that react to it.'*[243]

When expressing his opinion about Vrchlický, Březina wrote: *'… I measure the qualities of an artist according to the highest points of his inspiration. If in the whole book there would shine a single sentence, opening a new posibility of new perspectives or wording in a new, happier image the truth painted already on ancient Egyptian monuments …'*[244] In these quotations, Egypt is in keeping with the Renaissance tradition considered to be the root of education and source of primary knowledge. Like Bílek, Březina valued Oriental knowledge over the Classical.

However, similar concepts seem to be absent from his published poems. Březina's poems often contain a motif evoking the Bible – Moses, Eliah, Gedeon.[245] A specialist on his work, Emanuel Chalupný, distinguished in his works and in his metaphors the *'deep tones of Indian Upanishads,*[246] *of Plato's world of ideas, Evangelical love of the neighbour, Mediaeval mystique, Kant's critical idealism, Schopenhauer's poetico-philosophical system …'*[247] but he does not mention Egyptian literature. In Březina's time, however, the analysis of Egyptian literary work was much less advanced than now, although we have seen what Julius Zeyer was able to achieve using period works. In this context, Březina's library could be of value, since its composition could indicate something more about the poet's interest in this ancient culture. His notes, aimed at a possible improvement of history lessons, which he compiled as a high school teacher,[248] suggest that he did not underestimate the importance of ancient history as a whole, although a specific stand towards ancient Egyptian history is missing.

Egypt in the metaphor

O. Březina's relationship to Egypt as the motherland of spirituality was similarly peculiar as that of Bílek (cf. the quotation of M. Dvořák). It is hard to tell whether it was precisely for this reason that his style includes a metaphor bound to a certain characteristic feature of ancient Egyptian culture, hieroglyphic writing: '*The things of this land … seen as a hieroglyphic writing of a single message … a creation developing over millennia … like a scroll on the scribe's cylinder, ever unrolled and rolled back again!*'[249]

This shows that the Egyptian topos was strong enough to enter the realm of imaginative language as a suitable metaphor. A similar phenomenon is perceptible also in the Biblical similes with an Egyptian content, which we can observe throughout the 19th century use of Czech. This may have been the root of Josef Jungmann's simile, whom his patriotic fervour led to write: '*The little Czech, being ousted from every office, cannot even become a wretched scribe, he is, like there by the Egyptians, doomed to the plough or bodkin of his fathers …*'[250] Hieroglyphs as a metaphor for decorative art appear already in Božena Němcová's *Babička* ('Grandmother').[251]

Also Julius Zeyer wrote in his speech on Vojtěch Náprstek: '*he never regretted the left Egyptian pots …*'[252] And Jan Neruda used the following Biblical simile: '*and a big wailing came out in the Czech lands, like once in Egypt, when the tenth strike happened*',[253] although in this case the use is a satirical one, because the great killing, which Neruda refers to, are the December pig-slaughterings. His works includes several traces of non-Biblical consciousness about ancient Egypt. Before he had the opportunity to visit the Egyptian pyramids, he had written, to add strength to his simile, that '*the Egyptian pyramids, magnificent cemeteries of kings, cannot impress a man more than the cemetery of Paris*'.[254]

Metaphorical expression is therefore often rooted in Biblical themes and belongs to common cultural basis, because the knowledge of Biblical history, whether acquired in the church or at school, was commonplace. Such a simile in itself thus does not express a special relationship to Egypt. Also set phrases and metaphors, for example about hieroglyphs or pyramids, do not have to indicate more than the use of a commonplace metaphor. Its very existence and the fact that it had entered general consciousness, however, prove the existence of historical awareness about Egyptian culture.

Translated literature

Although native Czech production has to be taken into account for the study of the importance of literary art in Czech historical consciousness, translations of foreign language specialised and belletristic works are of no lesser importance for the creation of historical awareness. One of the important authors toward the end of the 19th century was Georg Ebers, a significant, although contradictory, character of German Egyptology and German literature.

The personality of Georg Ebers became the subject of various studies of Germanists, literary scholars and Egyptologists.[255] The expert in historical novel Lukács even called Ebers a '*vulgar populariser of superficial and hackneyed Egyptology*'.[256] Even Adolf Erman, who belongs to the generation of positivist historicising Egyptology, did not always fully respect the scholarly qualities of his teacher. Ebers, however, grew up from the same positivist roots that he passed on to the following generation of scholars, including Erman. It is even possible to maintain that Erman was as 'guilty' of injudiciousness and from our own point of view indeed inadequate comparison of ancient Egyptian customs with today as Ebers,[257] although in one case, they appeared on the pages of popular novels, and in the other in specialised publications.

Ebers indeed wrote a number of popularising articles, but he did not therefore interrupt his specialised activities. Ebers' novels[258] and popular Egyptological books were widely distributed and translated even to Czech. The novel *Uarda* (I–III) was published in Czech translation of B. Frida in 1880, *The Egyptian Royal Daughter* ('Egyptská dcera královská', I–III, translated also by B. Frida), followed in 1881–1883.[259] *Uarda* is set in the time of Ramesses II, *The Egyptian Royal Daughter* is a story taken from Herodotus – the story of Nitetis, daughter of King Wahibre (the Biblical Hofra, which is the version of his name that Ebers employed in his novel) of the 26th Dynasty, whom King Amasis allegedly married to the Persian future conqueror of Egypt, Kambyses.[260]

Ebers' attempt to introduce the ancient Egyptians '*rein menschlich*'[261] (as purely human) may not have diverged too far from that of Zeyer, who also aimed at depicting excitements and passions that were considered generally human. Arne Novák even called the latter '*Zeyer the idealist, sinking in the myst of meta-psychology*'.[262]

The same 'fault' became later the object of critique of the positivist Egyptologist Adolf Erman. He himself, however, judged the ancient Egyptian mind no better and with no more understanding. Above all certain Erman's conceptions about ancient Egyptian religion, although he had tried to be somewhat less bold when forming of his hypotheses than for example Brugsch, border on arrogance, and measure antiquity against the values of a scholar of the beginning of the 20th century.[263] Erman himself wrote that '*the world five thousand years ago was no different from our own times, the same rules, that it obeys now, have steered it already then without mercy*'.[264] This sentence characterises Zeyer's and Ebers' literary work, to which Erman's work forms a pendant in the field of period historical knowledge.

Egypt on the theatrical stage

The presence of ancient Egypt in European theatre art, above all in the opera and in the ballet, can be traced far back in history. Already in the 18th century a number of works appeared, the setting or characters of which were in one way or another connected to ancient Egypt. We may mention for example the ballet of J. Rameau, *La naissance de Osiris* or Neumann's opera *Osiris*,[265] not to speak of the opera of J. Mattheson, *Die unglückselige Kleopatra, Königin von Ägypten*, first performed already in 1704.

Egyptologist Dieter Arnold[266] studied opera-related literature preceding the beginning of the 19th century and counted 26 occurrences of the motif called 'Sesostris', 36 times Cleopatra, twenty times Arsinoe and also twenty times Caesar, or more precisely works concerning the parts of life of the famous warrior and politician that were connected with Egypt. The works that are performed to these days include Händels *Caesar* from 1724. In 1728, Händel set to music also a motif entitled *Tolomeo*, i.e. Ptolemy.[267]

Egypt and her connection to Freemasonry, which in itself represents one of the forms of her reception, played toward the end of the 18th century an important role in Mozart's *Magic Flute* (Die Zauberflöte). Mozart was a member of the Freemason's lodge and some of the ideas of Freemasonry seem to be present in the text of *The Magic Flute*. The composer had encountered the Egyptian motif already in his youth, when he composed musical accompaniment for *Thamos, King of Egypt*[268] of Tobias Gebler. *The Magic Flute* is a very popular work and as we shall see, it has regularly appeared also on Czech stages. Only the stage of the National Theatre has hosted it twelve times since the construction of the present historical building.[269]

In the course of the 19th century, several Biblical themes set in Egypt have appeared in operas, and even some Egyptian themes with no relation to the Bible.[270] E. N. Méhul composed the opera *Joseph and his Brothers* (first performed in 1807), which also entered the repertoire of the National Theatre.[271] G. Rossini wrote 'Moses in Egypt' (*Mosé in Egitto*, Naples 1818, arranged as *Moïse et Pharaon ou le Passage de la Mer Rouge*, Paris 1827), which, however, did not appear on the stage of the Prague 'Golden chapel'. A new and probably also the most popular presentation of Egypt on the opera scene is to be found in G. Verdi's *Aida*, traditionally connected with the festive opening of the Suez canal, although it was not performed at this occasion.

However, *Aida* is not the last work of world music that chose Egypt as its setting or its part. In 1894, J. Massenet performed in Paris the opera *Thais*. The motif is the conversion of a rich courtesan of Alexandria to Christian faith.[272] Richard Strauss composed music to the ballet entitled *The Legend of Joseph*, which was also performed on the stage of National Theatre in Prague in two versions, both were, however, staged first in the 1920s.[273]

The question is whether any Czech composer chose a motif that would take him to such distant past. We know that in the beginning of the 20th century,

Robert Holzer, designs for the Magic Flute, 1887

Bohuslav Martinů had several times used a motif from Mesopotamian mythology – *Gilgameš* ('Gilgamesh'), or the ballet *Istar*. We do not, however, know anything about the Egyptian inspiration of any Czech nineteenth century composer.

An Egyptian theme appeared in Czech work first in 1939, in the form of the text to the melodrama for the harp or the piano of A. Srba *Nářek Ésetin* ('The Lament of Isis') written by the already then well-known Czech Egyptologist František Lexa.[274] On the other hand, the composer Leoš Janáček refused the Egyptian motif, although it had been offered to him.[275]

Egyptian inspiration in theatrical scenery

Egyptian motifs of course appeared above all there, where the motif itself required them. This was the case of *Aida*. The setting of some performances of *The Magic Flute* on the Czech stages also included Egyptian elements.[276] There was no lack of Egyptian inspiration in the setting of the performances of this opera on European stages, but it did not dominate in the first stagings.[277]

The Egyptian inspiration influenced also the setting of musical works, which did not have any direct link to Egypt. This phenomenon is known from both world[278] and Czech scenes. For example in the design for the stage decoration of the National Theatre for Goldmark's opera *Queen of Sheba*, the interior of the temple of Solomon is adorned with an Egyptianising portal.[279] Quite particular is the use of the Egyptian motif in the costume design for the allegory of the continent of Africa in the ballet *Excelsior*.[280] The design is not an original Czech one, the costumes were made directly after propositions from Milan. In several cases, though, they were slightly altered to be more consistent with the Czech environment.

The decoration of the staging of *The Magic Flute* and of *Aida* (above all on the stage of the National Theatre, where it is very well documented thanks to the preservation of archive materials) is a very important part of historical culture[281] of the end of the 19th and beginning of the 20th centuries. Already in the end of the 19th century we may speak of a true Czech theatre decoration,[282] not only about copying foreign patterns. Subsequent development in the course of the 20th century then shows, in different conditions of historical culture, further possibilities of treatment of a certain historical (*Aida*) and mythical (*The Magic Flute*) picture in the theatre.

The Magic Flute

The Magic Flute belongs to the most discussed works of W. A. Mozart. The story and the music probably relate to Freemasonry, although it is hard to decide to what extent. In short, the story of the opera is as follows:[283] The Queen of Night is trying to get back her daughter Pamina, who is held captive by the wise

175

Sarastro. The queen persuades Prince Tamino, who was saved by the members of her suite, to go and search for Pamina. To ease his journey, she gives him The Magic Flute and the fowler Papageno who possesses a magical glockenspiel. Tamino meets the priests of Sarastro and learns who had taken Pamina captive and why. The negative character of the Queen of Night is revealed to him and he and Pamina are to be initiated into the secret of wisdom and truth. Sarastro demands for them the protection of Isis and·Osiris. After numerous difficulties, Tamino is indeed initiated, while Papageno, who chose to undertake the test with him, 'fails' and is 'compensated' at least by a companion for life, Papagena. Pamina, too, is initiated, and the Queen of Night is finally defeated.

The fairy tale story was a good setting for the priest of Isis Sarastro, and the goddess Isis was known to most people above all from the connection with the Freemasons' liking of symbols considered Egyptian. The ways through which the period Egyptianising concepts entered the story of the opera include not only the symbols of Freemasonry, but also Terrasson's novel *Sethos*.[284]

The Magic Flute belongs to the so-called *singspiel*, an entertaining musical piece with a lot of changes of setting that also brought it great popularity. Egypt is present in Sarastro and his priests, who serve Isis and Osiris and have other characters of the opera, above all Prince Tamino and Princess Pamina, undergo mysteries and initiations. These phenomena were in the minds of 18th century Europeans unequivocally connected with Egypt (see Terrasson, *Sethos*).[285]

'Egyptian' elements on the stage necessarily reflected period knowledge. The stage setting (which is an indispensable part of theatre art and possesses its own informative value) in European theatres includes Egyptian elements first since the beginning of the 19th century. Text and story, however, reflect classical conceptions about ancient Egypt. Music is rather of church style, than being inspired by Egypt or connected with her, for example by means of some 'Orientalising' reminiscences.[286]

The Magic Flute enjoyed great success on Czech stage. Only in the time between the years 1792–1793, it was staged twenty times. It was translated to Czech by Václav Thám.[287]

The scene of the historical building of the National Theatre hosted *The Magic Flute* on the 23rd September 1887. The decoration was the work of Robert Holzer, the costumes of František Kolár, and the props of the Bittner brothers.[288] Both the costumes and props have been well documented.[289] R. Holzer created a relatively convincing illusion of ancient Egypt in terms of buildings, his landscape was somewhat more phantastic. Kolár designed the costumes of Sarastro and Tamino, both with Egyptian elements.[290]

Of great interest is the common use of props for *Aida* and *The Magic Flute* in the first decades of the 20th century. In the first performance of *The Magic Flute* on May 8th 1913 and during the following performances, a lot of the props used had, at least according to the preserved archive materials, been taken from the 1912 performance of *Aida*.[291] For example the setting '*Garden of the Queen of the Night*' is identical to that by the Nile from *Aida*.[292] The author of this stage setting was M. Gottlieb. He used stylised (resp. influenced by European manner) motifs of seated statues (Act I) and also the sphinx (Act II). The elaborate costumes combine traditional Egyptianising elements.[293] The use of the props from *Aida* indicates a conscious connection of *The Magic Flute* with Egypt.

Other evidence of a perceived connection can also be found in the work of František Kolár, who assembled a living picture for Mozart's jubilee, and his designed figures included also a group that represents the characters from *The Magic Flute.* One of them, in all likelihood representing Sarastro, has a staff and a beard corresponding to the stylised Egyptian patterns, but also a breast-plate in the form of an Old Testament collar of the High Priests.[294]

The following performance of 1921 that was staged in Stavovské divadlo (first performance on the 8th of May), reaches significantly beyond the limits of the historical culture of the 19th century, but it forms an interesting evidence for the gradual transformation of setting from description to evocation.

Pyramids appear on stage, some of them even bear inscriptions (sic).[295] The female figure with a composite Osirid crown,[296] which dominates the setting for Act I, represents a strong reminiscence. Similar indications appear in the following performances of the year 1932 (first performance on the 1st of January),[297] and 1939 (first performance on the 10th of May). Here we note the combination of motifs of Classical architecture with slim pyramids in the background. They resemble rather the pyramids over the private tombs of the New Kingdom in Deir el-Medina than the royal buildings of the Old Kingdom.[298]

Karl Gruner, the stage for Aida, Act IV, 1883

177

The subsequent performances of the 1950s to 1980s (1957, 1961, 1976, 1986, 1993) were limited to relatively questionable evocations, if the used motifs can at all be defined as inspired by Egypt.[299]

The very fate of the story of *The Magic Flute* is interesting. It has stimulated attempts to write a sequel, the last appeared in the 19th century under the title '*Nitocris*'. These, too, shared reminiscences of Egypt.[300]

Aida

The world premiere of Aida was performed on December 24th 1871 in Cairo, the European premiere then in the Milan La Scala on February 2nd 1872. The main part was sung by the Czech soprano Teresa Stolz, the composer's friend.

The creation of the opera is connected with the person of an important French Egyptologist of the 19th century Auguste Mariette. Egyptologists took part also in other performances, the new 1880 performance in Paris benefited from the consultation of Gaston Maspero.[301]

Mariette's lively interest in the performance, and the fact that he took part in its Cairo realisation, indicates that he was concerned with its historical credibility. He was interested in details. He demanded e.g. the singers playing the main male parts, who had, according to the vogue of the period, a moustache and a beard, to shave themselves.[302]

Of course, it was impossible to avoid all inconsistent elements, but Mariette was from the very beginning trying not to present a caricature of Egypt on the opera scene, or to change it in a spectacle. '*... he did not hide his fears from seeing "his" Egyptians changed into grotesque, carnival figures.*'[303] On the other hand, he was aware of the problems that the creation of credible costumes presented for the costume designers, since the costumes had also to fulfill the demands of a dress for singing and acting.[304] We must add that the Aida roles are until now considered very difficult and emotional.

The costumes were also the result of period dressing conventions. If we observe the designs of original costumes, for example for the Milan first performance in 1872 and the photographs of the protagonists in the same costumes, is seems that the ladies portrayed (Teresa Stolz and Marie Waldmann) wear period strengthened underskirts under their Egyptian dress.[305]

Despite that, we must say that Mariette's presence at the creation of the costumes was reflected at least in the precision of the original designs, the aquarelles today kept in the library of the Paris opera. Although they were in all likelihood not drawn by Mariette[306] himself, they have a lot of very nice details. For example the proportions of the so-called 'blue crown'[307] on the design of the dress of the king really correspond to the Egyptian pattern,[308] although the crown itself is yellow.[309]

Mariette's role in the preparation of the setting was sometimes put to doubt, however, his interest was attested in written documents. Also the fact that the aquarelles with costume designs for the Cairo premiere were given to the Paris opera by Mariette's family attest his active part in the creation of stage setting.[310]

His personal participation in the preparation of props for the Paris premiere is also to be noted. J. M. Humbert studied period reports and concluded, that Mariette used models based on *Description de l'Égypte* and even on his own finds[311] For example the shape of the dagger in the design for the costume of Radames[312] corresponds to the dagger of Queen Ahhotep, discovered by Mariette. The tomb of Queen Ahhotep has a rich past and the individual finds have an even more colourful history. For example at the Paris exhibition in 1867, the jewels astonished Empress Eugenie, who was later to become one of the leading figures in the celebrations of the opening of the Suez canal, and she wished to possess them. The Egyptian Khedive told her to contact Mariette, who was authorised to give her the gift, but he refused and for some time fell into disfavour of the Khedive. Despite that we find him later playing an important role in the realisation of *Aida*.[313]

Karl Gruner, the stage for Aida, Act I and IV, 1883

Mariette was also probably the author of the story, which was elaborated into the libretto by Antonio Ghislanzoni using a previous arrangement by Camille du Locle.[314] The story of Aida is hard to classify to a particular historical period of ancient Egyptian history, although such attempts have been made.[315] The story runs, in short, as follows: Egyptians and Ethiopians are at war. The Ethiopians are defeated and their king Amonasro is taken captive. His daughter, the slave girl Aida, is already in Egyptian captivity, and the commander of the Egyptian armies Radames is in love with her. However, princess Amneris, the daughter of the

179

Egyptian pharaoh, has already chosen Radames as her future husband. Aida's father pressures her to learn from Radames how to escape from Egypt. She tries to persuade him to escape through this way with them. Amonasro hears their conversation; all are however surprised by Amneris and the high priest Ramfis. Aida and her father flee; Radames is arrested and condemned for treason. He refuses Amneris' proposal to save his life by marrying her and dies immured in a tomb under the temple of Vulcan (sic), where Aida sneaks in to die with him.

The libretto of Aida is plagued with some illogical twists. For example, in Act III Aida sings praise on the green meadows, scenting woods and fresh valleys of her homeland, which is rather inconsistent with the idea of Ethiopia (Nubia). It reflects also the traditional concept of Egypt as ruled by priests (it is they who try Radames in the end), and also of Oriental cruelty – the convict is buried alive.

J. L. Chappaz[316] noted the weak logic of the idea that Aida, presented on the one hand as an insignificant slave girl, would so easily become a confidant of the princess. The image of ancient Egypt as presented in Aida could be greatly criticised from the point of view of modern historical science, however, we must accept it as part of the 19th century historical culture. What did Mariette think about the story, when he was so focused in terms of stage settings?[317]

The names of the characters may have created an 'Egyptian' impression of the spectators of that time. They do not lack a real basis. Mariette called his princess Amneris because he himself read the name of the Divine Adoratress Amenardis[318] as Amneritis. Radames can be traced back to Ramesses (Ramses), and Amonasro to the name of the Kushite king of the 3rd century BC Amanislo.[319] Gauthier[320] even used in his *Livre des rois de l'Égypte* the form 'Amonasro'.

As D. Arnold[321] noted, Mariette's own research could have been reflected in his story in an indirect way. For example, the catacombs under the temple of 'Vulcan' in Memphis could have been inspired by his discovery of the Serapeum. Princess Amneris was inspired by the statue of the Divine Adoratress Amenardis.

In her time Aida created a great impression and until now it remains in the repertoire of opera houses with great success. The connection of Verdi's music with magnificent reconstructions of ancient Egyptian festivals (which were quite reliable for their time) guaranteed a lasting popularity to *Aida*.

Also the composer tried to create as credible image of Egypt in Aida as possible. He collected information about ancient Egyptian musical instruments and all accessible details on ancient Egyptian temple rituals.[322] Despite that he did not manage to try to reconstruct ancient Egyptian music – but that was not his aim, he needed just a touch of authenticity and atmosphere.[323]

As a whole, however, Aida remained in the mind of the contemporary European audience as a magnificent spectacle, while certain precision was demanded as a consequence of growing numbers of visits to Egypt and the amount of accessible literature.[324] These demands were, however, limited. For example the costumes did not necessarily look too unacceptable for them, despite the fact that while the designs appeared credible, the practical realisation bore only traces of ancient Egyptian inspiration.

A model Egyptian landscape in European imagination, ruins, palms and the Nile

There is another contribution to the contemporary reviews of Aida, namely the article of Edward Said, entitled 'The Empire at Work: Verdi's Aida'.[325] E. Said, the author of the definition of Orientalism, criticised the insufficient elaboration of Mariette's stage setting (in his opinion being a consequence of a condescending attitude toward Egyptian culture and implanting European conceptions therein). Considering Mariette's painstaking work, this seems hard to explain. The above-mentioned adoption of the setting and costumes to the demand of the theatre can in no way be considered as lack of understanding for the Egyptian culture. Said thus seems to be somewhat overinterpreting in order to support his theory of colonialism and its manifestations.

However, Said's comment that Verdi's Aida, as well as the Cairo opera building, belonged to the world of Europeanised Ismailid Cairo, is well justified. Besides it, there was the contemporary indigenous Cairo, which, as most of Egypt, had no access to many of the Ismailid court festivals and celebrations for Europeans.

J. L. Chappaz distinguished two styles in the settings for *Aida*,[326] namely reproduction (or copying) of ancient Egyptian forms, and their transposition (or arrangement). In general, it may be also stated that for many years, it was commonplace for stage settings to react to new Egyptological discoveries. However, 20th century settings were sometimes schematic and used straightforward topoi, often connected with recent discoveries (for example the mask of Tutankhamun). The 19th century, which is of greatest interest for us in connection with Czech environment, is returning again and the last performances reflect it in the form of the style of rich, colourful settings.[327]

National Theatre performed Aida first in 1884,[328] the premiere was on the 15th of February. The 1884 props were in continuous use at least until the year 1900. The designs for the decorations came from Vienna (firm Brioschi, Burghardt, Kautsky) and they are the work of Karl Gruner. The costumes were prepared by František Kolár and the props by the Bittner brothers. Gruner's setting was very rich, until now we may see his colourful designs, although it is no longer possible to test their realisations.[329] The props made by the Bittner brothers include figures of ancient Egyptian gods, the Apis bull, an elephant and a camel.[330] Period press praised the setting for its quality and historical credibility.[331] The stage setting of the opera was indeed magnificent[332] and K. Gruner included in it a great number of authentic elements. The ordering of the scene was subject to certain stage rules, and we therefore cannot blame him for arranging Egyptian architectural forms in order to comply with these rules. Sometimes he dared a somewhat bolder stylisation, for example the oblique architraves on the design for the temple interior,[333] but on the whole he remained trustworthy. All his designs date to 1883.

The director Šubert was subsequently criticised for the imposing stage of *Aida*, which was interpreted as a liking for pomp. Precisely the stage settings like those for *Aida* and *Excelsior* were the bases for the critique of Šubert's work in immediately following times. For example, according to some critics, in the end of the 19th century stage setting was accorded too much importance in the National Theatre to an extent that it became the dominant part of the performances.

According to Hepner's list,[334] these designs were used at least until the year 1900. Further archive materials come first from 1912 (with a single exception from 1901). The file[335] containing Gruner's designs allows us to see the following scenes:

Plate I for Acts I and IV: pillared portico. In the middle is a seated statue on a stylised throne, in the background behind it is a courtyard with a pylon flanked with columns. The composite capitals of the columns have not been executed with 'archaeological' precision. Everything is painted with bright colours.

Plate III for Act II, scene 2: the architecture comprises above all pylons with ram-headed sphinxes. All is sunk in rich green vegetation. The area is roofed by cloths hung on poles that stand in front of two pylon-like gates opposite each other.

Plate V: a view through temple architecture with a stylised colonnade. Some doors, and above all door-jambs are oblique, in keeping with the view of a pylon or naos (i.e. shrine, once again with the so-called cavetto cornice). The figures and 'inscriptions' cover every free space, the motifs employed include for example the marching army.

Plate IX: Act II, scene 1: The walls of two subsequent courtyards are covered with stylised paintings. The courtyards are covered with cloths that are decorated with stars that had indeed decorated ancient Egyptian ceilings. Columns and semicolumns are topped with Hathoric capitals.

Plate XIII: Act IV. Interior with columns. Door-jambs and parts of architraves are oblique.

Plate XVII: Act IV. The Nile riverbank with a small temple – kiosk (perhaps designed after Traian's kiosk in Philae) sunk in greenery, in the background a view of the river.

The costumes of this period are documented for example on the photograph of E. Turolla[336] in the role of Aida from 1898. The singer is wearing a pleated skirt with hems, decorative fringes, a top of period proportions (it looks like shaped for a bodice), covered with small coins, and a wide collar.

In order to compare more stagings of Aida, for which we have accessible material, we must go beyond the limit of the 19th century. This will take us outside the historical culture of that time, but we will be able to see whether the above-mentioned distinction[337] between resemblance and evocation applies also to the Czech environment. Resemblance is typical for the 19th century, the 20th century is characterised by evocation, often reflecting current discoveries. The same was true of the Czech stage. The first settings of 1884, 1901 (if it was not an arranged older scene), and 1912 held on to a descriptive scheme. We have seen a detailed description of the design from 1883. We know only one photograph from the 1901 performance, depicting one of the scenes designed by K. Štapfer.[338] In case of the first performance on October 6th 1912 we possess the photographical documentation of the props and the costume of King Amonasro.[339]

The main arch of the scene, columns supporting an architrave with a winged sun disc, remained on their place for the entire time of the performance. Most columns had composite capitals. In selected scenes, some columns are decorated with paintings, the motifs of which include above all stylised 'war' themes. The style of the whole still corresponds to the 'resemblance' part of the scale, although it is, similarly to Gruner's design form 1883, plagued with small inconsistencies. For example the lamps decorating the temple rather resemble the hanging lamps of Cairo mosques. The statue in the temple scene resembles a royal statue with the *nemes* headdress. The scene on the Nile abounds in rich tropical vegetation and a background with a dazzling turn of the river, shaded with palm trees, and is an altered version of Gruner's scheme. We know but little about the costumes; one preserved photograph depicts O. Chmel playing the part of Amonasro. He is wearing a short tunic with a decorative hem, the upper part of the skirt is decorated with an element in the form of crossed wings. One of the costumes – that of Aida – can be with a certain level of probability detected on the photograph of Emmy Destinn in this part.[340]

The third premiere of Aida took part on the 10th of March 1934. The setting was made by J. M. Gottlieb,[341] here the scene was only an indication and highly simplified. We know, however, more details on costumes, we possess photographs depicting the main figures and the whole scene. Amneris received a costume (seen on the photograph of the singer of this part M. Krásová)[342] that was undoubtedly inspired by the bust of Nefertiiti, which corresponds to the trend of the time of the staging.

Aida's dress is of a glossy cloth with a decorative ornament. Š. Štěpánková playing the part of Amneris also wears a glossy cloth with an indicated belt and collar or necklace, but otherwise it could just as well be a period evening dress. Interestingly enough, in the same year, 1934, C. De Mille, the later director of another classical piece of Egyptomania, *The Ten Commandments*, was working on *Cleopatra*. His costumes, too, evoked rather period clothing than that of ancient Egypt.[343]

The most important parts of the costumes of this Prague performance of Aida are stylised belts and collars – necklaces, although a look at true ancient Egyptian dress reveals that these are not always its most characteristic features. This, however, may have been a deeply rooted opinion concerning Egyptian clothing; several decades ago, the main 'Egyptian' feature on pictures was the *nemes*-headdress.[344]

The setting is much simple and it is limited to evocations of ancient Egypt. The scene is closed by a curtain and the background corners include obelisks, there are entrances with cavetto cornice, etc. The choreography of the dance (led by A. Nikolská) is interesting. The figures that we see on photographs are almost caricatures of Egyptian reliefs and correspond to the contemporary Lexa's critique[345] of imitations of Egyptian dance. The props are, on the other hand, surprising – the shields of the soldiers are of historical shapes. The king is wearing the *nemes* headdress, the hair curls on the forehead correspond to Ptolemaic statues (a very good example is to be seen on the fragment of a granite statue of Ptolemaios VI).[346] The scene on the Nile riverbank has clearly stylised columns, in the scene of the tomb, the dominating feature of the scene is an outline of a pyramid.

Drama

The world drammatical literature includes also dramas that derive their theme in one way or another from Egypt. Among the most famous of them we find Shakespeare's *Anthony and Cleopatra*. The newer include *Caesar and Cleopatra* of G. B. Shaw. Both plays were performed also on Prague theatre scenes.

One of the newer performances of *Anthony and Cleopatra* (1917) in the Vinohrady Theatre under the direction of Hilar and Hrska became a source of polemics. In the time of its staging, however, historical credibility was no longer the theme, but the impression of an almost expressionist stage setting[347] on the spectator, who was literally flooded by a wave of *'momentary impressions'*, according to the critic A. Procházka.[348] Egypt appeared on scene only as an evocation of a richly coloured scene in the background, that repeats stylised outlines of ancient Egyptian reliefs.[349]

Although they no longer belong to the historical culture of the 19th, but to that of the 20th century, the subsequent drammatical stagings of *Anthony and Cleopatra* and Shaw's *Caesar and Cleopatra* are also very interesting, including the most recent ones.

G. B. Shaw's play *Caesar and Cleopatra* was first performed in the National Theatre on October 3rd, 1917.[350] The setting was designed by K. Štapfer and the play was directed by K. Muška. The famous scene where Cleopatra meets the Roman commander under the Sphinx was characterised by a dominating figure of the Sphinx, stylised, however, into a caricature. Neither the costumes are characterised by a clear evocation or description of ancient Egypt.

Very interesting is the comparison with the setting of J. M. Gottlieb from 1925.[351] At that time, *Caesar and Cleopatra* was first performed on the 9th of October, under the direction of V. Vydra. The Sphinx is much more monumental and credible, its simplicity creates a better impression that the mocking description of her precursor from 1917. The monumentality and decorativeness of ancient Egyptian architecture are historically somewhat less acceptable as an image of Hellenistic Alexandria, especially as the stage is elaborated on large prospects of columned halls and porticoes. Only sometimes, the tendency to geometrical monumentality prevails, as for example in Scene 1,[352] where the setting is enclosed between huge inclined walls, perhaps belonging to temple pylons. The proportions of the columns that dominate the 3rd and 4th scene are more or less adequate to their Egyptian equivalents. The furniture on the scene almost creates the impression that its maker had studied the articles illustrating the discovery of Tutankhamun's tomb. The preserved drawings of the designs illustrate the colourful appearance of the stage. All in all the setting is a well-formed evocation of ancient Egypt including some descriptive elements.

The staging of Shakespeare's *Anthony and Cleopatra* inspired more diverging opinions among reviewers. The first performance in the National Theatre dates to the 3rd of March 1967,[353] that is outside the period of our interest. The play was first performed in Czech in Pilsen in 1909, and later in 1917 in the above-mentioned Vinohrady Theatre.[354]

Egypt also entered the content of a play of Czech authors, however, this happened as late as in the 20th century, and it was in the form of a parody. The 'Classical feerie in eleven scenes' *Caesar* of J. Voskovec and J. Werich (first performance 1932) includes of course also Cleopatra and characters of her

The post-Tutankhamun Czech Egyptomania in jewellery, 1920s

entourage. The queen is mocked as an *'operette figure of a disloyal wife whose amorous adventures steer the world'*[355] and the whole play is guided by *licentia poetica* rather than attempts at historical credibility.

The stage jewellery of Teresa Stolz for her role of Aida

Notes:

1 B. J. Kemp, *Ancient Egypt. Anatomy of a civilization*. London 1991; p. 103.

2 Ernst H. Gombrich, *Umění a iluze*. ('Art and illusion – A study in psychology of pictorial representation,' originally published in 1960), Prague 1985; p. 414.

3 Cf. Schäfer, *Principles,* pp. 306 and 308.

4 Basically the same analysis is to be found in Gombrich, *op. cit.*

5 *O historismu a dějepisectví* ('On historicism and historiography'), p. 34.

6 A model example is the painter of Dutch origin L. Alma-Tadema (for reproductions of his paintings, cf. e.g. Russell Ash, *Sir Lawrence Alma-Tadema*. 1995). Although his architecture may sometimes be found guilty of untrustworthiness, many objects that we can see on his paintings have been painted after museum pieces. For example on the picture entitled 'Joseph, the overseer of Pharaoh's granaries' from the year 1874, the wall in the background is decorated with the (misplaced, the setting is supposed to be 'Joseph's office') painting from the tomb of Nebamon, which is kept in the British Museum. Some Czech artists took no less meticulous care – J. V. Myslbek consulted J. L. Píč when creating the sculpture of St. Venceslas (Beneš, *op. cit.*, p. 109).

7 Cf. the treatises by a Hungarian scholar of art history G. Lukács. I have used the Czech edition of his work, *Umění jako sebepoznání lidstva*. ('Art as self-knowledge of humankind'), Prague 1976.

8 Its typical representatives are to be found precisely in the 19th century, the definitions of the genres are rather problematic and cannot be treated here in detail. A study of the historical novel can be found for example in G. Lukács, *Umění jako sebepoznání lidstva*, pp. 191f.

9 Lukács, *op. cit.*, p. 216. He maintains that W. Scott believed in the '*historically true ... period-rooted individuality of the spiritual life, morale, heroism ...*' (*op. cit.*, p. 208).

10 Cf. A. Grimm, *Joseph und Echnaton, Thomas Mann und Ägypten*. Mainz 1993. Already G. Flaubert used his own travel experience for his work, namely *Salammbo*, (cf. Krejčí, K., 'Foreword' to the Czech edition of *Pharaoh* of B. Prus, Prague 1957, notes to this edition were written by Zbyněk Žába, an important Egyptologist, and later a director of the Czech Institute of Egyptology).

11 For example among Czech scholars, Lexa noted first in 1923, when trying to distinguish the concepts of realism and romanticism in ancient Egyptian literature, that a work, that would distinguish these concepts of the ancient Egyptians, would have to include '... *a psychological assessment of the whole spiritual life of the ancient Egyptian, and today the material for that has not been collected, not to speak of its analysis.*' (Lexa, F., 'Realismus a romantismus ve staroegyptské literatuře beletristické' ['Realism and romantism in ancient Egyptian belles-lettres'], in *Beletristická literatura staroegyptská* ['Ancient Egyptian Belles-lettres'], Kladno 1921; p. 69.)

12 Krejčí, K.,'Foreword', p. 8.

13 Krejčí, K., 'Foreword', p. 8

14 Krejčí, *op. cit.*, p. 9.

15 A similar evaluation is to be found by H. Fischer (in the study *Der Ägyptologe Georg Ebers,* p. 94) in the context of period historical painting.

16 Beneš, Z., *Historický text a historická skutečnost* ('Historical text and historical reality'), Prague 1993. pp. 25-32. Also Beneš, Z., *Historický text a historická kultura* ('Historical text and historical culture'), pp. 83–92.

17 Beneš, Z., *Historický text a historická skutečnost*, p. 26.

18 Beneš, Z., *Historický text a historická kultura*, p. 109.

19 For the three types of historical text, cf. Beneš, Z., *Historický text a historická kultura,*

pp. 96–124, including an introduction to the semiosis of the text. For a comprehensive scheme of semiosis cf. Umberto Eco, *La struttura assente*. Milano 1968, 1980 passim, above all the entire part A on the general character of the sign, part B treats the iconic text; includes an analysis of various types of communication, and a classification of various types of signs and systems. There are English editions of his main treatises on semiotics, such as *A Theory of Semiotics* (1976), *Semiotics and the Philosophy of Language* (1984), and *The Limits of Interpretation* (1991) – the year in brackets is the first English edition.

20 Relevant passages can be found in the already cited literature (Beneš, Z., *Historický text a historická kultura, id., Historický text a historická skutečnost)* including references to further literature. There is to be recommended a series of works on ideas and theories regarding the reinterpretations, and new readings of a literary piece by Roman Ingarden, *The Literary Work of Art: An Investigation on the Borderlines of Ontology, Logic and Theory of Literature. With an Appendix on the Functions of Language in the Theatre,* translated and with an introduction by George G. Grabowicz. Evanston, Ill. Northwestern University Press, 1973 (With a short Ingarden bibliography.), furthermore *The Cognition of the Literary Work of Art*, translated by Ruth Ann Crowley and Kenneth R. Olson. Evanston, Ill.: Northwestern University Press, 1973. I have originally used the Czech edition – *Umělecké dílo literární*. Praha 1989; s. 246–247, s. 346ff.

21 Cf. Eco, U., *La struttura, l. c.*

22 Cf. Eco, U., *La struttura;* pp. 100ff. (scheme of semiosis).

23 For its analysis cf. Iversen, E., *Canon and proportions in Egyptian Art*. Warminster 1975 (2nd ed.); Schäfer, H., *Principles of Egyptian art*.

24 Cf. above Prisse d'Avennes and the erroneous painting of the Egyptian cosmetic spoon. For the mechanism of this influence see Gombrich, E. H., *Umění a iluze* ('Art and illusion'), passim. Gombrich stressed the role of stereotypes, that led for example to their depiction first of a general sign of a certain concrete entity, one that exhaustively characterised the category to which it belonged in the eyes of the contemporaries; particular signs, that were exclusively to be found by the entity in question, were then used only secondarily. Gombrich illustrates it on the example of the depiction of the Angel Castle, which was on a German early modern painting first characterised as a castle corresponding to the period conception, and only later has been augmented with a typical feature, known perhaps from descriptions – the angel on the roof.

25 For pictorial material see the exhibition catalogue *Die Ägyptomanie*.

26 *Egypt slovem i obrazem* I-II. Praha 1883. – a translation of his German original version *Aegypten im Wort und Bild* – from 1870s. I keep the Czech edition quoted here, because it was actually the source for the Czech environment, and as such is relevant to its study.

27 Humbert, *L'Egyptomanie*, etc.

28 Cf. also the quotation at the head of this chapter – Kemp, *Ancient Egypt, l. c.* A practical example of such an implementation of the criteria of one's own period to the historical source material was documented by Irena Lexová on one theory of Pierre Montet, in her work *O staroegyptském tanci* ('On ancient Egyptian dance'). Prague 1930; pp. 14–15.

29 Schäfer states that (after the English edition *Principles of Egyptian Art*, transl. John R. Baines, p. 7) „*We must always be aware that our understanding can never be complete. This is less because what is preserved, despite its profusion, remains, and always will remain, one-sided and full of gaps, or because we cannot waken a perfect human being from antiquity and incorporate him in our lives … it is far, far more because it is completely impossible for us to transport ourselves into the mind of a strange people. Such an aware-*

ness of limitations of insight or perceptiveness should never stop us from pressing forward as far we can. Research itself acquires from this barrier a particular, stimulating attraction. If no scholar can entirely free himself from himself and from the context in which he lives, this means that each individual will approach Egyptian art in his own way, which is racially, culturally, personally and temporally determined, and will by his agreement or disagreement conquer new areas or show known ones in a different light ... We must keep ourselves as far from the excessive enthusiasm which foists our own personalities onto the creations of ancient artists, as from a prim coldness – which is in the final analysis just as lacking in objectivity.'

30 For example the painting entitled 'Niljagd' (repr. in: *H. Makart und der Historismus in Budapest, Prag und Wien.* Ausstellungskatalog Schloss Halbturn, 1986) includes alongside fancifully dressed Egyptian women also cockatoo parrots and Guereza apes. His rendition corresponds to the period liking of exotism and his own inclination to the display of luxury on his paintings.

31 G. Wimmer, 'Orientreisen und Orientbilder', *Orient*, pp. 17ff. – '*Im Fall Ägyptens liegen Orientmalerei und Historienmalerei Seite an Seite.*'

32 *Europa und der Orient 800–1900*, passim.

33 *L'Egyptomanie*, end of the chapter 'Cléopatre, Amonbofis et les autres'.

34 G. Frodl specifically of Hans Makart, 'Wiener Orientmalerei', *Alte und Moderne Kunst* 26 (1981) no. 178–179; pp. 19–25. On p. 22. '*Er ist einer jener Künstler, für die der Orient ein gesellschaftliches Reiseabenteuer mit exotischem Austrich blieb. Der erotische Unterton, den die ägyptischen Bilder Makarts anschlagen (und nicht nur sie), wurde vom Publikum in diesem Fall gutgeheißen und begrüßt, da man wußte, daß im Orient freiere Sitten herrschten.*' Generally also Henri Marchal in the foreward to *Les Orientalistes I*, pp. 11–12; '*... pour échapper au puritanisme victorien ou au "moralisme bourgeois", les peintres transpossent sur un fond d'Orient onirique et voluptueux, les désirs, voite les phantasms – dévoilés en des odalisques lascives – que leur génération n'osait exprimer sous les poids des conventions.*' and also Herman de Meulenaere and P. and V. Berko, *Ancient Egypt in the 119 century painting.* Brussels 1992; pp 88 and 94, '*All Egyptianising paintings have one feature in common: the vision of Ancient Egypt they wish to transmit is that of a country of splendour, wealth and voluptuousness ...*'

35 Cf. Lynne Thornton, *Les Orientalistes I. Peintres voyageurs 1828–1908.* Paris 1983. The specific pages concerning the individual persons are quoted below. This book is an example of a great publication with a large amount of illustrative material, basic information concerning the individual works of art, and a bibliography to each one.

36 *Les Orientalistes I*, pp. 220–221.

37 *Les Orientalistes I*, pp. 242–243.

38 There is now a new comprehensive study by Martina Haja & Günther Wimmer, *Les orientalistes des écoles allemande et autrichienne.* Paris 2000, covering the theme in detail.

39 For personal data cf. *Allgemeines Künstler-Lexikon.* Vol. 3, München – Leipzig 1992; p. 149.

40 Cf. de Meulenaere, H. – P. & V. Berko, *Ancient Egypt in 19th Century Painting*, p. 132.

41 The details have not been revealed yet. Encyclopaedias of Czech artists do not include Ambros.

42 Frodl,'Wiener Orientmalerei', p. 24.

43 Cf. the representative sample of this type of paintings by H. de Meulenaere, *op. cit.*

44 Vlček, T., *Praha 1900*, p. 175.

45 Because of its general character, I consider this term to be well suitable also for the Czech cultural context, despite the fact that not all its manifestations have as yet been described. It was used also by Vlček, *Praha 1900*, p. 181.

46 A group (or generation) of artists, who represented a new wave in Czech literary revival, and introduced into it foreign themes and works.

47 Above all Austrian researchers point out that the Danube monarchy is no exception to the general trend of 19th century Orientalism connected with historicism (*Orient. Österreichische Malerei zwischen 1848 und 1914*. Ausstellungskatalog, hrsg. von Erika Mayr-Oehring, Residenzgalerie Salzburg 1997; e.g. p. 309). A whole small 'Austrian school' of Orientalist painters was created in Vienna. It was founded by Carl Müller (1834–1892, Cf. *Orient*, pp. 194ff.), who even had his studio for some time directly in Cairo, cf. above. This artist is also of interest in the context of the Czech lands, since during the stay in Egypt he met the architect František (Franz, according to Austrian publications) Schmoranz. Brothers František and Gustav (Gustav Schmoranz [1858–1930], director of the National Theatre 1900–1922, director and artist, agreed with a meticulous and costly realisation of stage decorations. Cf. *Národní divadlo a jeho předchůdci*. ['The National Theatre and its predecessors'], Prague 1988; p. 440) Schmoranz lived for some time in Egypt. Cf. below the chapter on František Schmoranz.

48 Cf. the summary of Vlček, *Praha 1900*, pp. 181f.

49 Curl, 'Aspect'.

50 Obelisk – for a general introduction, cf. *Lexikon der Ägyptologie* IV; c. 542–545, and Iversen. *Obelisks in Exile*. Copenhagen 1968–1972, Habachi, *The Obelisks of Egypt*. New York 1977. For a comprehensive work on the sources for the research on the significance of the obelisk see Martin, K., 'Ein Garantssymbol des Lebens. Untersuchung zu Ursprung und Geschichte des altägyptischen Obelisken bis zum Ende des Neuen Reiches.' *HÄB* 3, 1977.

51 Just like the pyramids, it was subject to various stylisations, as we can see on numerous Baroque and Classicist paintings, where the obelisk belonged to the common iconography of scenes set into the Egyptian environment. Cf. Syndram, 'Das Erbe der Pharaonen', in *Europa und der Orient*, illustrations.

52 Cf. Koch, W., *Baustilkunde*. Munich 1994.

53 Jan Baleka, *Výtvarné umění, výkladový slovník* ('Fine Arts, terminological dictionary'). Prague 1997, entry 'obelisk' p. 244.

54 It was for example used in the decorations of the street of Paris at the occasion of the welcome greeting of Henri II and Catherina di Medici, in this case even adorned with 'hieroglyphs' according to period concepts.

55 The original design of the monument of Josip Plečnik was rather reminiscent of a very thin Ionic column. Plečnik did, however, otherwise use free inspiration by Egyptian motifs (thin pyramids on the temple of the Most Holy Heart of the Lord in the Prague Vinohrady district), and his student Rothmayer followed in his footsteps in this respect. Although their works belong to a much later period than the one we are now interested with, they form an integral part of the Czech context. The work of Plečnik cannot be neglected also for the reason that it seems to have inspired the contemporary architect Theimer (designs of their works were shown for example in the exhibition *Cesta na Jih* ['Journey to the South']. Prague 1999, Municipal House – and a catalogue of the same name).

56 Cf. *České sochařství XIX. a XX. století* ('Czech sculpture of the 19th and 20th centuries'). Prague 1963. Text by Anna Masaryková. Illustrations – Plate no. 57 and pp. 33, 39 passim.

57 Curl, *op. cit., 'during the Renaissance period many Egyptian or Egyptianising motifs were hardly recognised as having Egyptian origins until Athanasius Kircher and others began their investigations.'*

58 Hlavačka, M., *Cestování v éře dostavníku* ('Travelling in the era of the coach'). Prague 1996, fig. on p. 17.

59 The pyramids were understood in various different ways in European Mediaeval period. Besides the above-mentioned books of Morenz and Humbert, other important works treating the evolution of the significance and understanding of the pyramid are the final chapters of the large volumes of R. Stadelmann (*Die Ägyptischen Pyramiden*. Mainz 1991; pp. 264ff.) and M. Lehner (*The complete pyramids*. London 1997; pp. 240–243). For the symbolic importance of the pyramid, rooted in European cultural memory, and expressed also in literary works, cf. E. Staehelin, in *Fs Lichtheim*, pp. 889ff.

60 For a long time it remained the pattern of the European conceptions of the pyramids (E. Iversen, *The myth of Egypt*), which were so deeply rooted, that when the itinerary of Remedius Prutký, who had in his time really visited Egypt, was transcribed, a plate was attached to it containing an engraving of a pyramid, proportionally corresponding to that of Cestius and not to the Egyptian pyramids as Prutký saw them (Verner, *ArOr* 36, 1968).

61 The most impressive ones include for example the tombstone of Maria Christina, daughter of Maria Theresia, by A. Canova. (J. S. Curl, *Egyptian revival*, illustration for example in Lehner, *The Complete pyramids*, p. 243.)

62 The tombstone of J. Vratislav of Mitrovice in the Prague Old Town church of St. James. Fischer's 'Entwurf einer historischen Architektur' was probably inspired by the works of Athanasius Kircher (Morenz, *op. cit.*, p. 149).

63 Morenz, *op. cit.*, the question of any deeper interest of artists like for example Poussin remains open. Morenz writes: '*der Maler Poussin, der Architekt Fischer und der Goldschmied Dinglinger einen unverkennbaren Zug zur Gelehrsamkeit gemeinsam haben … es drängt sich aber die Frage auf, ob dieser Drang zur Wissenschaft nicht über das bekannte normale Studium überlieferter Werke durch den Künstler, und gerade den Künstler von Rang, weit hinausgehe …*', p. 150.

64 For an overview of relevant literature, cf. the entry 'Sphinx' in *LÄ*. E.g. Demisch, H., *Die Sphinx. Geschichte ihrer Darstellung von den Anfängen bis zum Gegenwart*. Stuttgart 1977, containing an illustrative overview of the changes of the form of the Egyptianising and Classicising Sphinx. Above all the illustrations are comprehensive.

65 Cf. Baleka, *Výtvarné umění*, p. 329, entry 'sfinga'.

66 There is an early mediaeval example in Prague – the paving of St. Lawrence's Church at Vyšehrad. The church itself does not exist any more, but the archaeological excavations brought us fragments of the paving tiles.

67 Besides the already cited work of Demisch, *Die Sphinx*, cf. also the article of J. M. Humbert, 'Postérité du sphinx antique: la sphinxomanie et ses sources', in: *L'Égyptomanie à l'épreuve*.

68 Cf. for example the above-quoted opinion of the authors of the entry 'Egyptian revival', in *Dictionary of art*.

69 Division after Friederike Werner, *Ägyptenrezeption in der europäischen Architektur des 19. Jh.* Weimar 1994, who gives also a relatively rich amount of material for each of the categories.

70 For museum decorations cf. also Christiane Ziegler, 'L'Égypte et le décor des musées européens au XIXᵉ siécle', in *L'Égyptomanie à l'épreuve*.

71 Further see Werner, *Ägyptenrezeption*, pp. 88ff.

72 Werner, *Ägyptenrezeption*, pp. 2f.

73 Cf. the relevant entries in Arnold, Dieter, 'Rundstab', 'Hohlkehle' and 'Pfeiler' in *LÄ* V, c. 320f; *LÄ* II, c. 1263; *LÄ* IV, c. 1008f. and Wildung, Dietrich, 'Flügelsonne', *LÄ* II, 277–279.

74 Carrott, *Egyptian Revival*, pp. 54ff.

75 Werner, *Ägyptenrezeption*, pp. 73f.

76 Cf. Renate Wagner-Rieger, (*Wiens Architektur im 19. Jahrhundert*. Wien 1970. After Vybíral, *Století dědiců* ['The century of heirs'], p. 20 and p. 168, note 40.) differentiates two phases of historicism in architecture. The typical trait of the first phase is the use of unified stylistic elements, the second is characterised by a marked syncretism and effectivity. In my opinion, Prague architecture gives good examples for both epochs. For the first one, we may cite the National museum, Rudolfinum, or National Theatre, for the second the renewal buildings of the Old Town and above all of Josefov (Both now form part of the historical core of the city, Prague 1).

77 Baleka, *Výtvarné umění*, p. 132.

78 Important observations on this are to be found in the work of Jindřich Vybíral, *Století dědiců a zakladatelů. Architektura Jižních Čech v období historicismu*. Prague 1999; p. 53ff., 59–61, 64–65.

79 Cf. Koch, *Evropská architektura*, p. 374 ff. – German original, Koch, *Baustilkunde*. München 1994.

80 Koch, *op. cit.*, p. 375. A great example is the agglomeration of representative buildings in Vienna in the area of the demolished fortifications. The parliament is built in the anticising style, the university in Neorenaissance style, the Votive Church is Neogothic.

81 In Prague for example the synagogue in the Jerusalem Street, further the synagogue in Pilsen.

82 Cf. the exposition of Friederike Werner, *Ägyptenrezeption in der europäischen Architektur des 19. Jahrhunderts.*

83 Humbert, *op. cit,* pp. 300ff.

84 Cimitero monumentale of Milano, Italy, hosts at least one pyramid and one tomb in the shape of a deformed pylon. The same is true about the Paris cemetery Pére Lachaise (Humbert, *L'Egyptomanie).*

85 Cited after J. S. Curl, 'Aspect'.

86 Cf. Muk, J. – Líbal, D., *Staré Město Pražské* ('The Old Town of Prague'). Prague 1996; chapter. 'Období historizujících slohů a secese' ('The period of historicising styles and Art Nouveau'), above all pp. 457ff and 466f.

87 For an interesting remark on this in part already at the time of its creation, but mainly subsequently, criticised concept see Marie Benešová, 'Nápodoba v architektuře 19. stol.' ('Imitation in 19th century architecture'), in *Divadlo v české kultuře 19. století* ('Theatre in 19th century Czech culture'). Prague 1985; pp. 227f. It stands against the otherwise usual one-sided critique of the historically decorated façades, which in no way reflected the internal structure of the building but bore their own semantic content.

88 Benešová, M., 'Nápodoba', p. 229.

89 *Historické vědomí v českém umění 19. stol., Uměnovědné studie III* ('Historical consciousness in 19th century Czech art, Art historical studies III'). Prague 1981.

90 A general explanation of the role of the decoration of buildings and memorials with motifs from national history can be found for example in Vybíral, *Století dědiců* ('The century of heirs'), pp. 149ff., on the basis of the case study of the history of the Žižka monument in Tábor, designed by Myslbek. In terms of Prague representative buildings – national representation (including the celebration of national past) – dictated the decoration of the National Theatre. Cf. František Žákavec, *Chrám znovuzrození* ('The temple of rebirth'). Prague 1938; passim.

91 For a comprehensive overview see Vybíral, *Století dědiců a zakladatelů*, pp. 11ff.

92 For reproductions of some drawings and a short overview of the works of the most important artists above all from the period of Czech Neorenaissance can be found in the work of J. Brožová, *Čeští architekti realisté 19. století. Výstava původních kreseb a plánů*

('Czech realist architects of the 19th century. Exhibition of original drawings and designs.'). Prague 1952. Some sketches of Czech architects were also to be seen in the exhibition 'Cesta na Jih' ('Journey to the South'; Prague Municipal house 1999 and the catalogue of the same name and date).

93 Designed 1858.

94 Matějček – Wirth, *op. cit.*

95 As a part of the painted ceilings with a Pompeian motif, executed in all likelihood by Pietro Isella (cf. Vlček, et al., *Umělecké památky Prahy* ['The artistic monuments of Prague']. vol. I).

96 Cf. the Baroque sphinxes of H. Demisch, *Die Sphinx.* Stuttgart 1977; Fig. 493f.

97 Vlček, *Praha 1900*, p. 64.

98 Vlček, *Praha 1900*, pp. 64-65.

99 Fanta, J. 'Naše Jubilejní výstava: Stavby a architektura' ('Our jubilee exhibition: buildings and architecture'),*Osvěta* 21, 1891; p. 751.

100 Cf. also the section on Julius Zeyer.

101 Otokar Fischer, *Činohra Národního divadla do r. 1900* ('The National Theatre drama until the year 1900'). Praha 1983; p. 278.

102 Reproduced for example in Javorin, A., *Pražské arény* ('Prague arenas'). Prague 1958; s. 331.

103 Viz Baťková, Růžena a kol., *Umělecké památky Prahy. Nové Město, Vyšehrad.* Praha 1998. For details on the construction and above all a concise art historical description of the National museum, cf. pp. 672f; house no. 1700.

104 After the Czech edition of this text had been concluded, there appeared an excellent overview of the history of the National museum, including history of its buildings; Karel Sklenář, *Obraz vlasti* ('The Image of Homeland'). Prague 2001. It is a lively text by an archaeologist and historian, which describes the character of the Czech national museum, namely, being a national monument as much as a museum. This is especially clear, when we follow Sklenář in his description of internal decoration of the museum (*Ibid.,* pp. 281ff.), which includes portraits of men considered important for the national consciousness, plus paintings representing key places (understood historically) of Bohemian landscape.

105 Cf. Ziegler, Ch., 'L'Égypte et le décor des musées européen au XIXᵉ siécle', in *L'Égyptomanie à l'épreuve* and id. together with Andreu, Guilemette and Rutschowscaya, Marie-Héléne, *L'Egypte ancienne au Louvre.* Paris 1997. pp. 17f.

106 She is wearing a headdress very similar to the hairstyles on New Kingdom and Late Period coffins, a necklace, pectoral, and armbands.

107 Satzinger, H., *Das KHM*, p. 62. Some of them can be identified with a certain level of precision – for example the statue of seated Isis, which is now in the Egyptian Museum in Cairo, CG 38 884 (cf. Leclant et al., *Egitto nel crepuscolo.* Milano 1981–1991; p. 151).

108 Arch. J. Schulz in the years 1885–1890.

109 Cited after the cat. *Výstava generace Nár. divadla v Praze* ('The exhibition of the National Theatre generation in Prague'), S.V.U. Myslbek, Prague, 1932.

110 Vlček, T., 'Orientální motivy v kosmopolitním a národním programu lumírovské generace' ('Oriental motifs in the cosmopolitan and national programme of the Lumír generation'), in *Povědomí tradice v novodobé české kultuře* ('The awareness of tradition in modern Czech culture'). Prague 1988.

111 Cf. the collection of František Schmoranz in the Architecture Archive of the National Technical Museum in Prague.

112 Attested also by the illustrations used by G. Ebers in his *Aegypten im Wort und Bild,* and also in its Czech edition *Egypt slovem a obrazem* (cf. *ibid.,* 'List of plates').

113 Vlček, *Praha 1900,* p. 180.

114 A new monograph on Mašek has been recently published – K. Fabelová, *K. V. Mašek.* Prague 2002, English summary on pp. 218–287.

115 Vlček, *Praha 1900,* p. 171.

116 Vlček, *Praha 1900,* p. 180 and p. 173 – Islamic influence in Mašek's work.

117 Koch, *op. cit.,* p. 380.

118 Celetná 33/U Prašné brány 1 a 3/Královdorská 6, house no. 1078/1079, Prague 1, Old Town. Cf. Vlček, *Umělecké památky Prahy I* ('Artistic monuments of Prague').

119 The double uraeus can be seen on Egyptian royal statuary and reliefs of the New Kingdom, often adorning headdresses of queens and goddesses, such as Mut of Thebes (the consort of Amun). There are examples of this use on Late 18th dynasty and Ramesside royal portrayals, like the Ramesside princess (Meritamun ?) in the Cairo Museum – CG 600. The Egyptian uraei, however, are often completed with two crowns, respective of Lower and Upper Egypt.

120 Prof. Faiza Haikal of the Cairo University considers this combination of Egyptian and Classical motif an attempt to symbolically encode the roots of European culture.

121 Dušní 11, Prague 1 – Josefov, built by the technical and building office of J. Limax (cf. Vlček, *op cit.*)

122 House no. 300/XII, Prague 2, Vinohrady, Wilsonova. For bibliography see Vlček et al., *op. cit.,* p. 795.

123 Vlček, T., *Praha 1900,* p. 110.

124 Reproduced e.g. in Vlček, *Praha 1900,* p. 157, fig. 165.

125 Reproduced and dated in Vlček, *Praha 1900,* p. 142, fig. 134.

126 *Umělecké památky Prahy* ('Artistic monuments of Prague') – *Nové Město, Vyšehrad,* p. 782, with an orientation plan of the cemetery on pp. 780 and 781.

127 The portico was designed by Mikuláš Karlach as a part of the composition of the cemetery in the style of the Italian Campo Santo (cf. Baťková, Růžena et al., *Umělecké památky Prahy* ('Artistic monuments of Prague') – *Nové město, Vyšehrad,* p. 778.

128 Cf. *Umělecké památky Prahy – Nové Město, Vyšehrad,* p. 778.

129 See the overview of J. M. Humbert. *L'Egyptomanie dans l'art occidental,* passim.

130 Historical motifs naturally did not appear exclusively in the 19th century, but the *'definition of the concept of historical paintings belongs fully into the 19th century'* (Pelikánová, Z., *Historické motivy v českém výtvarném umění v 70. a 80. letech 19. stol.* ['Historical motifs in Czech visual arts of the 1870s and 1880s'], Master's Thesis FF UK, Prague, 1983).

131 Quoted after Prahl, R., *Česká historická malba v XIX. století* ('Czech historical painting of the 19th century'). Exhibition catalogue Městské muzeum in Milevsko, 1978, with a short overview of the painters of that time.

132 *Manuscripts* is a common term used for two forgeries, two parchments claiming a Mediaeval origin, but in fact written in 19th century. These were used as a testimony proving allegedly ancient origins of the Czech independent state.

133 Pelikánová, *op. cit.*

134 R. Kuchynka, 'Josef Mánes a staré umění' ('Josef Mánes and ancient art'), reprinted in L. Hlaváček, *Josef Mánes a umělecká rodina Mánesů* ('Josef Mánes and the Mánes artist family'). Prague 1988, pp. 302 ff. Mánes noted above all important Czech buildings.

135 Cf. Hana Volavková, *Josef Mánes, malíř vzorků a ornamentu* ('Josef Mánes, pattern and ornament painter'). Prague 1981. pp. 122f.

136 Ševeček, L., *Josef Navrátil a český romantismus* ('Josef Navrátil and Czech Romantism'). 1986, catalogue of the exhibition of the Gottwaldov (now Zlín) regional fine arts gallery, no. 53. The painting is now deposited in the West Bohemian Gallery in

Pilsen. However, the catalogue of O. Macková – of the year 1974 (exhibition of the West Bohemian Gallery in Pilsen 1973–1974) does not mention Cleopatra among the exhibited works. Neither J. Brožová (in *Umění a řemesla* 6/1968, pp. 204f., 'Josef Navrátil a malovaná výzdoba českého interiéru' ['Josef Navrátil and painted decoration of Czech interiors']) mentions any link to an Egyptian inspiration, despite the fact that she does treat Classical inspiration.

137 Jaroslav Čermák (1830–1878) spent some time in Paris, but he did not become famous through his historical paintings, but rather with paintings 'in a South Slavic folklore setting, with special attention to Montenegro' (L. Hlaváček, *Mánes a umělecká rodina*, p. 159).

138 Mrázová, M., *Václav Brožík (1851–1901)*, exhibition catalogue of the Prague Municipal Gallery, 1976-77, mentions that he finally did not study in Munich by the famous author of narrative historical paintings and Makart's predecessor K. Piloty. However, it can still be maintained that he knew European historical painting – he spent many years in Paris and even became the member of the French Academy. Among the themes of his historical paintings, Czech themes prevailed – the life of Jan Hus, Prague defenestrations, etc. His foreign motifs include for example 'A party by Rubens'. Neither the catalogue of the *Výstava Jednoty výtvarných umělců* ('Exhibition of the Union of visual artists') in Prague, organised in 1928 in the Municipal House, includes any work, which would have had an explicitly Egyptian theme, manifested at least in the title.

139 Nowadays the large collected volume Marie Mžyková ed., *Křídla slávy* ('Wings of Glory'). Prague 2001, may be consulted. It was published to accompany the exhibition of the same name, in Prague Rudolfinum, and concerns precisely the contacts of this generation with the French environment.

140 Quoted after the catalogue *Výstava generace Národního divadla v Praze* ('The exhibition of the National Theatre generation on Prague'), Spolek výtvarných umělců Myslbek, 1932.

141 Mžyková, *Křídla slávy* II, p. 446–447. In *ibid* we can find other Orientalising Bible – inspired works by Josef Douba and others. Most of them are now lost, and known only due to period reproductions in various periodicals and catalogues.

142 Cf. on him in the journal *Dílo*, Vol. I, pp. 69f.

143 Cf. the traditional characteristics of Egyptian architecture by Friederike Werner, who also collected period quotations of classical works. See Werner, F., in Seipel, W., *Ägyptomanie*. Wien 2000.

144 These details are well apparent in the reproduction in the book of Fr. Žákavec, *Chrám znovuzrození* ('The temple of rebirth'). Prague 1938; p. 121. Commentary on p. 112.

145 Cf. Mžyková, M., *Vojtěch Hynais*. Prague 1990; p. 28.

146 See Mžyková, *Křídla slávy* II, p. 449.

147 There is still one piece of art to be consulted, as Mžyková, *Křídla slávy*, II, p. 444, states there is a work named *Antonius a Kleopatra* in City Museum of Dačice, made before Mucha left for Paris, but she connects this work with Classical inspiration. As it is, it would be one of the few that were made with such theme in Bohemia itself.

148 They can easily be compared to the Egyptian floral motifs, for example nos. 290 or 291 and 292 of P. Fořtová-Šámalová, *Das ägyptische Ornament*. Text von Milada Vilímková. Hanau 1963. Fig. 69.

149 Jiří Mucha, *Alfons Mucha*. Prague 1999; pp. 81, 114.

150 Mucha, *Alfons Mucha*, pp. 98–99, 107 – the preparation for the illustration of the work of the historian Seignobos on German history – *Scény a epizody z dějin Německa* ('Scenes and Episodes from the history of Germany'). In a similarly meticulous way he later studied also folklore by Čeněk Zíbrt, when working on Slovanská epopej ('Slavic epic', *op. cit.*, p. 319).

151 Mucha, *op. cit.*, p. 287.

152 My descriptions of Mucha's works are based on the reproductions in the book *Mucha* by D. Kusák and M. Kadlečíková, Prague 1992.

153 Mucha, *op. cit.*, p. 101.

154 Quoted after Mucha, J., *Alfons Mucha*, p. 253. Considering simplicity as one of the main characteristics of Egyptian architecture is considered to be a common, but erroneous opinion (according to Prof. Dietrich Wildung).

155 Mucha, J., *op. cit.*, p. 327.

156 Exhibition catalogue *L. Marold*, Prague, Municipal House, 1998. The list published here was based on an unpublished manuscript of the French researcher Druart. The fact that only French editions are mentioned, although many of the books, as the authors themselves acknowledge, were published also in German (and some even in Czech, although they do not state which ones) complicates the search for them to compare the illustrations.

157 Brabcová, J., *Luděk Marold*. Prague 1988.

158 Cf. Dvořáková, Z., *Josef Václav Myslbek*. Prague 1979; pp. 160ff.

159 Ladislav Šaloun sculpted a female head entitled *Egypťanka* ('The Egyptian') and the work of Otakar Španiel probably contains the motif of the sphinx. I was unfortunately unable to access the publication of P. Wittlich, *Sochařství české secese.* ('Czech Art Nouveau Sculpture') Prague 2000, where the work of Šaloun is reproduced.

160 The term congregation denotes a group of monasteries – abbeys, united under the leadership of an archabbot. The entire Benedictine order is thus divided into several congregations. For the Beuron congregation, cf. Harald Siebenmorgen, *Die Anfänge der Beuroner Kunstschule.* Sigmarigen 1983.

161 M. Kunštát, 'Podněty beuronské školy pro české umění na sklonku 19. století' ('The inspiration of the Beuron school for Czech art in the end of the 19th century'), in *Povědomí tradice v novodobé české kultuře* ('The consciousness of tradition in modern Czech culture'). Prague National Gallery 1988, collected volume of the conference.

162 M. Kunštát, *op. cit.*

163 Cf. Holub, K. – Šebová, M., *Beuronská umělecká škola v opatství Svatého Gabriela v Praze* ('Beuron school of art in the St. Gabriel abbey in Prague'). Prague 1999; p. 19.

164 Holub, K. – Šebová, M., *Beuronská umělecká škola v opatství Svatého Gabriela v Praze,* plates.

165 For the architectural history of the monastery complex of the Emaus, see Baťková et al., *Umělecké památky Prahy* ('The artistic monuments of Prague'), *Nové Město, Vyšehrad*, pp. 134f. and 293ff.

166 Baťková et al., *Umělecké památky Prahy, Nové Město, Vyšehrad*, p. 135.

167 Holub, K. – Šebová, M., *Beuronská umělecká škola v opatství Svatého Gabriela v Praze* ('Beuron school of art in the St. Gabriel abbey in Prague'), p. 21.

168 Werner, *Ägyptenrezeption*, passim.

169 Rokosová, L., *Mistr František Bílek, křesťan a umělec* ('Master František Bílek, a Christian and an artist'). Master's Thesis, Department of Church history, Hussite Theological Faculty of the Charles University, 1998/9.

170 M. Halířová, accompanying text to the exhibition 'Bílek's villa and its maker', Prague City Gallery, probably 1990s.

171 Rokosová, *Mistr František Bílek*, and also Lenderová, Milena, *Zdenka Braunerová*. Prague 1999, passim.

172 *František Bílek (1872–1941)*. Prague 2000 (Prague City Gallery), p. 23.

173 *František Bílek (1872–1941)*, p. 85.

174 Rokosová, *Mistr Františk Bílek, křesťan a umělec* ('Master Františk Bílek, a Christian and an artist'), p. 35.

175 Rokosová, *Mistr František Bílek, křesťan a umělec* ('Master František Bílek, a Christian and an artist'), p. 36.

176 *František Bílek (1872–1941)*, p. 273.

177 Quoted after Svobodová, *Cesta Františka Bílka*. Prague 1998; pp. 73–74.

178 Svobodová, *op. cit.*, p. 71 and F. Bílek – 'Confiteor umění', in *František Bílek (1872–1941)*.

179 From the lecture of Fr. Bílek 'O stavbě budoucího chrámu v nás' ('On building of the future temple within us'), printed in: F. Bílek, *Stavba budoucího chrámu v nás*. ('The building of the future temple within us'). Prague 1996; pp. 25–26, and passim on the significance of the colonnade.

180 For a general overview cf. the entry 'Säule', *Lexikon der Ägyptologie*, V. And also *Lexikon der Ägyptologie* III, c. 323–327, 'Kapitell'. One of the very interesting examples of the use of the lotus-formed column is the portico of the Ptahshepses mastaba in Abusir (Verner, M., *Preliminary report on Czechoslovak Excavations in the mastaba of Ptahshepses at Abusir*. Prague 1976).

181 P. Wittlich (*Česká secese* ['Czech Art Nouveau'], Prague 1982) states that he originally wanted to include in to the cycle of 38 paintings (resp. statues or sculpture groups, Bílek intended to create an alley of sculptures) themes from Adam and Eve, over the Flood, to ancient Egypt, Moses and many others.

182 Cf. *František Bílek (1872–1941)*, p. 246 – his French inspiration can be discovered according to period literature.

183 Quoted after Svobodová, *Cesta Františka Bílka* ('František Bílek's journey'), p. 11.

184 Vlček, *Praha 1900*, p. 214.

185 *František Bílek (1872–1941)*, passim.

186 *František Bílek (1872–1941)*, pp. 89–90.

187 Cf. H. Demisch, *Die Sphinx*. Passim, but mainly the last chapters.

188 Bílek understood and classified the woman somewhat differently in his spiritual context. The woman '*suffers with our creative effort... she, the all-seeing one, suffers enormously, but quietly fulfills her duties and remains silent*'. '*The mother of all living ones, the mother of all saints.*' Cited after *František Bílek (1872–1941)*, p. 225.

189 *František Bílek (1872–1941)*, p. 97.

190 Larvová, H., accompanying text to the collection of photographs of Bílek's works, published by the Prague City Gallery, cf. M. Halířová, accompanying text to the exhibition 'Bílkova vila a její tvůrce' ('Bílek's villa and its creator'), Prague City Gallery, probably 1990s.

191 Cf. the journal *Český svět*, Vol. IV, no. 32, in Prague 22. 5. 1908; 'K výstavě Fr. Bílka' ('On the exhibition of Fr. Bílek') – '*It seems there is growing in front of our eyes an Egyptian initiate, who undertook all tests of physical and moral character in order to penetrate the mysteries of nature and reached the award in the form of the crown of the magus, the reward of all knowledge.*'

192 The statue typologically resembles the kneeling statues of the 30th dynasty, but he may have used older kneeling statues as his models, such as those from the New Kingdom. For the first possibility cf. e. g. the period illustration in Perrot, G. – Chipiez, Ch., *Histoire de l'art dans l'Antiquité. Tome premier – L'Égypte*. Paris 1882; p. 718, fig. 483. Nectanebo II from the Louvre. It is, however, impossible to determine whether precisely this statue may have inspired Bílek.

193 Wittlich, P., *Česká secese* ('Czech Art Nouveau'), p. 289.

194 Friederike Werner, *Ägyptenrezeption in der europäischen Architektur des 19. Jahrhunderts*, passim.

195 *F. Bílek (1872–1941)*, p. 219.

196 Rokosová, *Mistr František Bílek*, p. 26 – for some time they even considered to become monks together.

197 Svobodová in her work 'Cesta Františka Bílka' ('The journey of František Bílek'), quotes as a good evidence their letters, where both positively reflect on their meeting Bílek, p. 4, on their friendship passim and also *František Bílek (1872–1941)*, passim. The editions of the letters are also eloquent (*Básník a sochař – Dopisy Julia Zeyera a Františka Bílka z let 1896–1901* ('A poet and a sculptor – letters of Julius Zeyer and František Bílek from the years 1896–1901'). Prague 1948. They, however, contain no mention of Egypt, although both surely had something to say to this theme. It appears, however, that this was not the way of Bílek's Egyptian inspiration. Moreover, many of his works with Egyptianising elements come from more recent times. Both Zeyer and Březina visited Bílek in Chýnov, and Bílek even illustrated Březina's poems.

198 Vachtová, L., *František Kupka*. Prague 1968; passim.

199 Elisée Reclus, *L'Homme et la terre*. Paris 1905, 1908, sociological study. For an overview of illustrations see *Kupka – Waldes*. Prague 1999; pp. 359ff.

200 For example the illustration for *L'Homme et la terre,* entitled 'Égypte' consists of two parts. One shows a procession of priests with a statue of a deity that the priests manipulate – a popular motif of the critique of religious illustrations. The statue with the head of a falcon corresponds in likeness and proportions to Egyptian models and also to illustration number 44 on p. 64 in Perrot, G. – Chipiez, Ch., *Histoire de l'art dans l'Antiquité. Tome premier – L'Égypte.* Paris 1882. The motifs from the heading of the chapter 'Histoire ancienne' are also similar. *Kupka – Waldes,* p. 361. The designs for illustrations are in the possession of the Waldes collections, in 1996 they were returned to the heir in restitution.

201 *Kupka – Waldes,* plates 224, 225.

202 *Kupka – Waldes,* Plate No. 116.

203 Prague National Gallery – inventory number NG O 12643.

204 Also '*Černý idol*' ('Black idol'), '*Revolta*' ('The revolt'), '*Zaujatost*' ('Interest'). Cf. Vlček, T., *Praha 1900*, p. 215.

205 Cf. *Kupka – Waldes*, p. 258, no. 7 and p. 327, and also Schloegl in Jaeger, B. – Staehelin, E., *Ägypten-Bilder. OBO* 150. Fribourg 1997; p. 167. One book of Edouard Schuré was also published in Czech, but first in 1927, namely the story *The priestess of Isis.* Even here, however, mainly on p. 78-79, he exposed his belief in the primeval knowledge of the ancient Egyptians.

206 Kupka definitely did not need an Oriental theme for depicting the nudes – browsing the catalogue of his work we can come across a very openly erotic paintings and drawings (cf. *Kupka – Waldes, passim*). So, in his case the interest in Oriental theme was given by the illustration theme itself, and his studies for it were thorough.

207 A selection of photographs appeared for example in *Nový Orient* 5/2001.

208 Published in Prague by E. Beaufort in 1908. The journey was undertaken in 1905–06.

209 As the author himself stated (on p. 115), '*My dear friend, Viktor Oliva, fulfilled my wish with enthusiasm and illustrated my book. I appreciate his help particularly, as he contented himself with that few photographs I have brought from that journey ...*' These photographs were most likely bought as a tourist souvenir, and not made by Guth himself.

210 The research conducted in this field may modify, or at least complement, Chapter I, since the Austrian *Matrikelbuch* and other documents suggest that the Czechs travellers to Egypt were far more numerous than it was hitherto believed. Moreover, they seem to have even taken part in touristic trips organised by Thomas Cook agency.

211 A shorter form of the article on Julius Zeyer was published in *Nový Orient* 4/2001, entitled 'Druhý život starověkého Egypta v díle Julia Zeyera' ('The alternative life of ancient Egypt in the works of Julius Zeyer').

212 Pavel Poucha, 'Orientální náměty v díle J. Zeyera', studie pramenná ('Oriental

motifs in the work of J. Zeyer'. A material study), in Zeyer, J., *Světla Východu, výbor z díla s orientálními náměty* ('Lights from the East. Selected works with Oriental motifs'). Prague 1958; p. 568. The pagination in Zeyer's works cited below refers to this edition (Zayer). For Zeyer's translation of the original work cf. *Spisy Julia Zeyera* ('The collected works of Julius Zeyer') *XXXIV,* pp. 331ff.

213 Zeyer, p. 138.

214 The relationship of Egyptian deities to their so-called sacred animals is still a matter of discussion. Classical authors often denounced this custom, understood as a belief in the representation of a deity by an animal, which is worshipped. It is, however, unclear how the Egyptians themselves understood the relationship between deities and 'their' animals. For relevant literature, cf. the individual entries for deities and animals in *LÄ* and Bonnet, *RÄRG,* a new overview in Redford, D. B., *Oxford Encyclopedia of Ancient Egypt.* Oxford 2001, vols 1–3.

215 Zeyer, p. 138.

216 Zeyer, p. 137.

217 Zeyer, p. 137. A similar formulation however appears also in the original old French story, cf. *Spisy Julia Zeyera XXXIV,* p. 332.

218 Poucha, *op. cit.,* p. 570.

219 Poucha, Pavel, 'Orientální náměty v díle J. Zeyera' studie pramenná ('Oriental motifs in the work of J. Zeyer'. A material study), in: Zeyer, J., *Světla Východu, výbor z díla s orientálními náměty*

220 Poucha, *op. cit.,* p. 539.

221 Poucha, *op. cit.* p. 573. M. Rolin, *Histoire ancienne des Egyptiens, des Cartaginois, des Assyriens, des Babylonies, des Médes et des Perses de Macedonies, des Grecs,* Tome I–VIII. Amsterodam 1733–1735, was one of the classical historical works on antiquity. Uhlemann, M., *Handbuch der gesammten aegyptischen Altertumskunde,* I–IV., Leipzig, 1857–58. This book was according to Poucha in Zeyer's library, which is now kept in the possession of the Náprstek Museum. M. Uhlemann was a private assistant professor of Egyptology in Göttingen between 1854–1862. Cf. Horn, J., 'Daten zur Geschichte der Ägyptologie in Göttingen', in *GM* 28, 1978. For Uhlemann cf. *Who was who in Egyptology.* London 1995, and also Brugsch, H., *Ägyptologie,* p. 127.

222 Poucha, *op. cit.,* K. Schwenck, *Die Mythologie der Aegypter.* Frankfurt 1855.

223 For an analysis of Plutarch's work cf. for example Hopfner, T., *Plutarch über Isis und Osiris.* Monographien des Archív Orientální, Bd. 9, 2 Vols., Prag 1940–41; Griffiths, J. G., *Plutarch's De Iside et Osiride, with Introduction, Translation and Commentary.* Cardiff 1970; Hani, J., *La religion égyptienne dans la pensée de Plutarque.* Paris 1976. See also the overview in *LÄ* IV, c. 1066–1067.

224 Cf. e.g. Macura, V., 'Sen o rozkoši' ('The dream of sexual pleasure') in *Český sen.* ('Czech Dream'), Prague 1998 or the collected volume *Sex a tabu v české kultuře 19. století.* ('Sex and taboo in 19th century Czech culture') Prague 1999; passim, above all the articles of V. Macura (corresponding in content to 'The dream of sexual pleasure'); D. Tureček a D. Mocná (the latter to the decadent atmosphere of the Art Nouveau turn of the century). The relationship of researchers in the 19th century to this theme concerning the studied cultures is therefore correspondingly careful (bordering perhaps on tabooisation, cf. the entry 'Erotik' in *LÄ* I) – we may for example find comments on the licentiousness of the Egyptians, derived from the knowledge of the first translated texts. We can find them also in the Czech Rieger's dictionary – cf. the section on encyclopaedias and dictionaries. The studies on moral life of the Egyptians concentrate, however, above all on the exposition of the rules and customs of family life. Adolf Erman (*Aegypten und aegyptisches Leben im Altertum.* Tübingen 1887,), however, mentioned also Pap. Turin 145 /Cat. 2031/55 001

(*op. cit.*, p. 223; modern publication Omlin, J., *Der Papyrus 550001 und seine satirisch-erotische Zeichnungen und Inschriften.* Turin 1968), and was thus very critical of ancient Egyptian morale. If they were able to put something like this into somebody's grave, what kind of moral values could they have had, he asks.

225 Cf. Ranke, H., *Die Ägyptischen Personenamen.* Bd I. Glückstadt 1935; p. 161/20.

226 See Lichtheim, M., *Ancient Egyptian Literature* III. Berkeley – London 1980 and reprints, p. 125 ff.

227 Cf. the bibliography to the work in *LÄ* IV, 'Prinzenmärchen', c. 1108–1111.

228 Vachala, B., in *František Lexa, zakladatel české egyptologie.* AUC Philosophica et Historica 4–1984. Praha 1989.

229 Cit. Poucha, *op. cit.*, p. 573, note 26 – Ch. W. Goodwin, *The Story of Saneha. An Egyptian tale of four thousand years ago translated from the Hieratic text.* London 1866.

230 The illustrations were used also in the edition of the selected works '*Světla Východu*' ('Eastern lights') in 1958, the 'Egyptian' one on p. 136. According to T. Vlček, *Prague 1900*, p. 181, Jan Zrzavý was *'one of the artists who had the strongest form of a desire for a holistic dream, for a world lit by a common deep joy connected with the Orient ...'*

231 For the analysis of the symbolism of the sphinx in general, cf. Demisch, H., *Die Sphinx* and also Wiebke Rösch-von der Heyde, *Das Sphinx-Bild im Wandel der Zeiten* I–II. Rahden 1999.

232 *Čeští spisovatelé 19. a počátku 20. století* ('Czech writers of the 19th and early 20th centuries'). Prague 1989, p. 323.

233 Svoboda, *Antika a česká vzdělanost* ('Antiquity and Czech culture'), p. 207.

234 Svoboda, *l.c.*

235 A fictional story on the implementation and abolishment of the law banning the presence of women at the castle of Emperor Charles IV.

236 Cited after Fischer, *Činohra Národního divadla do roku 1900* ('National Theatre drammatical scene until 1900'). Prague 1983; p. 122.

237 The main source for Březina's opinions are his conversations with Gisa Picková-Saudková – *Hovory s Otokarem Březinou* ('Dialogues with Otokar Březina'). Prague 1929 (further G. Picková, *Hovory*).

238 G. Picková, *Hovory*, p. 139.

239 G. Picková, *Hovory*, p. 80.

240 H. P. Blavatskaya (1831–1891), 'theosopher' and author of the book *Isis Unveiled* (1877). Cf. also E. Hornung, *Das esoterische Ägypten.* Munich 1999; pp. 146ff.

241 G. Picková, *Hovory*, p. 31.

242 Cf. O. Březina, *Eseje* ('Essays'). Olomouc 1996; pp. 105ff.

243 Dvořák, M., *Tradice díla O. Březiny* ('The tradition of the work of O. Březina'). Třebíč 1993; p. 52.

244 Cited after E. Chalupný in the collection of articles *Stavitel Chrámu* ('Temple builder'). Prague 1941; p. 159.

245 Moses in a poem from 1887, Eliah and Gedeon in the prologue of *Tajemné dálky* ('Mysterious Distance'; mentioned by Emanuel Chalupný in the collection of articles *Stavitel Chrámu*, p. 27).

246 The influence of ancient Indian philosophy of the work of Otokar Březina was described by the Indologist Vincenc Lesný, 'Influence of ancient Indian philosophy on Czech poet Otakar Březina', in *India and the world, A monthly organ of internationalism and cultural federation*, 8, 1933, vol. II, nr 4 (April), Calcutta (Entry no. 108 in the bibliography of the works of Otokar Březina, *Stavitel chrámu*, p. 267, assembled by J. Riess).

247 E. Chalupný, *op. cit.* p. 248.

248 Cf. 'Editorial notes', in *Eseje* ('Essays'). Olomouc 1996; pp. 241–2.

249 O. Březina's essay 'Skryté dějiny' ('Concealed history'), published in the collection *Eseje*, p. 106.

250 J. Jungmann, *O jazyku českém*, ('On Czech language'), *Hlasatel český* ('Czech herald'), 1806, quoted after Lněničková, J., *Čechy v době předbřeznové* ('Bohemia in the pre-March time'), p. 131. It remains a question whether Jungmann did not rather refer to the presumed hereditary nature of arts and caste system, which were considered characteristic of the Egyptian society by period textbooks.

251 Božena Němcová, *Babička* ('Grandmother'), edition of 1961, p. 118.

252 *Spisy Julia Zeyera XXXIV*, p. 157.

253 *Masopostní odvary* ('Carnival decoctions'), 1874, after the edition *Obrázky z domova i ciziny* ('Pictures from home and abroad'). Prague 1983, p. 396.

254 *Na hřbitovech* ('At the cemeteries'), *op. cit.*, p. 129. His visit to Paris dates to the 1860s, of the Orient to the 1870s.

255 Fischer, H., *Der Ägyptologe Georg Ebers. Eine Fallstudie zum Problem Wissenschaft und Öffentlichkeit*. A list of older works can also be found here, including studies of Germanists.
Erman's critique of Ebers is, however, not so unequivocally negative as Fischer often states. Erman at times also valued Ebers, among others also for his role in the popularisation of Egyptology. Cf. Erman, A., *Mein Werden und mein Wirken*. Leipzig 1929; passim in the sections 'In der Wissenschaft', 'An der Universität'.
For the list of dissertations cf. Fischer, H. *op. cit*. So far, however, I was unable to access them – for the study of historical culture, some coud be of interest, such as for example '*Ägypten in der deutschen Literatur des 19. Jahrhunderts. Bogumil Goltz – Max Eyth – Georg Ebers*' of Rawhia Abd-l-Noor; cited by Fischer.

256 Cited after Fischer, *op. cit.*

257 Fischer, H., *Der Ägyptologe Georg Ebers*, p. 14. For the comparison of Erman and Brugsch see Köhler, U. in *GM* 12, 1974.

258 Corresponding to the definition of the historical novel, cf. Müller, H., 'Thesen zur Geschichte des historischen Dramas und des historischen Romans (1773–1888)', in *Geschichtsdiskurs 3*.

259 The data on the publishing dates of both novels come from the article of B. Vachala in *František Lexa*. p. 68.

260 Herodotus, III, 1–2.

261 Characterised by Fischer, H., in *Ebers*.

262 Novák, Arne – Novák, J. V., *Přehledné dějiny literatury české* ('A comprehensive history of Czech literature'). Brno 1995 (reprint of the original edition); p. 692.

263 For a discussion of the romantism of Ebers and positivism of Erman cf. Fischer, H., *G. Ebers*, pp. 14ff. On Erman see also U. Köhler in *GM* 12, 1974 and Koch, Klaus, *Das Wesen altägyptischen Religion im Spiegel der ägyptologischen Forschung*. Hamburg 1989.

264 Cited after Fischer, *Ebers*, p. 14. '*Die Welt war vor fünf Jahrtausenden nicht anders als sie zu unserer Zeit ist, dieselben Gesetze, denen sie heute gehorcht, herrschten schon damals in gleicher Unerbittlichkeit.*'

265 Iversen, *The myth of Egypt*. Copenhagen 1968.

266 Arnold, D., 'Moses und Aida', *Ägypten. Dauer und Wandel*. Mainz 1985.

267 Holden, A., ed. *The Viking Opera Guide*. London 1993. Entry 'Händel'.

268 *Die Ägyptomanie (Ausstellungskatalog)*. Wien 1994, chapter 'Ägypten in der Oper'.

269 Source: *Soupis repertoáru Národního divadla 1881–1983* ('List of the repertoire of the National Theatre 1881–1983'). ND publishing, Prague 1983.

270 Cf. also J. P. Bartoli in *L'Égyptomanie à l'épreuve de l'archéologie*. Paris – Bruxelles 1996.

271 Performed in 1892, cf. *Soupis repertoáru ND*, entry 509.

272 The reproduction of the designs for stage decorations *(International Dictionary of*

Opera, s.a., London, the relevant entry) suggests, that despite the temporal setting somewhere in late Roman, if not Byzantine, Egypt, many of the elements used were characteristic of the period image of the Egypt of the pharaohs, above all in the costumes (headdresses etc.). A similarly Egyptianising design is reproduced in *Die Ägyptomanie*, chapter 'Ägypten in der Oper'.

273 *Soupis repertoáru*, entries 2015, 2208.
274 Jiřina Růžová, 'Bibliografie děl Františka Lexy' ('Bibliography of the works of František Lexa'), no. 77, in *František Lexa*, Prague, 1984 (1989), AUC Philosophica et historica 4.
275 Jaroslav Vogel, *Leoš Janáček*. Prague 1997; p. 351.
276 This custom is, however, not the rule, as is shown for example by the new performance by the Brno opera in 1999.
277 *Die Ägyptomanie, l. c.*
278 Eg. Holden, A., *The Viking Opera Guide*, p. 931, reproduction of a painting of a scene from the opera of C. Saint-Saens, *Samson and Dalila*.
279 Plate 21, file 173/83 archive ND (archive of the National Theatre), designed by the Vienna company Brioschi-Burghardt-Kautsky. By coincidence, Alfons Mucha has shortly worked for the same company. However, if these stage decorations come from the year 1883 or later, he surely did not design them, since he had left the company already in 1881 (Kusák, D. – Kadlečíková, M., *Mucha*. Prague 1997, 'Introduction').
280 File 'Excelsior I' Archive ND, the depicted figure is wearing a blue-and-white striped headdress, earrings, it is leaning against a staff crowned by a winged sun disk and an ibis, and a striped skirt around the waist, tied to a knot in the front.
281 Cf. Beneš, Z., *Historický text a historická kultura* ('Historical text and historical culture'). Prague 1995, passim.
282 Ptáčková, V., *Česká scénografie XX. stol.* ('Czech scenography of the 20th century'). Prague 1982.
283 There is a number of works on the Magic Flute, monographs, articles and chapters in syntheses on Mozart, in English there are e.g. H. C. Robbins Landon, *Mozart and the Masons*. London 1991, Katherine Thomson, *The Masonic Thread in Mozart*. London 1977, Jacques Chailley, *The Magic Flute, Masonic Opera: An Interpretation of the Libretto and the Music*. Trans. Herbert Weinstock, New York 1971.
284 E. Staehelin, in *Fs Lichtheim*, pp. 911ff. also analyses the Egyptian rite in Freemasonry itself. For the background of *The Magic Flute* she cites also Morenz (*Die Zauberflöte*), who saw here a connection with the *Aithiopika* of Heliodorus. The musicologist P. Nettl, who worked in Prague for some time (one of his books was published here) also studied *The Magic Flute*, and analysed the links of the opera to Freemasonry.
285 Cf. also Staehelin, in *Studies … presented to M. Lichtheim* (*Fs Lichtheim*).
286 For an analysis see Morenz, *Begegnung*, p. 153.
287 Buchner, A., *Opera v Praze* ('Opera in Prague'), Prague 1985, p. 78.
288 Hepner, V., *Scénická výprava na jevišti Národního divadla* ('Stage decoration on the National Theatre scene'). Prague 1955; p. 135.
289 Archive ND, file 173/83, plate 7, 11 etc.
290 Hepner, *op. cit.*, p. 80.
291 Archive ND file *o 155* f.
292 *Ibid.*
293 Photographs of the actors in the roles of Sarastro and the 'Speaker' were preserved in the quoted file *o155* f.
294 Reproduced on Plate 5 in the book of A. Chaloupka, *Česká divadelní dekorace* ('Czech theatre decoration'). Prague 1939.
295 Archive ND file *o 155g*.

296 *Lexikon der Ägyptologie*, entry 'Krone'.

297 Archive ND file *o155h*, stage decorations by František Kysela.

298 Archive ND file *o 155 ch*, stage decorations by František Muzika.

399 Archive ND files *o 155 i* to *o 155 m*.

300 E. Staehelin, *Fs Lichtheim*, pp. 916–917.

301 Chappaz, J. L. 'Mettere in scena Aida', in *Come ci vedono, L'Egitto antico della riscoperta e dell'immaginario.* Torino 1993; p. 37.

302 Cf. the exhibition catalogue *Die Ägyptomanie.*

303 Chappaz, *op. cit.* '*Ma fin dall'inizio Mariette non nascose i suoi timori di vedere i "suoi" Egiziani trasformati in figure grottesche e carnevalesche.*'

304 Chapter 'Ägypten in der Oper', *Die Ägyptomanie*, For details cf. J. M. Humbert, 'Mariette Pacha and Verdi's Aida', *Antiquity* 59, 1985; pp. 101–104. P. 103 – '*Mariette's major concern was therefore to be as faithful as possible to the archaeological models: the scenery was a scrupulously exact reproduction of the real thing and so were the costumes, although for these he nevertheless accepted the adaptations made necessary by the singer's physique and by the requirements of the stage.*'

305 Cf. the reproductions in G. Verdi, *Aida. Texten* … etc. Reinbek bei Hamburg 1985, designs for the Milan first performance on pp. 183 and 185. Photographs on pp. 175 and 178, especially apparent on the picture of Tereza Stolz, on p. 175. In the case of Mrs. Waldmann on p. 178, the general impression of the vulture headdress was somewhat altered by her period hairstyle.

306 Although it is not wise to discard this possibility entirely. He was originally a drawing teacher. Cf. J. M. Humbert, 'Mariette Pacha and Verdi's Aida'. He also proved his understanding for creating scene decorations in the 1867 exhibition in Paris, where he designed the Egyptian exhibition halls (Humbert, *op. cit.*, p. 103).

307 On ancient Egyptian headdresses cf. *Lexikon der Ägyptologie*, and Abubakr, Abd-el Monem Joussef, *Untersuchungen über die ägyptischen Kronen.* Glückstadt – Hamburg – New York 1937, passim.

308 Simpson, W. K., 'Mariette and Verdi's Aida', *Bulletin of the Egyptological Seminar*, 2, 1980.

309 Reproduced for example in the catalogue *Die Ägyptomanie*, p. 289, in colour.

310 Simpson, *op. cit.* Before him, this are was studied by for example Elisabeth Riefstahl, J. M. Humbert (*Revue Musicologique*, 62, No. 2, 1976) and Salah Abdoun (*Genesi dell'Aida*, Quaderni dell'Istituto di Studi Verdiani, No 4, 1971). Bibliography after Simpson, *op. cit.*

311 Humbert, '"Aida" zwischen Ägyptologie und Ägyptomanie'. G. Verdi, *Aida. Texten…etc.* Reinbek bei Hamburg 1985, p. 117.

312 See Humbert, *L'Egyptomanie*, p. 290.

313 Rosalie David, *The Experience of Ancient Egypt.* London 2000; p. 122.

314 Verdi himself took part in creating the text, he was satisfied with the 'Egyptian sketch' as he called the theme. After reading it, he stated '*behind that, there is the hand of an expert, thoroughly familiar with the stage*'. Quoted after Southwell-Sander, P., *G. Verdi.* Bratislava 1995.

315 For example in the programme of the performance of the National Theatre Opera in Brno (first performance 9. 10. 1993), we find a large quotation from the older programme of the year 1978 by E. Bezděková some notes to the Egyptian conquest of Nubia in the New Kingdom and to the position of the priesthood. It may, however, be argued that if the colourful royal court and festivities in Act II of the opera remind us today of New Kingdom Egypt, the war with Ethiopia reflects either the clash of Amosis II with the king of Kush or the battles of the 25th Dynasty. It is most likely that the story of Aida is a typical love story, for which it was necessary to

find a very interesting setting. Verdi himself stated that the motif was not entirely new, which can also be supported with evidence from theatre history. It is also possible that the story reflected some period social problem; rather than by any concepts of the power of the Egyptian priesthood, it may have been inspired by the period problem of the relationship between Italy and the church, as is the opinion of Bezděková in the cited theatre programme. J. M. Humbert worked more with Mariette's own notes – and believes, that Mariette may have been inspired by the reign of Ramesses III, the time of military campaigns, but also of a conspiracy, which may have inspired him to write the court scene in Aida. Humbert, ' "Aida" zwischen Ägyptologie und Ägyptomanie', G. Verdi, *Aida. Texten* … etc.

316 Chappaz, *op. cit.*

317 For notes to the story of Aida see also Morenz, *Begegnung*, p. 179 and Humbert, *op. cit.*

318 Amenardis – name of two 'divine adoratresses' (of Amun) from the time of the 25th, resp. 26th, dynasties. Bibliography: overview in *LÄ*, I, col. 196–199, 199–201, further *LÄ*, entry 'Gottesgemahlin'; Sander-Hansen, C. E., *Das Gottesweib des Amun.* København 1940, p. 9 (Amenardis I); K. A. Kitchen, *The Third Intermediate Period in Egypt.* Warminster 1986, passim.

319 Arnold, D., 'Moses und Aida'.

320 Simpson, W. K., 'Mariette and Verdi's Aida', 1980, p. 116.

321 Arnold, D., *op. cit.*

322 Humbert, '"Aida" zwischen Ägyptologie und Ägyptomanie', p. 112ff.

323 Humbert, '"Aida" zwischen Ägyptologie und Ägyptomanie', p. 116.

324 Humbert, '"Aida" zwischen Ägyptologie und Ägyptomanie', p. 118–119.

325 E. W. Said, *Culture and Imperialism.* London 1994; pp. 133–159.

326 Ibid., *op. cit.*, p. 38.

327 Chappaz, *op. cit.* For example in one of the performance of 1927, the motif of the recently discovered bust of Nefertiiti appeared, and since the UNESCO campaign to save Abu Simbel, the façades of the temples of Ramesses II dominated also opera scenes. Chappaz concludes that '*L'Apporto dell'archeologia egizia alle realizzazioni di Aida in ultima analisi di una povertà desolante e stupefacente per l'egittologo.*' that is, that the contribution of Egyptian archaeology to the opera scene is in the end surprisingly and unfortunately small from the point of view of an Egyptologist.

328 Hepner, V., *Scénická výprava na jevišti Národního divadla.* Praha 1955 records no other stage decorations until this time.

329 ND archive file 173/83, pp. 1, 3, 5, 9, 13, 17. The decorations themselves were destroyed during WWII (1945 airstrike) – personal communication of the employees of the ND archive.

330 Hepner, *op. cit.* p. 124. The camel is an anachronism in ancient Egypt, but it was in all likelihood tightly connected with Egypt in the minds of period spectators.

331 Hepner, *op. cit.*

332 *Výtvarná práce na jevišti Národního divadla 1881–1941* ('Visual art on the stage of the National Theatre 1881–1941'), catalogue of the exhibition of the Union of visual artists Myslbek. Prague 1941.

333 Plate no. 13 of the quoted file. Also the 'hieroglyphic' inscriptions, sketched on the designs, are repeated groups of stylised signs, on the final appearance of which on stage we may only speculate. Anyway, from far away, which is how stage decorations are perceived, the impression was probably convincing enough.

334 Hepner, *op. cit.*

335 173/83, ND Archive, plates 1, 3, 5, 9, 13, 17.

336 Buchner, A., *Opera v Praze* ('Opera in Prague'), p. 133.

337 Chappaz, *op. cit.*

338   File *o 4 e* to year 1912 contains a loose photograph described as scene from year 1901 according to K. Štapfer.

339   Material of the ND archive, file *o 4 e.*

340   Holzknecht, V. – Trita, B., *Ema Destinnová*. Prague 1972; p. 100, fig. 71. 'Aida in all likelihood from a later period'. The decorations in the background correspond to the preserved photographs from the performance (AND *o 4 e*).

341   File *o 4 f*, ND archive.

342   *Ibid.*

343   Humbert, *L'Egyptomanie*, p. 290

344   E.g. H. Makart, *Niljagd*, see above.

345   As he stated for example in the introduction to the work of his daughter Irena Lexová, *O staroegyptském tanci* ('On ancient Egyptian dance'). Praha 1930. I. Lexová dedicated a short chapter in her work to modern reflection of Egyptian dance, 'Poznámka o egyptských tancích moderních tanečnic' ('Note on the Egyptian dances of modern dancers'), *op. cit.*, p. 60, where she notes that during her studies she had not met a single depiction of fitful movements and wrought hands, which modern dancers consider to be Egyptian. However, she did find similar shapes in Etruscan art. The photographs of the performance of Aida in 1934, however, include similarly wrought positions of hands.

346   The head of a granite statue, extracted from water at Aigina. Now in the National Museum of Athens, Inv. ANE 108. Cf. the citation after Hölbl, G., *Geschichte des Ptolemäerreiches*. Darmstadt 1994; p. 162.

347   Ptáčková, *op. cit.,* p. 23.

348   Ptáčková, *l. c.*

349   Ptáčková, *op. cit.,* colour plates.

350   Documentation ND Archive, archive set no. *91a*

351   Documentation ND Archive, archive set no. *91b.*

352   ND Archive no. *91b,* file of the original designs of Gottlieb.

353   Documentation ND Archive, archive set no. *30a.*

354   Theatre programme *Antonius a Kleopatra* ('Anthony and Cleopatra'), ND 1967.

355   Pelc, J., *Zpráva o Osvobozeném divadle* ('Report on the Liberated theatre'). Prague 1982; p. 108.

Papyrus v Egyptě nebyl věcí lacinou, a proto psali i žáci cvičili se v psaní na střepech nádob nebo hlazených kusech vápence. Na tomto mateřidle Egypťané také psali dopisy, dodací poznámky, účty, stvrzenky a t. d. Náš snímek zadržuje vyblednuvší kus vápence, popsaný hieratickým písmem (psaným od pravé ruky k levé), obsahující nadpis a počátek nauky, kterou napsal král Amenemhet pro svého syna.—Hieroglyfický a fonetický přepis (psaný od levé ruky k pravé) našeho hieratického textu vyhlíží takto.

šḏjt ꜣjt.n ḥm n njśwt bjtj Śḥtp-jb-Rꜥ sꜣ Rꜥ ꜥmn-m-ḥꜣt mꜣꜥ ḥrw
ꜣḏf m wḏw.t mꜣꜥ.t n sꜣf nb-r wr, ḏd.f:
ḥꜥ m ntr śrm n sꜣḏ.t-y n.k

Překlad zní (tečkované značky, které doplňují na této své kresbě, jsou v původním textu zničeny): „Nauka, kterou napsala Jeho Milost král Horního a Dolního Egypta Sehetepjebre syn Reuv Amenemhet ospravedlněný a kterou proslovil jako poselství pravdy pro svého syna, pána celého světa. On řekl: ›Až budeš zříti, jsa bohem, buď posluchem toho, co ti hodlám říci---". Nápis pochází z konce 18. nebo začátku 19. dynastie (r. 1300 – 1150 př. Kr.)

podobu mumie s jejich vlastním obličejem, které se proměnily ve skutečné živé bytosti, dokonale shodné se svými pány, přihlásili se za ně a vykonali za ně práci, jestliže jejich páni k ní byli voláni; jmenují se vešebti. Aby vešebt věděl, za koho má pracovati, bývá zhusta jméno jeho majitele na něm napsáno, nebo i vyryto, na našem je napsáno:

śḥꜣ wśjrw ḥrj ꜥḥ Nfr-ḥtp mꜣꜥ ḥrw

V překladu: Osvícený Usirev vrchní představený stáje Neferhotep ospravedlněný.

V hrobě kromě skutečných obětí, vyskytují se také modely obětí z dřeva, hlíny nebo kamene, které čarami mění se na oběti skutečné. Častými jsou hliněné obětní kužele, do jejichž základny jest vryto jméno jejich majitele. Na našem kuželu bylo původně vytlačeno:

ḥm-ntr 4-[nw] n ꜥmn Nfr-ḥtp mꜣꜥ ḥrw

Egypťané měli několik různých názorů o posmrtném životě; podle jednoho mrtví žili v západní říši Usirově (říše Osiris), a byli nuceni také pomáhati při nutných pracích, bez nichž stát se neobejde. Čárami pomáhali si k tomu, aby se vyhnuli nejtěžším pracím. Zrobili nebo dali si zrobiti sošky, mající

„čtvrtý prorok Amona, Neferhotep ospravedlněný". Později na levé straně bylo ještě vyraženo:

ḥm.t.f   což zní v překladu „jeho manželka".

12

IV. Egypt as a hobby

Collections and libraries

'Che antichità egiziane siano state precocemente apprezzate e quindi avidamente e amorosamente ricercate (e imitate!) significa uno loro capacità di inserimento immediato entro strutture valutative che sono le nostre ...'[1]

If an individual's interest in ancient history and art was not transformed into a scholarly interest, and if the general situation was favourable, it mostly resulted in the creation of a specialised collection and library. Current vogue also sometimes stimulated above all the higher levels of society to collects objects or books of a certain specialisation. Both the European nobility and the ever richer bourgeoisie had enjoyed a long tradition of collecting, and individual interest in exotic peculiarities and artistic objects had been filling cabinets of curiosities and kunstkammers ever since the Renaissance.[2] The collections gradually ceased to be mere sets of curiosities, and they acquired a specific task – to preserve works of art as objects of scientific study.[3]

In the course of the 19th century the interest in monuments from the Orient rose to such an extent that a lot of antiquities dealers began to literally pillage not only antiquities markets, but also archaeological sites. Egypt had a lot to offer in this respect, both as a result of the wave of Egyptomania that flooded Europe after the Napoleonic expedition, and because of the easy accessibility of her monuments. In terms of the history of the discovering of Egyptian monuments, the first half of the 19th century is called 'the time of the consuls', after the title of diplomatic representatives of European powers, who did not use their positions only for political agitation. Many of them, such as for example the British consul Henry Salt and the French representative with a Piedmont origin Bernardino Drovetti, gathered large collections of works of art which they subsequently offered for sale to European courts or public museums. This is how the collections of the Louvre and of the Turin museum came into being. The private collectors in Britain and France did not stay aside and above all many noble families assembled considerable collections of antiquities. The Austrian monarchy did not stay behind in this respect, despite its somewhat more distant links to the Near East. Austrian diplomats, above all Joseph von Hammer-Purgstall,[4] contributed with their gifts to the enlargement of the Emperor's collections in Vienna. Individual collections were not limited to the territory of residential Vienna. Some collectors can be found also in the Czech lands, above all in the second half of the 19th century.

In the course of the 17th and 18th centuries, noble families in the Czech Lands were founding their collections, comprising, however, above all of paintings.

In the 19th century, industrialists like Vojtěch Lanna appear among the collectors, in the end of the century also artists such as Julius Zeyer, Jiří Karásek, Emmy Destinn, or Alfons Mucha. In the time of the so-called First Republic, more collectors appear among the high state officials.

Egyptian antiquities, shortly aegyptiaca, could have entered these collections as curiosities, objects of systematic interest, or as souvenirs from voyages. The large collection of Pallme, which is now in the possession of the Náprstek Museum, indicates a more systematic interest. The collection of the writer Jiří Karásek from Lvovice reflects his interest, and so does his library, which contains specialised publications. Emmy Destinn, a famous singer of the role of Aida, was for sure captivated by the magic of Egyptian objects. Cyril Dušek, the first Czechoslovak ambassador in Egypt, also possessed a collection of aegyptiaca, that subsequently became part of the collection of the Karásek gallery, which was later in 1922 donated to the Sokol movement.[5] The rich private entrepreneur Zdeněk Macek met a number of important figures and collected souvenirs from visited sites. He also dwelled in Paris and one of the objects of his collection is even recorded as a gift of Jean Cocteau.[6]

A number of other private persons brought souvenirs from their voyages to Egypt, and these objects subsequently became parts of other small collections that we now know of.[7] The following two chapters include an overview of these collectors' activities.

The Collectors in the Castle[8]

Among the largest and also most important collections are those of the Archduke Joseph Ferdinand, given to the Olmütz museum, and the Metternich collection, until today kept at the Königswarth castle. The Archduke Joseph Ferdinand Salvator[9] (1872–1942), son of Ferdinand IV (the dethroned Grand Duke of Tuscany), was a passionate hunter, and in 1903 he undertook an expedition to Egypt, using the cover name of Count Buriano, thus joining the large number of leading Hapsburg figures of that time who took part in hunting expeditions to Orient. In 1910 he donated his collection of aegyptiaca to the museum of his garrison town in Olmütz.[10]

The collection of K. W. L. Metternich contained above all gifts of Muhammad Ali and belongs undoubtedly to the most important of its kind, despite the fact that one of its most significant objects – the so-called Metternich stela – is missing.[11] There exists a list of the objects contained in this collection, and some of them have even been published in detail.[12] The most important ones include the coffin and mummy of the seal bearer Qenamun from the 18th Dynasty.[13]

The aristocratic collectors in the Czech Republic include also the Berchtold Counts[14] (their collection is now deposited in Buchlov), Count Herberstein (collection at the Libochovice castle), Princes of Schwarzenberg (with their collection at Orlík), Count Colloredo-Mansfeld (the collection now deposited at

Opočno), and the Archduke Franz Ferdinand d'Este, whose collection is now located at the Konopiště castle. These collections were founded above all as sets of souvenirs from journeys (the Buchlov collection), or from gifts (the Metternich collection). The Náprstek museum now hosts parts of other aristocratic collections. Some of them were donated to the museum by their original owners, such as Count F. Colloredo.[15]

... and below

People of common origin, if they were interested, were also able to acquire a collection of aegyptiaca. Often they bought souvenirs on their journeys, that then remained in the possession of the family as unique curiosities. Sometimes the antiquity made its way into the Czech lands through peculiar ways, as was the case some objects in the collections of Zdeněk Macek or Jiří Karásek. Collectors could also have had a more specialised interest, inspired for example by a prolonged stay in Egypt. Small gifts and parts of estates, which now complete the collection of the Náprstek Museum in Prague, the museum specialised in the Oriental art, come also from small private collections, and were acquired originally either as gifts, or as souvenirs from journeys.[16] Examples of this second category can be found in the collections of the Náprstek Museum originating from the possession of the travellers Richard Štorch[17] and Bedřich Machulka.[18]

Richard Štorch, a traveller and hunter with an outstanding business talent,[19] visited Egypt several times, and although he did not become a real expert in Egyptian antiquities, we know that the Oriental environment interested him in many aspects, and not just as a source of money. Besides his collections of antiquities and game, he also took a number of photographs of Oriental women, that we have already mentioned in the chapter on photography.

We meet Egyptian or Egyptianising objects also in the possession of other personages. Some expressed their interest in the Egyptian culture in several mutually complementary ways. Egyptian and Egyptianising monuments can be found in the possession of Julius Zeyer, dr. Jan Palacký[20] and Justin V. Prášek[21]. Emmy Destinn, too, was a collector; fragments of her collection of aegyptiaca are to be found in the Náprstek Museum, alongside parts of other private and aristocratic collections.[22]

Emmy Destinn, Czech opera singer of international fame, whose civil name was Emilie Pavlína Kittlová (1878–1930), originated from a family with a broad cultural background. Her father, Emanuel Kittl, had travelled the Middle East together with Jan Neruda;[23] he had sponsored the journey that allowed this Czech writer to reach out beyond the limits of national themes.

The career of Emmy Destinn began with studies by the singer Marie Loewe-Destinn and the actress Otýlie Sklenářová-Malá. Despite her initial failure, she finally became in 1898 an opera singer in Berlin. She acquired fame playing various parts in the operas of Verdi, Wagner and Puccini. Her other famous parts include Salome of Richard Strauss, for which Destinn demanded a special costume in the Berlin opera, which indicates a possible Egyptian inspiration;[24] or Aida, in which she excelled in the beginning of 1905 on the London and New York stages, and since 1908 also in Prague.[25]

Her lifestyle, filled with a number of interests, was unusual for many of her contemporaries, but her passion for collecting was well in the trend of her time. Just like other contemporary artists, she surrounded herself with an environment full of curiosities, in her case sometimes even with a morbid touch. Reminiscences of the Emperor Napoleon I and his time[26] – the first glorious era of Egyptomania – form an important part of her collection. Destinn collected above all Empire style furniture and portraits of the Emperor. Her collection, however, included also true aegyptiaca. The Egyptian objects that had adorned her peculiar collection can today be found in the possession of the Náprstek Museum in Prague. They include a necklace with a scarab pendant and a papyrus bearing a Coptic text.[27]

Of some interest is also the collection of O. Pallme.[28] Also the traveller Jaroslav Kořenský[29] attained the objects from his collection as a result of his interest in the areas of the Orient. He became famous for several travelogue essays and books concerning this area.[30]

Only some of the collectors acquired their aegyptiaca on a journey to Egypt. This is the case, besides Mr. Holzmeister,[31] whose collection was originally located at Moravská Třebová, and of course Mrs. Štorch and Machulka, also of W. Riecken, who had bought his mummy, which is now kept in the Náprstek Museum, directly in Egypt.[32] Museums acquired through donations other objects from private possession of dr. Barth (Dvůr Králové nad Labem), dr. K. Fischer (Jablonec nad Nisou), Mr. Stifter (Křtinec), O. Schier (Brünn, in 1970 transferred to the Náprstek Museum),[33] but also from specialists such as František Lexa or Ludmila Matiegková.[34] The Memorial of National Literacy hosts the collections of J. Karásek, Z. Macek, or E. Lešehrad. The first group of travellers and occassional collectors possessed above all singular objects, specialists and collectors with a more particular interest then owned more structured sets of works of art.

These collections of various origin generally did not remain in the possession of the owners and their families, but they were donated or transferred to the collections of museums. The search for their origin or time of their creation is therefore an uneasy task. As the acquisitions of the Náprstek Museum indicate, collectors of aegyptiaca did not disappear with the beginning of the 20th century.

One of the most interesting characters of the Czech collecting community was Jiří Karásek from Lvovice (civic name Jiří Antonín Karásek, 1871–1951).[35] He therefore deserves special attention. Karásek was a Czech writer in the end of the 19th and beginning of the 20th centuries. He is one of the typical representatives of Czech decadence. Among others, he founded and coedited the journal

Moderní revue ('Modern Revue'), which was published between the years 1894–1925. He built a large collection of Czech literary works, sketches and designs, paintings, graphics and archive documents, the so-called Karásek Gallery, which is now part of the collections of the Memorial of National Literacy at Strahov. His personal library, too, indicates the large scope of his interests.

Many of Karásek's works were inspired by Classical Antiquity. He also argued about artistic reflection and reception of Classical Antiquity with J. S. Machar. This discussion, however, was rather about a clash of two conceptions of Classical Antiquity itself, and not the clash of the literary conception, which creates 'its own' antiquity, with the scholarly conception, which aims at studying it. Reviewers of Machar and Karásek write with justification that *'Their conception of Classical Antiquity is not historical, although both aspired to deeper knowledge, they were not satisfied with second hand information, but studied ancient views and modern works on Classical Antiquity. This fact, however, is not to be overestimated. It is the right of the poet to create his own, subjective "Antiquity", despite the state of historical knowledge.'*[36]

Karásek himself characterised the atmosphere of the literary circles that were inspired by Antiquity and exotic countries as follows: *'...the very exoticism of art is motivated by the Czech reality. It marks a protest and escape from its grey dullness, a reation of one's own world within ...'* The writers of that time included for example Julius Zeyer. It was a time of searching and creating exotism, even in the setting of the Czech lands and Prague.[37]

The variegated interests of Karásek from Lvovice found expression also in his collecting activities. It is interesting to observe how his various interests were reflected in the composition of his library and collections. We will focus on the part that indicates Karásek's interest in ancient Orient.[38] The collections of the so-called Karásek Gallery were kept, in compliance with the decision of the collector and his family, in Tyrš's house,[39] and they were transferred from here first after the state had taken over the premises in 1948. After that they entered the collections of the Memorial of National Literacy.[40]

The collection includes also several aegyptiaca. The original list included more objects than can now be found. Some of them were probably lost or destroyed in the course of the transferring of the content of the magazines. The last great move happened in 1993. We will hardly ever be able to determine the age, genuineness or artistic value of a 'part of coffin lid'[41] or 'ushabti of the stable foreman Nefferhoter (sic)'[42] that purportedly came from the time of the 28th dynasty, or the further mentioned scarabs and fragments of statuettes. Despite that, many objects with clear dating and provenance can still be found here. Considering the extent of Karásek's interests, it would not be surprising if some objects of his collections would not be of the quality that mostly characterises collections of special interest. In several cases we may even doubt their genuineness. We do not yet know too many details about the process of acquisition of the collection. Part of it probably entered the possession of Karásek's Gallery within the collection of the first Czechoslovak ambassador in Egypt, Dr. Cyril Dušek. These objects were presented to the Czech public by František Lexa.[43] Other objects of today's Karásek collection, excluding those of Dušek, are listed in the old inventory under the numbers 1783–1812. The description 'Greek object' or 'Egyptian work of art' that we find attached to some of them is not always correct.

The objects include above all small amulets, ushabti,[44] and small items of daily use.[45] The antiquities of Karásek's collection consist above all of those the production of which was probably most frequent in the Late Period.

Karásek's collection is exceptional, since only few such private collections of a larger extent (not considering the aristocratic collections)[46] were assembled on Czech territory at the turn of the 19th and 20th centuries. Its role in the overall Czech cultural environment of that time is also unique. The generation of Dušek and other contemporaries of Karásek had grown in the cultural environment of the last decades of the 19th century, when Czech lands grew nearer to the European interest in the world and in the history of the Orient. Despite the fact that Karásek's collection was formed (as the donation of Dušek's collection indicates) first in the course of the first decades of the 20th century, it is connected with the overall change of cultural climate, which was no longer concerned only with aspects of the national past.

The objects contained in the collection of Jiří Karásek from Lvovice are mostly identical to those that we can commonly find in European collections. Above all the collections of many European regional museums are of a very similar character. Many parallels for the objects of the collection were found in the catalogues of French regional museums.[47] Larger museums, of course, also possess numbers of these smaller objects, but they do not (yet) exhibit or publish them very frequently. The reason is obvious, small museums' collections often comprise only of these objects. They may be based on precisely such collections as that of Karásek, which is, however, of a later origin than its European counterparts. The creation of such a collection was common in Europe about a hundred years earlier.

Libraries

Similarly as in the case of collections, we may distinguish between libraries of aristocratic owners and private persons of non-aristocratic origin. This expression of interest in ancient Egypt is, however, unlike the collections, little known and the acquisition of relevant material is more difficult. We do possess information on the most important libraries – as the Metternich library at Königswarth or Chotek at Kačina Castle are great concepts of Czech cultural history. Both were founded in the first half of the 19th century.

We cannot neglect cloister libraries, for example the Strahov Monastery Library is alongside the above-mentioned aristocratic libraries one of the three places in the Czech Republic that possess the very important work of modern study of ancient Egypt – *Description de l'Égypte* of the Napoleonic scholars.

Sometimes the libraries contain some precious collections of works that are connected with Egypt. For example in the Metternich library we find besides the *Description of Egypt* also a number of other eighteenth-century works.[48] In the case of the composition of private libraries during the 19th century, we still have more questions than answers.

Private libraries, of which the most accesible are once again those that belonged to famous individuals, reflect the accessibility of contemporary literature. Karásek's library contains several interesting works of period Egyptology, such as the original books of Maspero, Mariette, or Chipiez.[49] Besides that Karásek also followed Czech production, he possessed the works of Lexa, but also the Czech translation of a book by Petrie.

Also Zeyer's library contained some standard works of his time (see above), and gave its owner a good basis for his literary works, inspired by antiquity. Emmy Destinn, whose baroque bookcases now adorn the study of the Prague Clementinum (the main building of the National Library of the Czech Republic), personally made an inventory of her library in 1912.[50] Also its content, hitherto unresearched, is of great interest.

This little overview of libraries that include or may include works connected with Egypt, closes our insight into the private sphere of Czech collectors and famous characters of Czech culture. Here and there we meet a person with a more specialised interest. More often, the possession of Egyptian antiquities and knowledge of Egyptian culture belonged to the general cultural background. The travellers and visitors of Orient collected aegyptiaca as exotic souvenirs from their journeys.

Notes:

1 S. Donadoni, 'Classicità dell'arte egiziana', in *Atti del convegno Internazionale 'L'Egitto fuori dell'Egitto'.* Marzo 1990, Bologna 1991 (ed. C. Morigi Gori, S. Pernigotti, S. Curto). Transl.: *'The fact that Egyptian monuments were valued very early and searched for (and imitated!) with passion and bewilderment means, that they are able to directly enter our own system of values ...'*

2 Cf. J. M. Augusta, *Rukověť sběratelova.* ('Collector's manual'). Prague 1927, reprint 2000; p. 11. This book is a relatively detailed introduction into the subject of collecting, and includes an extensive bibliography of older publications, regarding Czech collectors' tradition. A small, not specialised but witty, overview of important collecting activities in the world and in the Czech lands can be found in the book *Sběratelství* ('Collecting')., Prague 1983.

3 J. M. Augusta, *Rukověť sběratelova,* p. 3.

4 J. von Hammer-Purgstall (1774–1856), began his studies at the Orientalische Akademie. Cf. Kaiser, R., 'Joseph von Hammer-Purgstall', in *Europa und der Orient. Ein Lesebuch.* Berlin 1989.

5 There now exists a very good work on the complex history of Karásek's collections – the catalogue of the exhibition *Sen o říši krásy* ('Dream of the realm of beauty'). Municipal House, Prague 2001; there are both Czech and English editions.

6 The statue of a 'woman with a child', as it is described in the list of the collections of the Memorial of National Literacy Strahov, inv. No. 51/64–206, and acquisition no. 51/64. The object itself is not currently accessible, the information was derived from the catalogue of the collections of the Memorial of National Literacy Strahov. The material was made accessible to me thanks to the courtesy of Dr. Dačeva and Mgr. Mejstříková.

7 In many cases we know the names of the donors from the entries in the card catalogue of the Náprstek museum.

8 In describing the now publicly accessible collections, I relied mostly on their list, included in the master's thesis of M. Verner *Veřejné sbírky staroeg. památek v ČSSR* ('Public collections of ancient Egyptian monuments in Czechoslovakia').

9 For details on the life of the members of the Hapsburg family and for further bibliography cf. Brigitte Hamann (Hrsg.), *Die Habsburger, Ein biographisches Lexikon.* Wien 1988, from where I have also derived bibliographical data.

10 M. Verner, *Veřejné sbírky staroegyptských památek v ČSSR* ('Public collections of ancient Egyptian monuments in Czechoslovakia'). master's thesis.

11 Bibliography: Verner, M., 'The seal-bearer Qenamun', ZÄS 1974 pp. 130ff. and Strouhal, E. – Vyhnánek, L., 'Radiographic Examination of the Mummy of Qenamun the Seal-Bearer', ZÄS, 1974, pp. 125ff.

12 Verner, *Veřejné sbírky staroeg. památek v ČSSR,* id. *Altägyptische Särge in der Museen der Tschechoslowakei.* CAA Lief. 1. Cf. also Verner in ZÄS 1977.

13 Verner, M.. 'The seal-bearer Qenamun', ZÄS 1974, pp. 130ff.

14 The mummy of Nefersobek , inv. no. 1999, was acquired by Josef Vratislav of Mitrovice, brother-in-law of Zikmund Berchtold, the owner of Buchlov, directly during the journey of the Lord of Mitrovice through Egypt. Strouhal E., – Vyhnánek, L., *Sborník Národního muzea v Praze,* series B, XXXV. 1979, no. 1–4, p. 54.

15 Mummy inv. no. P 634 Náprstek museum collections, (Strouhal – Vyhnánek, *Sborník Národního muzea v Praze,* series B, XXXV. 1979, no.1–4, p. 38).

16 Browsing through the card catalogue of the museum, one can find a large number of names, moreover, some smaller collections that were originally located in regional

museums reached the Náprstek museum in terms of the unifications in 1960s and 1970s. Their original location was researched by M. Verner, *Staroegyptské památky*. cit.

17 E.g. inv. No. P 8, Náprstek museum.

18 Náprstek museum inv. no. P 345 and P 346.

19 For a short biography cf. Martínek, Jiří – Martínek, Miloslav, *Kdo byl kdo. Naši cestovatelé a geografové* ('Who was who. Our travellers and geographers'). Prague 1998; pp. 428–429.

20 The son of František Palacký, important Czech historian of the 19th century, already known to us as a university professor of geography (cf. above).

21 To Zeyer's estate belong the bronze triad of Osiris, Isis and Horus and the fake P 485. Fayence necklace P 346 is recorded as coming from the estate of J. Prášek. The collection of Jan Palacký was more numerous – the numbers P 2406 to P 2410 of the Náprstek museum are assigned above all to eye inlays.

22 For information on the collections of NpM in Prague and the problems of its acquisitions of the Egyptian collection I am indebted to Mrs. Adéla Macková.

23 Holzknecht, V., Trita, B., *Ema Destinnová*. Prague 1972; p. 13.

24 Reproduced in Holzknecht, *op. cit.,* p. 87, for example the lower hem of the skirt is adorned with lotus flowers alternating with closed buds.

25 Holzknecht, *op. cit.,* p. 98.

26 Holzknecht, *op. cit.,* p. 227, and fig. 169.

27 Card catalogue of the Náprstek museum, inv. no. P 2397, acquisition no. 30/69 (jewel) and inv. no. P 2459, acquisition no. 30/69, made accessible to me thanks to the courtesy of dr. Barochová, dr. Součková and other employees of the Náprstek museum.

28 Included in the collection of the Náprstek museum, the large number of objects makes it impossible to list here a complete overview of inventory numbers – for orientation – P 2316f., P 2401f., P 2411–2418 passim, P 2484f. Source – card catalogue of the Náprstek museum, the so-called 'red cards'. It was unfortunately impossible to find any details on the author.

29 Cf. the card catalogue of the Náprstek museum inv. no. P 2454, P2880 – P 2890 passim, and foll.

30 Publication of these is now in preparation.

31 Cf. Strouhal – Vyhnánek, *Sborník*, p. 60.

32 Strouhal – Vyhnánek, *Sborník,* p. 62, inv. no. P 629.

33 Strouhal – Vyhnánek, *Sborník,* p. 64, inv. no. P 630b.

34 Mostly originally in the possession of the Czech Institute of Egyptology and the National Museum, since the 1970s in the Náprstek museum. Some relevant archive material can also be found in the Memorial of National Literacy Strahov.

35 Cf. *Čeští spisovatelé 19. a poč. 20. století* ('Czech writers of the 19th and beginning of the 20th centuries'). Prague 1982.

36 *Antika*, pp. 366–367.

37 Cf. Vlček, *Praha 1900*, p. 181.

38 For some details on the history of Karásek's collection I am indebted to Mr. Závodský (Institute of University History, Charles University) and to the employees of the Memorial of National Literacy at Strahov.

39 Cf. Augusta J., *Rukověť*, p. 7.

40 For the information I am indebted to the employees of the Memorial of National Literacy, Dept. of artistic collections. The details on the odyssey of the collections can now be found in the catalogue of the exhibition *Sen o říši krásy* ('Dream of the realm of beauty').

41 Inv. no. 1842.

42 Inv. no. 1939.

43 It is interesting to note that Dušek's collection occupied exactly the Russian Egyptologist Prof. Lukjanov, whom we have met above in the letters of Dušek's wife Pavla. These – they are cited in above in the section on travelogues – allow us to reconstruct his influence on the collection of Dušek.

44 Briefly – kind of 'substitutes' for the deceased, for whom they fulfilled any tasks that may have been demanded from him in the afterworld. These statuettes appear in greater numbers approximately since the Second Intermediate Period, the concept itself is in all likelihood older; cf. above all H. Schneider, *Shabtis I–III*. Leiden 1977, with an analysis of production, dating criteria and ideological background of the use of ushabti.

45 The definition of amulet is still gradually made more precise – generally they are objects with a protective or power-giving function. For an extensive bibliography cf. *Lexikon der Ägyptologie.* Wiesbaden 1972, Bd. I, 'Amulette'; W. Petrie, *Amulets.* London 1914; M. Hüttner, *Mumienamulette im Totenbrauch der Spätzeit.* Wien 1995; also Müller-Winkler, C., *Die ägyptischen Objekt-Amulette.* Orbis Biblicus et Orientalis – Series archaeologica 2, Fribourg 1987, and other works cited there. A recent comprehensive overview is to be found in C. Andrews, *Amulets of Ancient Egypt.* London 1994.

46 Cf. M. Verner, *Veřejné sbírky staroegyptských památek v ČSSR* ('Public collections of ancient Egyptian monuments in Czechoslovakia'). Sine anno, Prague, Faculty of Arts, Charles University, and id., *Altaegyptische Saerge in den Museen und Sammlungen der Tschechoslowakei; CAA, Tschechoslowakei.* Lief. I, Charles University, Prague 1982.

47 Cf. *Collections égyptiennes. Musées départementaux de Seine-Maritime.* Rouen 1987, or *Loin du Sable. Collections égyptiennes du musée de Beaux Arts et de l'archéologie de Besançon.* 1990.

48 L. Varadzin, personal communication.

49 Maspero, call number XII A 29, Mariette, XII A 13, Peurot and Chipiez, call number XC 15, Lexa – more works, e.g. *Staroegyptské čarodějnictví* ('Ancient Egyptian witchcraft'), Petrie – translation of his *Arts and crafts* ('Umění a řemesla'), call number XII D2 86. Source – catalogue of Karásek's library, Memorial of National Literacy Strahov.

50 Holzknecht, *Ema Destinnová*, ill. 173, p. 234.

V. Conclusion – Egypt in Czech historical culture

When historicism was at its peak, history was indeed an integral part of period culture. How could the past and its perception – historical culture – address the society of that time? Despite all that has already been said, the answer to this question is not straightforward. An artistic expression, or a particular theoretical concept neither expresses the general opinion, nor has an overwhelming cultural impact. Egypt in particular poses a number of questions of her own – it was not European history (for we now observe a part of Europe) *stricto sensu.*

It is not only the question of how closely the researchers in the past, i.e. the 19th century, approached the conceptual world of the ancient Egyptians and their civilisation. Even now, when we are using historical anthropology[1] and the history of mentalities to apprehend how people of the past conceptualised and created their world, we cannot say that we really understand ancient Egyptians or can explain their culture without exceptions. We cannot do this precisely even in the case of people, who are much closer to us in time and space. In this respect, all of us in the historical research are bound by our sources – and in this case more than in any other also by our abilities to interpret them.

We are rather concerned with the thinking of our ancestors about a past very different from their own. They were relatively well informed about their own history, but could the same be said about what was outside their homeland's past? Further we are also interested in the general atmosphere of the period, which influenced their concept of ancient Egypt. Last but not least, it is intriguing to note what aspects of period interpretations are alive until today and why.

It is important to see to what extent the interest in history was interconnected with its everyday application in national consciousness. Czech environment apparently did not experience the same internalisation of Biblical stories – which stimulated most of the Anglo-Saxon (but also German) interest in Egyptian history.[2] Here, too, a connection to the Near East as part of one's own history, so natural in case of France, was missing. Let us not forget that the French did not connect Egypt only with Napoleon, but also with St. Louis.

If a 19th century man was to take history for his own, it must have immediately influenced him. And there were several dimensions in which it could have attracted his interest: on the general human level as a story, on the specialised level as an object of research, and finally from the point of view of cultural politics through its use for the topicalisation of certain, e.g. national, features. In case of the ancient Near East, it would seem that the 19th century Czech could have mostly appreciated the first dimension. The other dimensions were dominated by national history and Classical Antiquity. Neorenaissance and the Sokol movement attest the connection with Classical ideas. Ancient Orient played above all the role of decoration, or that of a curiosity.

National histories were of great importance for 19th century Europeans. For most learned men and politicians, history is a source of national identity. The identity of a nation has at that time formed a very important part of collective identity. National past acquired greater importance above all because first now did the knowledge of the past develop in new dimensions. Historiographers are no longer concerned with the histories and genealogies of clans and dynasties, but with histories of whole tribes, nations and states. History thus became more accessible and more interesting for wider levels of society.[3]

The support of national identity by referring to the glorious past belongs to the cultural politics of the time. Czech national revival is no exception in this respect,[4] as was clearly shown above all by Miroslav Hroch in his research on European national movements. The only difference lies in the fact that while great history is commonplace for a great nation, small nations use it to defend their existence.

Let us have a look what does this interest mean for historical culture. National past becomes one of the central points in the cultural environment of the time. Historical consciousness has, in keeping with central European development, an important position in Czech society of the 19th century. We can try to distinguish historical consciousness as a whole from the historical consciousness connected with one's own past, the fulfilment of this task would, however, require a special study.[5]

Czech historical culture was until now treated above all in studies related to the role of Czech historical consciousness in the national movement of the 19th century and in the general formation of Czech society of that time. Also expressions of artistic reflection of national history are being studied. Excellent examples of such reflections are to be found in Mánes' illustrations of the fake Manuscripts and the paintings of idealised national history in the National Theatre.

History became 'an argument for the existence of the nation' (Hroch), and therefore fakes such as the Manuscripts fitted well into the concept of the nascent theses on the old age of the nation and Czech contribution to world history. Czech historical consciousness and also historical knowledge were clearly focused on national past, studied from the linguistic as well as archaeological point of view (J. E. Vocel).[6]

No significant changes happened at the Czech University in the field of historical science for quite a long time.[7] Period interest in history, however, grew, and the relationships to some periods of history changed,[8] above all in terms of national history. The number of historians specialised in Classical and Oriental Antiquity (and thus also in Egypt), or at least paying some attention to it, rose first in the end of the 19th century. For a long time, there was no independent chair of Ancient history at the Prague university.[9] Similarly also numerous popularising works of Czech authors about this area, that in all likelihood influence the formation of historical consciousness, appear first toward the end of the century.

In many European countries, the interest in Egypt was preceded or accompanied by interest in Classical Antiquity. This is true both for the Empire Style France, and for the Victorian Britain. Czech lands, too, showed some interest in Classical antiquity, it is still, however, a question whether here too it was also accompanied by an interest in pre-Classical antiquity, i.e. not only Egypt, but also Mesopotamia etc. So far it seems that it was not.

Classical Antiquity, however, served in the Czech historical consciousness as a formative paradigm, to which the national movement turned for inspiration.[10] The role of Classical Antiquity was connected with the fact that numerous patriotic scholars followed Herder to consider the Slavonic element as one corresponding to the Greek element of the ancient world. Vladimír Macura write in this connection that *'classical stylisation completes large areas of Czech revival culture'*, but *'Czech culture… followed the Classical paradigm only on surface, it assumed a Classical mask for its own functions, used Classical Antiquity not as an immediate source of values, but much more as a means … for fulfilling its own internal needs, in the way that* (despite the real state of affairs) *was most suited to the given needs'.*[11]

In the second half of the 18th century, members of the aristocracy became interested in collecting Classical objects and also in the cultural heritage of Classical Antiquity.[12] This state parallels that in France and Britain, although not to the same extent and intensity. In the beginning of the 19th century chief figures of the national revival, Jungmann, Šafařík and Kollár, appealed to the Classical ideal. J. Zumr considers this first wave of Classical inspiration for national revival as based on Neohumanism, so characteristic for the German environment.[13] It is interesting to note that no such boom of classical archaeology and philology as at that time characterised German universities, happened at the Prague University. History in general, including ancient history (to which archaeology was considered to form an auxiliary discipline) had for a long time derived its importance as part of the study of law, and not as an independent discipline.

This was among others the result of period education. Above all in the teaching of Classical languages, there is a clear distinction between Austrian and German schools before 1848. After 1848, Austrian school system was reformed[14] after the Prussian model, which was, similarly like other school systems in German countries, based on the principles of Neohumanism.[15] These included also the stressing of the teaching of Greek as the language of the ideal (or rather idealised) Greek nation.[16]

Another wave of interest above all in Czech cultural heritage was stimulated by Miroslav Tyrš at the time when he declared Neorenaissance for his programme, also outside building and architecture. Tyrš wished the principles of Athenian democracy to inspire Czech culture.[17] In following this ideal, he was true even to the Greek ideal of Kalokagathia.

Generally, above all in the second half of the 19th century, Antiquity was rooted in Czech historical consciousness to a great extent also thanks to the 'classical gymnasiums' (secondary schools),[18] at least for those who had studied there. Martin Svatoš,[19] on the other hand, notes that people like Vojtěch Lanna, owner of a collection of Classical art, formed their relationship to Classical Antiquity through visiting art galleries and museums outside Czech territory rather than during their secondary school studies.

Classical Antiquity had a permanent position in the national movement as an argument for Slavonic exceptionality (Herder).[20] It did not, however, possess a leading position, since the paradigms of national movement could make use of a large number of scenes from national history, which in itself was one of the main arguments for national existence.

What was said above indicates that the situation in the Czech environment was not favourably inclined[21] to a deep and concentrated interest in ancient history as a whole, thus including also the Near East. Which does not, of course, mean that there would be no personality with such an interest in the 19th century, for example among artists or at the university. The overall cultural orientation, however, supported above all around the middle of the 19th century the dominance of other themes in contemporary historical consciousness.

The history of ancient Orient became more accessible in the course of the second half of the 19th century through educational literature. Above all J. V. Prášek was active in the popularising of the activities and discoveries of scholars. Contemporary dictionaries did also reach a reasonably high level, since their authors worked with accessible period literature on Oriental antiquity. Some of the ideas of contemporary specialists were taken over to Czech educational works and textbooks. In case of Egypt, these include above all insights about Egyptian society and culture and ancient Egyptian state system. The connection with Biblical context is no longer very common in specialised international Egyptological literature; it is, however, still present in the works of Czech authors. Some of them, though, were able to follow the growth of knowledge in disciplines such as ancient Oriental philology and history, and record it in their articles and publications. In some cases, such as the general encyclopaedic *Ottův slovník naučný* ('Otto's Educational Dictionary'), we can even see a cautious approach to hitherto insufficiently studied phenomena, that science was only beginning to understand. Textbooks, too, that were in part directed to secondary schools, brought a great deal of information on ancient Oriental cultures, that was also acquired in books of foreign provenance.

Oriental studies at the Prague Czech university were limited above all to philological disciplines – Oriental history and archaeology become the centre of attention first in the time of the First Czechoslovak republic. The question is, whether this was the result of better conditions for an overall development of the university, or because of the presence and possibility of development of able personalities. The suitable conditions for the creation of a chair of ancient history at the Prague Czech university had long remained unused, above all after the breach of the university to its Czech and German part, despite the existing interest. We may hypothetically explain this situation with personal disputes, but the reason could just as well have been the belief of contemporary Orientalists – philologists, that the university lacked a really educated personality to lead the subject. Anyway, Czech public thus had, due to the absence of local university programme in ancient Oriental history and languages, only indirect possibilities of accessing information.

Oriental decorativeness impressed Czech visual arts the same way as the contemporary presumed spiritual dimension of Oriental cultures. This dimension – internal spiritual content of the manifestations of ancient civilisations, which is of course the personal interpretation of the artist – is to be found above all in the works of František Bílek. František Kupka then employed standard artistic historicism in book illustrations, based on personal study of ancient works of art. Other artists, too, used Egyptian ornament as decoration, but it seems that for them it was only one of the possible choices from a whole repertoire. Czech interpretatons of the Orient are nonetheless original indeed, since they lack the narrative Orientalising historicism, which was so typical for a number of other artists in many European countries, including other parts of the Austrian monarchy and Vienna itself. The artistic community of the Czech lands, above all painters and sculptors, did not stand in the second half of the 19th century in any way outside current European trends. There was, however, no space for Egypt in the structure of Czech art of that time, except for a few cases.

General public connected Egypt above all with mysteries and undefined luxury. This is seen in the literary image of Egypt, and sphinxes, hieroglyphs and pyramids functioned as synonyms for an impenetrable and somewhat incomprehensible civilisation.

Significantly, the duality of ancient Egyptian civilisation that stems from its ambiguous evaluation, corresponds to the duality ascribed to the whole Oriental world. Orient as a whole was in the opinions of 19th century Europeans '...overestimated for ... its spirituality, stability, long duration...' as well as considered 'anti-democratic, primitive, counter-progressive and barbarian'.[22]

Egypt, too played on the one hand the role of a source of knowledge, which other cultures, including European, related to, and on the other it was presented as a model of a despotic state that suppressed its own people. The conservatism of the ancient Egyptian civilisation was also considered its characteristic trait, for a long time also among expert historians – these opinions were based on the presumed immutability of ancient Egyptian culture. They were, however, not universally accepted, as we can see in the more sophisticated opinions of Miroslav Tyrš.

These judgements are not very different from some contemporary Egyptological works. Therefore, we cannot consider them lagging behind. Still, Czech production of educational literature, where these opinions were presented – despite the fact that these were often textbooks – was often dependent on secondary literature, and did not always work with primary sources (this was of course not true for all authors, among the exceptions, we can mention Prášek and Šembera).

Artistic reflection, too, is to an extent dependent of period level of knowledge, but in the case of the appreciation of Oriental spirituality, it was influenced more by current international literature of esoteric character.

The place of Egypt in Czech historical culture at the turn of the 19th and 20th centuries can be summarised as follows: ancient Egyptian culture was present in the historical consciousness, but not as a topical and lived history. Egyptian history included few stories that the 19th century Czech could identify with, if we do not consider the romantic emotions that books of Georg Ebers aroused in the readers. The place of Egyptian antiquity within the system of values important for Czech historical identity of that time was not important enough for it to manifest itself very profoundly in the historical consciousness, but neither was it unimportant enough to be totally lacking. Egyptian history was an accessible part of education. Ways to knowledge of it were not closed, although there were only indirect ways to become acquainted with current state of Egyptology. Egypt found a place in artistic inspiration above all in Art Nouveau, and in a peculiar way by František Bílek. It appears that Egyptian culture was considered somewhat distant and exotic. Its creators were people with all their vices and virtues, but their existence did not appeal directly to Czech minds. It was impossible to say about them 'these are our ancestors'. They were only ancestors on the very long journey of the development of human culture and witnesses of Biblical times.

Notes:

1 Cf. Richard van Dülmen. *Historische Anthropologie*. München 2000.

2 An excellent period formulation in the context of the exploration of ancient Mesopotamia is to be found also in Friedrich Delitzsch, *Bábel a Bible*. (Babel und Bibel) Praha 1903; s 1–2. (The Czech edition is quoted as it is important to note that this book was translated and therefore accessible to a broader public, and that the interest was also sufficient to let this translation be made) *'It is remarkable to what extent now in Germany, England and America, the three countries of the Bible, as these lands are not without justification called, the Old Testament ... is being studied ...'*. The relevance of these conclusions for Egypt is evident not only in the early development of Egyptology in these countries, but also in other period materials. Cf. also Ebers, *Egypt in text and image*, passim.

3 Cf. Petráň, J., 'Ke genezi novodobé koncepce českých národních dějin' ('On the genesis of the conception of Czech national history'), in *Problémy dějin historiografie II; Acta Universitatis Carolinae – Philosophica et Historica* 5, Studia Historica XXVI. Prague 1982 (1986); pp. 67–89. For example, the originally above all aristocratic interest in family history evolved into a more general interest in the past of the nation or of the state. Notes on the role of the national past in the formation of the national identity are to be found also in E. J. Hobsbawm, *Nations and nationalism since 1780, programme, myth, reality*. Cambdridge 1990.

4 cf. Hroch, M., *V národním zájmu* ('In the interest of the nation'). Prague 1996 or id., *Na prahu národní existence* ('On the threshold of national existence'). Prague 1999, passim.

5 It would concern for example the determination of the share of world versus state or national history in education, the existence of books on home and foreign history, the presence of the works of foreign historians in Czech libraries, etc. It would also include a comparison of the extent to which Czech historising painters and artists in general chose themes from Czech history, and to what extent they turned to themes from the past of other countries. The latter point can be roughly illustrated on any greater corpus of works of Czech artists with a historical theme, such as, to take a characteristic example, those of V. Brožík. While it cannot be maintained that he would not be, as a member of the French Academy, well acquainted with contemporary themes of European painting, most of his works with historical themes had been inspired by Czech history; famous exceptions include 'Julie Šamberková v úloze Messaliny' ('Julie Šamberková playing the part of Messaline'), or 'Slavnost u Rubense' ('A celebration by Rubens'). Cf. also the repeatedly emphasised importance of national themes in Volavka, V., *Malířství devatenáctého století* ('Nineteenth century painting'). Prague 1941; p. 16 and passim.

6 Kutnar – Marek, *Přehledné dějiny*, pp. 234–236 and Štaif, J., *Historici*, (see note 8 below), p. 91.

7 Hroch, M., *Na prahu národní existence* ('On the threshhold of national existence'). Prague 1999; p. 141.

8 Hroch, *op. cit.* Through time, the relationship to certain periods gets in a way codified, and they become significant for the national movement. Cf. for example J. Štaif, *Historici, dějiny a společnost* ('Historians, history and society'). Prague 1997; passim, e.g. 'Dějiny, společnost a nacionalismus' ('History, society and nationalism'), p. 79, or 'České dějiny jako polemika mezi Čechy a Němci' ('Czech history as polemics between Czechs and Germans'), pp. 142ff.

9 Kazbunda, *Stolice dějin na pražské univerzitě*, Vol. II.

10 Macura, V., 'Sen o Lakedaimonských' ('The dream of the Lakedaimon'), in *Český sen* ('Czech dream'). Prague 1999.

11 Macura, V. 'Atický – Jónský – Dórský' ('Atic – Doric – Ionian'), in *Znamení zrodu* ('The sign of birth'). Jinočany 1995; p. 133.

12 J. Zumr, 'Úloha antiky v ideových koncepcích české společnosti XIX. stol.' ('The role of Classical Antiquity in the ideological conceptions of 19th century Czech Society'), in *Villa Lanna. Antika a Praha 1872* ('Villa Lanna. Classical Antiquity and Prague 1872'). Prague 1994.

13 Zumr, *op. cit.*, pp. 16–25.

14 The so-called Exner-Bonitz educational reform, cf. Svatoš, Martin, *Česká klasická filologie na pražské univerzitě 1848–1917* ('Czech classical philology at the Prague University 1848–1917'). Prague 1995; pp. 18ff. This reform included also the establishment of faculties of arts as independent full-fledged components of universities, not as two- or three-years 'prep schools' for the study at other faculties, which they had been hitherto (in the old system they connected to six-years secondary schools, which were in the new system replaced by eight-years schools.)

15 Cf. Svatoš, Martin, *Česká klasická filologie na pražské univerzitě 1848–1917*, pp. 19ff.

16 Besides the originally most promoted Latin, which was of course kept in the schedules.

17 Zumr, *op. cit.*, pp. 25f., id in: *Antika a česká kultura* ('Classical antiquity and Czech culture'), pp. 466–467, 508–509.

18 M. Svatoš, 'Výuka antickým jazykům...' ('The teaching of ancient languages...'), in *Villa Lanna*. On a conference of professors of east Bohemian secondary schools in 1886 in Kolín, Prof. Král thematised the problems of the absorbing of the complex knowledge concerning classical culture by contemporary students *'They can relatively well translate ... some passage of a Classical work and they are able to tell several literary-historical reports on Classical authors that are commonly being studied at schools; but they have a very faint idea on Greek and Roman literature in general, and their knowledge of history (above all when they know that no exam awaits them) is insufficient.'* – after Svatoš, M., *Česká klasická filologie* ('Czech Classical philology'), pp. 167–168.

19 Svatoš, M., 'Výuka' and also *Česká klasická filologie* ('Czech Classical philology'), pp. 157–159. The teaching of Classical languages at secondary school was often reduced to mere grammatical exercises, that failed to fulfil the role ascribed to it, namely, that of a stimulus of a complex development of the personality and above all of general philological development. Despite the fact that this 'school tradition of Classical antiquity' (Svatoš, *op. cit.*, p. 158) was not always favourably reflected, one of its aims was realised – general knowledge of Classical languages was in the course of the existence of the monarchy maintained as a unifying element of the educational system (Svatoš, *l.c.*). It is the more surprising, therefore, that Prague Faculty of Arts did not have an independent chair of ancient history, which, or at least its Classical component, otherwise belonged to the foundations of contemporary culture (Marek, J., *Jaroslav Goll*. Prague 1991; pp. 140–141).

20 This opinion is connected above all with the book *Ideen zur Philosophie der Geschichte der Menschheit*, 1784–1791.

21 It is interesting to compare this with the situation in Britain and France. Both of these countries had a political interest in the Orient and many of their citizens had the opportunity to visit Oriental countries. Neither Austria was, however, isolated from the Orient. The theme of period Orientalism can be mentioned again, being a second factor influencing the formation of the long-time reflection of Egypt (although the influence of Orientalism is, unlike that of Egyptomania, questionable). As far as the general relationship to the Orient is concerned, Czech lands experienced a differently oriented, but early wave of interest – in India. Cf. Macura, *Znamení zrodu* ('The sign of birth'), pp. 48–49.

22 Cf. Said, *Orientalism*, p. 150.

František Kupka, 'Egypt'; for E. Reclus, 'L'Homme et la terre'

Appendix I
Historical Culture

'Geschichte ist eine universelle kulturelle Praxis ... Geschichtsbewustssein ist die geistige Aktivität, durch die Vergangenheit gedeutet, Gegenwart verstanden und Zukunft erwartet wird.'[1]

History today is often first met in school curriculum, mimicked as a list of names and numbers. Seldom will a textbook mention the people in the background, and if it does, then they are portrayed as a king or soldier, as a type, not an individuum. However, now textbooks may change and pay more attention to individuality, but this is not an easy task.

The second place where we are often able to meet with history, is seemingly much more sociable – namely books, theatre plays, even movies. There are moving, breathing, living people wearing strange costumes, and acting on a stage set amid pieces of architecture and furniture more colourful, or more sinister than our own. They represent, they play for us a story, a narration, which we perceive as belonging to the past, although it seems often to us that they resemble the people of today, and thus we think human beings could have not changed much throughout the ages.

We are attracted by the past, or what we call so, we like to believe we can encounter the past in ruins of castles and temples, revive it in cunningly done museum exhibitions, feel it while we read authentic ancient texts or even fictions set in the past centuries. Probably, we like the sensation of having touched the past, and maybe we feel attracted by the immense abyss of time we are diving into, whereas our own life is so short and tied to a few decades. But is this a real encounter with the past?

The reply of a historian today, after (or almost after, for it is far from being concluded entirely) a discussion about the sense of history writing, is NO. Not that he would be the one consecrated to history as a mystery, one belonging to a high order, and thus being able to enter into communication with the past. Neither he can touch the past, however immense tasks he may try to perform in order to do that.[2] What he can do is something different, something that, in opinion of modern historians still does a good apology for their *métier*.[3]

A historian is specialised in a work of mediating between the past and present. The past itself is untransmittable experience, inaccessible to an historian but through the sources, remnants and fragments, legends and myths.

Before I continue, I would like to answer an obvious question, which can still be heard sometimes – from the students, for example. That is, what for? An apology for history is still required. This has been done better and more aptly elsewhere. Nevertheless, I would like not to avoid it – the past, however inaccessible directly, is our identity, it is our source, it helps us if not to take examples and precise models, then to orientate ourselves in the world. It offers us a wide space in time, which should enrich our lives by new experience, by dimensions unknown to the present, by horizons, which put our life-world into doubts, and on the other hand which can reaffirm the values of humanity. Like the shadow, the past can cast doubts and engender fears, but like the shadow of a familiar shape, it can reaffirm our attitudes. In both cases, it can help us to find a way through the variances and discrepancies of our own world – 'history is for human self-knowledge', as put by Collingwood.[4]

There are many ways how to insert the past into the present, which, in turn has been born out of it. It has been said that the past is somehow inherent to all cultures, and it has been decided to call this relationship of past and present history.[5] Modern history is being developed chiefly during the last two centuries, and it has been reflected mainly, though not exclusively by a number of European scholars. This is maybe due to the fact that history as a science has been paid a considerable attention in 19th century Europe, where most discussion about the scholarly and scientific character of historical research started.[6] The historian and history is thus often seen as a prerogative of the western world. By now, many historians set out to show that it is not the case actually, and offered a more nuanced view of history, understood as a sort of a common shared cultural feature, a common seed, which, nonetheless, bears a fruit different in shape and taste, according to which culture and time cultivates it.[7] When studying these processes of history making, historian is now in the same position as whenever studying other phenomena of human mind.

The historian is bound to his sources, and although he cannot be utterly objective and free from any inherent value measures of his own, he tries to be at least free enough to be able to see limits of his own, while reading the sources. What he finds in them, depends both on the actual character of these and on the historian, his abilities and his (dis)interpretative capabilities. He is often pressed to the reading that would be clear to his contemporaries, but which introduces into the old texts and testimonies something that is not proper for THEIR era. This happens, e.g. when he has to use modern names, or words borrowed from a modern language, to describe an ancient reality, which did not name its own phenomena. In the case of history and history writing, this seems sometimes exactly to be this case.

History is like a systemised attempt to deal with the past, but there are inherent dealings with the past, unsystemised as they may be, like the collective memory, tradition, or whatever name we like to call them. It has been called cultural memory.[8] Then, history can be viewed as a specific activity, which operates within a framework of cultural memory.[9] This Appendix is devoted to a short description of this framework.

Otherwise, we can speak about historical culture, in the sense of history forming a part in a cultural pattern. It is practically a question of naming the phenomena. In the beginning of Part I it was mentioned that Egypt played an important part in European historical culture. What, though, does this term mean? Historical culture, then, is another word that denotes the result of historical thinking, the ideological getting to grips with the past and with history,[10] which forms its accessible part.[11] I suppose we can use this term fruitfully for the 19th century. In this respect I would like to introduce a selection of works, however, contextually, relevant to Czech, or Central European, historical thinking of the period.

'Because one can think and contemplate about history even outside historical science, we call that phenomenon when a man is occupied with the past (all that happened) and with history (the accessible past) historical thinking. This phenomenon is to be found everywhere where a thinking man approaches the past, it includes records, simple memories, but also works of art, contemplations of philosophers or speeches of publicists.'[12] It includes, therefore, everything that expresses consciousness of the past and a relation to it.

There are two main aspects of Czech historical thinking of the 19th century. The first is the formation of historical science and therefore also of modern historical culture, for which historical science is a determining element. The second in the role of history, respectively historical consciousness, in the process that was especially important for Czech lands in the 19th century, namely, national revival. This process is one that the Czech nation shares with many other European nations that gradually created their cultural and political identity.[13] The relationship to the past – and above all to national past – was intertwined with questions that the whole society, or at least its politically and socially active part, was asking.

Historical culture includes a number of aspects of historical thinking that differ according to what extent they reflect current state of knowledge or, to the contrary, to what extent they are 'socially' or 'politically' engaged etc. In order to attain a certain level of clarity, a scheme of historical culture has been elaborated, that explains its various manifestations and levels.

I. The Scheme

It seems at place to quote the explanation of Zdeněk Beneš,[14] based on the works of the Polish scholar Maternicki and of the German historian Hardtwig, in its entirety. 'We can search for the historical culture of a certain level or society or group, of society as a whole or of an individual (or of a certain level of society as a group of individuals, as seems suitable in the case of school historical education) … individual historical culture arises from the historical culture of the society. Historical culture … subsumes also all institutions connected in any way with the production, storage and distribution of historical information in the society. These include above all schools, museums, libraries, archives, galleries, mass media (news, radio, television), but also theatres, cinemas – and also the cultural phenomena with which these institutions work: the book and conditions for its distribution, both specialised publications and belletristic

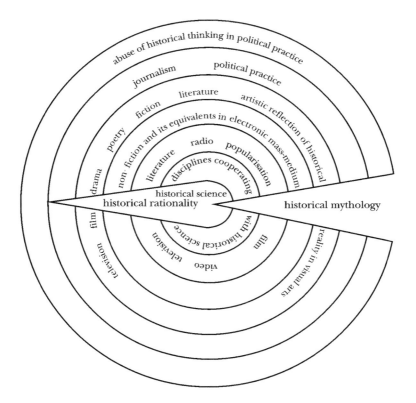

In the diagram:
- abuse of historical thinking in political practice
- journalism
- political practice
- fiction
- literature
- poetry
- artistic reflection of historical
- non-fiction and its equivalents in electronic mass-medium
- literature
- radio
- popularisation
- drama
- disciplines cooperating
- film
- historical science
- historical rationality
- historical mythology
- television
- film
- within historical science
- television
- video
- reality in visual arts

literature in its entire scope, drama, film, visual arts. And in part at least also political institutions (political parties and the executive) that use historical information for their political aims and intentions, or (as our experience with authoritative political systems has taught us) manipulating with their production and distribution ... Historical culture is such an inherently specific historical socio-cultural phenomenon, that must therefore also be studied on defined historical material ... In the first place, it is necessary to reflect the fact that historical culture is part of the general culture of (a given) society. As such it is above all a semiotic system ... '[15] Precisely this general dimension of the influence of historical thinking in the 19th century is an important part of the study of historical culture of that time.[16] The past is a presumed part of our individual and common memory.[17]*

The basic definition and delimitation of historical culture[18] is as follows. The simplified basic division includes three parts,[19] historical knowledge, historical consciousness, and historical awareness. Each of them includes a whole scale of particular manifestations.[20]

From the point of view of historical rationality, 'the highest level of historical culture' is historical knowledge, or historical science. Historical rationality allows it to create a more precise impression of historical reality. This fact is in itself problematic. Historical rationality is a term employed for the structure of the specialists'[21] approach to the past. If we speak of historical rationality as a whole, most often it is Gadamer's 'sense for history' that is meant. This includes *'the willingness and ability of a historian to understand the past, sometimes even the "exotic" past, in terms of its own context and sources. To have a sense for history means to consistently overcome the inherent naivity, that would lead us to judge the past according the so-called commonplace measures of our own world, through the eyes of our own institutions, our own values and acquired truths'.*[22]

Historical rationality may be complicated by the different mentality[23] of the epoch treated by the historian, for example an art historian or historian of religion may often express value judgements that concern more his own period than the one he is describing.[24] Scholars try to keep to the principles of historicism to the extent that they attempt *'not to influence the determination of the sense, meaning and function of the source by anything that would divide it from the time of its creation, from its temporal and factual content'.*[25] This principle is, however, sometimes hard to apply in cases when it is extremely complicated to reconstruct the particularities of the source to its context as well as the very socio-cultural system itself.

The other elements of historical culture are also its integral parts, but historians differ in their evaluation.[26] Historians, too, influence the process of the formation of historical awareness and consciousness. In the words of Georges Duby, *'... even historians have the right of imagination. However, it is their obligation never to manipulate, abuse or twist sources from the past ... If it is our opinion that history ought to serve a sober understanding of the present, we must distribute knowledge of it as much as possible through the press, television or film. On the condition that we avoid any kind of underbidding ... the public does not mind difficulties. Historians ... must present the important aspects ... they must try to present to the public the truth about the past and enable them to understand what people bore in their minds at various historical moments.'*

'Nowadays, historical novel, that treats history as a setting for an artificially developed story, is very successful.' To answer the question, whether they prepare readers to accept more serious works, he says: *'I do not think they perform any service for us ... to the contrary'* and concerning this, he states, *'this proves the necessity to continue in the quest for sobriety and historical precision against mystifying errors'.* G. Duby values above all *'when knowledge of history is allowed to keep their complexity'.*[27] He thus describes in other words the principles of Gadamerian sense of history. Outside the sphere of historical knowledge, the sense of history is sometimes missing. This way we finally approach that which stands outside this sphere, but still belongs within the limits of historical culture. Historical knowledge is connected with historical consciousness, which itself is connected with historical awareness. Historical consciousness appears to have a central position in terms of historical thinking in general. Inherent in it is the very fact of the awareness of the existence of the world in time.[28] Several different types of consciousness can be distinguished – that of historicity, of time, of reality – from which then historical consciousness, and thus historical culture, are gradually formed.[29] Several studies were dedicated to the formation of historical consciousness.[30] Miroslav Hroch uses 'historical consciousness' as a general term to denote *'on the one hand ... scattered isolated*

pieces of information, on which the unreflected myth is based, a collection of feelings and a priori value judgements without any real system (although sometimes possessing a certain inner logic[31]) and with a strongly irrational character, on the other hand we meet a more or less systematic, critical reflection of past development and its causal context, while this analytical reflection need not always correspond to the level of knowledge of modern science. The elements that belong to the first ... mythological side of the scale, could be called historical awareness, while elements belonging rather to rational reflection compose critical historical consciousness in its narrower sense.'[32]

The tripartite scheme of historical culture contains a third element, historical awareness. What are the mutual relationships of these elements?[33] In short, we may understand in historical consciousness a past event, understood at first as a present event dressed in a historical costume. Its semiosis[34] takes place in the context of the present, not in the context of its own time. However, the historical consciousness has the prerequisites to distinguish historical facts from historical fiction. Although it does not work with scholarly criticism (while not even this contains all ideals of total reflection[35]), it does not lack the ability to make this distinction.

Historical awareness has no such ability, it creates or maintains historical 'myths'. These may be very persistent, or even artificially preserved, *'as possible methods of manipulation with public opinion'.*[36] It should be stressed here that the term 'myth' as used here does not always denote 'true myths' in the sense of creating a guide story for a culture or a society.[37] 'Myth' can even mean a contortion of history, created with the purpose of manipulation. Moreover, the use of history as a counterpart and fertile source of fairy tales and myths in general[38] is a separate question, which desires special attention, but is already outside the scope of the present work.

According to the synthesis of Z. Beneš,[39] historical mythology, as an important component of historical culture, is not in itself specific to those areas of historical culture, considered non-scientific, since it stands outside historical science.[40] Mythological approach to the past is understood above all as a type of thinking that contains emotionally intuitive elements (J. M. Meletinsky).[41] It differs from the specialised approach to the past of a historian, who should be guided by historical rationality. Historical mythology may have an internal logic, but it is often led by a priori judgements (Miroslav Hroch).[42] Below, we shall return to historical mythology in connection with historical memory, which is another term that covers approximately both historical consciousness and awareness.[43] Even historical science, though, may create mythological fiction about history, or it can be employed in its creation, and thus lend it more authority (at least in modern conditions of historical culture).[44] This proceeding is suitable above all in the cases where fictions are created in order to manipulate. Then we talk about a *'non-scholarly'* approach.[45]

In defining historical culture of a certain period, we may identify several clichés of current historical mythology with respect to the contemporary level of knowledge. The basic criterion, however, lies in current specialised historical literature and contemporary historical approach. In our case, the problem could be summarised as follows: we must be interested both in what people could have known about ancient Egypt, and what of this they accepted into their historical consciousness and awareness.

'Historical communication' takes part in the context of the overall sociocultural situation,[46] which is formed by the context of period culture, level of education, etc. The extent and often also the fragmentary nature of sources presents a great problem for any attempt to trace both of these areas at the same time.

Historical culture is an important part of culture as a whole, playing the part of a bearer of common cultural identity in the form of signs that bear meaning for the society that uses them.[47] This common identity is borne by historical culture as a whole, as historical science and as historical mythology. To a certain extent, historical mythology may be connected with memories and common memory, which (independently of the fact whether the period historical culture is based on historical science or not), is dominated by other elements than those that modern historical science subsumes under the term 'historical knowledge'. Shared cultural memory may thus be another term that combines elements of historical consciousness and awareness (Jan Assmann, cf. below Tradition, memory, topos and myth).

II. The development of historical thinking

In the time and space of various cultures, the concept of history changes. Its basic role, however, remains the same – *consciousness of the past*[48]or *historical consciousness (Geschichtsbewusstsein) forms cultural identity.*[49] Consciousness of the past, which deals with the past without feeling the need to precisely date it or support with evidence of primary sources, can be distinguished from historical consciousness that forms a more systematic (and chronologically coherent) idea of the past. They can be differentiated to the extent that the philosophical term *consciousness (or, sense) of the past* is to be connected rather with the relationship to the past, while *historical consciousness* concerns the content of this relationship.

What forms of historical thinking amount to historical consciousness? 'Historical' must not necessarily mean 'respecting the principles of historicism',[50] (*Is history the same as the past?*[51]), but only 'relating to the past or to history'.[52]

In terms of Momigliano's definition of historicism, general interest in history may be equivalent to the first point of historicism – 'general interest in human activities'.[53]

This interest was not necessarily the same in various times and cultures,[54] 1. the intensity, 2. the formulation of the importance for the identity, 3. the tradition of one's own past, and 4. the perception of time, may have differed.

We should now try to imagine the development of historical culture which resulted in the form presented in Part I of this volume, i.e. above all modern

European historical culture. Jörn Rüsen proposes to call this process a *gradual rationalisation or historisation of the concept of the past.*[55] The scheme of development that he suggests is based on extensive evidence, above all from the development of historical thought and historical science. Modern historical thought[56] is defined as the result of the development of historical method and the role of history in science and society in the course of the last two centuries.[57] These were defined and formed gradually, on the basis of the knowledge of past development of the approaches to the past; they were not born at once in the form, as we know them now.[58]

This section has shown that the 'rationalised' history of today does not mean a single form of consciousness of the past that deserves the name of history. The ancient Egyptians themselves are perfectly entitled to have had a 'history', although their approach to the past differed widely from our own. This attitude corresponds to Momigliano's point 1. 'general interest in human activities', adding to that a proud adherence to the heritage of their culture, whether carried by literature, religion, or by their kings.

Their desire for history led them as far as to historicise gods, or at least some divine and semi-divine beings.[59] They inserted the first, mythic rulers of Egypt into the king-list designed for archive use ...

Yet how far does this stand from what we are used to know as history?

III. Tradition, Memory, Topos, and Myth

The role of the past and history in the formation of the cultural identity of the community can therefore be delimited and identified in several ways, from the sociological, psychological, or historical point of view. In terms of the formation of contemporary culture we may say that for the 19th century European society, 'its memory[60] is of crucial constituting importance'. Memory is another key term that can be used to classify the complex process of historical thinking and its manifestations. As we shall see below, memory is a way of bridging that which the above-described scheme has termed historical consciousness and awareness. While we have hitherto tried to describe what historical consciousness amounts to, we shall now attempt to see how it works.

I believe that here it is possible to take up the thesis of the Egyptologist Jan Assmann about a bipolar scale, one end of which is formed by memory, in this case collective (i.e. bearing the system that forms one of the supports of the identity of the society that uses it), and the other by history, or the study of it. The study of history belongs to the traits of the culture of the society, respectively to the traits of modern European society,[61] and specialised history is an authority concerning the sources of identity in the culture of the 19th century.

According to Assmann, '*Memory*[62] *and history are poles of the same range of activities, some of which are closer to one pole than to the other. It is important to keep the two poles apart in order not to lose sight of their constant interaction. Memory tends to inhabit the past and to furnish it with images of its own making, whereas history in its radical form of positivism tends to neutralise the past and to make it speak in its own voices, strange as they may sound'.*[63]Assmann adds that little has struck greater blow to the traditional image of Egypt than Egyptological discoveries.[64]

The tendency to inhabit the past may be connected with the phenomenon that has been described by the Czech researcher Jaroslav Marek[65] – that history presents an opportunity for identification: *'History presents the man, whom his lifespan limits to several short decades, with a magnificent panorama of human destinies, with which he may identify himself'.*

This definition also enables us to understand the gradual nature of the change of the image of historical reality (in our case the image of ancient Egypt, which is the focus of this work). If we have identified ourselves with a certain conception of the past, for example with a certain way of acting of a particular historical figure, which is for us a symbol of national courage, this figure keeps its symbolical nature despite the fact that new research or hitherto unknown facts prove with all authority of a specialised science the exact opposite. This is the paradoxical importance of modern historical science, since although it had become the norm in the course of the last two centuries and although its institutionalisation in the 19th century corresponds to the growth of the interest in the past as a significant element in the identity of the society and the nation, the traditional patterns, in which this very identity began to be formed, did not disappear.

Czech historian Dušan Třeštík speaks in the same context as Assmann's 'memory'[66] of the so-called 'second history'. *'Second history, though, tends not to understand history, but rather to embrace it',* it is *'the need of the social man'.*[67] The past of second history needs not to be continuous and chronologically systematic, but it is important as an identification element of the community. Despite the terminological difference, the concept corresponds approximately to part of Assmann's 'memory' or 'cultural memory'.[68]

This does not mean that memory does not 'see' for example the chronological system of history, i.e. that it does not perceive the past as a temporal dimension. Rather we can say that memory as a category operates with fragmentary past, resp. with fragmentary history,[69] not due to a lack sources that would lead to know it, but because it cannot span all accessible past. It is not the object of its interest.[70] Memory is further connected with historical mythology, historical science with historical reality. They can support and complement each other. History supports memory, but it has a more authoritative position in the modern scheme of historical culture.[71] Memory is also not trying to understand the fact that past events belong to their own time – memory actualises them in its own context, and creates thus basically a living tradition, permitting new interpretations of history, rather like reinterpretations of a work of art. Here, too, it is true that history may be viewed as important and inspiring, without its being understood at all in any 'historical – rational way' (cf. above – Hroch – the irrational perception of history), just as works of art need not necessarily be understood within the intentions in which they were created.[72] The bearers of cultural memory or 'second history' need not have a clear conception[73] of the past and its chronological order, but they internalise above all the content of stories that are being transmitted to them. They may identify with the heroes and thoughts of these stories. Therefore, historical memory is necessarily fragmentary, it chooses only those parts of history that are most bearing for identity.

All this implies that where Assmann speaks of memory, Beneš of historical consciousness and awareness and Hroch of historical consciousness, they in all likelihood have in mind differing nuances of the same richly structured process that takes place in the scope of historical thinking.

This relationship to the past often fulfils the task of explaining the connection of present and past events and presents a lot of material for study. It contains also stories with which hearers can identify themselves, each in his own way. It is therefore an important dimension of human existence that necessarily contains rational knowledge and emotional experience. Here it is important to note that the historian, too, shares this dimension of identity and identification in his work, and certainly takes part in both traditional and emotional experience with the past.[74]

In the end of the excursus on historical thinking or collective memory, which forms one of its components, I consider it useful to reiterate several points that are of crucial importance for the maintenance of collective memory (in many ways it corresponds to that which we have already said about historical culture). We have already indicated how this memory is being transmitted, i.e. what supports historical consciousness, namely, the central role of historical science and all its influence in education etc. What are, however, the places of common memory,[75] which support its maintenance outside official historiography and which may also support historical myth: oral tradition and storytelling, personal memories, memorials, artistic reflection, commonly celebrated festivals, memorial places connected with historical events?

We may presume that such memorial places are most perceived if they are connected to national history. I base this conclusion on the fact that one of the most important functions of history is to support for national existence, as we have already mentioned above. This would explain, for example, why Britain or France accorded to ancient cultures a more important position among their 'memorial places', because Egypt for sure was a physical place of memory for the French – it was the land of Napoleonic expedition,[76] not to mention the crusades of St. Louis. The German Egyptologist Helck does not hesitate to speak about a continuous French interest in Egypt[77] that finds its roots in much older periods and that can in the 19th century be explained by the uninterrupted contacts with Egypt.[78]

It is impossible to neglect the lasting strategic importance of Egypt for both European powers in the course of the 19th century. Both these powers also belonged to the few states that entered the 19th century with an already mature national identity, no longer perceived the need to fight for it,[79] and could thus direct their attention also to non-European cultures. Such stimuli, and above all this strong basis in the form of a stable national identity, were lacking in the Czech lands.

In addition, there is another moment, probably less accentuated in the Czech lands – the phenomenon commonly called Orientalism. Czech (as well as Austrian)[80] Orientalism should be considered worth a separate research; Orientalism itself is, furthermore, a term that lacks a concise definition of its inner structure. After all the discussion that has recently arisen around Orientalism,[81] it seems not in place to dedicate a special section to it here. I would prefer to consider it a specific part of European historical culture, containing European experience and mis/understanding of the Orient.

French and British Orientalism mirrors the close contacts of these countries with the Orient. Central Europe should then be expected to have a different degree of acquaintance with the Orient and thus a different development of Orientalism. 'Different', though, does not mean 'lesser' or 'weaker', since the Central European experience included a long-term neighbourhood with the Ottoman Empire.

Orientalism as a complex approach includes scholarship, art, and historical mythology, possessing most probably similar qualities and similar weaknesses as historical culture, of which it even could form a part.

IV. Summary

In the analysis of the phenomenon of historical culture we have used a large number of various specialised terms. In this work, the term historical culture is used in terms of the tripartite scheme 'knowledge – consciousness – awareness'.

Disregarding philosophical implications – it is historical thinking that plays an important role in the formation of collective, or cultural memory (these terms can for our purposes be considered partially alternating), which has a decisive importance for the cultural system, 'the network of meanings' (Bedeutungsgewebe)[82] of a given society. Historical thinking is a thinking that forms the relationship to the past, but not in a homogeneous way in one level. This gives rise to historical culture, a term that spans a wide functional field covering historical mythology and historical rationality. Historical rationality has a specific role compared to other elements of the functional field of modern historical culture, resulting from the formation and normative function of historical science. Historical science does not mean the fall of historical myth, which may be very alive and include its own, well elaborated structure of argumentation.[83]

The process of the tradition of the past is moreover in our specific case complicated by the fact that the meeting with ancient history in the 19th century – thanks to new scholarly disciplines – meant for modern Europe a meeting with something that, while it lived in its own historical culture, was also made accessible once again. Another problem lies in the fact that the whole confrontation of ancient Egypt with any other time and space is extremely difficult to describe in correct terminology.

Only the Europe of Classical Antiquity had the privilege to be confronted with Egyptian culture while this was still 'alive'. The Classical image of Egypt itself then also became an object of reflection of other generations until the decipherment of the hieroglyphs, when Egypt ceased to be an enigmatic memory and became once again a culture that was directly able to pass on its heritage and to enable posterity to read its traces.[84]

Sources

We must consider whether we want to follow the state of knowledge regarded as specialised in the frame of the period, or whether we want to consider the general view of Egypt in a certain period. In the latter case, however, we shall not be able to disregard current state of knowledge, because it forms part of the cultural discourse of the given epoch.

I believe that the more general context of the perception of Egypt in 19th century culture should not be neglected, and I consider it more easily traceable if the frame of period historical culture is taken into account. Historical culture is an extremely complex phenomenon and this book attempts to present a *complete image of Egypt* in period context despite the fact that partial studies are scarce and some materials must be collected directly from primary sources. The review of all archive and library funds is not included in this work, in some cases, it is even not possible and we must wait for the completion of their catalogues.

What does all this mean? When I consider for example the reception of Egypt in Czech architecture, my aim is not a complete list of all buildings that contain in their conception of decoration an Egyptian or Egyptianising motif. I describe a selection of these buildings. At the same time I search for connections that might have stimulated the use of Egyptian topics.[85]

Similarly in the case of textbooks and literature, the aim was not to excerpt all such books that were published in the period of our interest. Once again, a selection was made in order to illustrate whether certain themes change or persist, whether some stereotypes occur repeatedly, etc. In this second part a complete overview of the given period would have been a better solution, it would, however, in my opinion amount to an independent volume.

The sections dedicated to the historical culture or to Egypt in historical science (Historia magistra vitae) do not of course comprise complete studies on these themes, that are usually referred to in literature, but they are syntheses that enable an easier linking of the exposition on the Czech environment. The same is true of phenomena of European or Czech cultural history and the figures of their protagonists (for example artists) that are usually recorded only with respect to the selected theme.[86]

The problem of Egypt versus Europe can be approached from several points of view. We may follow the various complications of the perception of Egypt in European historical culture, both diachronically and synchronically on various

14 Beneš, Z., *Historický text a historická kultura*. ('Historical text and historical culture'). Prague 1993; pp. 154–155.

15 For an overview on semiotic system and its function cf. – Terence Hawkes, *Structuralism and semiotics*. University of California 1977, Umberto Eco, *La struttura assente*. (1ˢᵗ ed. 1968) Milano 1980 as basics, furthermore Eco – *Theory of Semiotics*, revised edition in 1976, *The Limits of Interpretation*, 1991 and others.

16 Social aspects of the development of historiography are mentioned in the works of a number of historians of historiography, for Czech 19th century cf. Štaif, J., *Historici, dějiny a společnost* I–II. (Historians, history, and society) Prague 1997.

17 Cf. Assmann, J., *Das kulturelle Gedächtnis*. München 1997. The term 'memory' may also be understood in the context of the categories of historical consciousness and awareness, which will be explained below, or it can be defined separately, as J. Assmann does it – both terms seem to basically denote the same concept.

18 The philosophical implications, connected with the contemplation of history (the problem of the reflection of the perception of time and mutability in time) will mostly not be considered here. Anthropological dimension of time and space study cf. an overview 'history and anthropology' in Barnard, A. – Spencer, J., *Encyclopedia of Social and Cultural Anthropology*. London and New York 2003, p. 272ff.

19 Beneš, *op. cit.*, pp. 150ff.

20 Beneš, Z., *Historický text a historická kultura* ('Historical text and historical culture'). Prague 1993.

21 Historical science itself meets and borders with the methods of other scholarly disciplines, which may, but needs not complement it. This process leads to the use of the knowledge of one discipline in other disciplines, and enables the linking of a large number of known facts in order to create a more vivid image of the past. Importantly, it is not only the connection to the knowledge acquisition structures of other disciplines, but also generally with the structures of other areas of culture (Beneš, *op. cit.*, p. 158). The most prominent among these is art, where history can be met as inspiration – but the genres of art have their own rules according to which they are structured.

22 Cf. Gadamer, *Problém dějinného vědomí*, s. 7–8, 17.

23 For the term *mentality* cf. above in the chapter Historia magistra vitae. This problem is actually also a question of history of terminology. Cf. Beneš, Z. in *ČČH* 93/1995; Horský, J. (ed.), *Kulturní a sociální skutečnost v dějezpytném myšlení* ('Cultural and social reality in historiographical thought'). Ústí n. Labem 1999, with further bibliography. The first larger Czech works on this theme are to be found in the contributions of J. Slavík and F. Kutnar at the 2ⁿᵈ congress of Czechoslovak historians 1947; ed. Kostlán, A., *Druhý sjezd československých historiků (5.–11. října 1947) a jeho místo ve vývoji českého dějepisectví v letech 1935–1948* ('Second meeting of Czechoslovak historians [5.–11. October 1947] and its role in the development of Czech historiography in the years 1935–1948'). Prague 1993. There is, of course, a number of works devoted to that question either in history or in social sciences in general see e.g. works by Clifford Geertz, Ruth Benedict, or Richard van Dülmen.

24 Kemp *(Ancient Egypt. Anatomy of a civilization*, p. 103), but above all Hornung *(Der Eine und die Vielen*. cited after the Italian translation *Gli dei dell'antico Egitto*. Roma 1992; p. 26), in part also Hermsen *(Discussions in Egyptology* 34, 1996). For the terminological history cf. also Horský, J., 'Dějezpytec a pojmosloví' (Historiographer and terminology), in *id.*, ed. *Kulturní a sociální skutečnost v dějezpytném myšlení* ('Cultural and social reality in historiographical thought'). Ústí nad Labem 1999.

25 Hroch, M. et al., *Úvod do studia dějepisu* ('Introduction to the study of historiography'). Prague 1985; p. 174.

26 Le Roy Ladurie, cited by Beneš (*op. cit.*, pp. 157–158) considers it paradoxical that we are often 'prepared' for historical knowledge by other elements of historical culture, while Beneš considers it natural considering the rising difficulty of reception of the individual constituents of historical culture.

27 As mentioned in one of his interviews in *Magazin littéraire* 189, November 1982.

28 Cf. J. Marek, *O historicismu* ('On historicism') p. 33. J. Marek also has a somewhat different opinion concerning what should be termed historical thought. He considers historical thought to be a narrower sphere than historical consciousness, *op. cit.*, p. 36. In the conception applied in the present volume, these two terms essentially overlap. Another analysis of historical consciousness from a different aspect is to be found in J. Pešková, *Role vědomí v dějinách* ('The role of consciousness in history'). Prague 1997, pp. 26f.
Also M. Hroch turned his attention to the definition of historical consciousness, e.g. in his article 'Některé metodologické poznámky ke studiu úlohy historického vědomí v národním hnutí XIX. stol.' ('Some methodological notes to the study of the role of historical consciousness in the national movement of the 19ᵗʰ century'), in: *Historické vědomí v českém umění 19. stol.* ('Historical consciousness in Czech art of the 19ᵗʰ century'). Prague 1981 (pp. 61ff).

29 Beneš, *op. cit.*, p. 171.

30 Beneš, *op. cit.*, p. 171f.

31 Here it could be concluded that the rationality of science was replaced by the rationality of the myth. Both structures could of course be the theme of a separate discourse. The former from the point of view of the history of scholarship, the second from the point of view of the phenomenon of 'mythical' thought. In addition we should then follow a discourse on mythical thought starting with Ernst Cassirer and others.

32 Hroch. M., 'Některé metodologické poznámky ke studiu úlohy historického vědomí v národním hnutí 19. stol.', p. 62. He returns to the definition also in the essay 'Několik poznámek k problému: historické vědomí a zájem rodícího se národa' ('Some notes to the problem: historical consciousness and the interest of the nascent nation'), in *Husitský tábor*, 8, 1985. pp. 185ff.

33 Beneš, *op. cit.*, pp. 170–177, passim.

34 Cf. Umberto Eco, *La struttura assente*, pp. 100ff. (the scheme of semiosis), and passim.

35 '...*the ideal of a total reflection, which would be able to clearly differentiate that what we see from that what we think, mean and presume, may be unrealisable, but as an expression of the striving to the maximum clarity it remains valid and foremarks possibilities ...* 'J. Patočka, cited in Z. Beneš, *op. cit.*, p. 171. On historian's objectivity, respectively his striving to it, cf. – Marek, J., *O historicismu* ('On historicism') passim, e.g. p. 57. For a critical approach see e.g. D. Třeštík, *Mysliti dějiny* ('Thinking history'). Prague 1999; pp. 208 ff.

36 Beneš, *op. cit.*, p. 176.

37 Cf. use of that word by Collingwood, *The Idea of history,* p. 14ff.

38 See J. R. R. Tolkien 'On fairy stories', in *The Monsters and the Critics.* London 1997, 1ˢᵗ edition 1983.

39 Beneš, *op. cit.*, pp. 168–169.

40 Even in historical science it is possible for example to dogmatise a theory or a method, the selection of methods or the line of exposition, and thus make them a myth (or to create a myth with their help). We may of course also mythologise by means of an inadequate interpretation. There exists extensive literature on the question of historical thought and historical myth. Eg. H. Samsonowicz – 'Co to jest mit' ('What

is a myth'), in O *'historii prawdzivej'* (On 'true history'). 1997 includes a synthesis of approaches to historical myth.

41 Beneš, *op. cit.*, p. 176.

42 Hroch in *Historické vědomí* ('Historical consciousness'), p. 62.

43 Cf the definition of J. Assmann cited below. The resolution of the question of the identical nature, resp. overlapping, of various terms is the result of consultations with Prof. Z. Beneš.

44 Where, according to Jorn Rüsen (*Konfigurationen des Historismus*. Frankfurt (M). 1993; p. 22), specialists and the general public are separated.

45 Z. Beneš, *op. cit.*, pp. 158–159. Non-scholarly is such methodology which, while it may be working with scholarly tools, uses them to mainly manipulative ends, which is inconsistent with their primary function of acquisition of knowledge.

46 Beneš, *op. cit.*, p. 80.

47 Cf. below Hermsen, *Discussions in Egyptology*, 34, 1996.

48 There, however, exists also a philosophical analysis of the term historical consciousness, namely Pešková, J., *Role vědomí v dějinách* ('The role of consciousness in history'). Prague 1997.

49 See fittingly Jörn Rüsen, 'Einleitung: Für eine interkulturelle Kommunikation in der Geschichte', in *Die Vielfalt der Kulturen*. Frankfurt (M) 1998; pp. 22ff.

50 For historicism as a term, cf. e.g. Momigliano, Arnaldo, *Historicism revisited*. Mededelingen der koniklijke nederlandse Akademie van wetunschapen, Afd. Letterkunde, Nieuwe Reeks, 37/3, Amsterdam 1974: *'historicism is the recognition that each of us sees past events from a point of view determined or at least conditioned by our own individual changing situation in history'*. Momigliano further cites Georg G. Iggers – entry 'Historicism' in *Dictionary of the History of Ideas*. New York 1973, where Iggers (on pp. 456ff.) describes various ways in which the term historicism had been interpreted. In the most general meaning of the word, as understood by the German scholars (Meinecke) *'... as an outlook on the world (Weltanschauung) which recognises the historical character of all human existence, but views history not as an integrated system but as a scene in which a diversity of human wills express themselves'*.
The problems and evolution of historicism, and its relationship to historical science are treated in Iggers, G., *Deutsche Geschichtswissenschaft*, München 1971; p. 12, note 1 – an overview of the most important works on this terms – including citations to the analyses of Croce, Meinecke and Troeltsch. For a concise treatment see Rüsen, J., *Konfigurationen des Historismus*. Frankfurt (M) 1993, above all 'Historismus als Erkenntnisprinzip und Wissenform – einige Gesichtspunkte.' (pp.17ff.). He defines various uses of the term historicism as one denoting 19th century historiographical thought, as a term of art history, and finally also as a term denoting historical thought in the sense that the latter accentuates the individuality of each historical epoch, its autonomous explanation and its possible genetic links. Mainly the works of Marek and Rüsen include also the analysis of the influence of historicism on period society, science, (not only historical) and of the relativising influence of historicism.
A somewhat different probem is the definition of the term 'historicism' and the discussion concerning it K. R. Popper, *The Poverty of Historicism*.

51 Pešková, *Role vědomí v dějinách*, p. 10.

52 Historicity is for example according to Hegel an important sign of everything human – cf. Pešková, J., *Role vědomí v dějinách* ('The role of consciousness in history'), passim. Can this historicity be equalled with historicism, understood as a historically critical approach? – Historicism is here once again understood chiefly in terms of the definition of A. Momigliano, namely:
' 1/ a general interest in past human deeds

2/ pleasure in discovering new facts about the human past
3/ awareness that the information we have about the human past raises problems which affect the credibility of the information itself and therefore the substance of the past
4/ an effort to make sense of selected facts of the human past that is, to explain and evaluate them.'

'... *Historicism is the recognition that each of us sees past events from a point of view determined by or at least conditioned by our individual changing situation in history.'* in Momigliano, A., *Historicism revisited,* Amsterdam 1974. For other possible definitions of historicism, see above, note 50, G. Iggers.

53 Cf. the previous note, sub 1/.
54 Other cultural times and spaces had of course been analysed in terms of the historical perception of the worlds by modern European culture. Here, we cannot neglect the so-called 'Spirit of the year 1949', apparent in the two fundamental works that were published in this year – Eliade's *Mythe d'éternel retour* and Löwith's *Meaning in History,* cited after Assmann, J., 'Denkformen des Endes in der altägyptischen Welt' in *Das Ende. Figuren einer Denkform.* Poetik und Hermeneutik, XVI., München 1996. This opinion concerns above all the specific historicity of time in the Judeo-Christian environment and the possible differences in the perception of historicity (e.g. in the fundamental perception of time and time) in other cultures. There exists an extensive literature on the theme, also in connection with ancient Egypt. J. Assmann addressed this question several times in terms of the analysis of historical consciousness and cultural memory, cf, for example Assmann, *Zeit und Ewigkeit.* Abhandlungen der Heidelberger Akademie der Wissenschaften, Jr. 1973/ I. Abh., Heidelberg 1975; Assmann, J., *Stein und Zeit. Mensch und Gesellschaft im alten Ägypten.* München 1991; Assmann, J., *Ägypten. Eine Sinngeschichte.* Wien – München 1996, Frankfurt 1999; Hornung, E., in *MDAIK* 15, 1957; Hornung, E., *Geschichte als Fest.* Darmstadt 1966; Redford, D. B., *Pharaonic King-lists, Annals and Day-books. A contribution to the Study of the Egyptian Sense of History.* Missisauga 1986; Wildung, D., *Die Rolle ägyptischer Könige im Bewusstsein ihrer Nachwelt, MÄS* 17. Berlin 1969. For some notes, see again Assmann, J., *Ma'at. Gerechtigkeit und Unsterblichkeit im alten Ägypten.* München 1990; mainly pp. 262ff. Interesting is Sylvia Schoske's use of the term 'Historisches Bewusstsein' to denote the transfer of iconographic patterns in the time of the New Kingdom – cf. Schoske, Sylvia, 'Historisches Bewusstsein in der ägyptischen Kunst. Beobachtungen an der Münchner Statue des Bekenchons.' *Münchner Jahrbuch der bildenden Kunst.* III. Folge. Bd. XXXVIII. 1987.

This discussion, which rather belongs to the space of the philosophy of history, concerns European historical culture secondarily, in enabling us to better characterise historical consciousness and its results in these cultures, and may prevent its inadequate explanations.

The very awareness of time was historised by some philosophers, such as Henri Bergson. Bergson's views were of course reflected in the historical community (for an analysis and ciritique of his views, cf. J. Popelová, *Tři studie k filosofii dějin* ['Three studies on the philosophy of history'] Prague 1947). Can, however, this concept of individual consciousness be applied to collective consciousness? Are, first of all, the terms 'collective consciousness' and 'collective memory' justified at all, or were the adjectives just mechanically added without any adequately defined content of the term being present? This question was asked already by Marc Bloch, when the sociologist Maurice Halbwachs began to use the terms *mémoire collective* and *conscience collective.* Bloch himself, however, applied the term *mémoire collective,* cf. Burke, P., 'Geschichte als soziales Gedächtnis', in Assmann, A. – Harth, D., *Mnemosyne, Formen und Funktinonen der kulturellen Erinnerung.* Frankfurt 1993; pp. 289ff.

Archive sources

Prague

Archive of the National Museum, Prague, Czech Republic (Archiv Národního musea, further ANM), Karton (file) 5, estate J. V. Prášek;

ANM, Karton 7, J. V. Prášek;

ANM, Karton 6, J. V. Prášek;

ANM, estate of Cyril Dušek, Karton (file) 1, 2, 4;

ANM, estate of J. Petrbok, not filed and numbered, information leaflets and booklets of Austrian Lloyd, Triest;

Archive of the Charles University, Prague Czech Republic (Archiv Univerzity Karlovy, further ACU), *Přehled přednášek kteréž se odbývati budou na c. k. české Karlo-Ferdinandské univerzitě v Praze* (A list of lectures held at the Imperial and Royal Charles University in Prague). Call numbers B 900/2, 1882 – 1892; B 901/2 , 1892 – 1902; B 902, 1902 – 1908; B 929, 1908 – 1912; B 930/3, 1912–1917; from 1918 onwards the lists are not bound into booklets;

The National Museum in Prague, Prague, Czech Republic, Section Náprstek Museum, Card archive – register cards with description and call numbers of objects in museum collections;

The National Technical Museum, Prague, Czech Republic, Archive collection of Franz Schmoranz junior and senior;

Archives of the National Theatre, Prague, Czech Republic, files *Aida, The Magic Flute, Antonius and Cleopatra, Caesar and Cleopatra;*

Archives of Memorial of National Literacy, Prague, Czech Republic, fund Emanuel Lešehrad, Jiří Karásek ze Lvovic, Zdeněk Macek;

Vienna

Austrian State Archives, Haus- Hof- und Staatsarchiv, Vienna, Austria, Estate Anton von Prokesch-Osten, Schachtel, IIII, XVII, XVIII, XXVI;

Austrian State Archives, Haus- Hof- und Staatsarchiv, Vienna, Austria, Staatskanzlei, Ägypten.

Abbreviations

Journals and publications

ÄA	– Ägyptologische Abhandlungen, Wiesbaden.
AEB	– Annual Egyptological Bibliography, Leiden.
ÄAT	– Ägypten und Altes Testament, Wiesbaden.
ArOr	– Archiv Orientální, Praha.
AUC	– Acta Universitatis Carolinae, Praga.
BdE	– Bibliothéque d'Étude, IFAO, Le Caire.
BIFAO	– Bulletin de l'Institut Français d'Archéologie Orientale, Le Caire.
CAA	– Corpus Antiquitatum Aegyptiacarum.
ČČH	– Český časopis historický, Praha.
ČČM	– Časopis Českého musea (Časopis musea Království Českého), Praha.
ČsČH	– Československý časopis historický, Praha.
DE	– Discussions in Egyptology, Oxford.
EPRO	– Études préliminaires aux religions orientales dans l'Empire Romain, Leiden.
FGrHist	– Jacoby, Felix, Fragmente der griechischen Historiker, 1951 - 1958 Leiden.
GM	– Göttinger Miszellen, Göttingen.
JARCE	– Journal of the American Research Center in Egypt, Boston.
LÄ	– Lexikon der Ägyptologie, Wiesbaden 1972–1992.
MÄS	– Münchner Ägyptologische Studien, Berlin, Mainz.
MDAIK	– Mitteilungen des Deutschen Archäologischen Instituts, Abteilung Kairo; Mitteilungen des Deutschen Instituts für Ägyptische Altertumskunde in Kairo, Berlin, Wiesbaden, ab 1970 Mainz.
OBO	– Orbis Biblicus et Orientalis, Fribourg - Göttingen.
OrSu	– Orientalia Suecana, Uppsala.
PES	– Pražské egyptologické studie, Praha.
RÄRG	– Bonnet, Hans, Reallexikon der ägyptischen Religionsgeschichte. Berlin 1953.
Schriften KHM	– Schriften des Kunsthistorischen Museums Wien, Wien.
Schriften ÖKI	– Schriften des Österreichischen Kulturinstitutes, Kairo.
ZÄS	– Zeitschrift für ägyptische Sprache und Altertumskunde, Leipzig.

Institutions

AND	– Archive of the National Theatre, Prague.
ANM	– Archive of the National Museum, Prague
CEFRES	– Centre Français de Recherche en Sciences Sociales, Prague.
FF UK	– Faculty of Arts, Charles University, Prague.
IFAO	– Institut Français d'Archéologie Orientale, Le Caire.
ND	– The National Theatre, Prague.
NpM	– The Náprstek Museum, Prague.
PNP	– The Memorial of National Literacy. Strahov Monastery, Prague.
ÚHSD	– The Institute of Economic and Social History, Faculty of Arts, Charles University, Prague.

Selected Bibliography

Agstner, R., *Der Ballhausplatz und Nordafrika. Studien zum Präsenz von Österreich (Ungarn) in Kairo, Kosseir, Luxor und Bengasi.* Schriften Öki Band 11. Kairo 1995

Agstner, R., *Die Geschichte der Konsulate in Suez, Ismailia und Port Said 1844–1956; 125 Jahre Suezkanal – Österreich (Ungarn) und seine Präsenz am Istmus von Suez.* Schriften Öki Kairo, Bd 10. Kairo 1995

Agstner, R., *Die österreichisch-ungarische Kolonie in Kairo vor dem ersten Weltkrieg – Das Matrikelbuch des k. u. k. Konsulates Kairo.* Schriften des Öki Kairo, Bd. 9. Kairo 1994

Ampolo, C., *Storie greche.* Torino 1997

Antika a česká kultura. Praha 1978

as-Sayyid Omar, M., Anton Prokesch von Osten. *Ein österreichischer Diplomat im Orient.* Studien zur Geschichte Südosteuropas 11, Frankfurt(M) 1993

Assmann, A. – Harth, D., *Mnemosyne, Formen und Funktionen der kulturellen Erinnerung.* Frankfurt 1993

Assmann, J., 'Denkformen des Endes in der altägyptischen Welt' in *Das Ende. Figuren einer Denkform.* Poetik und Hermeneutik, XVI., München 1996

Assmann, J., *Ägypten. Eine Sinngeschichte.* Wien – München 1996, Frankfurt 1999

Assmann, J., *Ma'at. Gerechtigkeit und Unsterblichkeit im alten Ägypten.* München 1990

Assmann, J., *Stein und Zeit. Mensch und Gesellschaft im alten Ägypten.* München 1991

Assmann, J., *Zeit und Ewigkeit.* Abhandlungen der Heidelberger Akademie der Wissenschaften, Jr. 1973/ I. Abh., Heidelberg 1975

Assmann, J., *Moses der Ägypter.* München 1997

Assmann, J., *Egypt ve světle teorie kultury.* Praha 1998

Assmann, J., *Das kulturelle Gedächtnis.* München 1997

Aufrére, S. – Foissy-Aufrére, M. P., *Egypte et Provence.* Avignon 1985

Baleka, J. , *Výtvarné umění.* Praha 1997

Baltrušaitis, J., *La Quête d'Isis.* Paris 1967

Beneš, Z., *Historický text a historická kultura.* Praha 1995

Blumenthal, E., 'Mut-em-enet und die ägyptischen Frauen' in *Thomas Mann Jahrbuch 6.* 1993

Bode, Ch., hrsg., *West Meets East.* Heidelberg 1997

Borowsky, P. et al., *Einführung in die Geschichtswissenschaft.* Opladen 1975

Briony L., 'Two Interpretations of Domestic Islamic Interiors in Cairo: J. F. Lewis and F. Dillon,' in P. Starkey and J. Starkey, *Travellers in Egypt.* London–New York 1998

Brugsch, H., *Die Ägyptologie. Abriss der Entzifferungen und Forschungen.* Leipzig 1891

Brugsch, H., *Mein Leben und mein Wandern.* Berlin (2. ed.) 1894. Reprint Osnabrück 1975

Budil, I. T., *Mýtus, jazyk a kulturní antropologie.* Praha 1998

Burke, P., 'Geschichte als soziales Gedächtnis' in Assmann, A. – Harth, D., *Mnemosyne, Formen und Funktinonen der kulturellen Erinnerung.* Frankfurt 1993

De Meulenaere, P., *Bibliographie raisonnée des temoignages oculaires imprimés de l'expedition d'Egypte* (1798 – 1801). Paris 1993

Donadoni, S. – Donadoni–Roveri, A. M. – Curto, S., *Egypt from Myth to Egyptology.* Milano 1990

Duby, G., *Vznešené paní ze 12. století II.* Brno 1999

Duff Gordon, L., *Letters from Egypt.* London 1983 (reprinted 1986)

Ebers, G,. *Egypt slovem i obrazem ve spolku s vynikajícími umělci předvádí G. Ebers,* české od spisovatele autorisované vydání řídí dr. Otokar Hostinský. Praha 1883

Eco, U., *La struttura assente.* (1ed. 1968) Milano 1980

Eco, U., *Trattato di semiotica generale*, Milano 2000

Edwards, A., *A Thousand Miles up the Nile*. London 1982 (Ist ed. London 1877)

Erker-Sonnabend, U., *Das Lüften des Schleiers – Die Orientenfahrung britischer Reisender in Ägypten und Arabien. Ein Beitrag zum Reisebericht des 19. Jahrhunderts*. Hildesheim – Zürich – New York 1987

Europa und der Orient 800–1900. Ein Lesebuch. Gütersloh – München 1989

Europa und der Orient 800–1900. Gütersloh – München 1989

Frank, K., *Lucie Duff Gordon. A Passage to Egypt*. London 1994

Frodl, G., 'Wiener Orientmalerei im 19. Jahrhundert', *Alte und Moderne Kunst 26*, 1981, no. 178–179

Geschichtsdskurs, Bd 2, Anfänge des modernen historischen Denkens. Frankfurt 1994

Gran-Aymerich, É., *Naissance de l'archéologie moderne. 1798–1945*. CNRS eds. Paris 1998

Grimm, A., *Thomas Mann und Aegypten*. Mainz 1993

Grimm, A., *Joseph und Echnaton. Thomas Mann und Ägypten*. Mainz (2te erw. Auflage) 1993

Grimm, A., *Ägypten. Die photographische Entdeckung im 19. Jahrhundert*. München 1980

Helck, W., *Ägyptologie an deutschen Universitäten*. Wiesbaden 1969

Hellmuth, L., 'Tradition and Major Aspects of Oriental Studies in Austria in the 19th century', in *Orient – Österreichische Malerei von 1848 bis 1914*. Ausstellungskatalog-Residenzgalerie Salzburg, Hg. von Erika Mayr- Oehring

Hogg, J., *Travels of Lady Hester Stanhope 1–3*. Salzburg Studies in English Literature 105:4–6. Salzburg 1983

Horn, J., 'Kleine Bibliographie zur Erschliessung der Literatur der Reiseberichte über und Landesbeschreibung von Ägypten' in Minas, M. – Stöhr, S. – Schips, S. (hrsg.). *Aspekte spätägyptischer Kultur* (Fs E. Winter). Mainz 1994

Hornung, E., *Das esoterische Ägypten*. München 1999

Hornung, E., *Geschichte als Fest*. Darmstadt 1966.

Horský, J. (ed.), *Kulturní a sociální skutečnost v dějezpytném myšlení*. Ústí n. Labem 1999

Hossam, M. Mahdy 'Travellers, Colonisers and Conservationists' in P. Starkey – J. Starkey eds. *Travellers in Egypt*. 1998

Hroch, M., a kol., *Úvod do studia dějepisu*. Praha 1985

Hroch, M., *V národním zájmu*, Praha, 1996

Hroch, M., 'Několik poznámek k problému: historické vědomí a zájem rodícího se národa' in *Husitský tábor*, 8, 1985

Hroch, M., 'Některé metodologické poznámky ke studiu úlohy historického vědomí v národním hnutí XIX. stol. ' in *Historické vědomí v českém umění 19. stol*. Praha, 1981

Hroch, M., *Na prahu národní existence*. Praha 1999

Humbert, J. M., 'Postérité du sphinx' *L'Égyptomanie à l épreuve de l'archéologie*. Paris – Bruxelles 1996

Humbert, J. M. , *L'Égyptomanie dans l'art occidental*. Paris 1989

Iggers, G., 'Historicism' in *Dictionary of the History of Ideas*. New York 1973

Iggers, G. G., *Deutsche Geschichtswissenschaft*, München 1971

Iversen, E., *The Myth of Egypt and its hieroglyphs*. Copenhagen 1961

Jacoby, F., *Fragmente der griechischen Historiker III*. E. J. Brill, Leiden 1958

Jánosi, P., *Österreich vor den Pyramiden*. Wien 1997

Rüsen, J., 'Einleitung: Für eine interkulturelle Kommunikation in der Geschichte' in *Die Vielfalt der Kulturen*. Frankfurt (M) 1998

Kalfatovic, M. R., *Nile Notes of a Howadji. A Bibliography of Travelers' Tales from Egypt from the Earliest Times to 1918*. London 1992

Kalista, Z., *Cesty ve znamení kříže*. Praha 1941

Kazbunda, K., *Stolice dějin na pražské univerzitě I–III*. Praha 1962–1967

Kees, H., 'Geschichte der Ägyptologie' in *Handbuch der Orientalistik* I.1. Leiden 1959

Kemp B., *Ancient Egypt. Anatomy of a civilization*. London 1991

Kovárna, F., *František Bílek*. Praha 1941

Kurth, K., 'Ägyptenbilder im Quattrocento: Biondo und Alberti', *Proceedings of 7th International Congress of Egyptology*. Leuven 1998

Kutnar, F. – Marek, J., *Přehledné dějiny českého a slovenského dějepisectví*. 2. vyd. Praha 1997

L'Égyptomanie à l'épreuve de l'archéologie. Paris –Bruxelles 1996

Le Tourneur d'Ison, C., *Mariette Pacha*. Paris 1999

Lichtheim, M., 'Views of Egypt in English Romantic Poetry' in *Form und Mass; Beiträge zur Literatur, Sprache und Kunst des alten Ägypten*. *AÄT* 12/1987

Marek, J., 'Kultura jako téma a problém dějepisectví'. *ČČH* 90, 1992

Marek, J., *O historismu a dějepisectví*. Praha 1992

Momigliano, A., *Historicism revisited*. Mededelingen der koniklijke nederlandse Akademie van wetunschapen, Afd. Letterkunde, Nieuwe Reeks, 37/3, Amsterdam 1974

Morenz, S., *Begegnung Europas mit Ägypten*. 1968, 1969

Mostyn, T., *Egypt's Belle Epoque. Cairo 1869–1952*. London 1989

Mukarovsky, H. G., et al., *Leo Reinisch. Werk und Erbe*, Österreichische Akademie der Wissenschaften. Philosophisch-historische Klasse, Sitzungsberichte 492. Bd., Wien 1987

Österreichisches Biographisches Lexikon 1815–1950. Pet – Raž. Wien 1983

Opgenoorth, E., *Einführung in das Studium der Geschichte*. 5. Ed. Paderborn 1997

Orient. Österreichische Malerei zwischen 1848 und 1914. Ausstellungskatalog, hrsg. von Erika Mayr-Oehring, Residenzgalerie Salzburg 1997

Orr, M., 'Flaubert's Egypt: Crucible and Crux for Textual Identity' in *Travellers in Egypt*. London 1998

Osterhammel, J., 'Neue Welten in der europäischen Geschichtsschreibung', in *Geschichtsdiskurs* Bd 2.

Otruba, M., *Znaky a hodnoty*. Praha 1994

Pánková, M., *Architektonická malba v díle Ludvíka Kohla*. Praha 1971

Pánková, M., *Ludvík Kohl*. Praha 1984

Panofsky, E., 'Titian's *Allegory of Prudence:* A Postscript' in *Meaning in the Visual Arts*. 1982

Pávová, J., *Rukopisné památky české provenience k poznání zemí severovýchodní Afriky v 18. a 19. stol.* Master's thesis 1984, FF UK

Pešková, J., *Role vědomí v dějinách*. Praha 1997.

Pfeiffer, I., *Reise in das Heilige Land, Konstantinopel, Palaestina, Aegypten im Jahre 1842*. Wien 1995

Popelová, J. *Tři studie k filosofii dějin*. Praha 1947

Redford, D. B., *Pharaonic King-lists, Annals and Day-books; A Contribution to the Study of the Egyptian Sense of History*. Mississauga 1986

Rees, J., *Writing on the Nile: Harriet Martineau, Florence Nightingale and Amelia Edwards*. The University of Birmingham – Institute for Advanced Research in the Humanities – Occasional Paper no 4. 1992

Rees, J., *Writings on the Nile*. London 1995

Rossi, A., *Grenz(en)erfahrungen*. MA thesis, Innsbruck 1993

Roullet, A., *Egyptian and Egyptianising Monuments of Imperial Rome*. EPRO 20, Leiden 1972

Rüsen, J., 'Der Kampf der Identitäten im Felde der Geschichtskultur.' *Die Vielfalt der Kulturen*. Frankfurt (M) 1998

Rüsen, J., *Konfigurationen des Historismus*. Frankfurt (M) 1993

Said, E., *Culture and Imperialism*, London 1994

Said, E., *Orientalism*. New York – London 1978, 1991,1995

Sattin, A., *Lifting the Veil. British Society in Egypt 1786–1956*. London 1988

Satzinger, H., 'Der Werdegang der ägyptisch – orientalischen Sammlung des Kunsthistorischen Museums in Wien', in *Egitto fuori dell'Egitto*. Bologna 1993

Satzinger, H., *Ägyptische Kunst in Wien*, Wien s. a

Satzinger, H., *Das Kunsthistorische Museum in Wien*. Mainz 1994

Sharafuddin, M., *Islam and Romantic Orientalism*. London and New York 1994

Scharabi, M., *Kairo. Stadt und Architektur im Zeitalter des europäischen Kolonialismus*. Tübingen 1989

Schmidt, S. J., 'Gedächtnis-Erzählen-Identität' in Assmann – Harth, *Mnemosyne*

Schoske, S., 'Historisches Bewusstsein in der ägyptischen Kunst. Beobachtungen an der Münchner Statue des Bekenchons.' *Münchner Jahrbuch der bildenden Kunst*. III. Folge. Bd. XXXVIII. 1987

Syndram, D., 'Das Erbe der Pharaonen. Zur Ikonographie Ägyptens in Europa' in *Europa und der Orient*

Šimeček, Z., 'Rožmberské zpravodajství o nových zemích Asie a Afriky'. *ČsČH*, XIII, 1965

Štaif, J., *Historici, dějiny a společnost* I–II. Praha 1997

Thissen, H.–J., 'Horapollinis Hieroglyphika, Prolegomena' in *Aspekte spätägyptischer Kultur*. Mainz 1994

Thornton, L., *Les Orientalistes I. Peintres voyageurs 1828–1908*. Paris 1983

Toledano, E. R., 'Social and economic change in the "long nineteenth century"' in M. W. Daly ed. *The Cambridge History of Egypt II. – Modern Egypt from 1517 to the End of the Twentieth Century*, Cambridge 1998

Třeštík, D., *Mysliti dějiny*. Praha 1999

Vachala, B., 'Giovanni Kminek-Szedlo, der erste tschechische Ägyptologe', *ArOr* 54, 1986

Vachala, B., 'Literární odkaz starověkého Egypta ... etc.' in *František Lexa, zakladatel české egyptologie*. Praha 1989 (1984)

Vachtová, L., *František Kupka*. Praha 1968.

Vatikiotis, P. J., *The History of Modern Egypt. From Muhammad Ali to Mubarak*. Baltimore 1991 (fourth ed.)

Verner, M., *Aegyptiaca. Anatolian Collection of Charles University*, Kyme I. Praha 1974

Verner, M., *Altaegyptische Saerge in den Museen und Sammlungen der Tschechoslowakei; CAA, Tschechoslowakei*, Lief. I, Univ. Karlova, Praha 1982

Verner, M., *Veřejné sbírky staroegyptských památek v ČSSR*, sine anno, Praha FF UK

Von Habsburg, Rudolf, *Eine Orientreise vom Jahre 1881 beschrieben von Kronprinzen Rudolf von Oesterreich*, Wien 1885.

Weber, M., *Metodologie, sociologie a politika* (Havelka, M. ed.). Praha 1998

Werner, F., *Ägyptenrezeption in der europäischen Architektur des 19. Jahrhunderts*. Weimar 1994

Wildung, D., *Die Rolle ägyptischer Könige im Bewusstsein ihrer Nachwelt*, MÄS 17, Berlin 1969

Williams, C., 'A Nineteenth century photographer: Francis Frith' in Starkey P. – Starkey, J., *Travellers in Egypt*. London 1998

Wittlich, P., *Česká secese*. Praha 1982

Wortham, J. D., *British Egyptology 1549–1906*. Univ. of Oklahoma 1971

Illustrations credits

p. 13 Courtesy of the Archive of the National Museum, Prague.
p. 22 Courtesy of the Archive of the National Museum, Prague.
p. 28 Archive of the Czech Institute of Egyptology, Francis Frith, 1880s. Kamil Voděra.
p. 44 Archive of the Czech Institute of Egyptology, "Aegypten. Wie man es am besten bereist". 1920s. Kamil Voděra.
p. 47 Archive of the Czech Institute of Egyptology, Kamil Voděra. After G. Ebers, *Egypt slovem i obrazem,* Praha 1883.
p. 48 Archive of the Czech Institute of Egyptology, Kamil Voděra. After G. Ebers, *Egypt slovem i obrazem,* Praha 1883.
p. 49 Archive of the Czech Institute of Egyptology, Kamil Voděra. After G. Ebers, *Egypt slovem i obrazem,* Praha 1883.
p. 52 Archive of the Czech Institute of Egyptology, "Aegypten. Wie man es am besten bereist". 1920s. Kamil Voděra.
p. 57 Archive of the Czech Institute of Egyptology, Kamil Voděra. After G. Ebers, *Egypt slovem i obrazem,* Praha 1883.
p. 59 Archive of the Czech Institute of Egyptology, Kamil Voděra. After G. Ebers, Egypt slovem i obrazem, Praha 1883.
p. 67 Archive of the Czech Institute of Egyptology, Kamil Voděra. After G. Ebers, *Egypt slovem i obrazem,* Praha 1883.
p. 68 Archive of the Czech Institute of Egyptology, Kamil Voděra. After G. Ebers, *Egypt slovem i obrazem,* Praha 1883.
p. 69 Archive of the Czech Institute of Egyptology, Kamil Voděra. After G. Ebers, *Egypt slovem i obrazem,* Praha 1883.
p. 72 Courtesy of the Archive of the National Museum, Prague.
p. 73 Archive of the Czech Institute of Egyptology, Kamil Voděra.
p. 74 Archive of the Czech Institute of Egyptology, Kamil Voděra. After G. Ebers, *Egypt slovem i obrazem,* Praha 1883.
p. 75 Courtesy of the Archive of the National Museum, Prague.
p. 92 Courtesy of Petr Meissner, Antikvariát Meissner, Prague, and the Waldes Collection.
p. 94 Archive of the Czech Institute of Egyptology, Prague.
p. 95 Archive of the Czech Institute of Egyptology, Prague.
p. 96 Archive of the Czech Institute of Egyptology, Prague.
p. 97 Archive of the Czech Institute of Egyptology, Prague.
p. 99 Archive of the Czech Institute of Egyptology, Prague.
p. 104 Archive of the Czech Institute of Egyptology, Prague.
p. 113 Archive of the Czech Institute of Egyptology, Kamil Voděra. After G. Ebers, *Egypt slovem i obrazem,* Praha 1883.
p. 130 Archive of Set Out, Roman Míšek, Prague.
p. 136 Archive of the Czech Institute of Egyptology, Kamil Voděra. After G. Ebers, *Egypt slovem i obrazem,* Praha 1883.
p. 139 Archive of Set Out, Roman Míšek, Prague.
p. 140 Archive of Set Out, Roman Míšek, Prague.
p. 141 Archive of Set Out, Roman Míšek, Prague.
p. 143 Archive of Set Out, Roman Míšek, Prague.
p. 145 Archive of Set Out, Roman Míšek, Prague.

p. 147 Archive of Set Out, Roman Míšek, Prague.

p. 149 Archive of Set Out, Roman Míšek, Prague.

p. 154 Courtesy of Alena Bílek and City Gallery Prague.

p. 155 Archive of Set Out, Roman Míšek, Prague.

p. 156 Courtesy of Alena Bílek and City Gallery Prague, Jan Malý.

p. 157 Archive of Set Out, Roman Míšek, Prague.

p. 159 Courtesy of Alena Bílek and City Gallery Prague, Blanka Lamrová.

p. 160 Courtesy of Alena Bílek and City Gallery Prague, Blanka Lamrová.

p. 161 Courtesy of Alena Bílek, Jan Pospíšil.

p. 162 Courtesy of Petr Meissner, Antikvariát Meissner, Prague, and the Waldes Collection.

p. 163 Courtesy of Petr Meissner, Antikvariát Meissner, Prague, and the Waldes Collection.

p. 164 Courtesy of Petr Meissner, Antikvariát Meissner, Prague, and the Waldes Collection.

p. 165 Courtesy of Petr Meissner, Antikvariát Meissner, Prague and the Waldes Collection.

p. 174 Courtesy of the Archive of the National Theatre Prague, Kamil Voděra.

p. 177 Courtesy of the Archive of the National Theatre Prague, Kamil Voděra.

p. 179 Courtesy of the Archive of the National Theatre Prague, Kamil Voděra.

p. 181 Archive of the Czech Institute of Egyptology, Kamil Voděra.

p. 206 Courtesy of the Archive of the National Museum, Prague.

p. 226 Courtesy of Petr Meissner, Antikvariát Meissner, Prague, and the Waldes Collection.

pp. 8, 54, 63, 70, 150, 166, 185, 186, etc. Archives of the authors.

Index of Personal Names

The columns of Villa Bílek

An Egyptianising lady with a basket (Seifertova Street, Prague)

Hana Navrátilová

Egyptian Revival in Bohemia 1850–1920

Orientalism and Egyptomania in Czech lands
Published by SET OUT – Roman Míšek
Tyršova 11, 120 00 Prague, Czech Republic
1st edition Prague 2003
Text © Hana Navrátilová, Roman Míšek
Translation © Renata Landgráfová, Hana Navrátilová
Photos © Photographers and Institutions as indicated
Cover design Roman Míšek
Editor Hana Vymazalová
Printed by ÚJI Zbraslav, Prague
Printed in Czech Republic